The
Wisdom of
Sri Chinmoy

THE WISDOM OF SRI CHINMOY

BY

SRI CHINMOY

BLUE DOVE PRESS
SAN DIEGO • CALIFORNIA
2000

The mission of the Blue Dove Foundation is to deepen the spiritual life of all by making available works on the lives, messages, and examples of saints and sages of all religions and traditions as well as other spiritual titles that provide tools for inner growth. These books are distributed in our *Lights of Grace* catalog, our bookstore, and also on our website: www.bluedove.org. We carry all available books by Sri Chinmoy.

For a free 68 page catalog contact:

The Blue Dove Foundation
4204 Sorrento Valley Blvd, Suite K
San Diego, CA 92121
Phone: 800-691-1008 or 858-623-3330
E-mail: bdp@bluedove.com
Website: www.bluedove.org

FIRST EDITION

Special thanks to Emily Scheese, Mary Kowit and Gigi Orlowski for unstinting dedication in the production of this edition.

Front and back cover photographs by Ranjana Ghose

Cover design: Wendi Hall
Text design: Wendi Hall & Sandy Shaw

ISBN: 1-884997-23-6

Library of Congress Cataloging-in-Publication Data

Chinmoy, Sri, 1931-
    The wisdom of Sri Chinmoy / by Sri Chinmoy.
        p. cm.
    ISBN 1-884997-23-6
     1. Spiritual life--Self-help. I. Title.

BL1237.36 . C5996 2000
294.5--dc21   00-040407

TABLE OF CONTENTS

INTRODUCTION

In a world where few feel totally at ease, Sri Chinmoy offers a plan for world and soul survival. Sri Chinmoy's deep love for God is known worldwide. Long revered as a spiritual force for peace at the United Nations, this humble God-directed author asks people of this planet to look within, to rediscover the essential truths of spirituality that have so blessed his extraordinary life.

The name Chinmoy, meaning "full of divine consciousness," bespeaks the mission of this deep soul. He lives to be an unconditional instrument of God. He trusts God. There is a sympathetic oneness with God and people throughout his reflections. He becomes sad when he thinks of how people have used religion to separate themselves from one another.

Sri Chinmoy suggests that the spiritual life's goal is self-transcendence. While man reaches up to God, God in turn reaches down to man. The connection occurs and deepens as each person aspires to open himself to the Light of God, the Will of God and a higher state of consciousness.

He is a champion of peace, attracting believers from all religions to see the oneness of the world. He suggests that true religions are recognized by forgiveness, tolerance, compassion, oneness and brotherhood.

His work lends itself to a wide audience. Christians, Jews, Muslims and other believers will find many passages in his works of deep insight and helpful suggestion.

For those trying to find their way, he proposes a form of prayer that includes: concentration, the focusing of all attention on a small object to become more aware; meditation, reflection on and identification with the vaster universe and the larger issues; and contemplation, an awareness of God so complete that one feels the oneness and love that comes from God and lives in each person and in all creation.

Sri Chinmoy does not shrink from the exigencies of everyday life. While he does promote soul growth and inner peace, he follows a long tradition of religious teachers who implore truth-seekers to exhibit and live a life of "dynamism" that is transformative of this world.

Sri Chinmoy believes in reincarnation. He articulates the notion that the soul progresses to a higher state in each incarnation. He roots his teachings in prayer and encourages his readers to adopt a "cheerful acceptance of the world with a view to transforming the fate and face of the world." He beckons Westerners to avoid trying "to possess the world" while encouraging Easterners to see that "austerity is not the answer."

Sri Chinmoy believes that God will save our world. The Light of God is stronger than the forces of evil. While he has deep confidence in God, his tranquil reflections portray an urgency which calls out to mankind: "Wake up! Grow deeper! Love in such a way that 'God's Will be done.'"

I find his works to be personally helpful. In an age when stress is real and it is hard to find the proper amount of time to pray, Sri Chinmoy reminded me that placing God at the center of my life, my work and my prayers will help me to make this a better, more peaceful world and to become the person of faith and love that I am called to be.

Monsignor Thomas J. Hartman
Diocese of Rockville Center, New York

Jeff Blom (Sevak Ram)
Blue Dove Press
4204 Sorrento Valley Blvd, Suite K, San Diego, CA 92121

My Dear Sevak Ram,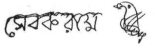

    I wish to thank you from the very depths of my gratitude-heart for your manuscript of my writings. I am extremely proud of you and your assistant, Andy Zubko. You have compiled my writings with utmost love, concern, faithfulness and devotion. As you know, over 1300 of my books have been published, most by our in-house Aum Publications. I wish to tell you that the manuscript which you both created is unparalleled. It is a true labor of love, revealing both your remarkable attention to detail and tremendous spiritual depth. I gladly approve of the title for the book which you have recommended, *The Wisdom of Sri Chinmoy*.

    My students who have read through the manuscript were delighted, and many told me they could not put it down. Your kind appreciation of my service for world peace touched me very deeply. My dear Sevak Ram, you and I are in the same boat. How soulfully you have devoted your life to promoting the cause of true spirituality by publishing and distributing the writings of humanity's beloved saints, sages and spiritual Masters. It is only the transformation of each and every individual on earth that can and will create peace on earth. Your delightful Blue Dove Press publications spread most fragrant peace-flowers and most delicious peace-fruits to the peace-hungry seekers throughout the length and breadth of the world.

    Once again, my heart of infinite gratitude and my life of infinite pride I am offering to you.

Yours in the Supreme,

Sri Chinmoy

Sri Chinmoy

A NOTE FROM THE COMPILER

What a sheer delight it was to bask in the illuminating words of Sri Chinmoy for hours and days and months at a time, handpicking these eternal gems of wisdom from among his 1,300 published books. What grace! Indeed, Sri Chinmoy is a vast ocean of grace. This cannot be denied. Like the Buddha, Sri Krishna, the Christ, Sri Ramakrishna and other great spiritual figures before him, Sri Chinmoy offers the seeker whatever is asked of him, and much, much more, beyond all imaginings. I can only suggest that in the reading of this book you throw away all your concepts of name and form, throw away your mind's fixed ideas and definitions, and leap into the ocean of Sri Chinmoy's consciousness. How exhilarating to merge in this boundless and fathomless ocean; how refreshing! Thank you, Sri Chinmoy, for a life-transforming experience...

—Andy Zubko

THE
WISDOM OF
SRI CHINMOY

ASPIRATION

Question: How does one increase one's aspiration or as you say, "the hunger for God" ?

Sri Chinmoy: What is most important is to try to develop a genuine hunger for God's love, God's compassion and God's blessings. There are two ways to increase one's inner hunger. One way is to cry for God like a helpless child crying for his mother. The other way is to offer one's actions to God while keeping a cheerful attitude. With both these ways the seeker will make real inner progress.

Question: What is the difference between desire and aspiration?

Sri Chinmoy: Desire is a wild fire that burns and burns and finally consumes us. Aspiration is a glowing flame that secretly and sacredly uplifts our consciousness and finally liberates us. Thirst for the Highest is aspiration. Thirst for the lowest is annihilation. Desire is expectation. No expectation, no frustration. With desire killed, true happiness is built. Aspiration is surrender. Surrender is man's conscious oneness with God's Will.

Desire means anxiety. This anxiety finds satisfaction only when it is able to fulfill itself through solid attachment. Aspiration means calmness. This calmness finds satisfaction only when it is able to express itself as all-seeing and all-loving detachment.

In desire and nowhere else abides human passion. Human passion has a dire foe called judgement, the judgement of the divine dispensation. In aspiration and nowhere else dwells man's salvation. Man's salvation has an eternal friend called Grace—God's all-fulfilling Grace.

Look at the strength of a bubble of desire! It has the power to engage our entire life for its use alone. Look at the strength of an

3

iota of aspiration! It has the power to make us feel that God the Infinite is absolutely ours. And something more: that God's infinite love, peace, joy and power are for our constant use.

Question: *How does one replace desire with aspiration?*

Sri Chinmoy: One day a disciple came up to his Master and said, "Master, this mind is horrible, horrible, horrible. I can not take it anymore. It is all meanness, jealousy, hypocrisy and lower vital thoughts."

The Master said, "My son, why do you speak ill of your mind? The mind is not bad; it is only that desire is entering into your mind and agitating it. The mind is not torturing you; it is you who are torturing the mind. Desire comes and wants to play with the mind or strike the mind to get some sound from it. Therefore, the mind starts defending itself and tries to kill you. A snake usually remains peaceful, but if you go and bite the snake, then naturally the snake will come and bite you or kill you. Very rarely will the snake bother you otherwise. So do not blame the mind. Blame your desire that strikes the mind."

The disciple said, "Then how can I get rid of desire?"

The Master said, "Desire has to be replaced, and this is possible only through aspiration. Empty the vessel of desire and fill it with aspiration. It is like emptying a vessel of dirty, filthy water and filling it with clean, pure water."

"How can I do that, Master?" asked the disciple.

The Master answered, "You can do it only by seeing what happens to those who have not emptied their vessels. They suffer unbearably, beyond their imagination. And those who empty desire-ignorance from their inner vessel and fill the vessel with aspiration-wisdom not only make themselves happy, but also make the Beloved Supreme happy. Not only are they fulfilled, but God Himself is fulfilled in and through them.

"So do not blame the mind. Blame desire that comes to torture the mind. Truth to tell, blaming desire is also not the correct way. One should bring into one's system something that will slowly, steadily and unerringly remove desire-life and replace it with its own reality. And that is aspiration. Replace desire with aspiration. Then you will have a heart of illumination and a life of perfection."

Question: *How can we best utilize our outer time to better our inner aspiration?*

Sri Chinmoy: Right now our time means our earthbound time. Now, we have to know why we have this limited time. Time and life came into existence together. They were very close to each other but unfortunately, when life started playing its role on earth, it became short-lived, and in the same way, time, being a friend of life, also became short-lived. Still, they know that their Source is the Eternal.

You are a seeker. When you pray, concentrate and meditate, you have to feel that each second is infinitely more important than you thought it was previously, before you entered into the spiritual life. This second you can use either for meditation or for gossip or for cherishing impure and undivine thoughts. So when you consciously use time to do something divine, you are entering into the divine time. Divine time means timeless time. When you are consciously thinking of something divine, immediately eternal time comes and shakes hands with you. Usually it does not stay in human beings, because when it stays, it has to stay in doubts, worries, anxieties, jealousies and so forth. But each moment, if you want to go upward through your aspiration, then the eternal time becomes your friend, and then earthbound time and eternal time can become friends.

Now, when you have prayed, meditated and played your part in the spiritual life, if realization is still a far cry, then you do not have to be impatient or worried, because God's hour has not yet struck. You have played your part and you have to feel that God has also played His part in and through you: you are the instrument. Even when your conscious mind wants to make you feel miserable that you have played your part and still God-realization is a far cry, you have to feel that God's hour has not yet struck. Then you will not feel miserable.

Very often we think of a date and set a deadline for our realization. We feel that on such and such a date, perhaps after ten, twenty, forty or fifty years, we shall realize God. Then, even though it is we who have imagined the date and have created this time limit for ourselves, when that time passes by and we have not achieved our realization, we curse our aspiration and we curse God. But if we feel that God has to choose the hour, then we can be happy.

To come back to your question, if you aspire consciously, and if you consciously pray and meditate, you will see that you are using your time most divinely.

Question: *Is there a specific way to accelerate realization?*

Sri Chinmoy: Yes, there is a specific way, and it is called conscious aspiration. God must come first. There must be no mother, no father, no sister, no brother, nothing else but God, only God. True, we want to see God in humanity, but first we have to see Him face to face. Most of us cry for money, name, fame, material success and prosperity; but we do not cry for even an iota of inner wisdom. If we cry sincerely, devotedly and soulfully for unconditional oneness with our Inner Pilot, then today's man of imperfection will be transformed into tomorrow's God, perfect Perfection incarnate.

Aspiration, the inner cry, should come from the physical, the vital, the mind, the heart and the soul. Of course, the soul has been aspiring all the time, but the physical, vital, mental and psychic beings have to become consciously aware of this. When we consciously aspire in all parts of our being, we will be able to accelerate the achievement of liberation.

Question: *How do we aspire?*

Sri Chinmoy: We aspire through proper concentration, proper meditation and proper contemplation. Aspiration covers both meditation and prayer. In the West, there were many saints who did not care for meditation; they realized God through prayer. He who is praying feels he has an inner cry to realize God, and he who is meditating also feels the need to bring God's Consciousness right into his being. The difference between prayer and meditation is this: when I pray, I talk and God listens; and when I meditate, God talks and I listen. When I pray, God has to listen. But when I meditate, when I make my mind calm and quiet, I hear what God has always been saying to me. Both ways are correct.

Question: *Is it possible to achieve perfection through aspiration?*

Sri Chinmoy: Each time you aspire, your perfection is increasing. Inside your aspiration, perfection is growing and glowing. Sincere aspiration means the opening of the perfection-lotus. A lotus, you know, has many petals. Each time you aspire most soulfully, one petal of the lotus blooms. And when one petal blossoms, it means perfection is increasing in the entire lotus.

Right now, your idea of perfection, your goal, is realization. That is your height of perfection. But when you realize God, at that time your aim will be to manifest God through your nature's transformation. Realization is transformation into perfection; but complete perfection is the transformation of the human nature into the divine nature. There have been quite a few Masters who never cared for the transformation of their nature. This is a more difficult task than realization. But nature's transformation is real perfection, for by bringing down divinity into your earthly human nature, you will be perfecting your outer life, which is a portion of the outer world.

Question: *How can I play my role in life with aspiration?*

Sri Chinmoy: Early in the morning, when you leave your bed, you can say to the Supreme, "O Supreme, make me unconditionally devoted to you so that I can serve You in Your own way." Then, before your breakfast you can repeat it again. As soon as you are through with your breakfast, say it once more. When you go to school or to work, you can again repeat it. Before performing any action, consciously pray that you will be able to serve the Supreme most devotedly and unconditionally. Each time, the vibration of your prayer will last for two minutes, six minutes, or ten minutes, depending on its soulful quality. But every time you offer this prayer you renew the vibration. Soon it will be like a bell. After you have started ringing the bell, it will become automatic and you will feel that the bell is ringing inside you constantly.

AUM

Question: I am curious about the meaning of these three letters which you pronounce "AUM."

Sri Chinmoy: AUM is a Sanskrit syllable, or you can say, a complete word. We have, in India, the Trinity: Brahma, Vishnu and Shiva—the Creator, the Preserver and the Transformer. "A" represents Brahma, the Creator; "U" represents Vishnu, the Preserver; and "M" represents Shiva, the Transformer. AUM is the breath of the Supreme. The Indian sages, seers and Yogis of yore chanted AUM and they got their souls' illumination and liberation. Even now, most of the seekers in India chant AUM most devotedly. They will achieve their realization by chanting AUM, the power infinite.

Question: What is the meaning of AUM?

Sri Chinmoy: AUM is a syllable that has a special significance and a creative power. AUM is the Mother of all mantras. When we chant AUM, what actually happens is that we bring down peace and light from above and create a universal harmony within and without us. When we repeat AUM, both our inner and outer beings become inspired and surcharged with a divine feeling and aspiration. AUM has no equal. AUM has infinite power. Just by repeating AUM, we can realize God.

When you chant AUM, try to feel that it is God who is climbing up and down within you. Hundreds of seekers in India have realized God simply by repeating AUM. AUM is the symbol of God, the Creator.

When you repeat AUM, please try to observe what actually happens. If you repeat the name of a cat, a dog or a monkey, or even of an ordinary person, you get no inspiration. But when you utter AUM, which is the symbol of the Creator, the life-breath of the Creator, you immediately get an inner feeling, the feeling that inspires your inner and outer movements to enlarge your vision and fulfill your life here on earth. This is the secret of AUM. If you want to cherish a secret all your life, then here is the secret. Please chant AUM and everything will be yours.

Question: *When you instructed us in meditation, why did not you give us the word AUM instead of God?*

Sri Chinmoy: Everything has its own time. I have now told you about the significance of AUM and the other day I told you about God. You have to know in which word you have more faith. When one person says God, all his love, faith and devotion come to the fore. In other persons, this may not be so. In your case, I told you to repeat the name of God because you go to church and pray in the Christian way. So far you have been familiar with God.

Question: *How do we chant AUM?*

Sri Chinmoy: The sound of AUM is unique. Generally we hear a sound when two things are struck together. But AUM needs no such action. It is *anahata*, or unstruck; it is the soundless sound. A Yogi or spiritual Master can hear AUM self-generated in the inmost recesses of his heart.

There are many ways to chant AUM. When you chant it loudly, you feel the omnipotence of the Supreme. When you chant it softly, you feel the delight of the Supreme. When you chant it silently, you feel the peace of the Supreme. The universal AUM put forth by the Supreme is an infinite ocean. The individual AUM chanted by man is a drop in that ocean, but it cannot be separated from the ocean, and it can claim the infinite ocean as its very own. When one chants AUM out loud, one touches and calls forth the cosmic vibration of the supreme Sound.

It is best to chant Aum out loud, so its sound can vibrate even in your physical ears and permeate your entire body. This will convince your outer mind and give you a greater sense of joy and achievement. When chanting out loud, the "M" sound should last at least three times as long as the "AU" sound.

No matter how grave a person's mistakes, if he chants AUM many times from the inmost depths of his heart, the omnipotent compassion of the Supreme will forgive him. In the twinkling of an eye, the power of AUM transforms darkness into Light, ignorance into knowledge and death into immortality. Everything that God has and everything that God is, within and without, AUM can offer because AUM is at once the life, the Body and the Breath of God.

Question: You have said that we can increase our purity by repeating AUM five hundred times a day. But for me to repeat AUM five hundred times a day is very difficult. Can you advise me what to do?

Sri Chinmoy: If it is difficult for you to do it in one stretch, then do it in segments. At ten different times you can repeat it only fifty times. Say that during the day you drink ten glasses of water. If you try to drink all ten glasses at once, you will not be able to do it. So you drink one glass now and after an interval of an hour or two, another glass. Then you can easily drink ten glasses of water. Instead of chanting AUM five hundred times all at once, early in the morning you can repeat it fifty times. Then, in an hour's time, do another fifty. Each hour if you repeat AUM fifty times, it would not take you more than a minute or two each time. Since you can easily offer two minutes in an hour to God, you can do your chanting in this way.

AVATAR

Question: What is the difference between a Yogi and an Avatar?

Sri Chinmoy: A Yogi is a fully realized soul. Higher than a realized soul is a partial Avatar, an *Angsha* Avatar. Higher than a partial Avatar is a full Avatar, a *Purna* Avatar. A Yogi can deal with a few people, a section of humanity; an Avatar can deal with the entire world. A Yogi silently acts; an Avatar acts dynamically and speaks confidently. A Yogi is a plant; an Avatar is a huge, tall tree.

An Avatar is a direct descendant of God: a real, solid portion of the Divine which constantly operates in the Highest and also in the lowest. An Avatar has the capacity of a huge sea, while a Yogi has the capacity of a river or a pool. When Yogis want to raise the consciousness of humanity, they will sometimes be affected by the ignorance of the earth. But an Avatar will remain in the Highest and the lowest together, and even in his lowest, his ability to function is not affected. An Avatar has infinitely more capacity than a Yogi in bringing about the total transformation of humanity.

Again, even an Avatar of the highest order may not or cannot function always from the highest level of consciousness because of the world's ignorance, darkness and imperfection. The earth's consciousness is not aspiring, and most human beings do not want his Light. Look at the Christ. Who cared for him? Very few. Look at Sri Krishna. Who accepted him? Very few!

According to Indian philosophy and spiritual teachings, an Avatar is a direct descendant of the Supreme who can commune with Him directly at will. Most of the Yogis cannot do that; it will take them two or three hours to enter into their highest consciousness in order to commune with God. Communion with God in the twinkling of an eye they do not have. Only the Avatar's communion with God is of this type.

An Avatar is a human being; he talks, eats, breathes and does

11

everything else like a human being. But when he enters into his Highest, if ever you can have even a glimpse of his consciousness, your whole life will be an object of complete surrender at his feet. Even if he kicks you, throws you aside, you will remain like a faithful dog, because in him you have got a matchless treasure which nobody else on earth will be able to give you. One has to have a very, very high standard of spiritual consciousness in order to get even the faintest glimpse of an Avatar's height. His consciousness can never be expressed or explained.

To have an Avatar as one's Guru is to have the greatest blessing that man can ever have. Sri Ramakrishna used to say, "If God is a cow, then the udder, which gives the milk, is the Avatar." A great aspirant will say that God in the form of an Avatar is more compassionate than God Himself. The aspirant says, "If I do something wrong, in God's case there is judgement, there is the law of Karma. But with the Guru, it is different. He has only deep affection for his dearest disciples. So when the actual punishment comes to me, the Guru will take the punishment." If the seeker prays to God and cries to God most sincerely and powerfully, then God may forgive him instead of punishing him. But if one has an Avatar as his Guru, and if he has the closest connection with the Avatar, then this Guru actually takes the punishment on the disciple's behalf.

Also, when there is one Avatar on earth, he embodies the consciousness of all other Avatars that came before him. Sri Ramakrishna said, "He who is Rama, he who is Krishna, in one form is Ramakrishna." In the West, unfortunately, you recognize only the Christ as an Avatar. Either you accept him or you reject him. If you accept him, then there can be no other for you. But in this you are making a mistake. The Christ, the Buddha, Sri Krishna and others all came from the same room. If you take the Christ as the divine, infinite Consciousness, then you cannot separate Sri Krishna, the Buddha or Sri Ramakrishna from the Christ. The Supreme entered into the form which you call the Christ; He entered into the form which you call Sri Krishna; He entered into the form which you call Sri Ramakrishna.

Question: Was Swami Vivekananda an Avatar?

Sri Chinmoy: Swami Vivekananda was not an Avatar. He had only a few glimpses of the truth that Sri Ramakrishna lived. Vivekananda was a great *Vibhuti*, one who is endowed with a special power of God, who acts most dynamically in the world atmosphere. *Vibhutis* are leaders of mankind who awaken the slumbering consciousness.

We cannot call Napoleon a *vibhuti*, but what Napoleon accomplished in the material world, Vivekananda accomplished in the spiritual world. The most powerful, dynamic power acted in human form in Vivekananda. Vivekananda's real mission was to spread the message of his Master, Sri Ramakrishna. Ramakrishna achieved, but he did not manifest much. He did not care for worldly achievement or the so-called manifold development. The present-day world needs the mind. The mind need not even be intellectual; it may be just an ordinary mind that can understand basic things. But Sri Ramakrishna did not care even for this ordinary mind. So Vivekananda collected the fruits of the tree that was Ramakrishna and offered them to the world. He came to the West at the age of thirty and brought abundant light to the West.

At the time of Sri Ramakrishna's passing, Vivekananda still doubted his Master's spiritual height. He said inwardly, "If you tell me that you are a great Avatar, I will believe." Ramakrishna read his mind and said, "Naren, you still doubt me? He who is Rama, he who is Krishna, in one form in this body is Ramakrishna." Rama was an Avatar, Krishna was an Avatar, and Vivekananda's Master embodied them both.

Vivekananda was not an Avatar; he cannot be put on the same footing with Sri Ramakrishna. I have great love and admiration for Vivekananda. My connection with him in the inner world is very close. Unfortunately, here in the West I encounter some spiritual people and swamis who belittle Vivekananda and his achievement, and dare to say he was not realized. But all I can say is that those who belittle Vivekananda are not worthy of washing his feet. God-realization he certainly had; he was very advanced.

The height of an Avatar cannot be judged by an ordinary person. It is like a dwarf trying to scale the height of a giant; it is ridiculous. But let us not think of a spiritual Master's height. Let us only think of his presence in our heart. When we can feel his presence in the depth of our heart, he can be our help, our guide, our inspiration, our aspiration, our journey and our goal.

Question: Will you explain the difference between an Avatar and a perfect Master?

Sri Chinmoy: An Avatar is a direct representative of the Supreme, a representative of the highest order. A perfect Master is also a representative of the Supreme. So if one is a real Avatar, then he is a perfect Master; and if he is a perfect Master of the very highest order, then he is also an Avatar.

Again, everybody's Master has to be perfect to that particular seeker. Your Master is perfect to you and somebody else's Master is perfect to him. Every Master should be claimed by his disciples as perfect. In that way only can he move himself forward. Otherwise, the disciple is not going to learn anything. Spirituality is not like a school lesson, where your teacher knows a little more than you. Although your geography teacher has many shortcomings, just because you have to study geography, you have to go and surrender to him and learn from him whatever he knows.

But in the spiritual life, when it is a matter of inner light, inner knowledge and inner wisdom, you have to feel that your Master is perfect. If you do not have the feeling that your Master is perfect, then you cannot go far. If from the very beginning you feel, "No, he knows only a little more than I do; he is not all perfect," then you will not be able to progress.

If the disciple does not see perfection in the Master, then how can he have perfection in his own life? If he sees the very thing that he wants manifested in someone else, then only will he strive to achieve it. But if he does not see the thing that he wants inside his Master then it is absurd for him to stay with the Master. He has to go to some other Master in order to see perfection.

In the case of an Avatar, it is a totally different matter. An Avatar is a direct descendant of God, so he has to be perfect in the absolute sense because he represents the Highest. Other Masters also are descendants of God, but you have to know that there is a great difference between a professor with a Ph.D. and a kindergarten teacher.

BEAUTY

Question: What do you mean by "outer beauty, but inner ugliness"?

Sri Chinmoy: Once a great sage named Eurba was walking along the street with his daughter, Kundala. She was very, very beautiful. As they were walking, another sage, Durbasha, saw them. Durbasha practiced austerities most soulfully, but his temper was of the quickest. He cursed people constantly and everyone knew of his temper.

When Durbasha saw Kundala, he immediately fell in love with her. He asked Eurba, "Please tell me who she is."

"She is my daughter."

"Your daughter?"

"Yes."

"Is she married?"

"No. She is not married."

"She is so beautiful."

"Yes, she is beautiful, but only physically is she beautiful. Inside she is always quarreling and fighting with the members of the family. Inside she is ugly, ugly, ugly. She is jealousy incarnate."

"I do not know about her inner bad qualities and I do not care to hear about them. I am so full of admiration for her physical beauty. Please, please, please give me your daughter."

Eurba said, "No, I will not give her to you. I do not trust you. Once you see how quarrelsome and jealous she can become, you may throw her out after you are married. Although she is very undivine, I have that much sympathy for my daughter that I do not want her to suffer this kind of fate."

"I promise that no matter what she does, I will not use my occult power. I will never destroy her, because I am so fond of her physical beauty."

Eurba said, "Are you sure you will not destroy her one day

15

when you get angry with her?"

"No, no, no. I promise you, I will give her everything and try only to please her. If she wants me to give up prayer and meditation, I will do so. I will give up everything for her. I will not even meditate on Lord Krishna, who is dearer than the dearest to me, if that is her wish. Once I get her, she will become my dearer than the dearest. She will be my all."

Eurba said, "I cannot believe it."

"Please! Love is blind. I love this girl more than my life. She is so beautiful. Please give her to me."

Eurba finally agreed and in due course, Kundala and Durbasha were married. Durbasha totally forgot about spirituality. He did nothing spiritual at all. He was always with his beautiful wife, bound by her physical beauty. Kundala was constantly complaining, scolding Durbasha for everything. Even when he had not done anything wrong, she scolded him. Durbasha said, "I gave up everything for you. My prayer, my meditation, my Krishna, my Beloved Lord—all I gave up for you, and still you are always scolding me."

"Who asked you to give up Krishna and spirituality, you fool? Nobody would have married you, but I agreed to marry you."

Durbasha said, "And nobody would have married you! You are so ugly inwardly. Your father was so right. In spite of knowing how bad you were, I married you."

"Who asked you to marry me?"

"My love for your physical beauty."

"Physical beauty? Look what you have done! You have ruined my physical beauty. You said if you married me, you would please me. Are you pleasing me in any way? I am asking you to do many things, but you are not pleasing me. I am asking you to make me very rich."

"How can I make you rich?"

"You have spiritual power, occult power. Make me very rich. I want to have many servants. I want to have a beautiful palace. If you cannot give me these things, I will go on scolding and insulting you."

Durbasha said, "Enough! Enough! I cannot tolerate you anymore. I am destroying you with my third eye."

As soon as Durbasha opened up his third eye, Eurba came and said, "My boy, my boy, I told you that my daughter was so undivine.

In spite of knowing that, you wanted to marry her, so I gave her to you. But do not destroy her, do not destroy her. Give me back my daughter. Since I brought her into the world, I will bear the burden the rest of my life. I do not want her destroyed."

Durbasha said, "Either take her away, Eurba, or I am going to destroy her immediately."

Eurba took back his daughter and said, "God gave you to me, my daughter, and God wanted me to marry patience. My name will be patience and nothing else. As long as I stay on earth, I will show you my infinite compassion and infinite forgiveness. What else can I do? If God blessed me with you, I shall pay the penalty for the rest of my life."

Question: *What do you mean by "body's beauty fails; soul's beauty sails"?*

Sri Chinmoy: In order to achieve liberation, Nigamananda had been practicing severe austerities in Benares for quite a few months. One day he was extremely hungry, but he had nothing to eat. In silence he said to the goddess of plenitude, Annapurna, how is it that I do not have any food to eat?

Just then a very ugly, elderly woman with filthy clothes brought him a bag and said to him, "Please hold this bag of food. Let me go and bathe in the pond nearby. Then we shall eat together."

Nigamananda waited two or three hours, but there was still no sign of her returning. Finally he opened the bag and saw most delicious food and fruits inside. He ate everything himself.

That night in a dream Nigamananda saw the goddess Annapurna. She said to him, "So you see, nobody remains hungry. I feed everyone."

"You feed everyone? Nigamananda exclaimed. When did you feed me? I invoked you when I was hungry, but an ugly, dirty, old woman gave me food. You are so beautiful and luminous!"

The goddess explained, "It was I who came to you in that form."

"Why did you do that?" he asked.

"I wanted to show you that all forms are mine, said the goddess. Still you care more for physical beauty than for the soul's beauty. So I wanted to show you that even ugly people can have good hearts. From now on try to feel that physical beauty has nothing to do with a kind, sympathetic heart."

The beauty of the body ultimately fails. The beauty of the soul eventually sails in the boat of perfection-oneness towards God's Satisfaction-Shore.

BELIEF

Question: Does belief come spontaneously or by effort?

Sri Chinmoy: Belief comes spontaneously. Belief comes by effort. In the spiritual life, a sincere, advanced and surrendered seeker can and will have spontaneous belief. Belief by personal effort, without the divine grace and God's unconditional protection, cannot be as effective as spontaneous belief. We have two principal organs: the eye and the ear. Our eyes quite often, if not always, believe themselves. Our ears very often believe others. These are our human eyes and our human ears. But the divine eye, the third eye, will believe only in the vision of Divinity, and the divine ears will believe only in the truth of reality. When we listen to the inner command, when we have the capacity to grow into constant obedience to our Inner Pilot, we feel within and without the presence of spontaneous belief. Belief is the reality of our inner obedience. This is divine belief, spontaneous belief. Belief by effort is a restricted, disciplined human understanding.

Belief is power. A real seeker of the infinite Truth knows this. An insincere and unaspiring seeker is aware of the truth that belief is power, but he cannot go beyond understanding or awareness; whereas a sincere, genuine, devoted and surrendered seeker knows that belief is dynamic power, and he has this power as his very own.

We see a tree. The tree bears flowers, and soon afterwards we see fruits. The flower is the harbinger of the fruit. In the spiritual life, belief is the flower. Belief is a divine angel which enters into us as the harbinger of the Lord Supreme.

If we do not have belief, we can develop belief. How? We can do it by mixing with sincere spiritual people who care more for God than for pleasure. There are also people who care only for God in human beings, and if we mix with those people we can cultivate belief. When we have belief, we can walk with God in His Garden of Light and Delight.

19

BODY

Question: The body is mortal, while the soul is eternal. What is the importance of having a body?

Sri Chinmoy: The soul is eternal and the body is perishable, true. But we have to know the supreme importance of three things: first, the embodiment of Truth; second, the revelation of Truth; third, the manifestation of Truth. It is on earth and through the physical body that the soul can manifest its own divinity which is the infinite peace, infinite Light, infinite bliss. This earth is the field of manifestation and at the same time, this earth is the field of realization. God-realization can be achieved only here on earth and not in other spheres, not on other planets, not in other worlds. So those who care for God-realization have to come into the world. The soul has to accept the body because the body is absolutely necessary here on earth for the manifestation of the soul's divinity.

On the one hand, when the soul leaves the body, the body cannot function; the body dies. On the other hand, when the soul wants to manifest, it has to be done in the body, with the body. So we have to know what we actually want. If we want to negate the body, destroy the body, what can the soul do? It has to leave the body. But if we want to achieve something here on earth and if we feel the necessity of establishing the Kingdom of Heaven here on earth, then it has to be done with the conscious help of the body. The body is the instrument of the soul. In the *Katha Upanishad* it says: "The soul is the Master, the body is the chariot, the reason or intellect is the charioteer and the mind, the reins." The body needs the soul, the soul needs the body. For the realization of the highest and deepest Truth, the body needs the soul; for the manifestation of the highest and deepest Truth, the soul needs the body.

Question: *Could you explain the difference between the body-reality and the soul-reality?*

Sri Chinmoy: Once Troilanga Swami was walking along the street near an Indian King's palace. This King was a great admirer of his. When the King heard that Troilanga Swami was nearby, he himself ran out and brought him into the palace. The Master was naked, so the King's attendants put very nice, expensive clothes on him and he looked extremely beautiful. Then they fed him most delicious food. The King and his party were blessed by the Master and they had a long conversation with him, although ordinarily he was a man of few words. Sometimes he would not talk at all for months.

When Troilanga Swami left the palace to go back to his cottage, some of the palace guards watched him from the distance. When he was practically out of sight, three hooligans attacked him and took away all the expensive robes that had been given to him by the King. The guards came running and arrested the hooligans. Then they begged Troilanga Swami to come to the King's palace once again, and he agreed.

When the King heard what had happened, he was about to punish the hooligans and put them in jail. But Troilanga Swami said, "No, do not do that. To me there is no difference whether I have the clothes or not. My soul is not affected at all when I do not have any clothes. Long before you gave me clothes, I had my soul inside my body, and this is the only real thing. What shall I do with the things that do not fulfill any need of my soul?" So the hooligans were allowed to go free and the Master peacefully went on his way.

The body-reality needs decoration, ornamentation and embellishment for its satisfaction. The soul-reality needs only its oneness with infinity's immortality for its eternal satisfaction.

CHOICE

Question: *Master, you say there is one, basic choice to make in life—what is that choice?*

Sri Chinmoy: It is up to you to think of yourself as the body or as the soul. If you think of yourself as the body and do not aspire, then in the spiritual life you are already dead. But if you think of yourself as the soul, that means you have already developed an inner connection with God.

Question: *What is it that one needs to look for in choosing a Master?*

Sri Chinmoy: What you need is inner guidance and outer assurance; you need somebody to guide you and constantly give you encouragement, inspiration and aspiration so that you can march along according to your soul's highest inner cry. Keep up your inner intense cry for a teacher. Then tomorrow or a few days later, you will find him. You should not miss any opportunity to go and see spiritual Masters when they give talks and hold meditations. Whoever gives you inner joy and satisfaction is your teacher.

Question: *Are you saying that joy is the most important factor in choosing a Guru or Master?*

Sri Chinmoy: The Guru who gives you boundless joy is your Master. Suppose four persons are walking down the street and you see all four of them. One will immediately attract your attention and you do not know why. The others are there, but your soul has an inner affinity with one in particular. Similarly, you may go to a spiritual Master and when you look at him, you may feel that he is someone you knew before. You may feel that something is telling you from within, "I know this man."

22

You may feel a tremendous familiarity, even in his outer gestures. You may feel, " This is someone who was very close to me, but now I have forgotten him." This is the connection between your soul and the soul of a particular Master. Everybody has a soul. If you immediately get an inner response from a Master's soul, then you can rest assured that you are meant for his path. If you get the utmost thrill in your inner being when you see him, then he is the right person.

Question: Are there any other methods we can try when selecting a Guru?

Sri Chinmoy: In selecting a Guru, there is one thing you can try. Write down the names of all the Masters that you have come across or heard of or found out about in books you have read. There will be about six or seven names. Then, take the name of the first spiritual Master on the list and, as you repeat his name, place your right hand on your heart. Try to feel the sound in your heart as you repeat the name seven times. Go down the list, and as you repeat the name of each Master, try to feel your heartbeat. If you feel joy, delight or ecstasy, instantly give the Master a grade. You have to feel what kind of joy you are getting from repeating his name, and then rate it on a scale.

If you get no response, no joy, no inspiration when you repeat the name of a particular Master, then you are in a perfect position to give him zero out of a hundred. If you get a tremendous response from the name of a Master on the list, if you are thrilled all over, if his very name sends enormous palpitations from the soles of your feet to the crown of your head, you are bound to give him ninety-five or even a hundred.

Question: We are letting our heart make the choice!

Sri Chinmoy: Yes, then you know without a doubt that this one is your Master. He is meant for you and you are meant for him. If he is not near you, but in India or elsewhere, then you have to go there or, if it is meant to happen, circumstances will bring your Master here. If you are destined to be a disciple of a particular Master, God will without fail either take you to him or bring him to you.

Question: Is it not then destiny or fate that chooses your disciples?

Sri Chinmoy: Whosoever is destined to be my disciple will eventually become my disciple. Whosoever is not destined for me may come to me for six months but he may see nothing in me. I cannot blame him, because I am not meant for him. So if you do not see anything in me or if you do not feel that this path is for meant for you, please do not be disappointed. There are many paths for you to choose from.

Question: And what about the devotees who have chosen to stay with you?

Sri Chinmoy: Those who are my disciples see something in me and that is why they stay with me. They are doing the right thing for themselves. If you do not discover what you want here, you should look somewhere else. I am not rejecting you—far from it. But I feel that you are wasting your precious time.

Question: Does it matter to you when a devotee does or does not choose you as a Master?

Sri Chinmoy: No matter who your teacher is, I want you to realize God. That will give me the greatest joy. It is not who takes you, but where you go that is important: whether you stay in ignorance or enter into the sea of Light. When I see an aspirant swimming in the sea of Light, that gives me the greatest joy. Who brought him is not what pleases me; only the fact that he is there, in the sea of Light.

CONCENTRATION

Question: What do you mean by "concentration"?

Sri Chinmoy: Concentration is the open secret of focusing all one's attention on a particular object or person in order to enter into and have one's identification with that object or person. The final stage of concentration is to discover and reveal the hidden ultimate Truth in the object of concentration. What concentration can do in our day-to-day life is unimaginable. It most easily separates our heart's Heaven from our mind's hell so that we can live in the constant delight and joy of Heaven and not in the perpetual worries, anxieties and tortures of hell while we are here on earth.

Question: What is the best point we can use to fix our gaze for concentration?

Sri Chinmoy: It depends on the individual. Some people find it easier to look at the flame of a candle and concentrate, while others find it easier to look at a beautiful flower. Still others prefer to look at the rising sun and concentrate. So if the individual gets a kind of inner joy when concentrating on a particular object, he should concentrate on that object in order to achieve his goal.

Question: My mind wanders, and I would like to know how I can better my concentration so that I can keep my mind focused on one point or on one thought.

Sri Chinmoy: Before you actually start your concentration, I wish you to repeat the name of God at least twenty times as fast as possible. "God, God, God..." In one breath, please try to repeat the word "God" as many times as you can. First try to purify your breath by repeating

25

God's name. The breath has to be purified. Unless and until our breath is purified, our mind will wander; thoughts will attack the mind mercilessly. After you have repeated God's name, I wish you to focus all your attention on a particular picture. You can focus your attention on a picture of a spiritual Master or look at your own picture or you can look at your reflection in the mirror. Do not feel that you are experiencing two bodies with one consciousness, but feel that you are feeling one body with one consciousness, even though the body in the mirror is a reflection of yourself. There should be no other thought besides this one, "God wants me; I need God. He will illumine me, my life; I shall fulfill Him, His mission." Then you will see that slowly and steadily God's divine thoughts are entering into you and permeating your whole inner and outer existence.

Question: When you speak, you close your eyes. Is this a kind of concentration or what is it?

Sri Chinmoy: When I was speaking, you observed me closing my eyes. It is not that I was concentrating; it was only that I was entering into various worlds. There are seven higher worlds and seven lower worlds. When I close my eyes and then open them, this blinking that you see indicates that my soul is moving from one region to another. During my talk, I was in a very high consciousness. Hence my soul got the opportunity to move from one plane of consciousness to another.

Question: Is it easier for you to concentrate while you are standing?

Sri Chinmoy: For a spiritual person like me, concentration can be done at any moment, at any place and in any position. I can concentrate even while I am running. I was a very good athlete in India. Even while running the fastest hundred meter dash, I used to concentrate. While I was pole vaulting—in the air—I was able to concentrate. So concentration can be done at any moment, at any place, in any position; it need not be done only while sitting. When the inner being compels us to concentrate, we concentrate. There is no hard and fast rule that one has to concentrate only while standing or while seated in the lotus position. When the inner being inspires us, we aspire, and this aspiration can be expressed either in the form of concentration or meditation.

CONSCIOUSNESS

Question: What is consciousness?

Sri Chinmoy: Consciousness is the inner spark or inner link in us, the golden link within us that connects our highest and most illumined part with our lowest and most unillumined part. Consciousness is the connecting link between Heaven and earth. Now, where is Heaven? It is not upstairs or somewhere far away. Heaven is in our consciousness. But it is the divine consciousness that connects earth with Heaven. The ordinary human consciousness will only connect us with something very, very limited and, at the same time, very fleeting. For one second we will be able to focus our consciousness on another person, and then our concentration disappears. But when we deal with the inner consciousness, which is the boundless, illumined, transformed consciousness, then our focus of concentration can go on, go on, go on.

It is not that only spiritual people have divine consciousness. Ordinary people have it also, but in them it is dormant. If they would concentrate, meditate and contemplate properly, this consciousness would come forward, and then they would have a free access to the soul, which is all Light, peace and bliss.

Consciousness is only one. It houses silence and it houses power. When it houses silence, at that time it houses its own true form. When it houses power, at that time it manifests its inner reality. A portion of the infinite consciousness that has entered into the gross physical and is possessed and used by the physical itself, we call the physical consciousness, the vital consciousness and the mental consciousness. In these there is a tiny portion of the infinite consciousness, but it is not the pure infinite consciousness that we speak of.

The eternal soul and the infinite consciousness must go together. They have a common friend, or you can say, a common father, and that is life, eternal life. One complements the other. The soul expresses its divinity through consciousness, and consciousness expresses its all-pervading power or silence through the soul. Consciousness and the soul can never be separated, whereas the body can easily be separated from consciousness.

What we, in our human life, call consciousness is usually only a feeling. When we perceive something subtle, immediately we call it consciousness, but it is not consciousness at all; it is a very subtle desire. We enter into the desire and immediately feel that this is our consciousness. Everything which is subtle in us and which we cannot define with words, we call consciousness; but consciousness is something totally different.

Awareness and consciousness are also two totally different things. If I talk with someone or mix with someone, then my mind becomes aware of his qualities. That is awareness. But consciousness is not a mental awareness or understanding. Consciousness is an inner revelation or an inner state of being. It is something infinitely deeper and more inward than awareness.

Question: What is the difference between human consciousness and divine consciousness?

Sri Chinmoy: Human consciousness is made up primarily of limitation, imperfection, bondage and ignorance. This consciousness wants to remain here on earth. It gets joy in the finite: in family, in society, in earthly affairs. Divine consciousness is made up of peace, bliss, divine power and so forth. Its nature is to expand constantly. Human consciousness feels there is nothing more important than earthly pleasure. Divine consciousness feels there is nothing more important and significant than heavenly joy and bliss on earth. Human consciousness tries to convince us that we are nowhere near Truth or fulfillment. It tries to make us feel that God is somewhere else, millions of miles away from us. But divine consciousness makes us feel that God is right here, inside each life-breath, inside each heartbeat, inside everyone and everything around us.

Human consciousness makes us feel that we can exist without God. When it is in deep ignorance, human consciousness feels that there is no necessity for God. We see millions and billions of people who do not pray or meditate. They feel, "If God exists, well and good; if He does not exist, we do not lose anything." Although they may use the term "God" in season and out of season, they do not care for the reality, the existence of God, either in Heaven or in their day-to-day earthly lives.

Divine consciousness is not at all like that. Even the limited divine consciousness that we have makes us feel that at every moment there is a supreme necessity for God. It makes us feel that we are on earth precisely because He exists. And when we cherish divine thoughts, the divine consciousness makes us feel it is He who is inspiring us to cherish these divine ideas. In everything the divine consciousness makes us feel that there is a divine purpose, divine aim, divine ideal, divine goal. In ordinary human consciousness there is no purpose, no positive goal; it is only a mad elephant running amuck.

In the divine consciousness there is always a goal, and this goal is always transcending itself. Today we regard one thing as our goal, but when we reach the threshold of our goal, immediately we are inspired to go beyond that goal. That goal becomes a stepping-stone to a higher goal. This happens because God is constantly transcending Himself. God is limitless and infinite, but even His own Infinity He is transcending. Since God is always making progress, we also are making progress when we are in the divine consciousness. In the divine consciousness, everything is constantly expanding and growing into higher and more fulfilling Light.

Question: Do we have control of our consciousness?

Sri Chinmoy: An ordinary man does not have control of his consciousness. But a spiritual man is able to control his. He is trying to lead a better life, a higher life, and in so doing, he is bringing down the Light of the beyond into the darkness of the present-day world.

Question: How do I work on my consciousness?

Sri Chinmoy: Do not think of doing anything. Just keep the door of your consciousness open to see whether it is a thief or a guest that is coming in. Allow in only those thoughts that you want. Keep out the lower thoughts. Open the door to higher, sublime thoughts. This is the first step in working on your consciousness. The following steps will come to you from within.

Question: *Could you please speak briefly about the different states of consciousness?*

Sri Chinmoy: There are three main states of consciousness: *jagriti*, *swapna* and *sushupti*. *Jagriti* is the waking state, *swapna* is the dream state and *sushupti* is the state of deep sleep. When we are in the waking state, our consciousness is focused outward; when we are in the dream state, our consciousness is turned inward; when we are in the state of deep sleep, our consciousness is roaming in the Beyond.

When we are in the waking state, the identification that we make with anything or anyone is *vaishwanara*, that which is common to all men. When we are in the dream state, we identify with *tejasa*, which is our inner brilliant capacity, our inner vigor. And when we enter into deep sleep, there we identify with and experience the subtle. In this third state it is not the mental consciousness, not the intellectual consciousness, but the inner, intuitive consciousness that we deal with. In *sushupti* there is no collective form; everything is indefinite. It is all infinite mass. In this state we get an experience of a very high order.

There is also a fourth state, *turiya*, which means the transcendental consciousness. This consciousness is neither outward nor inward; at the same time, it is both outward and inward. It is and it is not. It has the capacity to identify itself with anything and everything in the world and, again, it has the capacity to transcend anything and everything on earth. Furthermore, it constantly transcends itself. *Turiya* is the highest state of consciousness, but there is no end, no fixed limit, to the *turiya* consciousness. It is constantly transcending, transcending its own beyond.

The *turiya* state is like being at the top of a tree. When we are at the foot of a tree, with great difficulty we see a little bit of what is around us; but when we are at the top of the tree, we see everything around and below. So when we enter into the *turiya* state, we have entered into the highest plane of consciousness. From there we can observe everything.

In order to enter into the *turiya* state, for at least five or ten minutes every day we have to consciously separate our body from our soul. We have to say and feel, "I am not the body; I am the soul." When we say, "I am the soul," immediately the qualities of the soul come to the fore. When we are one with the soul, that state is a kind of *samadhi*. We can function in that particular state safely and effectively.

Question: *Are* Sat, Chit *and* Ananda *all on the same plane, or on different ones?*

Sri Chinmoy: Sat-Chit-Ananda is a triple consciousness. "*Sat*" is existence, "*Chit*" is consciousness and "*Ananda*" is bliss. You can separate them if you want to and, at the same time, you can take them as one. If one achieves existence, then inside existence he has consciousness itself. And if one has consciousness, then bliss is there. It is like an apartment or plot of land. You can give the plot of land one name or, if you want to divide it, each part of the plot can be called by a different name. But the reality of one is bound to be found in the other. They complement one another.

Sat-Chit-Ananda is the triple consciousness on the highest plane, and that plane is for the absolutely chosen few. To reach *sat-chit-ananda* is a most difficult thing. Hardly twenty or thirty Masters have reached it and stayed at that plane, and hardly one or two can embody it. Some Masters reached that plane and immediately came down because it was too high for them. It is much easier for people to reach the illumined mind or the super-mind, but Sat-Chit-Ananda is absolutely the Highest. That consciousness is almost impossible to attain, even for spiritual Masters.

Question: *Can a human being know the Infinite?*

Sri Chinmoy: Certainly. If you could enter into my consciousness, you would realize the Infinite.

Question: *But you are not infinite.*

Sri Chinmoy: You are seeing me now as a man, but if you enter into my consciousness, you will see the infinite Consciousness. If you meditate with me, I can enter into you and see the infinite Consciousness within you, but right now you do not have that power. You are not only a human being with hands and feet; you have come from God, and you have within you all the possibilities of realizing God.

Man in his outer life or his outer achievements is very limited. But the same man, when he enters into the inmost recesses of his heart, feels that there is something constantly trying to expand itself there. This is consciousness. This consciousness links him with the Highest Absolute. So when we ask how a man can achieve Infinity in his finite life, we must know that it is not in his physical body, in his arms or in his feet or inside his eyes that he will achieve Infinity. It is in his inner consciousness.

Question: There are seven planes of consciousness in the spiritual development. How can I determine which plane I belong to?

Sri Chinmoy: You can know which plane you belong to by throwing your outer mind into the sea of your aspiring heart, whose source is Consciousness. This Consciousness is the life-breath of all planes. The awareness of this Consciousness gives you the immediate recognition of your status where you were, where you are now and how far you still have to go.

After becoming aware of your plane, try to operate your daily activities from there. The easiest and most effective way of operating from that plane is to make your outer being a conscious and dedicated instrument of your inner vision and will.

In your case, let us suppose that you want to act from the intuitive mind, then once you have seen that plane and are conscious of it, you can try to remain there through your psychic aspiration and determined will. This is the real way to have mastery over a particular plane.

Question: When did you come upon the thought that there is an inner

Self within yourself? And after you discovered that you had an inner Self, were not you alarmed over the fact that you felt isolated from the rest of the world? And how did you make connections with other inner selves who were not aware that they had an inner Self?

Sri Chinmoy: I have known intuitively, from my early childhood, that there is a deeper Self within me. Each one of us has an inner Self. Some are conscious of this inner Self and some are not. Those who are conscious of this inner Self are, according to us, spiritually developed. What they can do in order to have a synthesis between the outer world and the inner world, between the outer being and the inner being, is to have a burning flame of aspiration. This aspiration is based on self-sacrifice, outer and inner.

Suppose you have found your inner Self and your inner life and the answers to the questions of your inner problems. But the person next door is utterly unconscious of the inner life and the inner world. Now it will be extremely difficult for you to have a kind of understanding with her and vice versa. She cannot come and enter into your consciousness. For her it is very difficult to enter into you.

Now, in order to have a bridge between you two, what you can do during your meditation or concentration is this: you know the person well, quite well. First you go deep within, and from there you bring forward all your sweet and subtle and harmonious feelings. It is all from within you. You bring forward all these subtle and delightful feelings and then consciously, during your meditation, you throw them into her: into her mind, into her body, into her heart. Then you have created a bridge between you and her.

Within your inner world, you are secure. You feel that the inner world has given you enormous confidence to cope with the outer world. You can go to her and speak to her on the spiritual life, the inner life, the life that gives you true happiness. She can try it for herself. In this world, everyone is running after true happiness and satisfaction. If one is satisfied after achieving something, the next day, again dissatisfaction comes in. One wants something more. Today's satisfaction will not be tomorrow's satisfaction. It will be tomorrow's dissatisfaction.

So first within yourself, just like watering a plant every day, you feed your inner being by meditation. Then you come to the outer world with your creative manifestation to form a bridge between your inner achievements and the outer world, where your future fulfillment will take place.

Question: How can we raise our consciousness when we feel threatened by negative forces?

Sri Chinmoy: When we are threatened by negative forces, we have to feel that we have the strongest friend within us, and that friend is the soul. Let us take shelter under the wings of the soul. Let us invoke the soul and pray for its guidance. If we call on this friend, naturally he will fight against the negative forces on our behalf; the soul will save us, protect us, illumine us and perfect us.

Question: Should one realize or reach the highest consciousness before mingling with unaspiring people?

Sri Chinmoy: First you have to realize the Highest. Only then can you dare to mix with unaspiring people. When you mix with unaspiring people, it is as if you are going to visit a mental hospital. Unless you yourself are very powerful, you will also be affected.

If you are aspiring, you need not reach the Highest in order to help other aspiring people. While you yourself are going high, very high, you can help your younger brothers who are aspiring but have not yet climbed as high as you. But it is stupidity for you to try to help people who are not aspiring at all. You will not be able to change their nature because they do not want to change.

To a seeker who is still unrealized God usually says, "You aspire, and while you are climbing up, if you see that somebody is a little behind you, then help him, inspire him, guide him so that he can also come up to the place where you are. But do not mix with unaspiring people, for if you do, then you will never aspire. If you do not aspire, then how will you realize Me?"

So let us be wise. First let us reach some height and mix with those who are aspiring. Then when we reach the Highest, if it is God's Will we can mix with those who are unaspiring.

Question: *What is inconscience?*

Sri Chinmoy: Inconscience is a state of consciousness where there is no light, not even a streak of light.

Question: *When you talk of mineral, plant, human and divine consciousness, what exactly do these terms mean?*

Sri Chinmoy: In mineral consciousness there is practically no light, and in plant consciousness there is only a streak of light. Limited light is or may be in human consciousness. But human consciousness is capable of housing unlimited Light, as is the case with very advanced seekers. Finally, the divine Consciousness embodies boundless, infinite Light.

Question: *If our consciousness is low during our dreams, is it harmful spiritually?*

Sri Chinmoy: If our consciousness is low and unaspiring at any time, it affects the seeker in us. The kind of dreams we have when we are in a low consciousness are detrimental to our inner life. If we have dreams from a low plane of consciousness, the best thing is to meditate more sincerely, more devotedly, more soulfully on the following day. In this way we can prevent these undivine dreams from entering into us again. Unaspiring dreams cloud our mental sky, damage our aspiring and dynamic vital and even try to destroy our physical health.

DEATH

Question: Is death the end?

Sri Chinmoy: Death is not the end. Death can never be the end. Death is the road. Life is the traveler. The soul is the guide. When the traveler is tired and exhausted, the guide instructs the traveler to take either a short or a long rest, and then the traveler's journey begins again.

In the ordinary life, when an unaspiring man wallows in the mire of ignorance, it is the real victory of death. In the spiritual life, when an aspirant does not cry for a higher light, bliss and power, it is the birth of his death.

What can we learn from the inner life, the life which desires the extinction of death? The inner life tells us that life is soulfully precious, that time is fruitfully precious. Life without the aspiration of time is meaningless. Time without the aspiration of life is useless.

Our mind thinks of death. Our heart thinks of life. Our soul thinks of immortality. The mind and death can be transcended. The heart and life can be expanded. The soul and immortality can be fulfilled.

When the mind and death are transcended, man will have a new home: Light, the Light of the beyond. When the soul and immortality are fulfilled, man will have a new goal: delight, the transcendental delight.

Today man feels that death is an unavoidable necessity. Tomorrow man will feel that immortality is an unmistakable reality.

Unfortunately, most of us cherish wrong conceptions about death. We think death is something unusual, something destructive. But we have to know that right now death is something natural, normal and, to some extent, inevitable. Lord Krishna tells Arjuna: "O Arjuna, certain is death for the born and certain is birth for the dead.

37

Therefore what is inevitable ought not to be a cause for thy sorrow."

The *Chandogya Upanishad* tells us something significant: "When the hour of death approaches, what should we do? We should take refuge in three sublime thoughts: we are indestructible; we can never be shaken; we are the very essence of life." When the hour of death approaches us, if we feel that we can never be destroyed, that nothing can shake us and that we are the very essence of life, then where is sorrow, where is fear, where is death? No death.

Question: *Is there life after death?*

Sri Chinmoy: Yes, there is life after death. Death is not and can never be the end. To me, life and death are like two rooms. During the day I work in the living room; death is my resting room. I equally need both in order to love, serve and please God.

Right now, death is something unknown, and most people are afraid of the unknown. But we have to realize that death is an important part of God's Cosmic Game and a natural step in our evolution. Let us say that an individual works very hard and makes considerable progress during his lifetime. But after playing the life-game for a certain number of years, he usually becomes tired. One cannot continue playing any game or sport without rest. We need rest so that we can start playing again with renewed energy and enthusiasm. So death is a well-deserved rest for the divine warrior who has been fighting hard on earth for the Lord Supreme.

Question: *What is meant by eternal life?*

Sri Chinmoy: There are two lives: one is the life that we are seeing here. We have a short span of life, say forty, sixty or eighty years; then we pass behind the curtain of eternity. Then there is an eternal life. This life existed before the creation, it exists now in the creation, then it passes through death and it goes beyond death and enters again into its own realm. So when we speak of life here, we think of the short span of life that we are seeing. But eternal life is not like that. It had no beginning and it has no end. It existed, it exists and it will forever exist. Through our meditation, when we realize God, when we stay in God, we become the possessor of that eternal life. Consciously we go beyond the veil of death and we remain in the eternal life, which has neither beginning nor end.

Question: *Is life after death a sort of consolation?*

Sri Chinmoy: Obviously it is not. I have just explained that life after death is the highest affirmation of Truth. In this life, you have not fulfilled even all your desires, let alone your aspirations. How can you do all this in one lifetime? Desire fulfilled today is bound to be followed by frustration tomorrow. Then man throws away desire like a dirty cloth; man enters into the field of aspiration. He wants to grow, he wants to have infinite joy, infinite Light, infinite bliss. These infinite gifts cannot be possessed by an individual in the course of one short span of life. For that we have to come back into this world. The soul comes back again and again in order to fully manifest its divinity here on earth. Because we cannot do all this in one short lifetime, the soul comes back and enters into various successive bodies in order to embody, fulfill and manifest the Divine.

Question: *Why is death necessary? Why can not the soul keep on progressing and evolving in the same body?*

Sri Chinmoy: Right now death is required; death is necessary for us. We cannot do anything for a long time at a stretch. We play for forty-five minutes or an hour and then become tired and have to take rest. It is the same with our aspiration. Suppose we live on the earth for sixty or seventy years. Out of sixty or seventy years we may meditate for twenty days or thirty days and, even then, for only a few hours. An ordinary human being may not aspire in his meditation for even one hour at a stretch. How can he have the aspiration or reality or consciousness that will take him to the eternal Truth or undying Consciousness all at once?

Right now death helps us in a sense; it allows us to take some rest. Then when we come back, we come back with new hope, new light, new aspiration. But if we had a conscious aspiration, a mounting flame burning within us all the time, then we would see that physical death could easily be conquered. A day will dawn when there will be no necessity for death. But right now we do not have that capacity; we are weak. Spiritual Masters, liberated souls, however, do have mastery over death, but they leave the body when the Divine wants them to.

An ordinary man who has shouldered the burden of a whole family for twenty, thirty or forty years will say, "I am tired. Now I need a rest." For him death really has meaning; the soul goes into the soul's region and enjoys a short rest. But for a divine warrior, a seeker of the ultimate Truth, death has no meaning. He wants to make his progress continuous, without halt. So he will try to live in constant aspiration, eternal aspiration. And with that eternal aspiration, he will try to conquer death so he can be an eternal outer manifestation of the Divine within him.

Question: *Is it possible for a man to learn what death is while still living, by actually entering into death?*

Sri Chinmoy: What death actually is one can easily know when one is in the very highest stage of meditation. Hundreds of times I have experienced what death is. I have also passed beyond death in my meditation many times when I have had to help my disciples. In trance one goes to many worlds, many planes, many regions beyond the domains and boundaries of death.

Sometimes we can actually follow a soul when the soul leaves the body, and then we can get the full experience of death while remaining in the body. I had my first experience of this with one of my sisters, who died when I was eighteen. I had this power, so I followed my sister's soul for about three hours in the world of death. What happens is that you feel that you are actually dead. Your body does not exist for you; only with your consciousness you are flying, flying like a kite. When you have this power, you can have the real experience of death in this world. During your meditation you can easily go. You can keep your body in the world of life and your consciousness-Light in the world of death.

Question: *You mention that death is an obstruction. I always thought you considered death to be a transition that just enables us to be reborn and make continuous progress.*

Sri Chinmoy: I have said that death is a transition. I have said that life and death are like two rooms: life is my living room, and death is my bedroom. When I say that death is an obstruction, I am speaking of death from a different point of view. What is an obstruction? An obstruction is something that prevents us from going farther. It is a limit which we cannot go beyond.

This life is a golden opportunity given to us by the Supreme. Now opportunity is one thing and achievement is another. Our spiritual evolution, our inner progress is very steady, very slow and, at the same time, most significant. Naturally there are people who for hundreds or thousands of incarnations will follow a normal, natural cycle of birth and death. Then one day, in God's eternity, they will realize God. But some sincere, genuine aspirants make a soulful promise that in this incarnation, here and now, they shall realize God. They say this in spite of knowing that this is not their first life or their last life. They know that there are people who have realized God and they do not want to wait for some distant future incarnation. They feel that it is useless to live without God-realization and they want to have it as soon as possible.

In such cases, if death comes and they are still unrealized, then death is an obstruction. If somebody who is destined to die at the age of fifty is aspiring soulfully, if he can push his death back, with the kindest approval of the Supreme, for another twenty or thirty years, then during this period what will he be doing? He will be continuing his sincere aspiration, his deepest meditation, his highest contemplation. He will be like a racer running towards his goal with no obstruction. During these extra twenty or thirty years he may reach the farthest end, where his goal lies.

But if death interferes, then he does not realize God in this life. In the following incarnation very few souls can immediately take up the thread of their past aspiration. As soon as one enters into the world, the undivine cosmic forces come and attack, and the ignorance, limitations and imperfections of the world try to cover the soul. In the formative years of childhood, one does not remember anything. A child is innocent, ignorant and helpless. Then, after a few years, the mind starts functioning. When one is between eight and twelve years old, the mind complicates everything. So for the first eleven, twelve or thirteen years of the next incarnation almost all souls, despite being very great and spiritual, forget their past achievements and deepest inner cry. Now there are spiritual Masters or great seekers who get a few high experiences in their childhood or who start thinking and singing about God at a very early age, but usually there is no strong connecting link between the soul's achievement on earth in its previous incarnation and these childhood years in the present incarnation. There is a link, a very subtle link, but this link does not function significantly for the first twelve or thirteen years.

Some souls do not regain the aspiration of their past incarnation until the age of fifty or sixty. From the spiritual point of view, these fifty or sixty years in their following incarnation are absolutely wasted time. So in this incarnation if one loses fifty years, and if in the past incarnation one has lost twenty or thirty years, then it is eighty years wasted. In this case I say that death is a real obstruction. We have to remove that obstruction with our aspiration, our unbroken aspiration. Aspiration should be like a bullet. It should pass through the death wall.

But even though it may take some time, eventually the inner being will come consciously to the fore and the person in his new incarnation will start praying and meditating on God most powerfully and sincerely. At that time he will see that nothing from his past has really been lost. Everything has been saved up in the earth-consciousness, which is the common bank for everyone. The soul will know how much it has achieved on earth; and all this is kept very safely inside the earth-consciousness, the earth-bank. You deposit money here in the bank. Then you can go to England and after six years or more you can come back and take out your money. The soul does the same thing after having left the earth for ten or twenty years. All the soul's achievements are kept here intact in Mother Earth. Then Mother Earth gives them back again when the soul returns to work for God on earth.

Nothing is lost except time, in most cases, during those few years of childhood. But it is better to realize God in one incarnation so that we do not lose our conscious aspiration again in this transitory period. If we can continue on earth for fifty to one hundred years with tremendous, sincere aspiration, then we can accomplish much. If we get help from a real spiritual Master, it is possible to realize God in one incarnation, or in two or three. If there is no real Master and if there is no aspiration, it takes hundreds and hundreds of incarnations.

Question: *When we are dying, what is the best thing to do?*

Sri Chinmoy: For a spiritual person, the best thing to do is to remember the presence of his Master. The near and dear ones should place a picture of his spiritual guide right in front of the seeker, and let the Master be with him spiritually when the seeker breathes his last. Let the Master be inside the very breath, the very last breath of the seeker. Then it is the duty, the responsibility of the inner guide to do what is necessary. Long before you leave the body your Master will have left the body. So you can meditate on the Master and he or she will help you.

Last year your father died. If you had been physically present, what you should have done at that time was to meditate most soulfully. Although your father was not consciously my disciple and had not accepted our path, who knows what he will do in his next incarnation? You knew that there was somebody who could have helped your father while he was dying, so you should have meditated on me. One always knows who can help in any situation. When somebody is sick, one calls the doctor. When somebody is in legal trouble, one gets the help of a lawyer. If you had wanted to help your father, immediately you should have thought of me and meditated on me. If you had tremendous aspiration or spiritual power, you would have given him all your spiritual strength. But your spiritual strength right now is your aspiration, and the source of your aspiration is inside this Master, your Guru. So if you want to help your dearest ones, you have to do it in this way.

But if you are speaking of other people, then in order to know what is best to do when they are dying, you have to know who gave them the greatest joy on earth, or in whom they had their greatest faith. If somebody had all faith in Christ, even though you may not follow the path of Christ, immediately you have to consciously and most devotedly invoke the presence of Christ. You have to help your friend at that time to increase his faith in Christ. You can repeat the name of Christ out loud, and bring him a picture of Christ and read from the Bible. In this way you will be able to help his aspiration. If somebody spiritual who knows me is dying, at that time you should read my writings and speak about me. But if it is someone who is just an acquaintance, you should increase his faith in his own way.

Question: *Is death painful?*

Sri Chinmoy: It depends on the individual. If the individual has not prayed and meditated and has not followed the spiritual life, then it is really painful to part with this life because he does not want to surrender to God's Will. First of all, it is not in him to know or feel what God's Will is. Also, he does not feel God's conscious Protection, Guidance and Concern, so he feels that he is totally lost. In this world he cannot do anything; in the other world all is uncertainty. If there is no aspiration, there is tremendous fear, for ordinary people feel that death is something totally unknown. They do not know where they are going. But seekers know that they are going to the Supreme, to the Lord's Abode. It is temporarily unknown to them, but that consciousness, that plane, is a realm of peace and rest. It belongs to the Supreme, their eternal Father. So they have no fear.

Then, of course, there is physical pain. At the time of death, even right up to the last moment, if somebody is suffering from a disease and if he cannot throw this disease into something higher or deeper, naturally his last days will be extremely painful. Even the last moment will be very painful because the death-being will come to him in a very destructive form. The death-force, death-being, appears before each individual in a different form according to his soul's achievement and realization on earth.

Ordinary people who are not aspiring, people who are absolutely wallowing in the pleasures of ignorance, will feel death as a terrible, ruthless being, a dark and awful figure. Sometimes the death-force has many subordinates which come before the dying person, and people very often see tigers or unimaginably huge beings, and become frightened. But sincere seekers see their spiritual Master or a luminous being, like an angel, taking them in a chariot. These seekers have worked hard on earth for many years and now Mother Earth consciously wants to offer them her blessingful and divine gratitude. Their Inner Pilot or their Guru takes them, but they see the benign Hand of God right in front of them, carrying them in His Golden Boat to the other shore. Some people see their long-departed relatives at the actual time of death. Their dearest ones come, and it is just like somebody who knows them is welcoming them to a new world.

When we are caught by the fetters of ignorance, there will be pain both within us and without at the time of our physical death. This pain is due to the ignorance in the human mind and human body which prevents us from entering into the realm of death and then going beyond the realm of death consciously and deliberately. But if the veil of ignorance is removed, then there can be no pain, either in death or in the world-atmosphere. If we can enter into the root of our suffering and pain, which is ignorance, and if we can transform ignorance with our soul's light, then death will be just like a passage leading us to another shore. This other shore is the Light eternal which guides, protects, shapes and molds us through eternity.

Question: When the physical being ceases to exist, what happens to your spiritual self?

Sri Chinmoy: When we die, our physical body, the physical sheath enters into the physical world and is disintegrated by burial or cremation. The vital sheath enters into the vital world. The mind enters into the mental world. Then slowly the soul goes back to its own region. There, usually, it stays for a few years. It depends on the individual soul—according to its necessity and according to its preparation. After taking rest for some time, the soul feels that the time is ripe for it to enter into the world once again to fulfill its divine mission. God-realization takes a good many incarnations.

Before the soul enters into creation, it tries to observe the environment, the situation and the family from above—which family it is going to accept. Then the soul goes to the Supreme for approval. Sometimes it gets this approval; sometimes the soul comes into creation merely with the knowledge of the Supreme. Again it starts its journey. It tries to unveil its inner divinity and at the same time, it tries to manifest the Divine in the field of creation. So this is how the process of reincarnation continues.

We believe in reincarnation. We know that we have millions of desires to be fulfilled. At the age of four, I had many desires; at the ages of ten, twenty, thirty, forty, sixty, these desires are not yet fulfilled. Neither we nor God will be satisfied unless we are fulfilled. First we get our fulfillment in satisfying our desires in the ordinary human life. Then we have our fulfillment in achieving our higher aspiration. Right now, we want money, a name, fame and all this. Later we try to achieve Light, peace and bliss with our spiritual aspiration. In one incarnation, in one short span of life, we cannot do all that. We need many incarnations. That is why, according to our Indian philosophy, reincarnation is a positive fact and a positive truth.

Question: *Will there be a judgement of what has been done in this life after death? Will there be punishment, reward or a sentence? If so, will it be eternal?*

Sri Chinmoy: At the end of the earthly sojourn, the individual soul passes on to the other world and offers to the Absolute Supreme the quintessence of the experience that it had on earth. The Absolute Supreme, from his transcendental height, evaluates the soul's progress. But there is no hard and fast rule about punishment, reward or sentence. Whatever God does with the individual soul—although it may seem like a punishment or a reward—is done from His transcendental vision-Light for the progress of the soul. But even the worst possible human being will never be condemned to eternal punishment or torture.

The reason God created human beings was not to punish us but to love us and give us opportunities to transform ourselves steadily and unerringly into divine beings.

Question: *What should be the attitude of the dear ones when somebody close is dying?*

Sri Chinmoy: We are all like passengers on a single train. The destination has come for one particular passenger. He has to get off at this stop, but we still have to go on and cover more distance. Now we have to know that this hour of death has been sanctioned by the Supreme. Without the approval or tolerance of the Supreme, no human being can die. So if we have faith in the Supreme, if we have love and devotion for the Supreme, we will feel that the Supreme is infinitely more compassionate than any human being, infinitely more compassionate than we who want to keep our dear ones. Even if the dying person is our son, or our mother or father, we have to know that he is infinitely dearer to the Supreme than he is to us. The Supreme is our Father and our Mother. If one member of the family goes to the father and mother, the other members of the same family will never feel sad.

If we have taken to the spiritual life and want to have real joy, we must know that we can have this joy only by surrendering our life to the Will of the Supreme. Now we may not know what the Will of the Supreme is, but we do know what surrender is. If the Supreme wants to take somebody away from our life, we must accept this. "Let Thy Will be done." If this is our attitude, then we will have the greatest joy. And this joy does the greatest service to the one who is going to depart. When we totally surrender to the Supreme, this surrender becomes additional strength and power for the departing soul that is suffering here in bondage. So if we really surrender our will to the Will of the Supreme, then this surrender will verily bring peace, an abiding peace, to the soul that is about to leave the earth-scene.

Those who have started meditating and concentrating are getting glimpses of their past incarnations. If we believe we had a past and we know we have a present, then we can also feel that we will have a future. Knowing this, we have to be always conscious of this truth: that there is no death. In the *Bhagavad Gita* it is said, "As a man discards his old clothes and puts on new ones, so does the soul discard this physical body and take on a new body." When we know that the person who is going to die is just leaving aside this old body before accepting a new one, and if the person who is dying also has the same knowledge, how can there be any fear?

We do not know what death actually is; that is why we want to stay here on earth as long as possible. But real death is not the dissolution of the physical body. Real death, spiritual death, is something else.

Question: *I had a young friend who died just six weeks ago. The day before he died, he told his father that he would die the next day, and then he did. How could he know?*

Sri Chinmoy: Why not? Is he not God's child? At the time of death, if one thinks of God all the time, one may get the message from one's own inner being. When my own mother was passing away, I happened to be at my uncle's house, six miles away. My mother was suffering from goiter. Early in the morning she said, "This morning I am leaving the body. Where has Madal gone? Send for him." Then a cousin of mine brought me the message and I came. She took my hand, then gave me a smile, her last smile. She left about a minute after I arrived, as if she had waited for me. Now I must be truthful. My mother was very, very spiritual, and used to practice the inner life in the strictest sense of the term. But about your friend, I must say that hundreds and thousands of people have known in advance when they were going to die. And for spiritual people it is very easy. They often know a few months in advance.

Question: *Is it written on a person's palm when he will die?*

Sri Chinmoy: From the palm you cannot always tell when someone will die. If it is an accidental death, the palm may not be correct, but the forehead is always correct. It gives an immediate vibration. The forehead will have written on it what will happen to the individual tomorrow, and it will be visible on the nose if there is going to be an accidental death.

I once had a friend who was very fond of me. His name was Ravi. One day he was practicing javelin at six o'clock in the evening.

When I took the javelin from him I saw death forces in him. I thought, "Best thing is to forget about it, or pray to God." I did not want to know about it. The following day, I was going down some stairs, and he was near the staircase. There I saw the same force and I cursed myself, saying it was all my mental hallucination. An hour and a half later, I heard that he had had an accident. He was riding a motor bike behind a truck with his friend. They were following the truck. The truck lowered its speed, and this fellow thought he also was lowering his speed, but he pressed the handle the wrong way and increased the speed, so he dashed against the truck. The truck driver heard the sound. He took both of them to the hospital. They were put in one room. Ravi's mother came to see him, but she was not allowed in because the doctor said that both the cases were serious. I think he lived only for three hours. So an apparition came to me while I was practicing javelin. The day he died was the day of our javelin competition, but I did not go there; I only went to the funeral. In his case it was destined that he die.

Question: *When a person is sick and, medically speaking, there is no hope of recovery, is it good to tell the person he is going to die and to start helping him get ready for departure?*

Sri Chinmoy: This is a very complicated question; each case has to be considered separately. Most people want to live; they do not want to die because they do not know what death is. They think that death is a tyrant who will torture them in every way and finally destroy them. When somebody's karma is over and the Supreme wants that particular person to leave the body, if the person has vital hunger and unsatisfied desires even though the soul does not have these desires, then the person wants to stay on earth. He does not want to obey the Will of the Supreme. So what should you do when a person has this kind of standard? If you tell him that God does not want him to stay on earth any more, that he has had all the necessary experiences in this body, then he will misunderstand. He will say: "God does not want me to leave the body; it is you who want this." He will think you are cruel and merciless. So if you know that it is the Will of the Supreme that this particular person should leave the world, the best thing is to silently speak to the soul of the person and try to inspire him to abide by the Will of God.

But if the person is very spiritual and a sincere seeker, then he himself will say to his relatives and dear ones: "Pray to God to take me away. I have finished my play here on earth. Read me spiritual books—the scriptures, the Bible, the Gita. Let me hear only divine things, spiritual things, which will help me start out on my journey." There are many, many people in India who, when they feel that their days are numbered, say: "The sooner He takes me, the better." When my mother was dying, she read the Gita constantly during her last few days with the attitude, "Now I am going to the eternal Father. Let me prepare myself." A patient of that type receives greater joy in knowing and obeying the Will of the Supreme.

Question: Is it always best for doctors to keep people alive as long as possible, or does it depend on the individual case?

Sri Chinmoy: If a person is spiritual, the doctors and relatives should always try to keep him on earth as long as possible, because spiritual people are always fighting against death. If somebody has the capacity to utter God's name soulfully just once more during his life, then he will achieve something in the soul's world. That achievement will be added to the other achievements of this life and in his next incarnation his life will be a little bit better.

In India some people live for over two hundred years, but they do not have time to pray to God even once in six months or a year. From a spiritual point of view, these people are like a solid piece of stone. For them each additional year is just another waste of time. But if one can stay on earth even one hour more and invoke the Presence of the Supreme during that hour, then naturally it is better for that person to stay on earth. Even unconsciously if someone is thinking of God, then it is better for him to stay as long as possible on earth.

Question: Can you postpone with your will power the time of death?

Sri Chinmoy: Certainly. Spiritual Masters can postpone it indefinitely if it is God's Will. A spiritual person gets this power when he has attained to spiritual perfection, because then he is absolutely surrendered to God. A disciple comes to a Guru and surrenders entirely to him. Similarly, a Guru has to make absolute surrender to God the Infinite. In this surrender he becomes one with God. He does not break the Law of God; he only tries to fulfill it. If God says, "I want you to leave the body now," he leaves the body. But if he sees that some hostile forces are attacking him and are untimely causing his death, then he uses his power because God wants him to live on earth to help humanity.

Having this power is of no use if you just want to stay on earth for two or three hundred years to live an ordinary animal life. A turtle lives for hundreds of years, but that does not mean that it is better than a human being. What we need is direct illumination, the knowledge of Truth, the knowledge of Light and the knowledge of God. It is not the years, but the achievements, that count.

Question: *What happens to the vital at the hour of death?*

Sri Chinmoy: There are two vitals. One is the physical vital, the vital that is in the physical. The other is the vital proper, the vital which does not belong to the physical. It is not identified with the physical; it is totally separate. When the soul leaves the body, the human being decomposes into its five elements. The vital proper enters into the vital sheath. The mind stays for a short while with the vital, for a few days or a few months, and then it goes back to the mind's level, the mental sheath. The soul stays in the vital sheath for two months, six months, sometimes even a few years; it depends on the individual soul. Then it passes to the mental world and then to the psychic world.

When the vital is in the vital sheath, it may suffer considerably. If the vital is unlit and impure, then it is tortured there most mercilessly. When our third eye is open, we see that no human punishment is as severe or as cruel as the vital punishment. Again, if the vital has aspired in its own way to be one with the soul, if the vital listened to the soul when the seeker was on earth, then the vital does not suffer in the vital zone. If the individual is spiritually advanced, he suffers practically nothing, because he knows the ins and outs of that realm. If a spiritual Master intervenes, he can very rapidly take a soul to the other inner worlds. The fastest that a spiritual Master can do this is nineteen days.

In the vital region itself there are higher worlds and there are lower worlds. On earth we have countries, and there they are called worlds. Here we say that some countries are bad and other countries are nice. All the inner worlds other than the vital worlds are good worlds, although some are higher than others. But in the vital region, some worlds are not so nice. The higher the soul goes, from the lower vital to the higher vital to the psychic worlds, the better for it. In the higher inner worlds souls have better treatment and better nourishment. Everything is better.

Question: *Do the circumstances under which a person dies determine where he goes after he leaves the body?*

Sri Chinmoy: That depends mainly on the consciousness of the individual, and this consciousness is the gradually accumulated achievement of his entire life. Good disciples will go to a very high plane immediately if they can think of their Master at the time of death. If a mother is killed while protecting her child, her soul will go to a high world. When a soldier dies defending his country, he will go to a high world.

In India there was a time when the wives threw themselves into the funeral pyre of their husbands. People may say that this is suicide, and granted it is. But in these cases the wives did not go to the lower worlds where people who commit suicide usually go. These wives had tremendous love and devotion for, and oneness with, their husbands, and God blessed their divine qualities and granted them the grace to go to the worlds where they would otherwise have gone according to the development of their souls.

Again, there were other wives who were forced to do this by law. They did it out of fear, out of necessity, but not out of a feeling of love or oneness. For them, too, the treatment was not the same in the inner world as for those who willfully committed suicide. They, too, went to their respective places according to their soul's standard. But those who gave their lives out of joy and oneness naturally created a strong connection with their husbands which will be maintained in future lives.

Question: *When we go to the other world after leaving the body, are there any forms or is it all formless?*

Sri Chinmoy: When somebody dies, if the soul wants to come and see the relatives still on earth, the soul usually takes the form that it had on earth so that the relatives can recognize it. But great spiritual Masters can recognize the soul no matter what form it takes. Even if the soul takes the form of a column of light, the Master can use his third eye and immediately recognize the soul.

Question: *What happens to the souls that have retired from work on earth? Will they eventually fill up the other worlds?*

Sri Chinmoy: There is lots of room in the other worlds. There we deal with Infinity.

Question: *What happens to the soul of an animal after it leaves the body?*

Sri Chinmoy: It has its own world. Each soul has its own capacity. The soul of a saint will not go to the same place as the soul of a thief. The saint will go to a much higher world. It all depends on the consciousness that the soul has revealed here on earth. So, animals will go to a world that will suit them. They will not go to a world where the souls are very highly developed.

Question: *Do our souls ever leave our bodies for just a second while we are alive?*

Sri Chinmoy: For a few seconds during the day the soul may leave, but the consciousness of the soul remains in the body at that time. This is your room and your whole vibration is here. As soon as somebody comes here, he will immediately feel your vibration. But if you go away and do not come back, then there will be nothing here. If the soul stays away, then its own body becomes foreign; its own room is foreign. But when it is a matter of dying, the body, like a cage, is broken. What is the use of staying in a broken cage?

Question: *I have heard that seeing the relatives' and friends' tears gives great joy to the soul when parting from this life. Is this true?*

Sri Chinmoy: In general there are three types of human souls: first there are what we call most ordinary, unenlightened; then good but ordinary souls; then great, extraordinary souls. When an ordinary man dies, he looks all around to see whether his dear and near ones are crying for him. If he sees that nobody is crying, then he gets terribly disheartened and says to himself: "All my life I have helped them in various ways. Now look at this ingratitude!" These ordinary souls are so attached to their dear ones and so attached to earth that they become disheartened if at this last moment their dear ones do not acknowledge their previous love and sacrifice. There are even some unenlightened souls that take a malicious attitude if their relatives do not mourn for them and come back in disembodied form to frighten their dear ones after they have left the body. If there are children in the family, the deceased may assume the ugliest form and come in front of the children to frighten them.

The second type of person has been nice, sweet and extremely helpful to the members of his family, and when he is about to die he feels that there should be a bond of affection and attachment which lasts forever. This kind of person does not want to leave the earth-scene. He feels that it is attachment alone that can maintain the connection between this world and the other world, so he tries to draw the utmost affection and sympathy and concern from his dear and near ones. If he sees that his dear and near ones are not showing any sympathy or sorrow for his loss, or are not crying bitterly, then he gets a tremendous pang in his inner existence. He feels: "Here I want to establish something permanently, and I am not getting any help or cooperation from the members of my family." But it is not the so-called human love, it is not human attachment, that can create an eternal divine bond between the departed soul and the souls that are in the land of the living. The love that binds human beings can never last; it is like a rope of sand. It is only the divine love that can transcend all barriers.

Then we come to great souls, that is to say, spiritual Masters. When a Master leaves the body and sees that his disciples are crying bitterly over their loss, the Master feels sorry because the disciples do not recognize him fully as a spiritual Master. A spiritual person, one who has realized God, lives on all planes; his consciousness pervades all the worlds. So if his disciples cry bitterly for him, feeling that they will see him no more, then they are putting their Master in the same category as an ordinary person. It is like an insult. The Master knows that he will appear before the disciples who are sincerely praying to him or who are meditating and aspiring sincerely. He knows that he will be all the time guiding, shaping and molding them. He knows that he will be able to enter into them, and they will be able to enter into him. So naturally he feels sad if his disciples take the attitude: "Now the Master is gone and we will never hear him again. Our prayers to him will be in vain, so it is useless to pray. Let us go to some other Master or let us try to find another means to make spiritual progress." So spiritual Masters feel sorry when their dearest ones cry or shed bitter tears for them, whereas ordinary people get joy from this.

Yes, for a while the disciples can feel sad that they have lost their Master, that they will not see him in the physical frame. But that sadness must not last because the soul's joy, the soul's intense love and all-pervading concern, have to enter into the disciples who have sincerely accepted the Master as the sole pilot of their lives.

Question: Do spiritual Masters ever appear in the subtle body after their death?

Sri Chinmoy: In India, many spiritual Masters have proved to their dear ones that death is not the end by appearing most vividly in the subtle body. I will give you just one example. Perhaps you have heard of the great spiritual Master named Sri Ramakrishna. When he left the body, his wife became a widow. It is customary in India that when the husband dies, the wife stops wearing her bangles and jewels. But when Sri Ramakrishna's wife was removing her jewelry, her husband appeared before her so vividly and said to her, "What are you doing? You should not take off these bangles and jewels. On the contrary, from now on you should wear golden bracelets and golden jewelry. I am now immortal. Therefore, you should wear something more beautiful, more meaningful and more fruitful." There are many incidents like that, only they are not recorded.

Question: Does the soul ever linger on earth after death in order to help its near and dear ones?

Sri Chinmoy: Some souls do not waste much time. They just go away. They only wait for a few days to see if their relatives and friends care for them. After three or four days they have experienced enough.

Again, some wise souls stay in spite of being very bright and powerful. They want to see if they can help their friends and relatives before they enter into the mental world. If they can be of some service to their dear ones, they do it. They help them in many ways by inspiring them. Sometimes they come to a friend or relative in a dream with some light, and they give some inspiration. Or they come to them and say, "There is nothing lasting on earth. As I have left the body, so also you will have to leave. My time is expired. Now I cannot do anything more for God on earth. So the best thing is to achieve something for God on earth. Do not waste time. Do as much as you can." Before it leaves the body, each soul feels sorry that it has wasted time. We all waste time. The soul can also give people answers either through luck or through inner communication. So there are many ways the soul can help its near and dear ones.

Question: Why do people keep the body for a few hours or even for a few days after the soul has departed?

Sri Chinmoy: You can say it is because the relatives want to see the remains. They feel sorry because this body, this person, helped them or loved them during life. The father does not see the mother's soul during her lifetime, but he sees her body, so he is attached to the physical. That is why when she dies, he wants to keep the physical as long as he can. When the soul has left, the body is useless. It is just like the old, dirty dress you put in the wastebasket. If it is an ordinary soul, after it leaves the body, it hovers in the house or in the yard or somewhere nearby. God gives the soul a chance to see whether the family really cared for it, and the soul gives the family a chance to show whether they actually cared about its death. Then after a few hours, usually about eleven hours although it may be longer, the soul departs and does not come back again.

Question: *Even if a seeker has not realized God while on earth, will his soul see God or realize God after it leaves the body?*

Sri Chinmoy: Every soul is bound to see God, because the soul comes directly from God. When the soul leaves the body, it goes to the vital world, the mental world, the psychic world and finally to the soul's own world. Here it rests for a while. Then, before it comes down for its next incarnation, the soul will have an interview with God. The soul has to stand in front of the Supreme and say how much it has achieved in its past incarnation. It will see the possibilities of its coming incarnation and make promises to the Supreme. The aims and ideals that the soul expresses for its role in the world of revelation and manifestation have to be approved by the Supreme. Sometimes the Supreme Himself says: "I expect this from you. Try to accomplish it for My sake there on earth."

The soul that sees God and has a conversation with Him is like a stranger to us, for most of us have not seen the soul on earth. Unless we have free access to the soul, unless we hear the voice of the soul and try to listen to its inner dictates, it is simply impossible for us to realize God. After it leaves the body, every soul will see God in the sense that I see you because I am standing in front of you. But when one realizes God in the physical, here on earth, it is a totally different matter. Here the whole consciousness—the physical consciousness, the individual consciousness—merges into the infinite Light and bliss. When we read spiritual books or listen to others, we may feel that God is ours. But our conscious oneness is something else. When we consciously feel God as our very own, then at every moment in our inner life, our inner existence, we feel boundless peace. Outwardly we may be excited or talking, but in our inner life we are a sea of peace, Light and delight. When this sea of peace, Light and delight comes into our physical being, our physical consciousness, then our inner divinity can be manifested on earth. In Heaven we cannot manifest anything, and also, we cannot realize anything. If the soul does not realize God while it is here on earth in the shackles of the finite, it will not realize God when it is in its own world. Realization can only be achieved through the physical.

Question: Have you ever had to actually fight the death-forces to save somebody's life?

Sri Chinmoy: Just this last Sunday I came very late to morning meditation because I was fighting with three death forces that wanted to snatch away three of my close disciples. With two I was really successful, but with the third I was not at all certain what was going to happen. It was not until the following day that I got the assurance that the third one would also survive. Otherwise, that night you would have seen someone in the New York Center snatched away. He was going to have a heart attack. The funniest part of the story is that this person was there at the morning meditation, meditating while I was fighting with the death-forces.

Question: I work in a cancer hospital where people frequently die. Sometimes when people are dying I see a quality or a look on their face which is very similar to something that I see in your face. Can you tell me why?

Sri Chinmoy: When I am united with the Universal Consciousness, I am in everybody. There are many people on earth who are not my disciples, but they are sincere seekers. God-realized souls who are of the first class will see when sincere seekers pray to God at the time of their death, or when their days are numbered. I tell you, if they pray to God or Christ or any other Master, if they are really sincerely knocking at God's door, they can find shining there Buddha's face, Krishna's face, my face because of our Universal Consciousness. Who these people are, I cannot tell. There are hundreds and thousands who are not my direct disciples. But they knock at the Universal Consciousness, and there receive my light, my compassion. That is why you see my face on their face. They see me, and get help from my compassionate inner being. At that time, an illumined part of my being, of my inner existence, goes there to give them some consolation, some little illumination, so that in the soul's world they can have a better existence and can come back again to aspire. If you look at a dying person and if you see my face, then you will know that this person is a seeker. There is no need for him to be my disciple. But if he has extremely sincere aspiration, because of my Universal Consciousness, I can be there with him.

There are times when my disciples meditate most soulfully on me and identify themselves with me to such an extent that other disciples will see on them my face. Their power of concentration on me is so sincere, so devoted, so one-pointed and soulful, that right on their face the disciples will see my face, even if the person is a woman. This has happened several times.

Question: What is the difference between cremation and a regular burial?

Sri Chinmoy: The outer difference you know: when it is cremation, the body is burned; when it is burial, the body is put into a coffin and buried. Indians especially are fire worshippers. They feel that fire not only consumes everything but also purifies everything. For fire we have a god, whose name is Agni. We pray to Agni for purification and for Self-knowledge, and we also give our dead to him.

From the spiritual point of view, we know that the body has come into existence from five elements: earth, water, air, ether and energy. From five elements the physical sheath came into existence, and with the help of fire it will go back into the five elements. With cremation the physical body will dissolve with utmost purification, which here means transformation.

Again, those in the West who prefer burial also have their own spiritual interpretation. A kind of spiritual compassion comes because the body has served us so faithfully, and we say: "Oh, I utilized this body for so many years and never gave it any rest. Now the soul is not there; the bird has flown away. Let me give the body a chance to rest and have it put into a coffin." Those who care for burning the body feel that the body, which has done so many silly, evil things in this life, needs purification. And those who care for burial want to give the body a comfortable rest.

Question: How does giving your body to science alter you spiritually?

Sri Chinmoy: It is neither noble nor ignoble. It is only an individual choice. As you know, sometimes the body is cremated and sometimes it is buried. Once the soul leaves the body, the soul does not care what happens to the body. Once the bird flies away, only the cage remains. At that time we can do anything we want with the cage.

One individual gets satisfaction by saying, "After I die, I want to give my body to a hospital so that medical science can make some experiments which will be of great help in the future." But another person says, "Only let God's Will operate in and through my relatives. Let my relatives bury me if they want to; if they want to cremate me, let them cremate me." So he leaves it entirely up to the wishes of the relatives. Or an individual may say, "No, I want tradition to be carried on. I want my body to be buried or cremated in the normal way." But no particular way will necessarily please God more. God has given us the freedom to make an individual choice. If we want cremation, God will say, "Wonderful!" If we want burial, God will say, "Wonderful!" If we want our body to be taken to a hospital for experimentation after the soul leaves, God will in no way be displeased or dissatisfied with us.

Question: You have spoken about physical death. Could you say something about the kind of death and rebirth that occurs in the spiritual life?

Sri Chinmoy: When we wholeheartedly, sincerely and unreservedly accept the spiritual life, we feel that it is the real death of ignorance, of desire, of limitation. It is the death of our limited, strangling, unfulfilled and obscure consciousness in the vital. It is the vital that is craving to fulfill all kinds of desires, not the physical, so this death takes place in the vital plane. When we really launch into the spiritual life we have an inner death. This death is the death of our past, of the way we have formed our past.

We will build the edifice of Truth on aspiration, not on desires and worries or anxieties and doubts. The past wanted to show us the Truth in one way. But the past was not able to show us the Truth; that is why we are what we are in the present. Whether the present will show us the Truth or not, we do not know. But we think we will see the reality either in the immediate present or in the fast-dawning future, the future that is growing in the immediacy of today.

One of the mysteries in the spiritual life is that at every moment we are dying and renewing ourselves. Each moment we see that a new consciousness, a new thought, a new hope, a new light is dawning in us. When something new dawns, at that time we see that the old has been transformed into something higher, deeper and more profound. So in the higher spiritual life, at every moment we can see the so-called death of our limited consciousness and its transformation into a newer, brighter consciousness.

Question: I was actually talking more in terms of rebirth. How can I become like a child again and accomplish this spiritual rebirth?

Sri Chinmoy: This rebirth must take place in the mind, in the body and in the vital. It must take place in the innermost, unconscious part of yourself, that part which has been engulfed by ignorance, imperfection and limitation. When this spiritual rebirth takes place and you feel the dawn of a new consciousness in yourself, please try to become that consciousness and give it to your Master and to the Supreme, as you would offer a flower. When you are giving the flower, feel that it is not something you have plucked from a tree, but that it is your entire being which you are placing at the Feet of the Supreme. Then you will see this flower blooming petal by petal, and you will bloom inwardly with your inner fragrance, like a child. Deep within yourself a child will be growing and your outer age will disappear from you. But this will happen only when your aspiring consciousness has full mastery over your body, vital, mind and heart and has made your whole existence into a flower which you have offered at the Feet of the Supreme.

It is inevitable for each human being who has entered into the spiritual life to have a spiritual rebirth in this life. Everyone must feel that he is a conscious, dynamic instrument, a child of the Divine. Everyone has to feel this truth and become this truth. When it is done, the child is no longer a child; he becomes Divinity itself. And then God-realization is not only possible but inevitable. Only a child has the right to be in the lap of the Father, and the Father is eager to have the child in His lap. He is proud of having the child and the child is proud of having the Father.

Question: Do you think there is communication between the living and the dead?

Sri Chinmoy: There is a way to communicate with the dead. As a matter of fact, there are various ways. If one has occult power or spiritual power, one can easily communicate with anybody living or departed. What we call death is not the extinction of consciousness. It is only a transition. Today I am here; tomorrow I will be in New York. Similarly, now I am here on this earth; after some years, I will be somewhere else in one of the other worlds. Depending on the strength of our Self-realization, we can enter into the soul of a person who is either here or elsewhere; either in Heaven or in hell.

On earth we can make either a local call or a long-distance call to any part of the world. The telephone is the medium. Similarly, our conscious oneness with God or, we can say, our Self-realization, enables us to commune with anybody, whether here on earth or there in Heaven.

Question: Why is it that so many linger in pain for a long time before dying?

Sri Chinmoy: Many sick people want to die because their pain is unbearable. They want to be free from their suffering. But why do they still linger and suffer? It is because purification of their nature has not been completed. Through purification we enter into a higher life and a more fulfilling divinity. This is where the law of karma operates. In our past lives, we have done many things wrong. It is through this physical pain that we are purified. This experience is necessary, because through it a new wisdom dawns in the person's consciousness. But when someone suffers bitterly we should not think of his past actions, that he led a bad life and had a bad character, and for this he is suffering. No, let us become one with the experience that he is going through. When we are one with the experience, we get true satisfaction in our human existence.

Again, I have to say that the law of karma is not simple; it is very, very complicated. Some souls are very pure and spiritual, but still they suffer when they die. Is it because of their past wrong karma? No, it is because they identify with humanity and want to experience for themselves the bitterest kind of suffering. Most of the great spiritual Masters have had very painful deaths. Why? At their own sweet will they could have left their body, but they did not do it. Instead they contracted cancer and other serious diseases, and only after much suffering did they die. In their case, what they were doing was entering into humanity's suffering and trying to feel how humanity suffers. Unless we enter into the suffering of humanity, everything is theoretical; nothing is practical. But if ordinary people suffer, we see that it is the law of karma that is operating.

Nevertheless, if someone dies of sudden heart failure, that does not necessarily mean that he was very spiritual or religious. No, God wanted to have this particular experience through him, and perhaps through his loved ones, at that particular time. Here there is no question of good or bad, divine or undivine, but of what kind of experience God wanted to have in that particular person. Ultimately everything is an experience of God that we are seeing or having.

Question: Will we see you when we leave the body?

Sri Chinmoy: If you are my true disciple, you are bound to see me when you leave the body. That much I assure you. If you are my real disciple, you will not be able to die without my knowledge and consent. At that time I will stand right in front of you and take you in my chariot. I will carry you in a golden or silver or bronze chariot. You will see. This is the promise that great spiritual Masters give: they will come and take the souls of their disciples to the higher worlds.

Question: Will we see you after you leave the body?

Sri Chinmoy: You may see me in a dream for a minute or two. Spiritual Masters, when they leave the body, often open the third eye of their disciples for a few minutes.

Question: Will everyone see you in the inner world after death?

Sri Chinmoy: The soul's region is a big place, a vast place. The earth is also a vast place. If you had not come to my Center, I would not have seen you. In the inner world I move from one place to another. Now if my real headquarters is on the plane that a person is on, then certainly that person will see me. We will have a group of people there who truly love me and are sincerely devoted to me. We will dwell together in the same plane. But those who do not care for me, those who know nothing about me and have no connection with me will not see me, unless it is the express Will of the Supreme. Those people will see others at their own level of development. They will dwell with the ones whom they loved.

Question: Many people who have close calls with death often report a similar experience—coming face to face with a luminous being or a light which gives them a message. What are these beings?

Sri Chinmoy: Sometimes they are not beings at all, but the souls of deceased relatives. Sometimes they are old and friendly acquaintances from previous incarnations. Sometimes they are fate-making angels or deities. Sometimes they are fruitful imaginations of the seeker's soulful aspiration.

Question: A friend of mine, a lady who was very spiritual, passed away recently. Will her friends come to meet her in a beautiful Heaven?

Sri Chinmoy: If her friends were also spiritual and highly developed, naturally they will come to receive her if they themselves are still in Heaven. But if her friends left the body long before she did, who knows where they are now? They may be in the region of Heaven, or they may be still loitering in the vital plane, or they may have taken human incarnation already. But if they have passed through the vital world, the mental world and a few other worlds, and are now enjoying the blissful rest of Heaven, and if the souls still maintain their same sweet feeling for your friend, then naturally they will come to receive her and help her enjoy a life of bliss in Heaven.

My own mother happened to be a very, very spiritual woman. When my mother was leaving the body, a very close relative of mine saw in a dream that my mother's friends were coming in a golden chariot to receive her. When my father died, one of my uncles, who was away in the city, saw another uncle of mine and a few other people coming to take my father in a golden boat. There were many to receive my father and mother because both they and many of their friends and relatives were very spiritual.

In the case of almost all religious and spiritual people, the relatives do come. It is easier for spiritual people to come, because they have almost a free access to this world. When ordinary people who are not spiritual and aspiring leave the body, they do not go immediately to God. They stay in the vital world and suffer a great deal. When one disciple's father died, he went to the vital world where he was not treated well. He was having quite a few problems there until one of the vital beings asked him if he had known any religious or spiritual people in his life. He said, "Yes, I know my daughter's friend," who happened to be me. When my name was said, immediately the vital beings knew with whom he was connected, so he was released immediately. He was then able to leave the vital world, the world of torture, and go to a very good higher world.

When another disciple's father died, he went to a very high place, but he was not satisfied there. Her father had seen me only once, in Canada, but when he had, his whole body had been thrilled from head to foot with ineffable joy. So when he left the body and was not satisfied with the plane he was in, his soul came to me and said, "I want to go to a higher world." So I called on one of my own departed friends, Jyotish, to take him to the plane where he was living. Now he is extremely happy there, in this very high world. He sometimes comes to me and expresses his deepest joy.

Question: *Will the soul be able to have some kinds of experiences in the worlds it goes to after it leaves the body?*

Sri Chinmoy: As soon as the soul leaves this physical body, the physical body will be dissolved in matter. The body enters into the physical sheath, the vital enters into the vital sheath and the mind enters into the mental plane proper. The soul will go through the subtle physical, the vital, the mental, the psychic and then finally to the soul's own region. As it passes through each of these planes, the soul takes up with it the essence of all the experiences it had on earth.

The soul gets various kinds of subtle experiences in these other sheaths, but these experiences are not going to manifest in these worlds. If the soul gets some experience here on earth, the experience is bound to be manifested either today or tomorrow. In the soul's world there is no manifestation. Progress is there, but not in the sense of evolution.

We enter into the soul's world to take rest. But if our soul associates with a higher soul, a more illumined soul, then naturally we will be inspired. If, in the soul's world, we are near a spiritual Master or some other very great, significant, spiritual person, then naturally we will be influenced. The soul can aspire in any world. In the higher worlds it will have only aspiration, and this aspiration will eventually take the form of experience. Aspiration itself is an experience. But on earth, when the soul observes suffering or joy or the activities of the world, the experiences that the soul gets here are constantly leading it towards the fuller manifestation of divinity.

Question: *When the soul leaves the body after death, you said it enters into the vital sphere. What is the vital sphere?*

Sri Chinmoy: The vital sphere or region is simply a world, and that world is also within us. As we have the physical world, so also we have the vital world, the mental world, the psychic world, the soul's world and other worlds. When we go within, immediately after the physical is the vital world. This vital world is operating every day in us. Sometimes our physical consciousness will enter into the vital;

other times the vital world enters into the physical. Very often we enter into the vital world in our dreams. When the soul passes from one plane of consciousness to another in our dreams, the first plane it enters into when it leaves the physical is the vital. And when the soul leaves the body and the person dies, the first step on the soul's journey towards its own resting place, its destination is the vital world. Some souls suffer there, while others do not. It is like visiting a strange, new country. Some are fortunate enough to mix freely with the people of the new country and understand its culture in almost no time, while others are not so fortunate.

The vital that we have embodied here in this physical world is something solid. With our physical eyes we cannot see the vital, but in our feelings, in our inner perception, we can feel it. Again, with our human eyes we can actually see the vital movement and activity here on earth. This vital can take and has taken the real form of a subtle body. When the soul leaves the body and the body stops functioning, this form becomes formless; the vital form that we had during our lifetime enters into the vital sheath. The vital which had form enters into the formless vital. There it takes rest or disintegrates, while the soul travels back to its own region.

Question: What is it like in the vital world?

Sri Chinmoy: In the vital world immediately after the physical world, there is tremendous chaos and restlessness, insecurity, obscurity, dissatisfaction and a sense of incompleteness. Nevertheless, a tremendous power is operating in and through all these forces. This world is a portion of the passage through which the souls come into the physical world before birth and return to the higher worlds after death. This vital world is very chaotic. If you go there, you will see many broken and deformed things, as though a cyclone has hit the area. In this particular vital world the migrating beings are not usually happy. They become happy only when they have passed through it and entered into a higher vital world where a conscious aim and an upward urge are palpable.

DESIRE

Question: Speak to us about desire.

Sri Chinmoy: Desire is temptation. When temptation is nourished, true happiness becomes starved. Aspiration is the soul's awakening. The soul's awakening is the birth of supernal delight. It is only through high, higher and highest aspiration that one can get rid of all temptations, seen and unseen, born and yet to be born. Temptation is a universal disease. For a man without aspiration, temptation is unmistakably irresistible. But a true seeker feels and knows he can resist temptation and what he cannot resist is transformation, the transformation of his physical nature, his entire consciousness. Of course, this transformation is something he does not want to resist. On the contrary, it is for this transformation that he lives on earth.

Question: How can I separate myself from my physical desires?

Sri Chinmoy: First of all, since you have accepted the spiritual life, you have to ask yourself whether desire satisfies and fulfills you or not. In your inner being you will feel that it neither satisfies nor fulfills you. Before you actually desire, you have in mind the object or fruit of your desire, and you think that when you attain that object, you will be happy. Unfortunately, what you eventually get is frustration. When you enter into the physical or lower vital desire with your mind, you are caught. You enter into the very jaws of a devouring tiger. When you concentrate on desire, you can feel inwardly that in the beginning there is no light, in the end there is no light and in the middle there is no light. There is only darkness from the beginning to the end, and darkness means the absence of divine satisfaction. If you can feel this result before you actually desire, then you can easily turn your life away from desire.

You have to feel that what you want is aspiration and not desire. The moment one begins to aspire he feels true satisfaction. This true satisfaction comes because aspiration has the capacity to identify itself consciously and soulfully with the farthest corner of the globe, with the deepest and inmost being and with the highest transcendental Self. If you feel the real necessity of aspiration, you will see that physical, vital and mental desires will stop knocking at your heart's door.

At every moment you have to aim at your goal. If you want to concentrate and meditate on the sun as it rises early in the morning, then you have to face the east, and not some other direction. If you are looking toward the west and running toward the east, you will stumble. If you want to be certain of your goal of God-realization, then you will not look behind you or around you, but only toward the Light. You can conquer your physical desires only by running toward the Light. Do not think of your physical desires, but think only of your aspiration. If you can run forward with one-pointed determination, limitations and desires will fade away from your life. Aspiration is the only answer. For outer things you cry; for inner things you can also cry. If you can cry sincerely, you can fly spiritually.

When I think, I sink. When I choose, I lose. When I cry, I fly.

Question: *What happens when our desires are not fulfilled?*

Sri Chinmoy: Man has countless desires. When his desires are not fulfilled, he curses himself; he feels that he is a failure, hopeless and helpless. He wants to prove his existence on earth with the fruits of his desires. He thinks that by fulfilling his desires he will be able to prove himself superior to others. But alas! He fails, he has failed and he will fail.

Question: *Is it proper to have a motivation for achieving realization, such as the desire for liberation? Is this a proper motivation?*

Sri Chinmoy: Certainly it is a proper motivation. There are two different approaches to God-realization. One approach is to make a complete surrender to the Will of God. This surrender has to be dynamic. Otherwise, you will be like the millions of lethargic people on earth, wallowing in the pleasures of ignorance, who are waiting for realization at God's hour. It will take these people millions of years to realize God. For if they do not utilize the capacity God has given them, then why should God play His role? In dynamic surrender, we play our role and utilize the capacity God has given us; then we leave it up to God to give us what He wants when He wants. In dynamic surrender, we make a full personal effort and then pray for the divine grace. An ordinary person wants to achieve his goal by any means, by hook or by crook. But in the spiritual life, we do not do this. We use our patience.

The other approach is to have some idea of what we want when we are praying and meditating. Let us say I want to be good. This is quite legitimate. If I become good, that means there will be one less rascal on earth, and God's creation will be better. So I am praying to God to give me something which will help Him in expanding His own Light on earth. In order to be of some service to mankind and to please God in God's own way, we have to become good. But only when we realize God can we be of real help to Him. Unless we are realized, unless we are free from the meshes of ignorance, what can we give to humanity? Unless we have some peace, Light and bliss, how can we help either God or mankind?

The great spiritual Master Sri Ramakrishna used to pray, "O Mother Divine, make me the greatest of the Yogis." Ordinary people will say, "What kind of Master prays to be the greatest?" But this was not competition on Sri Ramakrishna's part. He knew that if he could become divinely great, then he could be of real service to mankind. So there is nothing wrong in praying for realization and liberation. If you do not have any motive, if you do not feel any inner hunger for God or for peace, Light and bliss, then God will say, "Sleep, My child, sleep, as millions and billions of other people on earth are sleeping."

Question: *Could you speak on the role desire plays in the movement toward God-realization?*

Sri Chinmoy: We often feel in our daily experience that desire is one thing and God is something else. Desire, we say, is bad in the spiritual life, for when we desire something, we feel it is the object itself that we desire. It is true that through aspiration alone we can realize God, but we have to know that God abides in our desire as well as in our aspiration. When we come to realize that desire also has its existence in God, we get our first illumination.

Our earthly journey starts with desire, and in the ordinary life we cannot live without it. But if we feel that we are not ready for the spiritual life just because we have teeming desires, then I wish to say we will never be ready for the spiritual life. We have to start our spiritual journey here and now, even while we are walking along the path of desire.

Let us take desire as an object and try to feel the Breath of God inside it. Slowly and unmistakably the Breath of God will come to the fore and transform our desire into aspiration. Then, if we apply this process to aspiration as well, we will come to feel that our aspiration and our earthly existence can never be separated.

Question: Is is sometimes better to have desire than to just be lazy?

Sri Chinmoy: There are two kinds of men on earth who do not have desire: those who have liberated souls and those who have dull, inert, lifeless souls. Liberated souls have freed themselves from bondage, limitations and imperfections. They have become free from ignorance and have become one with their souls in transcendental illumination. On the other hand, some human beings want nothing from life. They just wallow in the pleasures of idleness and lethargy; they have no aspiration for anything. So they will never, ever have illumination.

The great spiritual hero, Swami Vivekananda, was once asked by a young man how he might realize God. Vivekananda said, "From now on start telling lies." The young man said, "You want me to tell lies? How then can I realize God? It is against spiritual principles." But Vivekananda said, "I know better than you. I know what your standard is. You will not budge an inch; you are useless, you are practically dead to the ordinary life, not to speak of the spiritual life. If you start telling lies, people will pinch you and strike you, and then you will exert your own personality. First you have to develop your own individuality and personality. Then a day will come when you will have to surrender your individuality and personality to the divine wisdom, the infinite Light and bliss. But you have to start your journey first."

There is another story about a man who came to Swami Vivekananda and asked him about God-realization. Vivekananda said, "Go and play football. You will be able to realize God sooner if you play football than if you study the *Bhagavad Gita*." Strength is required in order to realize God. This strength need not be the strength of a wrestler or boxer, but the amount of strength required for normal day-to-day life is absolutely necessary.

There are some unbalanced persons who feel that they will realize God by walking along the street like a vagabond or by torturing their body and remaining weak. Their physical weakness they take as a harbinger of God-realization. The great Lord Buddha tried the path of self-mortification, but he came to the conclusion that the middle path without extremes is the best. We have to be normal; we have to be sound in our day-to-day life. Aspiration is not one thing and our physical body something else. Our heart's aspiration and our physical body go together; the physical aspiration and the psychic aspiration can and must run together.

Question: *Is it not the duty of a Master to try to please the wants and desires of his devotees?*

Sri Chinmoy: A spiritual Master tries to please his disciples on all levels. At times he succeeds, at times he does not. At times he gets a hundred out of a hundred from them; sometimes he gets zero out of a hundred.

It is not always possible for the Master to please his disciples. Sometimes a disciple feels that the Master is unkind or does not care for him if the Master does not give him what he wants. But if the Master does give him what he wants, the disciple's soul will feel miserable and will curse the Master. And the Supreme will hold the

Master responsible. He will say that the Master is consciously delaying the progress of that particular disciple. If a child wants to eat poison, the mother does not give him poison just to please him.

Question: *What desires then will you not be able to fulfill?*

Sri Chinmoy: There are many, many things that I will not be able to give you, whereas others will be able to give you these things or you may be able to get them from the outer world. I do not have the capacity to fulfill these kinds of outer desires. When it is a matter of fulfilling your desires or demands, I am not the person. But what happens is that, out of compassion, I try to fulfill them. I fulfill somebody's outer demand out of compassion. Then, when I see that that disciple is slowing down in his spiritual life, I feel that since I made the mistake, it is my responsibility. So I put that person on my shoulder and I run with him. Then, when I bring him back to normal speed, I say, "All right, now you go." But a few days later he will again slow down and fall. So I have to put him on my shoulders again.

DEVOTION TO THE GURU

Question: What is devotion? Just a desire to do everything possible for one's Guru?

Sri Chinmoy: For a disciple, devotion means his purified, simplified, intensified, consecrated, conscious and constant oneness with his Guru. The disciple must feel that the Guru is the spiritual magnet constantly pulling him towards the infinite Light of the Supreme. Devotion does not mean just a desire to do everything possible for one's Guru. Devotion is something infinitely deeper than desire. Devotion is the conscious awareness of Light in operation. In this Light, the aspirant will discover that when he does something for the Guru or the Guru asks him to do something for him, he has already been given more than the necessary capacity by the Guru.

Question: What are the manifestations of devotion?

Sri Chinmoy: The manifestations of devotion are simplicity, sincerity, spontaneity, beauty and purity. The manifestations of devotion are also one's intense, devoted feeling for the object of one's adoration and the feeling of one's consecrated oneness with the Inner Pilot.

Question: If we feel that we are not devoted enough, how can we increase our devotion?

Sri Chinmoy: If the aspirant feels that he is not devoted enough, then he can do four things to increase his devotion. He should try to love the Master more than he already does. He should try to feel that the Master loves him infinitely more than he thinks. He should try to develop more purity in his outer life. He should try to feel that

Devotion to the Guru • 75

the highest Truth can and will come to him from the Master and through the Master alone.

Question: *If one has aspiration but not devotion, does this hinder his spiritual progress?*

Sri Chinmoy: If the aspirant has aspiration and not devotion for the Master, certainly it hinders considerably the aspirant's spiritual progress. If the aspirant does not care for a Master and wants to aspire all by himself, then it is a different matter. He is not expected to show devotion to anyone. But here also I want to say that if he really aspires, then he has to feel that one day he has to reach his far-distant goal through devotion. In order to reach the goal, even without a Guru, he still needs conscious devotion to the goal itself, and if the aspirant feels that he has no need for this devotion, then he is hopelessly mistaken.

There comes a time in the spiritual life when one is bound to feel that devotion and aspiration can never be separated. Devotion is the candle, aspiration is the flame. No matter which path one follows, if his aspiration is not founded on one-pointed and surrendered devotion towards his highest goal, then the realization of the ultimate Truth will always remain impossible.

Question: *What happens to those people who attempt to insult a Master?*

Sri Chinmoy: One of Shyama Charan Lahiri's disciples was named Kali Kumar. He worked in an office and used to visit the Master quite often. Unfortunately, Kali Kumar's boss did not like the idea of his being devoted to a spiritual Master. His boss was a middle-aged man, and he wanted to be Kali Kumar's only boss, so he literally hated the spiritual Master.

One day, the boss followed Kali Kumar to his Master's ashram with the idea of insulting the Master. He wanted to complain that Kali Kumar was not as obedient to him as he was to the Master. Before the boss could say anything, however, Shyama Charan Lahiri started speaking to Kali Kumar. "Today I wish to show you something which may please you. Turn off the light." Kali Kumar turned off the light and they meditated for a few minutes. Then the Master said, "Can you see anything?" Both Kali Kumar and his boss saw a most beautiful young girl. Then the Master said to the boss, "Do you recognize her?" The boss was so ashamed and embarrassed.

"Is it not your lover?" Shyama Charan continued. "Your wife and children are so devoted and faithful to you. How is it that you have fallen desperately in love with this girl?"

Kali Kumar's boss cried and cried. "Please forgive me," he begged the Master, "I want to become your disciple. I want to be initiated by you."

Shyama Charan said, "I cannot initiate you right now. You have to wait for six months. If you lead a pure life for six months and remain faithful to your wife, I will initiate you."

The boss remained faithful to his wife for only three months; then he went back to his girlfriend, and after four months he passed away.

If you try to harass a real spiritual Master, then ruthless embarrassment will dog you. The spiritual Master will easily forgive you, but it will be most difficult, almost impossible, for your own soul to forgive you. Your soul knows that a true spiritual Master is not only your best friend but your only friend. When you harass a spiritual Master, you attempt to break the eternal friendship that shines between your soul and the spiritual Master; therefore, your soul does not approve of it at all. At that time, your soul invokes the cosmic Will or justice-Light to play the role inside your unaspiring and unlit life.

Question: Does an insult to a Master bring retribution?

Sri Chinmoy: One day Troilanga Swami was walking along the street naked when a magistrate and his wife saw him. The wife was horrified and wanted to have him arrested. As the guards were about to arrest the Yogi, Troilanga Swami suddenly disappeared. There were many people surrounding him, so everyone was surprised that he could escape. After a short time, he appeared in the same spot, smiling. The magistrate got furious. "Why do you do this kind of thing?" he shouted. He insulted the Master mercilessly, saying, "You are such an odd-looking fellow! Why do you move around naked? Do you have no sense? You create so much nuisance for us!" But he let Troilanga Swami go.

That night the magistrate had a dream. In the dream he saw a *sannyasi*, wearing the skin of a tiger and holding a trident, running towards him to kill him. The *sannyasi* said to the magistrate, "How did you dare to insult Troilanga Swami? He is such a great spiritual Master. I shall not let you remain in this sanctified city of Benares." The magistrate was frightened to death. He shouted out loud in his sleep, and his attendants came to his rescue and woke him up.

The following day the magistrate himself went to Troilanga Swami, placed himself at his feet and begged for forgiveness, which was immediately granted.

When one insults a God-realized Master, he incurs immediate retribution, not from the Master himself but from God, who loves the Master, His supreme instrument, more than He loves Himself. The Master forgives the culprits, for forgiveness is what he knows. But God, in spite of being His own eternity's and infinity's forgiveness, does not allow His chosen instrument to be ridiculed and insulted, for His instrument is he who is of God and for God alone. After all, what God wants is always the constant manifestation of His own Truth-Light-Beauty.

THE DISCIPLE-MASTER
RELATIONSHIP

Question: What are some things a disciple must do to receive the utmost from a spiritual Master?

Sri Chinmoy: Some disciples think that when their spiritual Master leaves the earth they have to become very strict with themselves in order to remain spiritual. It is their feeling that while the spiritual Master is still with them in the physical, they can enjoy themselves. I wish to say, no. These disciples are acting like children who feel that they should just enjoy life while their parents are on earth because when the parents are gone they will have to become very serious in order to earn their own livelihood. This attitude is wrong. While the Master is on earth, you have to do your utmost. When he is in the other world, you have also to do your utmost.

If one really wants to become a divine instrument, he has to work very, very hard all the time. Otherwise, some people may stay with the Master for twenty years and get nothing, while some who come later will get things in one year or in one day which the others who were with the Master longer have never got at all.

Question: Could you give an illustration of how a new disciple can get more from a Master than an old disciple?

Sri Chinmoy: Just today I was reading a story about a spiritual Master who advised two seekers to go and accept another Master. It happened that the second spiritual Master was unkind, rude and in every way insulting to the seekers when they came to him. Nevertheless, the two seekers would not leave this Master. Finally the Master said, "All right, come back tomorrow. I will speak to you then." The two seekers came the following day, but this time the spiritual Master would not even come out of his house. He sent one of his guards to tell them that he did not want to see them. The seekers said, "Just yesterday he scolded us, insulted us and promised to see us today. Please go and tell him." The guard said, "This spiritual Master is far above morality. He does not have to keep his promises." But the seekers pleaded with him. Finally they were granted permission to see the spiritual Master. When the Master saw that these same seekers had come again with tremendous aspiration, he asked them a few questions and told them about their future life. Then they wanted to have some spiritual blessings and love.

The spiritual Master said, "For spiritual love, you do not have to be near me. No matter where you are, if you are sincere, you will get it. If you are not sincere, you will be like this fellow beside me. For the past twelve years I have not been able to give him anything. But here is another one who is also my student. He has received considerably from me, although I have seen him only once before, many years ago. You two who have come here for the first time have also received much from me. But this man who has been with me for so many years has not received anything from me."

If one does not try to please the Master while he is on earth, how can one expect to please the Master in Heaven? He who sincerely pleases the Master now will please him in Heaven as well. If the disciple does not please the Master here and now, the Master will have no faith that that person will please him anywhere else. Pleasing one's Master has to be done all the time, like breathing. You breathe in and out all the time, everywhere. If you know how to please the Master when he is with you, then you will be able to please him after he has left the body.

Question: How can a disciple best please his Master?

Sri Chinmoy: A disciple can best please his Master if he does not expect anything from the Master. He will give and give and give and offer himself totally and unconditionally. Only then will the Master be most pleased with him. At that time the Master will give him infinitely more than he deserves.

Right from the beginning, the disciple's devoted, dedicated action should be absolutely unconditional. The disciple feels that his time, his effort, his capacity and his dedication are all his treasures. When he has given his treasures to the Master, he thinks that he has a legitimate right to expect the Master to give him peace, Light and bliss, which are the Master's treasures. But there should be no bargaining in the spiritual life. If the disciple gives something of his, he immediately expects something in return, because he is living in the world of give and take. But the Master knows what is best for the disciple and also when it is best to give it. If the Master gives something untimely, instead of illumining the unlit consciousness of the disciple, he will just break the inner vessel. The power of the Master is bound to illumine the disciple if the disciple has receptivity. If the disciple has no receptivity, then the Master's power will be of no use. On the contrary, it will be harmful. Very often when I touch and bless someone, I get such resistance or unwillingness to accept what I have to offer. And at that time what happens? I can force Light or power from Above into this adamantine wall of resistance, but it would only break.

So if you want to please the Master in a perfect way, then the word "expectation" should go out of your vocabulary. If you expect, you will expect in your own mental way: "I am doing this for the Master, so the Master will do something for me, or I will be his favorite." There are so many expectations. But beyond expectation is the divine Truth. The Master knows what to give and how to give. But the disciple has his own way of expecting something from the Master. So there is a conflict between the Master and the disciple.

By giving something to the Master, if you feel that you will be able to please the Master, to some extent it is true. But you can really please the Master by not expecting anything after you have given him something, for then the Master will be able to operate in the disciple in his own way. The Master will feel "He has given me his treasure, but he does not want anything from me. Now it is up to me to decide what to give. So I shall give him the best, the very best." But if somebody gives the Master something and then thinks that the Master will favor him in something, or say something very nice about him, then he has already begged for something in the inner world. So naturally the Master will try his best to give him that. But if he had left the choice to the Master, if he had given the Master the opportunity to give what the Master wanted, at that time the Master could have given him abundant peace, Light and bliss.

The best way to please the Master is to give what you have and what you are, but without the least possible expectation. In that way you get every divine thing in infinite measure from the Master and, at the same time, the Supreme in the Master can utilize you for His own purpose.

Question: How important is it to have faith in one's Guru?

Sri Chinmoy: Swami Satchidananda had a statue of a particular god. He asked his disciple Nigamananda to worship it, but Nigamananda did not care for this statue. One day the Master said to him, "Why do you not worship the statue which I worship? How is it that you do not see or feel anything inside my beloved Lord?"

Nigamananda said, "You may see your beloved Lord there, but I see only a piece of lifeless wood."

At this the Master became furious. He insulted Nigamananda mercilessly and told him, "If you show disrespect once more to my beloved Lord, I shall throw you out of my ashram! Be careful!" Then the Master left the room to attend to ashram business.

Nigamananda was humiliated and very angry. He immediately took the statue off the shrine and gave it a smart slap, exclaiming, "You! For you I have got such a severe scolding from my Master. You deserve my punishment." Then he placed it again on the shrine.

A few minutes later the Master came back and said to him, with a broad smile, "You said my Lord is a lifeless piece of wood, but does anybody strike a lifeless thing? Only when we see that someone or something has life do we get satisfaction by striking it. One does not speak to a lifeless thing, for a lifeless thing cannot understand or respond. No, you do see something inside the statue. I was so pleased when I heard you speaking to my Lord. My Lord not only has life, but embodies the universal and transcendental life. So from now on please worship this statue."

Nigamananda bowed to his Master and said, "Please forgive

me. I shall worship this statue, and inside the statue I shall see and feel you, Master."

The Master said, "That is absolutely the right thing for you to do, my son."

Faith is of paramount importance. One needs faith in infinite measure in one's Master. The human mind may sometimes find it difficult to believe in the Master's way, but the aspiring heart is always one with the Master's inner and outer operations. The seeker always has to remain in the heart. To have faith in one's Master is to feel God's own Presence here, there and everywhere. It is not what the object is, not who the man is, but whether or not one retains faith in one's Master's spiritual realization. Then one achieves success in the outer world and progress in the inner world convincingly, easily and rapidly.

Question: *Should one always consider his Guru the Highest?*

Sri Chinmoy: Once Nigamananda went to visit the Kumbhamela, India's most famous fair, which literally countless people attend. He was delighted to see his Guru, Swami Satchidananda, there. A different spiritual Master presides over each fair, and this time the great Master Shankaracharya, Satchidananda's Guru, was presiding over the fair. Everybody was full of adoration for Shankaracharya, who was sitting near Satchidananda.

When Nigamananda arrived, he bowed to his Master first and then bowed to Shankaracharya. Everybody was shocked. How was it possible for him to bow to Satchidananda first, when Shankaracharya was sitting right beside him? Some people said to Nigamananda, "You are such a fool! Do not you know how to discriminate?"

Nigamananda replied, "I do know how to discriminate. I tell you, nobody can be superior to one's own Guru. My Guru is and will always remain Highest to me. Therefore, I did the right thing by bowing to him first."

On hearing this Shankaracharya gave Nigamananda a broad smile and said to him, "You are right, my son, you are right." Then he asked Nigamananda a few spiritual questions which Nigamananda answered perfectly. Then Shankaracharya said to Satchidananda,

"What are you doing? Why are you not asking this disciple of yours to have his own disciples and to help illumine mankind? I clearly see that he is ready for that."

Then, in front of Shankaracharya and all the seekers who were nearby, Satchidananda declared, "My spiritual son Nigamananda has realized God. From now on he will accept disciples and illumine their minds and fulfill their hearts."

At the journey's start the Master is the boatman, the boat and the river. At the journey's end, the Master becomes the goal itself. A beginner-seeker sees the Master as the boat. When he crosses beyond the barrier of the mind, he sees the Master as the boatman. When he establishes his constant oneness with the Master, he sees the Master as the river. And when he becomes the most perfect instrument of the Master, he sees the Master as his goal itself. When the hour strikes for the disciple, the disciple also has to play the role of a Master, for progress must continue in the world of self-giving and God-becoming.

Question: How does one become part and parcel of the Master's inner circle?

Sri Chinmoy: I always say that I have first-class, second-class, third-class, fourth-class, fifth-class, sixth-class and seventh-class disciples. But no matter which class an individual belongs to, he must not try to become very close to me by hook or by crook, by grabbing or pulling me. Only by sincere devotion and dedication can one become close to his Master. Each person has to know who comes first and foremost in his life: whether it is the Master or any member of his family or any other person in the world. If the Master comes first in everything, in every action, then I tell you, that person is bound to establish an inseparable connection with the Master. If a seeker has become very devoted and has offered his unconditional surrender not to the Master's personality or individuality, but to the Master's divine Will, then that person will be part and parcel of the Master's inner circle.

Question: How may one distinguish the first-class disciple?

Sri Chinmoy: The really first-class disciple will never make any decisions for himself. The moment an individual makes his own decisions, he is millions of miles away from the Master. Whether you will drink a glass of water at five o'clock or six o'clock—that kind of decision you will have to make for yourself. That is a common sense decision. But anything you feel is important in your life should be done only with the Master's inner approval. First-class disciples do not make any decisions for themselves without first approaching the Master on the inner plane. They feel that everything will come from the Master. Inwardly they tell their Master what they are thinking of doing, and then they wait to see if the Master will care for it or not. Then, after some time, they know.

Question: How does one become a first-class disciple?

Sri Chinmoy: By serving, serving in every way possible. How do you serve? You serve through aspiration. And how do you get aspiration? In the beginning, you have to exercise your imagination. Imagination is not a bad thing; on the contrary, it is a very important thing for the scientist, for the poet, for everyone. In any field of life you have to exercise your imagination. Then you can do something; you can become something. With your imagination, you will try to spread the Light of the Supreme, that Light that I bring down to you.

Question: What is it like to be your first-class disciple?

Sri Chinmoy: For those who are first-class disciples, for those who are totally one with me, I know in the inner world what I am for them.

Just like a potter, I shape their inner life every day. I take the divine clay and I just mold it. There are some disciples who have that kind of connection with me. Their inner progress, their life, their everything, not only in this incarnation, but in all future incarnations will depend on me: not on the human being in me but on the Supreme in me. It is not that I want to lord it over them or that I just have more capacity than they do. No! It is they and the Supreme who have wanted me to have that kind of oneness with them.

It is through this oneness that the Master is manifested and the disciple is perfected.

Question: Which is better—one first-class perfect disciple or a million disciples of other classes?

Sri Chinmoy: One perfect disciple is infinitely more important than thousands and millions of lesser disciples. The only thing is, the perfect disciple that you will get is bound to come from that one million. He will not come ready-made, just thrown down from Heaven. It is like evolution. We come from the animal kingdom; at one time we were monkeys, donkeys, horses and so on. Now, there is such a difference. We have undivine qualities, but they are being transformed. When a human being conquers his undivine qualities, then he becomes divine. This transformation does not take place overnight.

You have had many, many animal lives and many human lives. Human life is, to some extent, more perfect than the animal life. But the divine life that you are growing into is coming slowly and steadily; it does not come all at once. In comparison, we are more divine, but we have to know that greater perfection comes from lesser perfection. A tiger's perfection is to devour many animals for food. But God's perfection is showing love, compassion and concern.

To come back to your question, one absolutely first-class disciple is a rarity in God's creation. But spiritual Masters have infinite appreciation, compassion, love, concern and pride for what the closest disciples have done. So on the spur of the moment they may say someone is a perfect disciple, but both they and the disciples know in their hearts if they are perfect instruments.

Question: How can one always remain a first-class disciple?

Sri Chinmoy: If a disciple can have a life of constant and conscious surrender to the Master, then he will always be most dear. If his surrender is constant and conscious, if he becomes a conscious, constant and surrendered instrument in the heart of his Master or at the feet of his Master, then he will always remain a first-class disciple. Otherwise, there is a possibility of his descending.

Question: *Are you saying that the Master plays the role of the bridge between the disciple's soul and the Supreme?*

Sri Chinmoy: In some cases the Master plays the role of the bridge between the individual seeker's soul and the Supreme. But for the dearest and closest disciples, the Master is more than a bridge; he is also the goal. The Supreme tells those souls, "Do not separate your Master from Me."

For the dearest and closest, the Master has to play the role of the Supreme Himself because at that time the Master is fully responsible for the realization, perfection and manifestation of those particular souls. The Master becomes absolutely the Inner Pilot for those individual souls who are his very close, very intimate, first class disciples: his inner circle.

Question: *And what does it feel like for a devotee to be a member of the Master's inner circle?*

Sri Chinmoy: When the disciple becomes a member of the Master's inner circle, rest assured that in his every action is bound to feel the Master's presence—even if he is just drinking a glass of water or going to the supermarket to buy something. If you are drinking water, you will see the Master's existence inside the water, and while the water is entering you, you will feel that you are the Master's existence. Then, when you are talking to the supermarket man, even if he is very nasty, you will see the Master's presence inside him. Only he has not been able to bring forward this divinity. The outer existence is very crude and rude, but in his inner existence you will feel the presence of your Master.

Question: *Who should come first, the disciple or the Master?*

Sri Chinmoy: Ramdas Kathiya Baba and his Master, Devadas Maharaj, were both heavy smokers, and they often took arsenic to keep themselves warm. One night Devadas asked his disciples to go and buy two rupees worth of arsenic, but his disciples had no money and they were also a little bit hesitant to go to town at that hour. Ramdas offered to go, but he had no money either. The Master said, "Do not worry. You just go to the town. There will be somebody there to give you some money."

Ramdas believed his Master and left without any money. When he reached the town, it was quite late and everything was dark. He saw a light in only one house, so he went and knocked at the door. When the owner opened the door, he was so happy to see a sadhu standing there. He said, "All day I have been thinking of offering two rupees to a sadhu, and now you have come. I am so grateful to you. Please take these two rupees."

Then Ramdas took the money and bought two rupees worth of arsenic. On his way back to the ashram he thought that since he had such a large quantity, he would take a very small portion and his Master would not notice it.

Ramdas was so happy to bring the arsenic and offer it to his Master, but Devadas Maharaj showed him a sad face. Ramdas said, "At this hour I went all the way to town and got you arsenic. How is it that you are sad?"

The Master replied, "I am sad because you come first in your life, and not me. You should have given me the full quantity; then I would have given some to you. Always think of me first. Only then shall I be pleased with you, and I shall give you not only much more than you need, but much more than you deserve."

The Master's faith in the disciple and the disciple's faith in the Master are of equal importance. But sometimes the Master does not reveal to the disciples all aspects of the reality-tree, for it may confuse the seeker's unripe mind. If he does not tell the story of the reality-life all at once, that does not mean that the Master is mean or not generous. But the Master feels that like a child the disciple has to receive things little by little so that he can assimilate everything.

When the disciple has to deal with the Master, the story has to be different, for no matter what he has or what he is, it will not confuse the Master's illumined mind. The Master gives to the disciple according to the disciple's limited receptivity and easily measured capacity, whereas if the disciple wants to give something to the

Master, he can do so unreservedly, for the Master's receptivity and capacity is immeasurable. Again, if the disciple does not give his whole existence to the Master, the Master does not become the loser—far from it. But the disciple weakens his capacity, shortens his vision of the Master and falls down from the reality-oneness with the Master. Finally, insincerity-dragon and ingratitude-insect threaten his aspiring existence.

So give to the Master unreservedly what you have and what you are. The Master will give you according to your need and according to God's need. The fulfillment of your need entirely depends on God's Will.

Question: How does a Master deal with a foolish devotee?

Sri Chinmoy: No matter how insincere, how stupid, how foolish or how unlit a disciple may be, the Master holds a very high opinion of him. He sees in each disciple the living Divinity of the Supreme. He sees, he knows, he feels that one day each disciple will be the perfect image of God and will realize God fully.

Question: How does someone become a perfect disciple?

Sri Chinmoy: In our spiritual life, say in meditation, we are pleasing God, but in our dedication, we are nowhere. Although we do not deserve help, with grace the Master makes us perfect. Sometimes it happens that the individual cannot surpass a certain point. At that time the Master gives him the capacity.

Unconditional grace makes the disciple perfect. Until he reaches his goal, along the way the disciple will time and again fail. Until he becomes perfect, he will delay the aspiring consciousness of humanity. But when he becomes perfect or realized, the disciple is bound to elevate the aspiring consciousness of humanity.

Question: If a Master retires from the earth-consciousness, should his disciples help others?

Sri Chinmoy: If a disciple gets help from his Master, he is not bound to help others. The relationship between a Master and a disciple is mutual and reciprocal. Because I give you compassion, you are giving me dedication. In the outer world, if I am the teacher and you learn something from me, then you become a teacher. If you learn the alphabet, then you can teach it. But in the spiritual life, it is not like that. Unless you have solid knowledge, you cannot teach. You will be able to teach Hatha Yoga, but if you want to teach real meditation, it is impossible because you will not be able to elevate the consciousness of seekers.

Question: Is protection guaranteed from a Master for a disciple's family?

Sri Chinmoy: A disciple of Ramdas Kathiya Baba had to go out of town on business for a few days. For various reasons he could not take his young wife with him, although she was terribly afraid of staying alone at night, so the Master said to the husband, "You tell your wife not to worry. I shall take care of her."

That night the young woman had a dream that her whole room was flooded with light. When she woke up and opened her eyes, she saw the Master in a corner of the room. It was not the Master's physical body she saw, but his luminous subtle body, but she felt that it was actually his physical body. The Master said to her, "My child, until your husband comes back, always feel that I will be here to protect you," and the Master's subtle body with its luminosity protected her until her husband returned.

Human responsibility is such that we can either minimize it or maximize it, contract it or expand it, decrease it or increase it. In the case of a spiritual Master, his responsibility only increases at every moment. A spiritual Master enjoys the increase of responsibility, for his responsibility is nothing short of a golden opportunity for him to manifest more divine peace, Light and bliss on earth.

In this case Ramdas showed that a spiritual Master takes care not only of his dear disciples, but also of those who are closely connected with them. The teacher accepts the student not only with what he is, but also with what he has.

DISCIPLINE

Question: How can one have a disciplined life?

Sri Chinmoy: A disciplined life can come from only one thing, and that is aspiration, the inner cry. When we cry for outer things, sometimes we get them, sometimes we do not. But if our inner cry is sincere, we see that fulfillment always dawns. A child cries for milk. He is crying in his cradle in the living room. The mother may be in the kitchen, but wherever she is, the mother comes running to feed the child with milk. Now why? The mother feels the cry of the child is genuine and sincere. Similarly, in the spiritual life we have an inner cry. If we have that inner cry, then it does not matter when we cry. It may be at noon, in the morning or in the evening. At any hour, that inner cry reaches God and God is bound to fulfill that inner cry. If one wants to discipline oneself, if one is dissatisfied with his loose life and if one feels that from a disciplined life he can have real fulfillment, perfection and satisfaction, then God is bound to help that particular sincere seeker. If there is an inner cry, then nothing on earth can be denied. No fruit can be denied an individual who has an inner cry.

As human beings, we cry for name and fame, for many things. But we do not cry for one thing which is of paramount importance, and that is God's inner Wealth. What is His inner Wealth? His inner Wealth is divine fulfillment, divine perfection. No human being is perfect. But our aim is to be perfectly perfect. This perfect Perfection can only come from self-discipline. Self-discipline is the precursor of self-discovery. Self-discovery is the harbinger of God-manifestation.

God is all ready. He is more than eager to offer His perfect Perfection. But for that perfect Perfection we have to grow into a mounting cry which we call aspiration, constant aspiration. When this flame of aspiration rises toward the Highest, it illumines everything around it which is dark. The higher it goes, the greater and more fulfilling is our manifestation.

Question: How important is discipline in spirituality?

Sri Chinmoy: When Ramdas was a young boy, one night he and his Guru, Devadas Maharaj, were meditating separately at different places. It was snowing heavily and the weather was extremely cold. Each one had an open fire in front of him to keep him warm. Ramdas meditated a few hours; then he fell asleep. When he woke up, he saw that the fire was totally extinguished. He was frightened to death, for he knew that his Master would be furious if he went to him to get a few burning coals. But at the same time he was unable to bear the cold weather. Finally he mustered courage and went to his Master for a few burning charcoals.

Devadas Maharaj came out of his trance and insulted Ramdas mercilessly. "Who asked you to leave your parents and your family if sleep is so important in your life?" he shouted. "This is my last warning. If you ever fall asleep again when you are supposed to be meditating, I shall not keep you as my disciple. You do not deserve to be my disciple."

Spirituality means discipline. Discipline means conscious progress. Conscious progress means the transcendence of nature. Man's transcendence of his nature is his awareness of his immortal Self for God-satisfaction in God's own way.

Discipline is always indispensable, especially in the beginning of the seeker's spiritual adventure. Today we call something discipline; tomorrow we call that very thing a natural and spontaneous habit. Today's forward movement carries us to tomorrow's door. Once we are at the door, we do not even have to knock at the door. The divine Owner opens the door from inside and then takes us inside to introduce us to three most important friends: Eternity's Beauty, Infinity's Delight and Immortality's Light.

Question: What attributes do we need if we are going to practice self-control?

Sri Chinmoy: For self-control we need simplicity, sincerity and humility. Simplicity has to feed self-control. Sincerity has to feed self-control. Humility has to feed self-control. We can say the breakfast of self-control is simplicity, the lunch of self-control is sincerity, and the dinner of self-control is humility. Unfortunately, we are living in an age when self-control is not appreciated. It has become an object of ridicule. A man is trying hard for self-mastery, and his friends, neighbors, relatives and acquaintances all mock him. They find no reality in his sincere attempt to master his life. They think that the way they are living their lives is normal. The man who is trying to control his life is a fool, according to them. But who is the fool? He who wants to conquer himself or he who is constantly a victim of fear, doubt, worry and anxiety? Needless to say, he who wants to conquer himself is not only the wisest man but also the greatest divine hero. Let the world find fault with you. Let the world laugh at you. Your sincerity is your safeguard. Your spiritual discipline will lead you to your destined goal. Everybody has the capacity and opportunity to become a king if he wants to. Who is a king? Not he who governs a country, but he who governs himself.

DOUBT

Question: Why is it easier to disbelieve than believe?

Sri Chinmoy: It is easier to disbelieve than to believe because disbelief is an act of descent, whereas belief is an act of ascent. Descending is easier than ascending.

It is easier to disbelieve than to believe because disbelief is an act of breaking, and belief is an act of building. Building is more difficult than breaking.

It is easier to disbelieve than to believe because disbelief is an act of our self-centered mind, whereas belief is an act of our self-giving heart.

Disbelief begins its journey in the doubting mind and ends in the destructive vital. Belief begins its journey in the illumining soul and continues to march in the vast kingdom of the aspiring heart.

A man of disbelief, with his eyes firmly closed, tells us what others are, what the world is and what he himself can do for the entire world if he wants to. A man of belief, with his heart's door wide open, tells us what God has done for him, what God is doing for him and what God will do for him.

Disbelief has a perfection of its own. Disbelief finds its perfection in the cyclone of separation. Belief has a perfection of its own. Belief finds its perfection in the music of universal oneness.

Disbelief tells the world, "Be careful, be careful. If not, I shall devour you." Belief tells the world, "Come in, come in, please. I have been eagerly waiting for you."

Disbelief hates the world. Why? It feels that the world is never of it and can never be for it. A man of disbelief always feels that this world does not belong to him and that he can never lord it over the world. This is precisely why a man of disbelief dares to hate the world.

A man of belief loves the world. Why? He believes that this world of ours is verily the aspiring body of God, the glowing dream of God and the fulfilling reality of God.

In the spiritual life, if one cherishes disbelief, one is simply lengthening the distance to the ultimate goal. But if a seeker has abundant belief in his spiritual life, in his own quest for the ultimate Truth, then undoubtedly he is shortening the distance. Finally, if his inner being is surcharged with boundless faith, then he feels that the goal itself, the goal of the beyond, is running towards him, and not that he is trying to reach the goal.

There comes a time when a man of disbelief, being totally frustrated, wants to kill the world around him out of exasperation. But to his wide surprise he sees that the wild ignorance of the world has already stabbed him. With his proud knowledge he wanted to kill the world; but before he could kill the world, the world and his own wild ignorance have killed him.

A man of belief wants to love the world. To his wide surprise he sees that his entire existence is in the very heart of the world. The world has already placed a throne in the inmost recesses of its heart for the man of belief to sit upon.

In our spiritual life disbelief is nothing short of a crime. When we disbelieve, we pour slow poison into our system; we kill our possibility and potentiality, and wallow consciously and deliberately in the pleasures of ignorance.

Why do we disbelieve? We disbelieve because we are afraid of oneness, afraid of the vast. We feel that when we enter into the vast, we lose our identity, we lose our individuality, we lose our very existence. But we forget the undeniable truth that when we enter into the vastness, it is nothing short of the enlargement of our divinized consciousness.

For an ordinary person, an unaspiring human being, it is extremely difficult not to disbelieve. An aspiring person, an aspiring seeker, knows that there is something within that is pushing him forward to the Light, to the reality, for his is the life of conscious awareness. An unaspiring person feels that something from without is pulling him backwards, pulling him to something unknown, to something that will bind him.

When we consciously disbelieve someone, we do not realize the fact that the inner magnet within us pulls the undivine qualities of that particular person into us. What happens when a person has achieved something but we do not believe it? The person and his achievement remain the same whether we believe it or not. But the person also has imperfections, limited capacity, impurity; and our disbelief is a magnet that pulls only his imperfections. If we have belief and if we offer our belief, then we have a magnet that draws the good qualities, the divine qualities, the illumining qualities of the other person.

When we disbelieve God, when we disbelieve the reality, God remains the same. But what happens is that ignorance gets the opportunity to envelop us more powerfully and more completely. When we believe in God, God's compassion gets the utmost opportunity to work in and through us most powerfully.

The deeper we enter into the spiritual life, the more we become aware of the capacity of disbelief and belief. Disbelief is nothing short of destruction. Belief is nothing short of a new creation. Each time we believe in something, we see the face of a new creator within and without us. And when we go one step ahead, when our inner faith looms large, then we see in us a perfected man and a liberated soul.

DRUGS

Question: *There are many people who claim that with the use of certain drugs they are able to get closer to God. Of course the Chinese have been using opium for centuries and centuries. How do you feel about using stimulants, drugs, etc., to stimulate the mind in order to get closer to God?*

Sri Chinmoy: Let me start out by saying that there are two ways of approaching the Truth. One way is that by meditation and prayer, we know the real Truth, we feel the real ecstasy, we see the real Light, we experience Existence-Consciousness-Bliss. These last three go together and we can come into that state only through meditation and oneness with God. But those who are taking drugs are putting the cart before the horse. They are deceiving themselves into thinking that they already know the Truth. At the same time, they are not aware of the fact that by taking drugs, they are damaging their inner, spiritual faculties which are of paramount importance in order to enter into God's kingdom.

Let me make it clear to you. If you throw me into a sea and plunge me, immerse me forcibly in the water, not allowing me to come to the surface, then what shall I see? All blank, all white. And that is what actually happens to those who have taken to drugs. Through the effect of chemicals, a violent change of consciousness is effected. They get an experience—all white! Even if it is a higher experience, they cannot sustain it unless they take another dose of chemicals. But when I pray, when I concentrate, when I meditate, I enter into the living Consciousness of God and I can learn to remain there. This is the positive and natural way of entering into God. God is natural and I am His son, you are His son; we have to follow the natural process. But by taking to drugs and using these artificial means, people are unconsciously, if not deliberately, negating the real Truth.

I have a few students who used to take drugs. They have had first-hand "experiences." They tell me now that when they were taking drugs, it was nothing but self-delusion and self-annihilation. Now what they experience is self-acceptance and self-fulfillment. So this is the difference that they have now discovered. Needless to say, I am proud of their present spiritual achievements.

To come back to your question, no one can come closer to God by taking drugs or stimulants. One can come closer to God only by loving God and meditating on God.

DUTY

Question: Speak to us about our duties in day-to-day life.

Sri Chinmoy: In our day-to-day life, duty is something unpleasant, demanding and discouraging. When we are reminded of our duty, we lose all our spontaneous inner joy. We feel miserable. We feel that we could have used our life-energy for a better purpose. Only a man devoid of common sense can say he does not know what his duty is. Each man knows his duty well, too well. It is up to him whether or not to perform it. Duty is painful, tedious and monotonous simply because we do it with our ego, pride and vanity.

Question: What priorities would you assign to the duties of a disciple?

Sri Chinmoy: Love your family much. This is your great duty. Love mankind more. This is your greater duty. Love God most. This is your greatest duty, the duty supreme.

An aspirant's life is the life that has to perform the duty supreme. His first and foremost duty is to realize God. There is no greater duty than this in his life here on earth. Time is fleeting; time does not wait for us. We have to be wise. We can utilize each moment for a divine purpose. We can utilize each moment in performing our soulful duty.

Question: How does one make duty pleasant and uplifting?

Sri Chinmoy: Duty is pleasant, encouraging and inspiring when we do it for God's sake. What we need is to change our attitude towards duty. If we work for the sake of God, then there is no duty. All is joy; all is beauty. Each action must be performed and offered at the feet of God. Duty for God's sake is the duty supreme. We have no right to undertake any other duty before we work out our own spiritual salvation. Did God not entrust us with this wonderful task at the time of our very birth? The supreme duty is to constantly strive for God-realization.

Question: *Could you tell us what an aspirant's duty to society is, if he has one, and how he should relate to his total society? Should he be withdrawn or should he contribute, and if so, what should be the nature of his contribution?*

Sri Chinmoy: It depends. First of all, we have to know the standard of the aspirant. If the aspirant feels that the inner life, the spiritual life, is of paramount importance, that he cannot do without it, then he has to devote most of his time to the inner life, the spiritual life, to God-realization. His inner being will tell him to what extent he can contribute to society. But if the aspirant is just learning the ABCs of the spiritual life, then I wish the aspirant to accept society as something important, needful and significant in his life, something that should be accepted along with the inner life.

Again, I wish to say that if he is a true aspirant, he has to go deep within in order to know how to help society. To help society is a wonderful thing. To be a philanthropist is a wonderful thing, and if that particular philanthropist goes deep within and gets the direct message from the inner being, from God, then only at that time will his help to society be really meaningful. Otherwise, the so-called help or contribution to society by an aspirant will be an act of self-aggrandizement, a feeding of his ego.

In order to realize God, one does not have to leave society altogether for good. If one leaves society, or in the larger sense, humanity, then how can one establish and manifest divinity here on earth? But one has to be wise in his spiritual search. He has to know that God comes first and then humanity. If one goes to humanity first and serves humanity according to his limited capacity or just to feed his ego, then he is not fulfilling God in society or in humanity. So to serve humanity properly, divinely, one has first to go to Divinity and from there, one has to approach humanity. At that time, the help will be most beneficial.

EGO

Question: Speak to us about the human ego.

Sri Chinmoy: The ego is that very thing which limits us in every sphere of life. We are God's children; we are one with God. But the ego makes us feel that we do not belong to God, that we are perfect strangers to Him. At best, it makes us feel that we are going to God, not that we are in God.

There are many thieves, but the worst of all these thieves is undoubtedly our ego. This thief can steal away all our divinity. Not only are our experiences afraid of this ego-thief, but even our realization, our partial realization, is afraid of it. We have to be very careful of the ego-thief.

Our human ego wants to do something great, grand and magnificent, but this unique thing need not be the thing that God wants us to do. It is always nice to be able to do great things, but perhaps God has not chosen us to do that particular thing. God may have chosen us to do something insignificant in the outer world. In the Eye of God, he is the greatest devotee who performs his God-ordained duty soulfully and devotedly, no matter how insignificant it may seem. Each man is a chosen child of God. Similarly, each man is destined to play a significant part in God's divine Game. When God sees a particular person performing the role that He chose for him, then only will He be filled with divine Pride. Our ego will try to achieve and perform great things, but in God's Eye we can never be great unless and until we do what God wants us to do.

The ordinary, common human ego feels that it has achieved everything and that it knows everything. This reminds me of an anecdote which Swami Vivakananda related to the Parliament of Religions in Chicago in 1893. It is called "The Frog in the Well."

It happened that a frog was born and brought up in a well. One

100

day a frog from the field jumped into the well. The first frog said to the other, "Where do you come from?"

The second frog said, "I come from the field."

"Field? How big is it?" said the first frog.

"Oh, it is very big," said the second.

So the frog from the well stretched its legs and said, "Is it as big as this?"

"No, bigger! Much bigger!" said the frog from the field.

The other frog jumped from one end of the well to the other and said, "This must be as big as the length of the field."

The second frog said, "No the field is infinitely vaster."

"You are a liar!" said the first frog. "I am throwing you out of here."

This shows the tendency of our human ego. Great spiritual Masters and sages speak of infinity, eternity and immortality. The beginner who is just starting his spiritual life will immediately ask, "Is infinity a little larger than the sky?"

The sage will say, "No infinity is infinitely larger than your imagination, larger than your conception."

Immediately the sage will be criticized because the ego makes us feel that what we have realized can never be surpassed by the realization and experience of others. The ego does not like to feel that someone else has more capacity or that someone else can do something which it cannot do. At one time ego will make us feel that we are nothing and at another time it will make us feel that we are everything. We have to be careful of both of our feelings of importance and our feelings of unimportance. We have to say that if God wants us to be nothing, then we will gladly be nothing, and if God wants us to be everything, we will be everything gladly. We have to surrender unconditionally and cheerfully to the Will of God. If He wants us to be His peers, we shall be. If He wants us to be His true representative on earth, we shall be. "Let Thy Will be done."

Question: How can I conquer ego?

Sri Chinmoy: Feel that your ego is a thief inside you. When you see a thief, what do you do? You chase him. Feel that a thief has entered into you, into your room of aspiration. Start chasing your ego, the thief. If you can really feel that your ego is a thief, a day will come when you will be able to catch it. It may not come all at once, but if you know that something is stolen and you have seen the thief, you will continue searching. Your search is bound to be rewarded one day. When you catch the ego, what will happen? Your sword of universal oneness will transform it.

Ego is separativity and individuality. Separativity and human individuality cannot live in the sea of oneness and universality. If we want to maintain our separate individuality, our life will end in destruction. A drop, before entering the ocean, says, "Here is the mighty ocean, the vast ocean. When I enter into it, I will be totally lost; I will be totally destroyed; I will have no existence!" But this is the wrong way of thinking. The drop should be spiritually wise. It should feel, "When I enter into this vast sea, my existence will merge with it inseparably. Then I will be able to claim the infinite ocean as part of myself." Who can deny this? The moment the drop enters into the ocean, it becomes one with the ocean; it becomes the ocean itself. At that time who can separate the consciousness of the drop from the consciousness of the entire vast ocean?

The human ego is constantly bothering us. But if we have the divine ego which makes us feel, "I am God's son, I am God's daughter," we will not separate our existence from the rest of God's creation. God is omniscient, omnipotent, omnipresent. If He is all, He is everywhere, and if I am His son, how can I be limited to one particular place? This divine ego or divine pride is absolutely necessary. "I cannot wallow in the pleasures of ignorance. I am God's child. To realize Him, to discover Him in myself and in everyone, is my birthright. He is my Father. If He can be so divine, then what is wrong with me? I came from Him, from the Absolute, from the Supreme; therefore, I should be divine too." This kind of divine pride has to come forward. The ordinary ego that binds us constantly has to be transformed. The divine ego, the divine pride which claims the universe as its very own, should be our only choice.

The ego deals only with the person and his possessions. If we deal with the Universal Consciousness, we become the entire universe. In this consciousness we do not act like a tiny individual who can only claim himself and feel, "This is my property. This is my capacity. This is my achievement." No, at that time we will say, "All achievements are mine. There is nothing that I cannot claim as my very own."

The easiest way to conquer ego is to offer gratitude to God for five minutes daily. Then you will feel that inside you a sweet, fragrant and beautiful flower is growing. That is the flower of humility. When you offer Him your gratitude, God gives you something most beautiful, which is humility. Once it has seen the flower of humility, the ego goes away because it feels that it can become something better: universal oneness.

The more we give, the more we are appreciated. Think of a growing tree. A tree has flowers, fruits, leaves, branches and a trunk. But the tree gets real satisfaction not by possessing its capacity but by offering its capacity. Only in self-giving does it get satisfaction. When it offers its fruit to the world, it bows down with utmost humility. When it offers shade or protection, it offers them to everyone without regard for wealth or rank or capacity. We also get real satisfaction by self-giving and not by keeping everything for our own use.

The ego always tries to possess things for itself. But when we transcend ego, we try to give everything for God's Satisfaction, for the world's satisfaction and for our soul's satisfaction. On the human level, the ego tries to get satisfaction by using things for its own purpose. In the spiritual life we transcend the human ego and then we use those things for a divine purpose, for the satisfaction of the entire world.

Question: *I feel that I am always competing with others. How can I overcome this?*

Sri Chinmoy: Try to feel your oneness with everybody. When you do, immediately you will expand your consciousness. If someone does something well, immediately you have to feel that it is you who have done it. He should also do the same when you do something significant. Whenever any individual does something very well, others have to feel that it is their conscious inspiration and aspiration that have enabled that individual to achieve this success. If we always have an attitude of teamwork, then we will be able to conquer the ego.

But the competitive ego should not be confused with divine pride. Sometimes we feel, "I am God's son, so how can I be so bad? How can I tell a lie? How can I be insincere? I am God's instrument, so how can I do this kind of thing?" This is also a type of ego, but this ego is not the challenging and destructive ego that makes us want to defeat everyone by hook or by crook and lord it over the whole world with our invincible superiority. The divine ego comes from our divinized consciousness, from our inner oneness with God. If we feel in a divine way that we are God's chosen instrument, then there can be no undivine ego in our life. First we have to feel this inwardly. Then in our actions we have to manifest it.

So whenever somebody else does something good, please feel that it is you who have done it. This is not wrong at all. You are not fooling yourself. Do not think, "Oh, I have not done it. My name is not so-and-so." Your name is the Universal Consciousness. There is only one Being and that is the infinite and all-pervading "I." So when any inhabitant of the universe achieves something, you can easily and most legitimately claim that you have achieved it, if you can just identify yourself with the Universal Consciousness.

Question: *In order to achieve the state of pure delight, one must drop the ego. What exactly is the ego?*

Sri Chinmoy: The ego always makes us feel that we are anything but divine. We are God's children, we are one with God, but the ego makes us feel that we do not belong to God, that we are perfect strangers to God. At best, it makes us feel that we are going to God, not that we are in God.

The ordinary human ego gives us the sense of separate identity, separate consciousness. No doubt, the sense of individuality, of self-importance, is necessary at a certain stage in man's development. But the ego separates our individual consciousness from the Universal Consciousness. The very function of the ego is separation. It cannot feel satisfaction in viewing two things at a time, on the same level. It always feels that one must be superior and the other inferior. So ego makes us feel that we are all separate weaklings, that it will never be possible for us to be or to have the infinite

Consciousness. Ego, finally, is limitation. This limitation is ignorance, and ignorance is death. So ego ultimately ends in death.

Question: How was the ego born? How did it come into being?

Sri Chinmoy: The ego came into existence from limitation. The moment the soul enters into the physical consciousness or the physical world, it comes down into a strange, foreign world. In spite of being a flame of the Divine and, in essence, omnipotent, the soul in the beginning finds it very difficult to cope with the world. And most of the time it has to endure unpleasant experiences in order to remain in the physical world and finally establish the Divine here on earth.

The ego, day by day, gets the opportunity to function independently and it gets stronger day by day and separates itself completely from the source of its absolute, divine fulfillment, the soul. The ego wants to crush and starve the divine in man, and the ignorance of the physical world feeds that limitation which is ego. The Divine, too, initially feeds the ego, but eventually illumines and transforms it into a perfect instrument of the Supreme.

Question: How do we weaken the ego and ultimately subdue it?

Sri Chinmoy: By thinking of God's all-pervading Consciousness. This Consciousness is not something that we have to achieve. This Consciousness is already within us and we have just to be aware of it. Further, while we are in meditation, we have to develop it and illumine it infinitely. In the meantime, to our wide surprise, the ego will be buried in the bosom of death.

ETERNITY

Question: Can you say something about eternity and the eternal life?

Sri Chinmoy: Being a spiritual man, I can say on the strength of my own inner realization that the soul does not die. We know that we are eternal. We have come from God, we are in God, we are growing into God and we are going to fulfill God. Life and death are like two rooms; going from life to death is like going from one room to the other. Where I am now is my living room. Here I am talking to you, meditating with you, looking at you. Here I have to show my physical body; I have to work and be active and show my life. Then there is another room, my bedroom. There I take rest; I sleep. There I do not have to show my existence to anybody; I am only for myself.

We come from the infinite life, the life divine. This infinite life stays on earth for a short span of time, say fifty or sixty years. At that time we have within us the earthbound life. But inside this earthbound life is the boundless life. After a while this life again passes through the corridor of death for five or ten or fifteen or twenty years. When we enter this corridor, the soul leaves the body for a short or long rest and goes back to the soul's region. Here, if the person was spiritual, the soul will regain the eternal life, the life divine which existed before birth, which exists between birth and death, which exists in death and, at the same time, goes beyond death.

Now while we are living on earth, we can place ourselves in the realm of eternal life through our aspiration and meditation. But just by entering into the endless life, we do not possess that life; we have to grow into it consciously. When we enter into the life of meditation, we must eventually become part and parcel of meditation. And when we are able to meditate twenty-four hours a day we are constantly breathing in the endless life. In our inner consciousness we

106

have become one with the soul. When we live in the body, there is death all the time. As soon as fear comes into our mind, immediately we die. As soon as some negative forces come, we die. How many times each day we die! Fear, doubt and anxiety are constantly killing our inner existence. But when we live in the soul, there is no such thing as death. There is just a constant evolution of our consciousness, our aspiring life.

EXPERIENCE

Question: Are all our experiences transitory?

Sri Chinmoy: In the outer world we do not remember in detail all of our experiences. They are real for a few days and then they are totally erased because they do not stay in our day-to-day consciousness. But we keep the essence of these experiences in our inner life. In the inner world, everything is recorded permanently.

Question: What about an experience we had in the inner world, such as an experience during meditation? Do we remember this consciously?

Sri Chinmoy: In the case of an ordinary seeker, when he has some inner experience, he does not consciously retain it, even though the essence remains in his inner life. Even if it is a high experience, after four years or so he totally forgets it. The experience is lost because the ignorance in his life swallows it. He says, "How can I have had such an experience? If I did have such an experience, how is it that afterwards I did so many wrong things? How is it that I did not meditate, I did not pray? That means it was not such a significant experience." His doubt devours the experience. But in the case of a realized person, he knows that whatever he saw or felt was absolutely true. Also, he can remember the inner experiences that he had even at the age of seven or eight, or in previous incarnations, because of his inner vision. But ask an ordinary seeker, and even if he has had only two major experiences in his life, it may take him an hour to remember, or he may not remember them at all.

Question: What is the difference between experience and realization?

Sri Chinmoy: The difference between experience and realization is this: a realized person can say, "I and my Father are one" or "God and I are one," whereas a seeker who has had many spiritual experiences can only feel that he is slowly but inevitably growing into the realization of God.

Experience shows us and tells us what we will eventually become—the possessor of God-Consciousness. But in realization, we come to know what we truly are—absolutely one with God, forever, throughout eternity.

Question: After one realizes God, does he remember all his experiences?

Sri Chinmoy: When one realizes God, it does not mean that he will remember all the millions and billions of outer experiences he has had during his lifetime. But his inner experiences, the significant higher experiences that he had in the inner world, he can bring to the fore at his command. If he wants to bring his whole inner life in front of himself, he can.

Question: Is the experience of the Beyond calm or excited?

Sri Chinmoy: The experience of the Beyond is calm, but it is not static. In it, dynamism and tranquility exist together. In one of the *Upanishads* we find this definition of the Beyond: "That moves and that moves not. That is far and that is near." How can something move yet move not? It seems impossible. But when you are in the Beyond, you will see the universe in movement and, at the same time, tranquil. There is also another description of the Beyond: the experience of the infinite. "Infinity is that. Infinity is this. From Infinity, infinity has come into existence. From infinity, when infinity is taken away, infinity remains."

Question: Are the kinds of experiences that Yogis have different from those ordinary people get in life?

Sri Chinmoy: Sri Aurobindo once said that the biography of a spiritual Master is all written inside. If you write the biography of an ordinary person, it can be thousands of pages long. If you want to write about his inner life, you will not be able to fill even one page. In the case of a spiritual Master, hundreds and hundreds of pages can be written about his inner life, but they are not written. A spiritual Master, who is dealing with the inner world, gives and receives hundreds of significant experiences every day. A Master's inner experiences are the predominant experiences of his life, whereas for an ordinary person inner experiences are a very rare occurrence.

Question: Are spiritual experiences absolutely necessary to realize God?

Sri Chinmoy: No. There can be many roads leading to the same goal. One road may have many beautiful flowers on either side; another road may have only a few blooms; a third road may have none at all. If each of three seekers selects a different road according to his soul's need and preference, each of them will reach the ultimate goal.

Of course, experiences do give you additional confidence in yourself. They also give enormous delight. They encourage you and energize you to march farther and farther. And while you are having the experiences, you may feel the presence of an invisible Guide within your being, pushing you towards the light of Truth so that you may be blessed with full realization. But you can also have full and complete realization without so-called "experiences." One's expanding consciousness, as one grows into God, is itself a solid experience.

FAILURE

Question: Spiritual seekers try to climb up the God-realization-tree with spiritual methods such as meditation, but sometimes fail. What happens to them?

Sri Chinmoy: People who fail while trying to climb up the God-realization-tree will not always continue to fail. They will definitely succeed one day, for no soul will remain unrealized and imperfect forever. Making spiritual progress is like developing a muscle. Slowly and steadily, through regular practice, we develop stronger muscles. That is also the way we develop our inner muscles, which are inspiration, aspiration and dedication.

Question: How can I overcome the fear of failure?

Sri Chinmoy: You have to know what failure is and what failure can do. Fear is bound to go when you know that failure is not something shameful, damaging, destructive or painful. Feel that failure is something natural. When a child starts to walk, he often stumbles and falls down. But he does not feel that stumbling is a failure. He thinks that it is a natural process to stand up for a moment and then fall again.

If you think of failure in that light, not as something that is against or totally distant from reality but as something that is forming, shaping, molding and becoming reality, then there cannot be any fear. We take failure as something contrary to our expectation and our God-realization. But failure is not contrary to our realization. Failure is something that is urging us towards our realization. What we call failure, in God's Eye, is only an experience.

Always take failure as an experience. Do not take it as a finished product or as the culmination of an experience, but rather as the process of an experience. If you think that failure is the end of your experience, then you are mistaken. In a long race, one may start very slowly, but then gradually he increases his speed and eventually he reaches his goal. If he thinks that since his start was slow, he will not be able to reach the destination, then he is making a deplorable mistake. If there is no failure, naturally you will run the fastest. But if there is failure, take it as an experience that is just beginning. The end will be success. And then who can say that you have failed?

FAITH

Question: *Speak to us about faith.*

Sri Chinmoy: First of all, faith is not credulity or blind belief. It does not mean that you must constantly believe in the impossible. No, that is not faith. Faith is a spontaneous feeling. It does not care for human justification. It is the eye that visions the future, and it is always in tune with a higher Truth. The door of faith is always open to the Truth beyond, and by virtue of faith, we transcend ourselves.

Question: *How may we strengthen our inner faith in God when we are beset with discouragements in our daily life?*

Sri Chinmoy: Please try to feel from now on that there is Somebody around you who does not want anything from you, but simply wants to see joy in you and around you. There is Somebody who does not want anything else from you except joy, inner joy and outer joy. He wants you always to swim in the sea of joy and delight. If you remain in joy—I do not mean outer joy, that is, going here and there, mixing with people, buying material things—but if you can have real joy, if you can feel the source of it, then you will automatically have faith in God.

When we are worried, or are afraid of something, we immediately try to create a kind of self-imposed faith in God. This is not true faith. In danger, we say, "God, save me, save me!" But we say this only to avert danger. This is an escape. This kind of faith does not last.

Spontaneous faith can come when we have inner joy, inner fulfillment. Everything is inside the person—his joy and his fulfillment. Who is the possessor of this inner fulfillment? It is God. We are just His devoted instruments. So when we feel spontaneous inner joy as part and parcel of our life, we can then have faith in God, the possessor of infinite joy. From now on, please try to feel your own inner joy. In regard to your outer frustrations, please do not try to unite them with your inner joy. Please separate your inner joy from the outer happenings. Then alone will you be able to strengthen your faith in God.

FEAR

Question: Why is it that I have a fear of the inner life?

Sri Chinmoy: Strange is this world of ours. Stranger is our human understanding. Strangest is our fear of the inner life. Most of us do not know what the inner life is. It is the life that lives to grow and grows to live.

You are afraid of the inner life. You feel that the moment you launch into the inner life you are lost, completely lost, in an unknown land. You may also think that in accepting the inner life, you are building castles in the air. Finally, you may feel that to accept the inner life is to throw your most precious life into the mouth of a roaring lion who will completely devour you and your outer life.

You have countless sweet dreams. You want to transform them into reality. In all your dreams you want to enjoy the world or you want to offer your momentous might to the world at large. You feel that if you embark on the inner life, you will be deprived of all those invaluable achievements. So now it is time for fear to make its appearance, and naturally you start shying away from the inner life. Fear starts torturing you. It tries to limit and bind you. Unfortunately, your life yields to this deplorable condition.

But if once, only once, with the help of your all-energizing meditation, you would carry your long-cherished fear into the inner world, you would see that fear loses its very existence there.

Question: How can we overcome the fear of death?

Sri Chinmoy: Conquering the fear of death depends on how much love you have for God and how sincerely you need Him. If you need someone, immediately you establish a kind of inner access to that

115

person. If your need for God is soulful, devoted and constant, then in the inner world you establish a free access to God's love, God's compassion, God's concern. And if you can always feel God's love, compassion and concern, then how can you be afraid of death? The moment you feel that you need God and He needs you, the moment you feel God inside you, before you and around you, then death no longer exists for you. When God is away from your mind, when God is not to be found inside your heart, when you feel that God is nowhere near you, at that time death exists for you. Otherwise, where is death? This physical body may leave the earth, but the soul, which is a conscious portion of God, will remain consciously in God and for God throughout eternity. It is up to you to think of yourself as the body or as the soul. If you think of yourself as the body and do not aspire, then in the spiritual life you are already dead. But if you think of yourself as the soul, that means you have already developed an inner connection with God. If you know that the soul is your real reality, you will not have any fear of death.

Question: *How can we overcome fear?*

Sri Chinmoy: Fear can be in the physical body, the vital, the mental and even the heart. First of all, one has to know where the fear looms large. If there is fear in the gross physical, then that person should concentrate on the navel chakra. If one can concentrate on the navel center and be one with the life-force, the life-energy in the physical, then one can conquer fear there.

If one wants to conquer fear in the vital, then one should concentrate on one's own inner being. But this is difficult for beginners, so I tell them that they should try to expand the dynamic vital in themselves. We have two types of vital. One is aggressive, and the other is dynamic. The dynamic vital wants to create something sooner than at once in a divine way, an illumined way. So if we can concentrate on that vital, or focus our attention on that vital, then we expand our consciousness in the vital. Then there can be no fear.

To conquer fear in the mind, one has to empty the mind daily. The mind is full of doubt, obscurity, ignorance, suspicion and so forth. Early in the morning you can try for ten minutes or so not to have any thoughts—good, bad, divine or undivine. If a thought comes, try to kill it. Then, after some time, allow only the divine thoughts which are your friends. In the beginning you do not know who your friend is and who your enemy is, so you have to be very careful. Later on, you can allow only your friends to enter. Your friends are divine thoughts, progressive thoughts, illumined thoughts. These thoughts will undoubtedly conquer fear in the mind on your behalf. Feel that your mind is like a vessel. First you empty it, and then you wait for peace, Light and bliss to descend. But if you do not first empty the vessel, then peace, Light and bliss will not be able to enter.

Question: *Why is there fear in the physical, the vital and the mind?*

Sri Chinmoy: Precisely because we do not want to expand our consciousness. I feel that I am separate from you. You feel that you are separate from me. That is why I am afraid of you and you are afraid of me. But when we realize the Highest, immediately we feel the length and breadth of the universe as our very own. In expansion only can we expel fear. If we expand our consciousness, then we become one with others. We feel that we belong to them and they belong to us. How can we be afraid of anybody when we represent divinity in humanity and others represent the same divinity in humanity? So there can be no fear.

The aspiring heart has no fear, but the unaspiring heart does have fear. The aspiring heart has a flame, a burning flame that mounts towards the Highest. Where there is Light, there cannot be fear. But to conquer fear in the unaspiring heart you have to take help directly from the soul. When you meditate on the heart center, every time you breathe in, try to feel that you are digging inside. This is not violent digging, but a divinely intensified feeling you have inside your heart that you are going deep, deep, deep within. Each time you breathe in, feel that you are going deep within. If you do this regularly, after a few days or a few months you are bound to feel a twinge or hear a very tiny sound. When you hear the sound, try to see if the sound is caused by something or if it is spontaneous. We need two hands to clap, but in the heart sound is not produced by two things struck together; it is automatic, spontaneous. When you can feel that kind of sound inside, like a celestial gong, then you are bound to conquer fear in your unaspiring heart.

Question: *I feel as if I have many enemies in life.*

Sri Chinmoy: If I ask you how many enemies you have you will say, "Quite a few." But I have to say you are mistaken. You have just one enemy and that is all, even though it seems like a host in itself. That single enemy of yours is fear, your unconsciously cherished fear. You are afraid of the inner life. You feel that the moment you launch into the inner life you are lost, completely lost like a babe in the woods. You may think that in accepting the inner life, you are building castles in the air. Finally, you may feel that to accept the inner life is to throw your most precious life into the roaring mouth of a lion who will completely devour you and your outer life.

FREEDOM/LIBERATION

Question: When we reach liberation, does the physical body change?

Sri Chinmoy: The physical, vital and mind enter into the psychic consciousness when we are liberated. We do not discard them, but the physical, vital and mind aspire along with the soul. The physical, before liberation, is obscure and impure. In order for liberation to take place, the physical has to be purified. The vital is usually aggressive; before liberation it must become dynamic. The mind is usually suspicious; before liberation it must become vast and loving. These divinized parts of man enter into the heart when liberation takes place, and remain there permanently. The appearance of the physical body will be basically the same, but it will have infinite purity and luminosity, which it did not have before.

Question: Is there any difference between liberation and realization, or are they absolutely identical?

Sri Chinmoy: There is a great difference between liberation and realization. Liberation is much inferior to realization. One can reach liberation in one incarnation, and realization in some later incarnation. Or one can become liberated and realized in the same incarnation. But it is not possible to be realized without first being liberated. Sometimes a great spiritual Master, if he is fortunate, will bring down with him a few really liberated souls to help him in his manifestation. Sri Ramakrishna, for example, brought down Vivekananda and Brahmananda. Some of these liberated souls who enter the earth-scene with the great Masters do not care for realization. They come just to help. Others, like Vivekananda and Brahmananda, want realization also.

A liberated soul is liberated from ignorance, from worldly,

119

undivine qualities. A liberated soul will inspire others with his presence. He will inspire them to be pure, simple, kind-hearted and loving. Tremendous purity and serenity will flow from him, and others will want to touch him, speak to him, look at his face. You can say that he is much more than a saint. True, worldly obscurities, impurities and other things will not enter into the liberated soul, or he will be all the time cautious so as not to allow them to enter into him. But a realized soul is much higher. He is consciously part and parcel of God.

A liberated soul knows that there is a special room where he stays and has his shrine. He knows that there is also a kitchen, which is all dirty and full of impurities. Ordinary human beings have no special room, no shrine at all. They are all the time locked in the kitchen, and naturally they cannot come into the room where the living deity is. The liberated soul is able to live in the room with the shrine, but he is afraid that if he enters into the kitchen, the undivine things there may attack him, and he will again become their victim as he was before his liberation.

But realized souls are extremely powerful. They know what they are and where they have come from. On the strength of their universal and transcendental consciousness, they can enter into the ignorance of humanity, into the earth-consciousness as such, and illumine it with their light. They do so only because of their infinite compassion, not because they still have some temptations or wrong forces in them. No! They enter into ignorance deliberately so that humanity can be radically transformed. But only realized souls of a high order accept this bold challenge.

A liberated soul is like a child, so beautiful and pure. But how long can you stay with a child? With his capacity you cannot go very far, or reach the Highest. A realized soul is like a mature person who can offer you tremendous aspiration, light and wisdom, the living reality. A liberated soul will inspire you to walk along the path. A realized soul will not only inspire you, but also guide you and lead you to your destination.

A realized soul is not only the guide, not only the way, but the goal itself. First he pretends he is not even the guide, but just someone to inspire the seeker. Then he comes and tells the seeker that he is the guide, but not the road. Gradually, however, he reveals that he himself is also the road. And finally he makes the seeker feel his infinite compassion and shows him that he is not only the guide and the road, but the goal as well, the seeker's own goal.

The realized soul touches the foot of the realization-tree, climbs up to the topmost branch and brings down the fruit to share with humanity waiting below. That is realization. But even the one who only touches the realization-tree and sits at the foot of the tree without climbing up or bringing anything down is far superior to the liberated soul.

But again, to reach liberation is no easy matter. It is very, very difficult to become freed from ignorance. Out of the millions and billions of human beings on earth, there may be ten or twenty or even a hundred liberated souls. But God alone knows how many realized souls exist. To realize the highest Absolute as one's very own and to constantly feel that this realization is not something you have actually achieved, but something you eternally are—that is called realization.

GOAL

Question: What is our goal?

Sri Chinmoy: Our goal is within us. To reach that goal we have to enter into the spiritual life. In the spiritual life, the thing that is most needed is consciousness. Without this, everything is a barren desert. When we enter into a dark place, we take a flashlight or some other light in order to know where we are going. If we want to know about our unlit life, we have to take the help of consciousness.

Man, in his outer life or his outer achievements, is very limited. But the same man, when he enters into the inmost recesses of his heart, feels that there is something which is constantly trying to expand itself. This is consciousness. This consciousness links him with the highest Absolute.

Consciousness is our real teacher, our dear friend and our sure slave. As a slave, consciousness carries our teeming ignorance to God. As a friend, consciousness tells us what the supreme Knowledge is. As a teacher, consciousness reveals to us the undeniable truth that today's imperfect and unfulfilled man is tomorrow's perfect and fulfilled God.

Consciousness sings. It sings the song of universal oneness. Consciousness plays. It plays the game of cosmic manifestation. Consciousness dances. It dances with God's fulfilling vision within and God's fulfilled reality without. Consciousness acts. It acts through man's crying, climbing and surrendering aspiration, and God's descending, protecting and illumining compassion.

When consciousness is all activity, it bows to God the Mother, its Source. When consciousness is all silence, it bows to God the Father, its Source. From the Mother it gets the mightiest power to make the supreme sacrifice for the unconscious earth. From the Father it gets the highest Light to illumine the unlit earth.

Consciousness itself is at once Light and power. As Light, it identifies with the pure inspiration and deep aspiration of our inner world. As power, it exercises its divine sovereignty over the darkest bondage and the wildest ignorance of our outer world.

The consciousness that the unaspiring body uses is called the hopeful consciousness. The consciousness that the unyielding vital uses is known as the hurtful consciousness. The consciousness that the uncompromising mind uses is called the doubtful consciousness. The consciousness that the uncovering heart uses is called the truthful consciousness. The consciousness that the unlimited soul uses is called the fruitful consciousness.

Question: I was wondering if it would help my progress if I kept thinking about my goal of God-realization.

Sri Chinmoy: A kindergarten student's ultimate goal is to get a Master's degree. Now, while he is studying the kindergarten lessons, if he constantly thinks, "Oh, I have to get my Master's degree, I have to get my Master's degree," it is foolishness on his part. He may know his goal, but if he thinks about it all the time, then he will not learn his present lesson well. There are some aspirants who think of God-realization although they are not ready even for basic inner awakening. There are some who think and speak of God-realization, whereas they are not yet ready even to learn the ABCs of the spiritual life.

God-realization, immortality, infinity, eternity: these are all big words right now. If you speak about these words, you will only be building castles in the air. They are a reality in their own plane, but that reality you cannot bring into your day-to-day life right now. So let the reality remain in its proper place. If you go on thinking of the goal all the time with your imagination, the goal will not be the way you are imagining it, and you are bound to be disappointed. Also, if you think of the goal all the time, then you will not pay proper attention to your present aspiration and you will unconsciously delay your progress. God-realization is your goal, but you have just entered into the spiritual path. You are walking along the right path, and this is good. Right now your main concern should be aspiration, inner progress, simplicity, sincerity, purity and humility.

God-realization is a difficult goal, but it is not impossible. After meditating for several years, some people feel that God-realization is impossible in this incarnation and say that they do not want it. It is like the story of sour grapes. Many people leave the spiritual path for this reason after following it for quite a few years. They find fault with God and with the Master's teachings, and become stark atheists. But this is very bad. Before you entered into the spiritual life, when you were wallowing in the pleasures of ignorance, at that time God forgave you because He knew that you were not aware of anything else. God said, "My child does not know anything better than ignorance." But after you have entered into the inner life, if you go back again to the ordinary life, thinking that God-realization either does not exist or is totally beyond your capacity, then the inner retribution for your ignorant and undivine actions is infinitely worse than it would have been if you had never left ignorance at all.

Right now the goal is a far cry, but you must not be discouraged. Step by step, slowly and steadily, you will reach the goal. From kindergarten you go to primary school, then to high school and then to the university. So do not be restless or impatient. Only God knows when His choice hour will strike for you. It is your business to aspire, and it is God's business to pour down His infinite compassion. When you play your role, God will play His role and make you realize Him at His choice hour. So let us walk along the path of reality. On the strength of our inner aspiration, the goal itself will come towards us.

Question: *Do we have to remove all materialistic goals in order to realize God?*

Sri Chinmoy: How we utilize the material life is what is of paramount importance. Matter, as such, has not done anything wrong to God; it is not anti-divine. It is we who use material things in a wrong way. We must enter into the material life with our soul's light. We can use a knife to stab someone or we can use it to cut a fruit to share with others. With fire we can cook and with fire we can also burn ourselves or set fire to someone's house.

We have to feel that matter and spirit go together. Matter has to be the conscious expression of spirit. If you say that matter is everything, that there is no spirit, no higher life, no inner reality, then I have to tell you that you are mistaken. There is an inner reality, there is an infinite Truth that wants to express itself in and through matter. Matter is asleep, and it has to be aroused. The material life has to be guided and molded by the spirit.

But first we have to understand what the material life is for. If by material life we mean lower vital enjoyment and the fulfillment of gross desires, then it is useless to try to accept the spiritual life simultaneously. But if the material life means the life of expansion—the expansion of the heart, the expansion of love—then matter and spirit can easily go together. In this material life we have to feel peace, Light and bliss. What we see right now in the mind is jealousy, fear, doubt and all undivine things. But in this very mind we can and we must feel harmony, peace, love and other divine qualities. If we want these divine qualities from the material life, then the material life can go perfectly well with the spiritual life.

The true material life is not just eating, sleeping and drinking. The material life is a significant life. And it eventually has to become a life of dedication. Right now in the physical we are trying to possess people and things. But the material life will have meaning only when we stop trying to possess and start trying to dedicate. When we dedicate ourselves to the Supreme, to the unparalleled goal of realizing God, only then will life reveal itself to us as the message of Truth, the message of infinity, eternity and immortality.

GOD

Question: What is God and what is the relationship between God and man?

Sri Chinmoy: God and man—this is the eternal question and the eternal answer. God is the living Breath and that living Breath is in man. Man has a goal and the name of that goal is God. In God is man's satisfaction, achievement and fulfillment. Through man is God's satisfaction, achievement and fulfillment. Man needs God to realize his true Self. God needs man to manifest Himself on earth.

Question: Are you saying that God and man are one and the same?

Sri Chinmoy: Yes. God and man are one and the same. God is man yet to be fulfilled in His infinity and man is God but he has yet to realize it.

I have to grow and God has to flow. I grow as a human being into His highest Consciousness and God flows into me and through me with His infinite compassion.

Question: Is God Father or Mother to you?

Sri Chinmoy: God is both my Father and my Mother. I meditate on my Father-God for my illumination and perfection. I pray to my Mother-God for Her compassion and affection. When I wish to hear the song of the infinite in the heart of the finite, I go to my Father-God. When I wish to hear the song of the finite in the soul of the infinite, I go to my Mother-God.

My heart's streaming tears in no time reach my Mother-God. My soul's beaming joys reach my Father-God sooner than the soonest. My Mother-God proudly tells the whole world who I am: I am

God's choice instrument. My Father-God smilingly tells the whole world what my ultimate goal is: my ultimate goal is to serve both my Father-God and my Mother-God unconditionally while they are transforming today's man into tomorrow's God.

Question: Why do you always speak of God in masculine terms?

Sri Chinmoy: When I say "Father," I do not exclude the Mother. God is both masculine and feminine. It is only that the term "Father" is more familiar in the Western world because the Christ always said "Father." So I use the term "Father" because it is familiar to you. In the East we approach the feminine aspect quite often. We think of the Supreme Goddess, the Divine Mother. We have so many goddesses: Mahakali, Mahalakshmi, Mahasaraswati and Maheshwari, so it is very easy for us to think of God in feminine terms. But when I am with you, I have to use a term which is quite familiar to you, for I feel that this will make it easier for you to share my experiences. In truth, God is both masculine and feminine. Again, He is neither masculine nor feminine; He transcends both. He is what He eternally is: His vision and His reality. This reality transcends both the masculine and the feminine form and, at the same time, it embodies both the masculine and the feminine.

Question: Why can you see God and I can not?

Sri Chinmoy: Now you are looking at me with your eyes open. You know that my name is Chinmoy and you are able to see me. Now (putting his hands over her eyes) I have closed your eyes. Can you see me? No, you cannot see me. When your eyes are shut you cannot see anybody in front of you or beside you. But when you keep your eyes open, you can see me, you can see your father, your friends and everyone.

You know that you have two eyes. With these two eyes you can see me, but at the same time, if you keep them closed you cannot see me. Now you have another eye and this eye is between your eyebrows. It is an inner eye, your third eye. In my case that eye is open. So I can see God. Everything that is within others I can also see. That eye is here between my eyebrows and I can see with it. Now, in your case, just as you cannot see anything when you have closed your two eyes, so also you do not see God because your third eye is closed.

If you pray to God every day, you will see that all of a sudden this inner eye will open up. Get up early in the morning and open your two ordinary eyes and see your mother and father and everything that is in your room and then pray to God. One day by your prayer, you will see that your third eye has opened. You will also be able to see God. So every day, pray to God to open up this third eye. Put your finger on this eye and pray, "O God, please open it." One day God will open it up and you will see Him just as you see me now.

Question: *Does God ever speak to you?*

Sri Chinmoy: Every day in the small hours of the morning my Mother-God says to me, "How are you today, My child?" And my Father-God says to me, "What are your plans today, My son?" Late at night when I am about to retire, my Mother-God tells me, "My child, sweet dreams, sweet dreams." And my Father-God tells me, "My son, do not dream of escaping from harsh reality. Fight bravely against ignorance-night. Be victorious! Your Mother and I are all for you."

A sweet conversation in my fragrance-heart-garden: I say to my Mother-God, "Mother, You forgive me almost immediately when I do something wrong. How is it and why is it that when I do something wrong, Father, instead of forgiving me, illumines me? And that He does so slowly—although steadily and unerringly. Why, why?"

My Mother-God says to me, "My child, your Father is the one who has to answer that question."

My Father-God says to me, "My child, your Mother's quick forgiveness does not necessarily change your nature, but My illumination can and does change your nature. Yes, it always does."

My Mother-God says to my Father-God, "But if I do not forgive My child first, how on earth are you going to illumine him?"

My Father-God, heaving a smilingly tearful sigh, says, "Oh, I see! I helplessly agree with You."

Question: Does God need man?

Sri Chinmoy: Definitely God needs man. God is both the Creator and the creation. Man is nothing other than the creation. God needs man to manifest His Light on earth, and man needs God to realize his own highest height. So God the Creator and God the creation undoubtedly need each other.

Question: But we are not realized—do not we need God more than God needs us?

Sri Chinmoy: We feel that we need God more than God needs us since we are not realized. This is wrong. God needs us equally, if not more. Why? He knows our potentialities, our possibilities, infinitely better than we do. We feel we can only go this far, but He knows we can go millions of miles. Our ignorance does not permit us to know what we actually are. We think of ourselves as useless, hopeless, helpless, but in God's Eyes we are actually His divine instruments. He wants to use us in infinite ways. This is His Dream, that He wants us to be not only infinite but also eternal and immortal. He knows we have the capacity because He gave us the capacity. Now He wants is to utilize our capacity.

Question: How should I go about reminding myself that I need God just as much as God needs me?

Sri Chinmoy: Always say, "I need God in order to realize my highest and God needs me so that He can manifest Himself in and through me." This is God's own supreme philosophy. Always feel, "Because of my ignorance, I do not know how to realize Him or fulfill Him; but God, because of His Knowledge, knows the infinite ways He will be able to utilize me for His manifestation.

Question: How does one go about pleasing God?

Sri Chinmoy: How to please God? I can please God by offering Him what I have and what I am. What I have is gratitude What I am is inspiration. If I want to please him more, than I must never consider my life a sad failure, but rather a constant experience of His. If I want to please Him most, not only in one but every aspect of life, than I must feel that, unlike me, He sees my life, inner and outer, as the Song of His own Life-Breath, the song of His own Perfection, growing into His perfect Perfection absolute.

Question: *Is it possible to hurt God?*

Sri Chinmoy: Do you know when you hurt God? You hurt God the moment you underestimate your inner capacity. You hurt God the moment you exaggerate your self-imposed outer responsibility. You hurt Him deeply when you cherish the futile idea that God-realization is not for you. To be sure God-realization is the mightiest affirmation, the greatest certainty at God's choice hour.

Question: *What is the difference between seeing God and realizing God?*

Sri Chinmoy: There is a great difference between seeing God and realizing God. When we see God, we can see Him as an individual or as an object or as something else. But we do not consciously and continuously embody Him and feel that He is our very own. When we see God, it is like seeing a tree. We do not at that time consciously embody the tree-consciousness. And since we do not embody it, we cannot reveal or manifest it. But when we realize something, at that time it becomes part and parcel of our life. We may see a flower, but only when we realize the flower do we actually become one with the consciousness of the flower.

When we merely see something, we cannot claim it as our very own, and that particular thing also will not claim us. Seeing is on the physical plane, while realizing is on the inner plane. Seeing does not last, whereas realizing does remain with us. If we see something, the vision may last for a short while; but when we realize something, this realization lasts forever.

Question: *How does the Supreme appear to you?*

Sri Chinmoy: Usually I see the Supreme in the form of a golden Being, a most illumined and illumining Being. Here on earth, when we say that a child is extremely beautiful, we are judging his form. But I wish to say that the Supreme is infinitely more beautiful than any human child we can see. This is the way I see the Supreme when I converse with Him. It is this form that I am most fond of. At the same time, my Beloved may assume the formless form. Other spiritual Masters prefer other forms, and the Supreme appears before them in those forms. In this way He has let us exploit His compassion.

Question: When you speak of seeing God face to face, what is your conception of God?

Sri Chinmoy: God is with form; He is without form. He is with attributes; He is without attributes. If an individual wants to see God as an infinite expanse of Light and delight, God will come to that person as an infinite expanse of Light and delight. But if he wants to see God as a most brilliant, most luminous being, then God will come to him like that. Of course, when I say God takes the form of a luminous being, I am understating the case. He is not merely luminous; He is something I cannot describe to you in human terms.

In my case, I have seen God in both ways—with form and without form. But when I speak of God, I speak of Him as a being, because this idea is easier for the human mind to grasp. When you say there is a form, a shape, it appeals to individuals. Otherwise, God becomes only a vague idea. If I say God is bliss, and if the seeker has not experienced bliss, then he will be hopelessly confused. But if I tell a seeker that God is like a person, an all-powerful father who can say this or do this, he can conceive of it and believe it.

When a human being thinks of some being greater than himself, immediately he thinks of it as similar to a human being. It is much easier to conceive of the idea of God through form. But I will never say that those who want to see God without form, as an infinite expanse of Light, delight, energy or consciousness, are wrong. I just feel that the other way is easier.

Question: *What is the nature of your relationship to the Supreme?*

Sri Chinmoy: Our relationship is that of Father and son. Out of His infinite compassion, He has kindled the flames of aspiration in me. These flames climb high, higher, Highest. My aspiration carries unconditional love, devotion and surrender.

Familiarity breeds contempt in the human life, but in the spiritual life the familiarity between the seeker and the Supreme Pilot only increases in intensity and capacity. Familiarity cannot diminish the sweetness, love and concern that flows between the seeker and the Supreme. On the contrary, familiarity only increases these qualities. When I deal with the personal aspect of the Supreme, He increases my love, devotion and surrender. He makes me aware of what He eternally is. The more familiar we become with Him, the more we establish our oneness, our ever-fulfilling oneness with Him.

The personal aspect cannot create problems for the true seeker. When two people become close, it often does not last because they see weaknesses in each other. But the personal aspect of the Supreme knows what we are. He does not think of us as imperfect; he takes us as His own infinite extension. He does not find fault with us either on the physical plane or on the psychic plane. It is He that is carrying us to the ever-transcending Perfection.

Question: *There are different ways of approaching God. If one person possesses three different kinds of qualities, will it affect his progress?*

Sri Chinmoy: Instead of hindering, it helps. But you have to give more importance to the particular path that inspires your being most.

For example: the attitude of service, the attitude of devotion and the attitude of quest for knowledge, taken all together, will help you make a balanced progress. But at some point in your life, you have to find the one that inspires you most. Each soul has its own way of moving. Here on earth, we are inspired to progress according to our soul's propensity. If you accept all the paths, it is a great help; at the same time, you have to choose your own soul's way, the way that gives you the greatest fulfillment according to your deepest aspiration.

Question: How can one reach God in one's lifetime?

Sri Chinmoy: Let us change the word "reach" and instead let us use the word "realize." When we use the term "reach," we feel that we have to come to a certain place. Now you are sitting over there and if you want to reach me, you have to come to me by either walking or jumping or flying. But when we use the term "realize," there is no separation. Where is God? God is deep within us. But God-realization in one life, in one short span of time, by one's own personal effort, is next to impossible. But along with one's personal effort, if the aspirant has absolute aspiration, one-pointed dedication, if he has the blessings, grace and concern of a very great spiritual Master who represents God to his disciples, and if he has been assured by his spiritual Master on this point, then in one life he can realize God.

If one does not have a fully realized Master, a Guru, but if his aspiration is most intense, then God's grace showers on him and God Himself plays the part of the human teacher, that is to say, the spiritual Master. If God sees that the particular aspirant is absolutely sincere and he deserves self-realization in this life, then, as I have said, God plays the part of a human Guru. Otherwise it is a spiritual Master who becomes a pilot and takes you across the ocean of ignorance to Light, wisdom, peace, bliss and plenitude.

You have got a Guru, so your problem is over, and your aspiration is most intense. I say it from the very depth of my heart that this Guru of yours will never fail you. You will always be in the inmost recesses of his heart. He will carry you, carry you to the golden shore of the beyond.

God-Realization/ Self-Realization

Question: *What is Self-realization?*

Sri Chinmoy: Self-realization means self-discovery in the highest sense of the term. One realizes one's oneness with God consciously. Now you have studied books and people have also told you that God is in everybody. But you have not realized God in your conscious life. When one is Self-realized, one consciously knows what God is, what He looks like, what He wills. Those who have not realized God will say, "God may be like this, God may be like that"; it is all mental speculation. But when one achieves Self-realization, one remains in God's Consciousness and one speaks to God face-to-face. He sees God both in the finite and in the infinite; he sees God as personal and impersonal. In this case, it is not mental hallucination or imagination; it is direct reality. This reality is more authentic than my seeing you right now in front of me.

Question: *How far are we from realization?*

Sri Chinmoy: *Avidyaya mrityum tirtha vidyaya amritam snute*—"By ignorance we cross through death; by knowledge we achieve immortality." This is indeed a major realization.

Realization means the revelation of God in a human body. Realization means that man himself is God.

Unfortunately, man is not alone. He has desire, and desire has tremendous power. Nevertheless, it fails to give him lasting joy and peace. Desire is finite. Desire is blind. It tries to bind man, who is boundless by birthright. God's grace, which acts through man for God's full manifestation, is infinite.

Realization springs from self-conquest. It grows in its oneness

134

with God. It fulfills itself in embracing the finite and the infinite. We are seekers of the Supreme. What we need is absolute realization. With a little realization we can at most act like a cat. With absolute realization we shall be able to threaten ignorance like a roaring lion.

The moment I say "my body," I separate myself from the body. This body undergoes infancy, childhood, adolescence, maturity and old age. It is not really me. The real "I" remains changeless always. When I say that I have grown fat or thin, I am speaking of the body that has grown fat or thin, and not the inner "I," which is eternal and immortal.

Realization says that there are no such things as the bondage and freedom, which we so often refer to in our day-to-day lives. What actually exists is consciousness—consciousness on various levels, consciousness enjoying itself in its varied manifestations. So long as we think that we are living in the bondage of ignorance, we are at liberty to feel that we can dwell in freedom as well, if we want to. If bondage makes us feel that the world is a field of suffering, then freedom can undoubtedly make us feel that the world is nothing but the blissful consciousness of the *Brahman*. But realization makes us feel *Sarvam khalvidam Brahma*—"All that is extended is *Brahman*."

In order to realize what realization is, we first have to love our inner Self. The second step is to love realization itself. This is the love that awakens the soul. This is the love that illumines our consciousness. Love and you will be loved. Realize and you will be fulfilled.

Realization is our inner lamp. If we keep the lamp burning, it will transmit to the world at large its radiant glow. We all, with no exception, have the power of Self-realization or, in other words, God-realization. To deny this truth is to deceive ourselves mercilessly.

We realize the Truth not only when joy fills our mind, but also when sorrow clouds our heart, when death welcomes us into its tenebrous breast, when immortality places our existence in transformation's lap.

How far are we from realization? We can know the answer by the degree to which we have surrendered to God's Will. There is no other way to know it. Also we must know that every single day dawns with a new realization. Life is a constant realization to him whose inner eye is open.

Question: *Why do we want to realize God?*

Sri Chinmoy: We want to realize God because we consciously have made ourselves avenues through which the fruits of God-realization can flow. Our very body is a divine machine; hence it needs oiling. Realization is a divine lubricant, which does its work most effectively.

Realization can be achieved by God's grace, the Guru's grace and the seeker's aspiration. God's grace is the rain. The Guru's grace is the seed. The seeker's aspiration is the act of cultivation. Lo, the bumper crop is realization!

Question: *Should we understand that the extent of Self-realization that we can achieve is subject to our effort and our will, or is it ultimately determined in some way by Something beyond our will?*

Sri Chinmoy: Two things go together—individual effort plus the divine grace. If I sleep all the time, God is not going to liberate me, but at the same time, if I feel that on the strength of my personal will, by hook or by crook, I will be able to realize God by exerting all my power, it is foolishness. God is on the third floor and I am on the first floor. There should be a rendezvous, a meeting place. I have to go to God; I have to go to the second floor with my personal effort, that is to say, with my tears, my soulful cry. Then God will come down from the third floor to the second floor with his infinite grace and compassion, and there we will meet together. He has to give what He has—His compassion, the flood of compassion—and I have to give my little personal effort and my tears, the flood of my tears.

A spiritual Master was once asked by her disciples how much personal effort she made in order to realize God. She said before she had realized God, she thought that her personal effort was 99% and God's grace was only 1%. She was working so hard in order to realize God. But when she realized God, she found that it had been just the reverse—that God's grace was 99% and her personal effort was only 1%. There she did not stop. Then she said, "My children, this 1% of personal effort was also God's grace. It was the divine grace which I got and others did not get. This grace of God allowed me to make that most insignificant personal effort."

Question: Can we actually feel our realization coming, or does it appear spontaneously and unexpectedly?

Sri Chinmoy: Real realization cannot dawn unexpectedly. Gradually, gradually we come to the point where we realize God. If one is on the verge of realization, he will know that it is a matter of days or months or years. Realization is complete conscious oneness with God. Now, if one does not have a limited conscious oneness with God, how can he attain an unlimited conscious oneness with God all at once? It is true that God can do everything, that He can grant realization without asking anything of the seeker. But if God gave you realization without your meditating and practicing the spiritual life, then everybody would expect it.

Some people get realization after only four or five years of meditation, whereas others who have been meditating for thirty, forty or fifty years are nowhere near realization. But you have to know that in the case of the person who realizes God after having meditated for only four or five years, this is not his first incarnation as a seeker. He started his conscious journey long before you may ever have thought of God. Now he is completing his journey to God-realization, while you perhaps have just started yours. Again, we have to know that even though we have meditated for many incarnations in the past and for a few years in this incarnation, it does not actually mean that we deserve God. It was God's grace that operated in our previous incarnations and it is God's grace that is helping us realize Him in this incarnation as well.

From your constant, lifelong meditation you can expect realization, but only at God's choice hour. You may want it immediately, but God may know that if you realize Him right now, you will be more harmful than helpful to mankind. So God has His own hour for your realization, and when that hour nears, you will be aware of it.

Question: *How do you personally know whether someone is realized or partially realized?*

Sri Chinmoy: When one is realized, one can easily know the realization of others. On the basis of my unity and identification with their consciousness, I can easily tell about others' realization.

Question: *How long would it take the average person who comes to a spiritual path to realize God?*

Sri Chinmoy: It depends on the sincerity or the commitment of the disciple-seeker. His meditation must be most sincere, devoted and fulfilling. If one can meditate eight hours or twelve hours a day most devotedly and soulfully, then there is every possibility that that person can realize God in the short span of one life. But if one meditates, say, for five minutes a day, even if it is most soulful, it may not be possible for that person to realize God in one lifetime. Still, it is more advisable to meditate for one minute most sincerely and devotedly, than to meditate insincerely for ten hours.

Again, there is no hard and fast rule. God's grace is there. If you get a spiritual Master of the highest calibre, you do not have to meditate twelve hours or sixteen hours a day. No, you just meditate an hour or two a day most devotedly, and with the Master's grace, you can make the same progress as you would have made meditating twelve or sixteen hours a day without a Master.

Question: *Is there a way to make the road to realization shorter?*

Sri Chinmoy: There are two roads. One is the road of the mind; the other is the road of the heart. The road of the heart is a shortcut. If we walk along the mind-road, very often we will have doubts. We will doubt our own aspiration, we will doubt our own experiences and we will doubt our own feeling for God. This moment we love God, the next moment we may not love God because God has not fulfilled our desires. On the mind-path we are constantly contradicting our own thoughts. This moment we are saying that the path is very good and making progress; the next moment, when our desires are not fulfilled and doubts enter into us, our progress stops.

The other path is the path of the heart. Once we love God, we jump into the sea of peace, Light and bliss. Like a drop that enters into the mighty ocean, we feel that we have become the ocean itself. If we use the mind, it will immediately think: "I will be destroyed in such a vast ocean." But the heart will say, "No, I will jump. If I jump, I will not be lost. I will only become the infinite." The heart is a child, and a child always has faith in his parents. So if we have a Master, we will have faith in him, and we also will have faith in God, for God will always be doing what is best for us. This is what we feel if we follow the path of the heart. The path of the heart is the shortest path.

Question: *What are the aspects of God that makes God-realization so difficult?*

Sri Chinmoy: God has two aspects—personal and impersonal. If you do not accept God in His personal aspect, then realization will be most difficult. If we take God in His impersonal aspect, as an infinite expanse of peace and Light, it will be extremely difficult to realize that aspect. But if we see the personal aspect, it is very easy to enter into the impersonal aspect. If you do not know a person and you hear his name, it will be difficult for you to establish any clear or close inner connection.

Question: *Is it possible to realize God without going to live in a cave?*

Sri Chinmoy: Not all spiritual Masters have gone to the Himalayan caves to realize God. I did not realize God in a Himalayan cave. Most spiritual Masters, such as Sri Ramakrishna, the Buddha, Sri Aurobindo and others, did not meditate in the Himalayan caves.

There was a time when it was necessary for people to withdraw from the world, but now it is not necessary at all. If you do not face the world, then the world will follow you and chase you like a thief. But why be afraid of the world? If you stand firm and accept the world, the world will salute you and say, "He has strength." If you are afraid of the world, then the world, like a lion, will devour you. But if you have the capacity to act like a divine hero and face the world, then God's compassion, God's Light, God's power will descend on you.

Spirituality is for the brave. God-realization is for the brave; it is not for the weakling. In almost all the Indian scriptures, the same thing is said: "The soul cannot be won by the weakling." Only those who have strength will march forward and see the goal.

Question: *What part of man achieves realization?*

Sri Chinmoy: When realization takes place, it is the entire being that realizes God. The soul has already realized God, but the soul is bringing to the fore its realized consciousness. It is entering into the heart and trying to permeate the heart with its divine consciousness. Then, from the heart, realization comes to the mind, from the mind to the vital and from the vital to the physical body. When it envelops the physical, the vital, the mental and the psychic, realization is complete.

Real realization makes one know that one is neither the body nor the mind nor anything else but the soul, which is a manifestation of the Divine. Each person, when he realizes God, will feel that he is a conscious portion of God. The physical is limited, but the soul is unlimited. When we speak of realization, we are referring to something unlimited, infinite. When we realize God, we go beyond the body-consciousness and become one with the soul's unlimited capacity.

Question: *I have read that realization is not an achievement but a discovery.*

Sri Chinmoy: True, realization is not an achievement, but a discovery. But when we discover something, it then becomes our achievement. The moment we discover something, it becomes part and parcel of our existence; and whatever becomes part and parcel of our existence becomes our achievement. Right inside discovery, achievement looms large. When a scientist discovers something, it becomes the property of the entire world, but it is still his achievement. Similarly, when one realizes God, although God has always been there and belongs to both the inner world and the outer world, God-realization is still the most significant achievement for any individual.

Truth and Divinity already exist inside us, but we neglect them. Because we do not use them, they have become foreigners to us. But the moment we discover them already within us, they become our own achievement. They become our achievement through our sincere personal effort and through God's constant inner grace.

Question: *Is realization a fairly common experience during any single generation of human beings? In India, for example, are there many realized spiritual Masters?*

Sri Chinmoy: There are millions and billions of people on earth, but only a very few of these are actually realized. If you feel there are hundreds of spiritually realized people on earth, then you are mistaken. The world is quite vast, but when it is a matter of truly realized persons, then I wish to say that there are only ten or twelve on earth right now. There are some swamis and teachers who have meditated and sincerely practiced Yoga for ten or fifteen years, and who are far superior to their students, but who are not actually God-realized souls. One need not have reached the Highest to teach a beginner, just as one does not need a Master's degree to teach kindergarten.

There are sincere and insincere Masters. Many insincere masters come to the West and exploit people. In India, also, false masters exploit seekers. But God will not allow a sincere student to be deceived forever. The seeker's own inner cry will take him to a real teacher. If it is God's Will, the student may get a really high Master who will take him right from the beginning to the Highest. Otherwise, he will get a Master who will take him only through kindergarten, and then he will have to find another teacher.

Question: *What is the difference between enlightenment and God-realization?*

Sri Chinmoy: Full enlightenment, complete and all-illumining enlightenment, is God-realization. But sometimes, when a seeker is in his highest meditation, he gets a kind of inner illumination or enlightenment, and for half an hour or an hour his whole being, his whole existence, is illumined. Then, after an hour or two, he becomes his same old self; he again becomes a victim to desire and undivine qualities. Enlightenment has taken place, but it is not the transcendental enlightenment which occurred in the case of the Buddha and other spiritual Masters. That kind of all-fulfilling, all-illumining enlightenment is equivalent to God-realization. God-realization means constant and eternal enlightenment, transcendental enlightenment. When we get God-realization, automatically infinite illumination takes place in our outer as well as our inner existence.

What some people call enlightenment is only a temporary burst of light in the aspiring consciousness. After a short while it pales into insignificance, because there is no abiding reality in it. Abiding reality we will get only with constant, eternal and transcendental illumination, which is God-realization.

Sometimes when we speak of enlightenment, we mean that we have been in darkness about a particular subject for many years and now we have inner wisdom, or now that particular place in our consciousness is enlightened. But this is just a spark of the boundless illumination, and that little spark we cannot call God-realization.

Question: Is technology acting as a hindrance to God-realization?

Sri Chinmoy: The answer is in the affirmative as well as in the negative. When modern technology is serving as an expression of the inner soul, when it feels that it has a connecting link with the inner life, the inner existence, at that time technology is a help to God-realization. But very often we see that technology and the inner life do not go together. The outer world with its success is running towards a different goal. We have to be very careful about this, for no matter how much success we derive from technology, the infinite fulfillment cannot take place if the soul is not there. Again, the soul is lame if the outer life does not keep pace with it through technological and scientific progress.

For the absolute fulfillment of God's vision and reality here on earth, science and spirituality must go together. From spirituality we can expect liberation and realization. From technology and science we can expect material perfection—the material embodiment of the highest Truth. When realization is inside material success, only then will the material world achieve permanence in eternal values. Again, if perfection is lacking in the inner world, then the material success has to inspire the inner realization to come and take the lead.

Question: *Once a seeker becomes advanced, do all the obstacles to God-realization vanish and does his realization become a certainty in this incarnation?*

Sri Chinmoy: Until you reach the goal, there is no certainty. You may even be only one step from the goal, and still you may fall. Even at the last moment you do not know whether you are going to win the race or not. Before God-realization, the last trial is extremely difficult. Many really sincere seekers are about to realize God, believe me, in the inner world there is no more than an inch gap, but hostile forces attack them mercilessly and they fall. Then it takes such a long time for them to get up again. Some people take six months or two years or four years; others may have to wait for another incarnation. So always be on the alert and run as fast as you can towards your goal. Do not stop until the race is won; otherwise, the pull of ignorance will take you back again to the starting point.

Question: *Is it possible to have complete knowledge and wisdom of God in one lifetime?*

Sri Chinmoy: It is absolutely possible to have complete knowledge of God, provided the aspirant has the most sincere aspiration. Also, the aspirant must have the capacity to hold the knowledge and wisdom of God. Third, the aspirant must have a very high spiritual Master, a God-realized Yogi of the first rank. Fourth, it must be the Will of God that the seeker receive this complete inner wisdom and knowledge. If all these four conditions are fulfilled simultaneously, then it is absolutely possible.

But if one just enters into the spiritual life and wants to realize

God without the help of a Master, it is impossible. For an ordinary human being, hundreds and thousands of incarnations are required. Even if one has a good Master, if the disciple is not one hundred per cent sincere, it may take six, seven, ten or twenty incarnations. But the very best disciples get realization either in one incarnation or in a few incarnations, under the constant guidance of the Master.

Occasionally someone realizes God without having a spiritual Master. How is it possible? In his past incarnation, perhaps he had a very, very powerful Master. In this incarnation his Master has not taken human incarnation, but from the inner world this Master is constantly guiding him, molding him and instructing him. The seeker knows that his Guru is instructing him during his dreams and during his meditation.

Then, of course, there is also another possibility. If a seeker has been meditating for quite a few incarnations and God is most pleased with him, and if the seeker is not favored with a spiritual Master in this incarnation, then God Himself plays the part of a spiritual Master, even during the seeker's waking hours and in his day-to-day life activities. If the seeker needs to drink a glass of water, God will tell him, "Go and drink a glass of water." And if he has to shut the windows, God will tell him. God will take the form of a very, very luminous being and will guide him in this way.

Question: If a seeker does not realize God in this lifetime, does this mean all his efforts will be lost?

Sri Chinmoy: If a seeker does not attain to spiritual perfection in this life, that does not mean that he will lose everything. When he does not complete his journey in this life, in his next incarnation he starts the journey where he left off. Nothing is lost. But unfortunately, for the twelve or thirteen years of his childhood, he will be captured by ignorance. Ignorance will stand right in front of him and devour him like a wolf. He will have to take strength from the inner world and then fight like a warrior in the battlefield of life to conquer ignorance once again. But one who has realized God and attained perfect perfection in his previous incarnation does not have to wait all these years. So it is better to conquer everything in this life, so that in our next incarnation we can travel forward from the very beginning.

Question: *Do you believe that a human being can realize God and become one with Him here on this material plane, which is so ignorant and dark?*

Sri Chinmoy: On the one hand, the planet earth is obscure, ignorant, inconscient; it does not care for anything divine. On the other hand, it has the tremendous inner urge to expand and transcend. God is aspiring through the earth-consciousness. Earth is the only place for people who want to be rich, either on the physical plane or on the spiritual plane. The life of desire and the life of aspiration are both possible on earth. Other worlds are for static enjoyment. In other worlds the beings are satisfied with what they have already achieved, whereas here nobody is really satisfied with what he has achieved. Dissatisfaction does not mean that we are angry with somebody or angry with the world. No! Dissatisfaction means that we have constant aspiration to go beyond and beyond. If we have a little light, we want to have more light, abundant light, infinite Light.

According to our Indian tradition, there are thousands of cosmic gods, and there are as many presiding deities as there are human beings. These presiding deities and gods remain in higher worlds—the vital world, the intuitive world or some higher plane. Right now they have more power, more capacity than we have, and they are satisfied with what they have. They do not want to go one inch beyond. But still, their capacities are limited in comparison with the Light, bliss and power of the Supreme. When we are liberated and realized, when we are consciously one with the Supreme's Consciousness, we will have infinitely more capacity than the deities and cosmic gods.

When the creation started, the souls that wanted to make progress followed a different path. They wanted the ultimate Truth, the infinite Truth. Even the cosmic gods, if they want to achieve infinite peace, Light and bliss, must come down to earth in human form and then realize God on the strength of their absolute love, devotion and surrender. Only here, in the physical body, can we pray and meditate and realize the Highest. Only this planet is in evolution. Evolution means constant progress, constant achievement. When one wants to make progress, when one wants to go beyond, then this is the place to come. It is here alone that God must be realized, revealed and manifested.

Question: How do you know that there is such a thing as realization, and how do you know when you are realized?

Sri Chinmoy: Many people have realized God. This is not my theory; this is not my discovery. Indian sages, Indian spiritual Masters of the hoary past, have discovered the Truth; and I also see eye to eye with them on the strength of my own realization.

When you eat a mango, you know that you have eaten it. You have eaten a mango and the knowledge of it remains inside you. If others say, "No, you have not eaten a mango," it does not bother you, for you know what you have done. As long as your hunger is satisfied, you do not need the approval or recognition of others. The delicious taste, the experience that you had, is proof enough for you. In the spiritual world also, when one has drunk the Nectar of realization, one knows that one has really realized God. One feels infinite peace, infinite Light, infinite bliss, infinite power in his inner consciousness. A realized person can see, feel and know what Divinity is in his own inner consciousness. When one has realization, he has a free access to God and a sense of complete fulfillment. When realization dawns in an aspirant's life, then he will know it unmistakably.

Question: When a person reaches the state where he achieves union with God, does his emotion or feeling of aspiration become so intense that it automatically expresses itself in terms of words?

Sri Chinmoy: There will be no words at that time. You cannot express union with God in words; you can only feel it.

Question: Even if they are words of praise and oneness with God?

Sri Chinmoy: Yes, there can be words of praise and union. Human seekers often do express their spiritual experiences in words of intense beauty. Many spiritual figures have told us what union with God is, and mentally we think we know. But God-realization cannot be expressed in the human tongue. One who has realized God is infinitely superior to an ordinary human being, and there are no human words to express his consciousness.

Question: *After a person realizes God, does he still act like an ordinary human being?*

Sri Chinmoy: When we use the term "realization," people are very often confused. They feel that a realized person is totally different from an ordinary person, that he behaves in a very unusual way. But I wish to say that a realized person need not and should not behave in an unusual way. What has he realized? The ultimate Truth in God. And who is God? God is someone or something absolutely normal.

When someone realizes the Highest, it means he has inner peace, Light and bliss in infinite measure. It does not mean that his outer appearance or outer features will be any different, for peace, Light and bliss are inside his inner consciousness. Even after a spiritual Master has realized the Highest, he still eats, sleeps, talks and breathes just as others do.

It is inside the human that the divine exists. We do not have to live in the Himalayan caves to prove our inner divinity; this divinity we can bring forward in our normal day-to-day life. Spirituality is absolutely normal, but unfortunately we have come to feel it is abnormal because we see so few spiritual people in this world of ignorance. But this feeling is a deplorable mistake. Real spirituality is the acceptance of life. First we have to accept life as it is, and then we have to try to divinize and transform the face of the world with our aspiration and with our realization.

Unspiritual people frequently think that a realized person, if he is truly realized, has to perform miracles at every moment. But miracles and God-realization need not necessarily go together. When you look at a spiritual Master, what you see is peace, Light, bliss and divine power. Enter into him and you are bound to feel these things. But if you expect something else from a realized soul, if you come to a spiritual Master thinking that he will fulfill your teeming desires and make you a multimillionaire, then you are totally mistaken. If it is the Will of the Supreme, the Master can easily make someone a multimillionaire overnight. He can bring down material prosperity in abundant measure, but usually this is not the Will of the Supreme. The Will of the Supreme is for inner prosperity, not outer affluence.

Question: *Once you said that when a seeker reaches the highest realization, automatically spiritual manifestation comes. Would you explain to me what you mean by that kind of manifestation?*

Sri Chinmoy: When one gets realization, if he remains in the world, automatically manifestation starts. When you stand in front of a liberated, fully realized soul, what happens? Immediately you will see the vast difference between yourself and that person. The first thing you will see in him is peace; in his eyes you will see infinite peace. From his body you will get a sense of purity, a purity which you have never felt before in your life or in anybody else's life. How is it that he is emanating purity, Light and divine power, while somebody else is not? It is just because he is fully realized. He may not say anything to you, but from his very presence you will get infinite peace, infinite bliss, infinite Light. Realization automatically shows its own capacity, which is manifestation. The inner realization of the Master is being manifested through his outer form, which is the body.

There is another kind of manifestation, which we find more on the physical plane: it is the manifestation of divinity on earth. This manifestation takes place when a spiritual Master deliberately tries to awaken spiritually hungry individuals. There are many people on earth who are spiritually hungry, but they do not have a Master or a spiritual path. So the Master tries to inspire them, kindle the flame of conscious aspiration in them and put them on a spiritual path.

When a spiritual Master, with the help of his dearest disciples, tries to manifest divinity on earth, sometimes people misunderstand him. They think he wants to convert everyone. But the Master's motive is not that of a missionary. Christian missionaries went to India and all over the world, saying, "There is only one savior, the Christ." But if the Christ is the only savior, then where does the

Buddha stand? Where does Sri Krishna stand? Where are Sri Ramakrishna and all the other great Masters? Each genuine spiritual Master is a savior, needless to say; but to say that he is the only savior, or that his path is the only path, is foolishness. If I say that my path is the only path, that if you do not accept me, you will go to hell, then there is no more stupid person on earth than I. On our path, we do not try to convert anybody; we try to inspire.

A realized Master never, never tries to convert; he only offers his realization in the form of inspiration to aspiring souls. That is why the Master has to act like a normal human being. If he does not act like a human being, if he does not eat and take rest and talk in a human way, then people will say, "Oh, you have gone far beyond us. It is simply impossible for us to be like you." But the spiritual Master says, "No, I do everything you do. If I can eat the same food, if I can mix with you the way you mix with others and, at the same time, not lose my highest consciousness, then how is it that you also cannot enter into the Highest?" This is how the Master inspires his disciples.

But inspiration is not enough. After inspiration comes aspiration. There is a great difference, a vast difference, between inspiration and aspiration. Aspiration is very, very high. The spiritual Master becomes one with his disciples, whose aspiration he has already kindled, and together they go to inspire the spiritually hungry world. In this way realization is transformed into manifestation.

Inside realization you will see manifestation. Manifestation is the outer form of realization, and one who is really spiritual will immediately feel the manifestation in the realization itself. If I have realized something and manifested it in the outer world, the heart of humanity feels it, but the physical mind may take a little time to perceive and understand the manifestation. In the field of manifestation, the Master is dealing with ignorant, unaspiring people or emotionally bound people who will not see the Master's full Light. But a great aspirant sees the realization and cannot separate the realization from the manifestation.

Question: What is the difference between revelation and manifestation?

Sri Chinmoy: Let me give you an example. Let us say that inside your pocket is a most delicious mango. You put your hand inside the pocket, bring out the mango and show it to me. This is revelation. Before, the mango was concealed, and now you have revealed it. Then you have to manifest it. How will you do that? You will cut it into a few pieces and share it with me and with others.

When you reveal God or Truth or Light to the world, it means that you have brought these things forward and they are there for all the world to see. But if nobody looks at what you have revealed, or if nobody accepts or understands it, then this is revelation without manifestation. Manifestation means not only to show what you have and what you are, but also to make the world see, feel, understand and accept it. This is the difference. Today's realization is tomorrow's revelation. Revelation is today's manifested realization and tomorrow's fulfilled manifestation.

Question: *Were the Spanish mystics God-realized?*

Sri Chinmoy: The term "mystic" is very vague and complicated. Not all of the Spanish mystics were realized, but some of them definitely were! Many of them just entered into the mystical world for a period of time and wrote poetry and so on. But why ask about only the Spanish mystics? There have been many mystics, but very few were realized. Again, when they became real God-lovers, real aspirants, at that time they were no longer mystics. From that point of view, I can say that a Yogi is infinitely superior to a mystic.

Question: *What is the difference between a mystical experience and God-realization?*

Sri Chinmoy: God-realization is infinitely higher than a mystical experience. In a mystical experience, you feel God's Presence as something very sweet and delicate, but a mystical experience is not a permanent thing. As soon as you achieve a mystical experience, you can lose it. But God-realization you cannot lose; it is permanent. Once you realize God, you never lose what you have.

Sometimes poets get mystical experiences. A poet can receive most sublime light and have a deep mystical experience. After completing his poems, however, the poet's consciousness may become undivine and he then cannot maintain his mystical experience. A mystical experience is not a permanent experience. But if God-realization takes place, then the mystical experience that one has will have abiding strength and can be permanent. So, there is a great difference between God-realization and mystical experience. God-realization is something infinite, eternal and real. Mystical experience is divine, but if mystical experiences do not come after God-realization, they do not last. A mystic is much inferior to a Yogi. There is no comparison. A Yogi constantly and unconditionally serves the Supreme and is continuously having God-experiences. A mystic is satisfied with experiences alone. He wants to enter into wisdom-Light, but he does not care for the world. The Yogi cares for the world. The mystic wants only experience and wants it to lead to a final merging in God.

God's Will

Question: *How can we know God's Will?*

Sri Chinmoy: In order to know God's Will convincingly, we have to meditate most soulfully and reach our highest state of consciousness. When we are in the highest state of consciousness, we will see that we have gone far beyond the domain of the mind, and the dance of thoughts has completely stopped.

Then, if we want to know if a certain idea or message is from God, the answer will come in a very soft, subtle voice or it will be written in a column of light inside our heart, which we will be able to read.

After discovering God's Will, if we are still in our higher consciousness, we will not be affected regardless of whether the message is encouraging or discouraging to our mind. If we are in an ordinary consciousness, we will have preconceived ideas about what is desirable and undesirable. If the message says that we will be successful, then we are happy, but if the message is perceived by our mind in a negative way, then we feel miserable. But once we are highly developed, even if the message does not appear favorable, we will not be disturbed. After knowing God's Will, we can go one step further and cheerfully accept God's Will.

Question: *What do you mean by "Justice is the execution of God's Will"?*

Sri Chinmoy: Early in the morning Ramdas Kathiya Baba was meditating in his garden when he saw a young man. "What do you want?" he asked the youth.

The boy replied, "I have come here to take some pomegranate leaves. My doctor has asked me to bring him some leaves of this plant so that he will be able to cure me."

"No, you can not take any leaves; they are my possession," said

Ramdas. "Go and ask your doctor to get them from someone else."

The boy could not believe his ears. "You are a spiritual Master. You have so many disciples. You should be generous. You can not part with a few leaves, a few insignificant leaves?"

Ramdas said, "I have not come here to learn your philosophy. Get out. If you do not leave this place, I shall break your head with my stick."

The young man became so angry that he wanted to strike the Master with his stick. Ramdas shouted until many people came. Then he explained, "This boy wanted to take away some leaves without my permission."

"I am asking your permission," said the boy.

"But I am not granting you permission," replied the Master.

What could the disciples do? They compelled the boy to leave without the pomegranate leaves.

Then the disciples said to Master Ramdas, "We shall never understand you."

"You do not have to understand me," Ramdas said. "Only do what I want you to do. I want justice-Light."

The disciples said, "We shall never understand you. At one moment you do not need anything. Even if someone places the whole world's wealth at your feet, you ignore it. But now you are fighting over a few leaves. When you receive nice gifts, like a child, you come and tell us how beautiful they are. The other day the girls from the King's family sent you a shawl. Everybody saw how happy you were to have it. You ran into the marketplace, telling everyone, 'Look, look, how beautiful this shawl is! And who has given it to me? The girls from the King's family.' This moment you act like an innocent child; the next moment you act like a cruel man."

Ramdas said to his disciples, "Do not judge me. You will never be able to fathom me. Only have faith in me and do whatever I ask you to do. This is the only way you will realize me."

What is justice? Justice is the execution of God's Will. God's Will is infinitely higher than man's mental grasp can reach. God is not bound by any law. He wants to enjoy the infinite in the finite. He wants to bring down the message of immortality into the very heart of death. A spiritual Master is God's representative. Out of His infinite

Bounty, God has granted him boundless peace, Light and bliss. The Master wants to share these gifts with the rest of the world.

The human mind did not know, could not know, that the young boy carried very impure vibrations which were affecting Ramdas Kathiya Baba's meditation. It was not really a question of a few pomegranate leaves. If the young man had not carried an impure vibration and disturbed Ramdas' peace with his impurity, perhaps the Master would have given him the leaves. But the teacher had every right to throw the boy out, for stealing is one kind of ignorance and carrying impurity is another. Why should a spiritual Master condone two acts of ignorance?

GRACE

Question: Master, would you speak to us about grace?

Sri Chinmoy: The Supreme is omniscient, omnipotent and omnipresent. He has various kinds of power, but His greatest adamantine power is His grace. The moment the Supreme uses His grace for an individual, He offers His very Life-Breath to the seeker, for the Supreme and His grace cannot be separated. Whenever we think of the Supreme, if we feel that it is through His grace that we are approaching Him, then we can be most successful in receiving Him.

The divine grace is constantly descending upon us. Those who are sincerely aspiring are conscious of this divine grace, but those who are not aspiring are keeping their heart's door permanently closed. If we feel the Supreme's grace, then we shall see that His infinite qualities, peace, Light and bliss, are already in the process of entering us, ceaselessly flowing in and through us and becoming part and parcel of our inner and outer life. We have only to follow the flow of grace to carry us into the Source which is the Supreme.

God's grace is like the rays of the sun. The sun is always there, but what do we do? We get up late. Instead of getting up at five-thirty or six o'clock, we get up at eight or nine o'clock. Then we do not get the blessing of the morning sun. And when we do get up, we keep the doors and windows all shut and do not allow the sunlight to enter into our room. Similarly, God's grace is constantly descending, but quite often we are not allowing the grace to enter our system. We have kept barriers between God's grace and our own ignorance. Only if we keep our heart's door wide open can God's Light enter into our existence. God's Light means God's grace. There is no difference between God's grace and God's compassion-Light. Every day we have to empty our inner vessel and fill it with God's

155

peace, Light and bliss. We have to feel that God's Light is there all the time and is more than willing to illumine us. Only then will we be able to utilize God's grace. Again, if we miss God's grace, we should not be doomed to disappointment. Today we have not allowed the sunlight to enter into our room, but tomorrow the sun will be there again. If today we have not allowed God's grace to enter into us, it is due to our ignorance. Tomorrow we will definitely be prepared for God's Light to enter into us.

Question: What is the difference God's compassion and God's grace?

Sri Chinmoy: Compassion and grace are the same thing, but compassion is much more intense. The same grace, when it has tremendous intensity is called compassion. Water is everywhere, but when there is a torrential rain, you can say compassion is descending. It is like a heavy downpour from Above, with tremendous force. Grace is also water, but water is here, there, everywhere. This is the difference between compassion and grace.

Question: What does God's compassion do when we resist God's grace?

Sri Chinmoy: When an individual resists God's compassion, God either waits indefinitely and uses his Patience-Power, or He uses more compassion. In His case He deals with infinite compassion. He does not accept any defeat. If we resist His compassion, He may use more of His compassion to conquer us, or He may allow us to stay for ten, twenty, fifty, sixty or a hundred years more in ignorance. He is dealing with eternal time. It is up to Him whether to force us to accept His Light in a different way. But this forcing does not occur in a human way. His forcing means that He will use more of the compassion-power which He has and which He is. From His infinite compassion, He will use more compassion; He will use more compassion in order to conquer our ignorance.

But if He meets with tremendous resistance, then He may change His mind. He may say, "No, he wants to sleep for another hundred years. There is no hurry in it." God will never withdraw his compassion for good, no matter how we resist His compassion.

Only we delay our onward, upward, inward progress by resisting God's compassion-power. For God's compassion-power is His magnetic power that draws us to His very Heart, which is all Light and Delight.

Question: *How important is God's grace in our spiritual progress?*

Sri Chinmoy: Before realization we think that our personal effort, our aspiration alone is responsible for our spiritual progress. At that time there is no such thing as grace for us. But after realization, we come to see that there is no such thing as aspiration. Our progress is all due to divine grace.

In the ordinary human life there is no end to our desire. Today we want one car, tomorrow two cars, the day after tomorrow three cars: our desire goes on and on. In the world of aspiration and realization there is no end.

From an iota of peace, Light, and bliss, we try to get a large quantity, then an abundant measure. But we have to know who has inspired us to leave the world of desire and enter into the world of aspiration.

Among the members of my family, my friends and all the people in the whole world, why is it that only I am aspiring? Who inspired me? Who compelled me to aspire? It was the divine grace of the Supreme that inspired me. How is it that my brother is not praying and meditating but I am crying to realize God? It is because of the highest power, the divine grace is operating in and through me. I have aspiration because God gave it to me. It is all His grace.

The sun is shining. It is up to us to open all the windows and the doors in order to receive the Light. Naturally, if we open up the doors and windows, then the sun will come in. Similarly, the divine grace is constantly showering down from above. Let us try always to receive it with our heart's door wide open.

Question: *Can God's grace change fate?*

Sri Chinmoy: Fate can and must be changed. For that, what is required is God's grace plus personal effort. There are some seekers who feel, "If I care for God's grace, what necessity is there to make personal effort?" But they are mistaken. Personal effort will never stand in the way of God's descending grace. Personal effort expedites the descent of God's grace. God can give us all that He wants without even an iota of personal effort from us. He says, "It is for your satisfaction that I ask you to make this little personal effort." When we can make this personal effort, our whole life will be supercharged with divine pride: "See what I have done for God!" Our conscious oneness with God, who is infinite, who is eternally immortal, prompts us to do something for our Dearest and not for our ego.

If we sincerely make personal effort, God is bound to be thrilled with us. Why? Because He can tell the world, "My child, My chosen instrument, has done this for Me and that for Me." Through personal effort we can make our existence on earth worthy and, at the same time, we can make God proud of us.

Ultimately, personal effort has to grow into dynamic self-surrender. When we offer the results of our aspiration and inner urge to God, that is called self-surrender. If we do not offer the results to God and just lie like a dead body at His Feet, letting Him work for us, in us, and through us, it is wrong. God does not want an inactive body, a dead soul. He wants someone who is active, dynamic and aspiring; someone who wants to be energized so that he can do something for God; someone who wants to realize God and manifest all the divine qualities here on earth.

Surrender is our ultimate achievement. There is no difference between God's grace and our unconditional surrender. God's grace and our unconditional surrender are like the obverse and reverse of the same coin. If God did not give us that kind of grace, then we could not make unconditional surrender. To achieve God's grace is a real achievement. To make unconditional surrender is also a real achievement.

Question: *How do I know if I have done something through personal effort or God's grace?*

Sri Chinmoy: You have to understand that grace is something we can never understand and will never understand unless and until we have realized God. Personal effort is also God's grace. There are many stories about how seekers think it is all personal effort and later come to realize that its was all God's grace. As long as we are not aware of God's constant grace, we have to use our personal effort. God has been crying for us as individuals to come out of the sea of ignorance.

God's grace is responsible for everything, but before we feel it, it is always advisable for us to make a conscious personal effort. If we do not consciously make a personal effort, then we will never be able to know the highest Truth, we shall see that personal effort is nothing but God's hidden grace. Without the Grace-Power, everything is out of reach. With the Grace-Power, everything is within easy reach.

There is a fixed hour when God will kindle our consciousness whether we have faith in Him or not. He waits for the choice hour and when the hour strikes, He comes and gives us what He wants to give. But that does not mean that we shall not aspire, that we shall live in the world of sleep and not make any personal effort. No! We shall go on like a true farmer and cultivate the soil with sincere dedication and regularity, and after we do our part, we will leave it up to God to decide when He wants to give us the bumper crop of realization.

When God uses His compassion, it is like a magnet from above pulling us up to the Highest. And when we use our surrender, this magnet immediately pulls God down into our living breath. So when our magnet and God's magnet come together, the hour of God dawns for us in our life of aspiration and self-dedication.

Question: *Is God's compassion the same as His love?*

Sri Chinmoy: God's love is for everybody. It is like the sun. A person has only to keep open the window of his heart to receive divine love. When God's love takes an intimate form, it is called compassion. This compassion is the most powerful attribute, the most significant attribute of the Supreme. God's compassion is for the selected few. God's compassion is like a magnet that pulls the aspirant toward his goal. It is a mighty force that guides, pushes and pulls the aspirant constantly and does not allow him to slip on the path of Self-realization. God's love comforts and helps the aspirant, but if the aspirant falls asleep, the Divine love will not force him to awaken and compel him to resume his journey.

God's compassion is not like human compassion. In a human way we can have compassion and pity for somebody, but this compassion does not have the strength to change the person and make him run from his ignorant condition toward the Light. In the case of God's compassion, it is a force that changes and transforms the aspirant and keeps him from making major mistakes in his spiritual life.

Love will stay with ignorance, but compassion will not. compassion has to be successful otherwise it may be withdrawn. It will stay for a few seconds, or for a few minutes or for a few years, but it has to report to the Highest Authority and say whether or not it has been successful or not. A time may come when the Highest Authority says, "It is a barren desert. Come back." Then compassion has to fly back to the Highest Authority, the Supreme.

Question: Am I correct in saying that we who are believers in God must grow in grace daily?

Sri Chinmoy: You are absolutely correct in saying that the believers of God must grow in God's grace daily. A true believer of God feels that his very existence on earth, his inner and outer achievements and fulfillments are entirely due to God's grace. Also he is truly fortunate to see that his so-called personal efforts too are an act of God's grace. At every moment he feels that without God's grace, he is nothing and with God's grace, he is everything.

Question: Is it ever possible for man to become omnipotent?

Sri Chinmoy: No, man can not become omnipotent. But God's unconditional grace operating in and through man can do things that are absolutely unimaginable. Needless to say, man is not the doer of these imaginable deeds. The omnipotent God is using man as an instrument. His own omnipotence He can manifest through man's pure and humble receptivity. If God, out of His infinite Bounty, wants to perform something extraordinary in and through you, He can do so.

GURU/MASTER/TEACHER

Question: Do you think that the aspirant needs a living Guru in order to achieve realization?

Sri Chinmoy: To be very frank with you, the necessity of a living Guru in order to realize God is not absolutely indispensable. The first person who realized God on earth, the very first realized soul had no human Guru. The poor fellow who first realized God had only God as his Guru.

If you have a Guru, it facilitates your inner spiritual progress. A Guru is a private tutor. At every moment in life's journey, ignorance tries to test you, examine you and torture you, but this private tutor will teach you how to pass the examination. If you have a private tutor, you know how much help you can get in order to pass the examination. Moreover, if you get a Guru, once you get him and once you are in his boat, he takes you to the Golden Shore. You on your part do not have to work as hard as you would have done without a Guru.

The Guru is approached by his disciple at any time, any hour of the day or night, in his suffering and in his joy. The necessity of a Guru for a sincere disciple is certainly of paramount importance. But at the same time, it is not indispensable. However, if someone is wise enough to want to run towards his goal instead of stumbling or merely walking, then certainly the help of the Guru at that time is considerable.

Again a true disciple feels that the Guru and the disciple are not two totally different beings. That is to say, he does not feel that the Guru is at the top of the tree and he is at the foot of the tree, that he is all the time washing the feet of the Guru. No, he feels that the Guru is his own highest part. If he has feet, than he has also a head. He feels that he and the Guru are one. The Guru is his own highest and most developed part. Therefore he does not find any difficulty in surren-

161

dering his lowest part to his highest part. It is not beneath his dignity to offer his lowest to his highest because he knows that both the highest and the lowest are his.

So to come back to your question: the need for a teacher. It is absurd to feel that for everything else in life we need a teacher but not for God-Realization. Again, God is in everybody. If you feel that you do not need human help, you are most welcome to do it alone. Why does one go to the university when he can study at home? He need not go to university, but he feels that there he will get expert instruction. If you want to make fast, faster and fastest progress in the spiritual life, then I must say that a Guru is almost indispensable.

Question: *You spoke of a Guru as someone to help make a shortcut in the search for realization. I find it hard to channel myself in that search. Could you recommend or direct me somehow in channeling my energies toward Self-realization?*

Sri Chinmoy: To start with, I wish you to study some spiritual books. Right now, do not think of realization, liberation or salvation. Those who, at the very beginning of their journey, use the terms "self-realization," "liberation," "transformation" all the time are just fooling themselves, to be very frank with you. Please do not think I am criticizing you or blaming you, but I wish to say that these are big words. Some spiritual Masters say that one should not utter these words at all at the beginning, words like "realization," "divinization," etc. These are all big, big words. Only when one is on the threshold of true liberation, one can use them, or when one is far advanced in the spiritual life. Otherwise, people just entering into the spiritual life who have not learned the ABCs of the spiritual life, say "I want God-realization, I want liberation." Very often I hear this from people and I feel so sad. Before they have actually started climbing the tree, they want the fruit from the topmost branch.

Please launch into the spiritual path and learn the ABCs of the inner life. For that, discipline is required. Just as you take exercises every day to develop your muscles, you should likewise meditate regularly without fail, for five or ten minutes, according to your capacity and according to the instructions given to you by a teacher. You have to feel the necessity of feeding the child within you. When the child cries, immediately the mother runs to feed the child. Similarly all of us have within us a divine child, the soul. This soul has to be fed, if we want spiritual fulfillment, if we want the manifestation of God here on earth. If we feed our outer body thrice a day, it is only sensible that we feed the inner child within us at least once a day. If we do that, we shall eventually feel the Divine and realize God.

Question: *Why do we need a teacher or Guru? Is it important to have a teacher to follow the spiritual path?*

Sri Chinmoy: In this world we cannot do anything without the help of a teacher. The teacher may be necessary for a second or for a year or for many years. If I want to learn music, at the beginning I have to go to a musician. If I want to learn how to dance, I have to go to a dancer. If I want to learn about the sciences, I have to go to a scientist. In order to learn anything in this world, we need a teacher at the beginning. Then how is it that we do not need a teacher to help us in our inner, spiritual life?

A soul enters into a human frame, a human body, and then the human being grows and completes his first year of existence, his second year, third year and so on. What have the parents done during these years? They have taught him how to speak, how to eat, how to dress, how to behave. He learns everything from his parents. The parents played their part in the formative years of the child.

Similarly, in the spiritual life, the spiritual teacher has to teach the student how to pray, how to meditate, how to concentrate. Then, when the student learns and he goes deep within, he can do all this by himself.

Right now I am here in Puerto Rico. I know that New York exists and that I have to go back to New York. What do I need to get me there? An airplane and a pilot. In spite of the fact that I know that New York exists, I cannot get there alone. I need help. Similarly, we all know that God exists. You want to reach God, but someone has to help you. As the plane carries me to New York, someone has to carry you to the Consciousness of God which is deep within you. Someone has to show the path in order to enable you to enter into your own divinity, which is God. So this is the answer—that at the beginning, we need a teacher.

Question: *It seems to me that it takes a certain amount of energy and desire to follow the path of your teachings. And what about the rank beginner on it? Sometimes you can not muster enough energy to get yourself going!*

Sri Chinmoy: You are right. Not only to follow my path, but to follow any spiritual path, one has to have some spiritual energy and aspiration. But if one has to wait for this dynamic and spiritual energy, then one will never start one's journey. So if you really want the spiritual life, just throw yourself into the inner life. Do not look either backwards or sideways. Look ahead and jump into the sea of spirituality. Start from where you are. If you have limited energy, if your aspiration is insignificant, then go deep within. You will get to the inner well, the source of aspiration.

You cannot become a multimillionaire overnight. You have to start with a penny. Similarly if you have a little aspiration, if you really care for God, then start uttering God's name once a day, early in the morning. Gradually you can transform the whole day into a repetition of God's name and make real headway towards your self-discovery. If you have a sincere cry for God, then you can start your spiritual journey, no matter where you are or what you have.

Question: *How can one recognize a God-realized spiritual Master?*

Sri Chinmoy: When you are with a God-realized Master, consciously or unconsciously you are bound to feel some peace, some Light, some bliss, some power because it is his very nature to radiate these things. He is not showing off; it is spontaneous, as the very nature of a flower is to emit fragrance. Every day you come in contact with thousands of people, but you do not get this from any of them.

A Master's outer body may be very ugly, but in his eyes you will see all divine qualities. And if his eyes are closed, you may observe nothing outwardly, but deep inside yourself you will feel an inner joy that you have never felt before. You have felt joy before, true, but the inner thrill that you will get the moment you stand before a real spiritual Master for the first time can never be described. And if the Master is your own Master, then the joy will be infinitely greater.

You are bound to feel all kinds of divine qualities in the spiritual Master, provided you have aspiration. Otherwise, you may sit in front of the spiritual Master, talk to him, have all kinds of intimate friendship with him, but you will get nothing. It is your aspiration that permits you to receive all the divine qualities of the Master. If you have no aspiration, no matter what the Master has, he will not be able to give it to you.

Also, when you speak to a real Master, your own sincerity has to come forward. This does not mean that you will always express your sincerity. You may tell lies in spite of the fact that your sincerity is pushing you, compelling you to tell the Truth. But when you are with a spiritual Master, you at least want to offer your sincerity, although insincerity may come and fight with you and sometimes prevent you.

When you are with a realized Master, you are bound to feel that the Master understands you; and not only that he understands you, but also that he has the capacity to comfort you and help you in your problems. Some people feel that there is nobody on earth to understand them. But, if they are lucky enough to find a person who understands them, they come to know that this person still cannot solve their problems because he does not have inner Light, inner wisdom, inner power. A spiritual Master not only understands your problems, but also has the capacity in infinite measure to help you in your needs.

When you stand before a Master, you will feel that he can never be separated from your inner or outer existence. You feel he is your highest part and you want to grow into him. You want to become a perfect part of his highest realization, for the very divine qualities that you are aspiring for—Light, joy, peace, power—a spiritual Master has in boundless measure.

Question: *How does one go about finding a Guru and how does one know they are making the proper choice?*

Sri Chinmoy: It is not a matter of knowing. It is a matter of feeling. Please go deep within, shed bitter tears and pray to God: "I have wasted my life, all my life; now You must tell whether I am meant to have a Guru." Then God will say, "Yes, you are meant." You will ask God, "Who is my Guru? I implore You to tell me." If you are totally sincere, then God will immediately answer your prayer. When a child cries bitterly in front of his mother, how long can she, if she is a real mother, deny him what he wants? You are a child of the Supreme. If you sincerely cry, it is a matter of hours or days. The Supreme will quickly make you feel which Master is meant for you.

Question: *Is there a difference between the realization of one Master and the realization of another?*

Sri Chinmoy: Masters are not all at the same level. A fully realized Master is he who is constantly one with God's Consciousness, constantly aware of his oneness with God. Again, there are half-realized or partially realized Masters. A few hours of the day, when they are meditating, they will be one with God, and the rest of the time they will be like ordinary human beings. Their oneness with God depends on what kind of realization the Masters have achieved.

God-realization is like a tree. One can run and touch the tree of realization and say, "I have realized God." But this realization is only touching the foot of the tree. One is very happy in touching the foot of the tree, for he has seen that the fruit is there, the leaves and branches are there; he can touch them, hold them, feel them, and he knows that he has reached his goal. But another person will say, "No, I am not satisfied. I want to climb up a little and sit on a branch. Then I will feel that I have reached my goal." He goes one step higher, so naturally his realization is superior. Again, there will be someone who will climb up to the topmost branch and eat the delicious fruit there. His realization is higher still. He has not only seen and touched the Highest, but has actually climbed up to the Highest. But he has no intention of coming down because he feels that the moment he comes down he will again be an ordinary person and will be caught in the meshes of the ignorant world. He feels that once he climbs down, he will not be able to climb back up again.

There is another type of realized soul who will not only climb up to the Highest for realization, but will bring down the fruits of the tree for the world. He will come back for manifestation. He says, "I am not satisfied with sitting at the top of the tree. This is not my goal. What I have received I want to share with humanity." He has the capacity to climb up and climb down at his sweet will. When he climbs down, he brings down compassion, peace, Light and bliss from above. And when he climbs up, he takes humanity with him. He places a few human beings on his shoulders and then climbs back up. He will leave those souls up there and come down again to take a few more up on his shoulders. His capacity is infinitely greater than that of the person who just comes and touches the tree. His realization is the fullest.

In India, there have been quite a few spiritual Masters who were partially realized. They touched the foot of the tree, but did not climb up to the topmost branch. They are considered very great by the aspirants, but when you compare their standard with that of Sri Krishna or the Christ or the Buddha, you have to say that those who only touched the tree achieved only a partial realization.

If a Hindu touches a drop of water from the Ganges, he will feel a sense of purity. But if somebody has the capacity to swim across the Ganges, naturally he will be more convinced that his entire body is purified. When it is a matter of realization, also, one can be satisfied with a drop of nectar or one can say, "No, I need the boundless ocean." Again, one can say, "This boundless nectar is not only for me; it is for everybody. I want to share it with others." The realization of the individual who actually has the capacity to share his highest realization with others is undoubtedly superior to that of the other two.

Sri Ramakrishna used to speak about the *jivakoti* and the *ishvarakoti*. The *jivakoti* is one who has realized God but does not want to enter into the field of manifestation again. A person who has a raft, a tiny boat, can cross the sea of ignorance himself, but he cannot take others. But the *ishvarakoti*, who has a big ship, can accommodate hundreds and thousands of human souls and carry them across the sea of ignorance. He comes into the world again and again to liberate mankind.

Question: *Do spiritual Gurus transfer all their power to one spiritual descendant?*

Sri Chinmoy: It is not quite like that. If the spiritual Guru is really great and has real power, it is quite possible that his power will be given to a spiritual descendant. Sri Ramakrishna had a spiritual descendant, Vivekananda. But at the same time he had a few more disciples who were spiritually great. Undoubtedly, Brahmananda was one of them. You can say that a Master might have one major disciple, but you cannot say that all his spiritual power, all his Light he gives to this one person, while others get next to nothing. It is not like that. When the Master realizes God, he represents the Divine to his particular disciples. Indeed, because he represents the Divine, his spiritual power, knowledge, peace, Light and delight are unlimited. Each disciple can get boundless Light, delight, peace and power. "When infinity is taken away from infinity, infinity still remains the same." This is what the Upanishads teach us.

Question: *So what you are saying is that each disciple is given according to his or her capacity to receive?*

Sri Chinmoy: Yes, one disciple can play the part of a leader and he can be described as the Master's spiritual descendant, but the Master's spiritual powers and achievements are given to each disciple according to his capacity and receptivity. The Master may make one disciple a leader, as Sri Ramakrishna did with Vivekananda. Everybody cannot be a leader. But even the leader will receive from the Master according to his own spiritual capacity and receptivity. There are many sincere disciples who do not have the capacity of leadership, but at the same time, they most sincerely aspire. If they are sincere they, too, can get anything.

Question: *How then can a devotee know that he or she is close and dear to the Guru?*

Sri Chinmoy: The moment the disciple feels that he has offered everything—his outer life as well as his inner life—to the Guru, he can feel that he is the dearest and closest. If he lives just because the Guru wants him to live; if he lives for the sake of the Guru, for the sake of the Divine, undoubtedly he will feel that he is dearest to his Master.

Question: But how does the devotee know this feeling is genuine?

Sri Chinmoy: If this feeling of his is absolutely true, nobody will have to reassure him on this point. No one will even have to tell him. If any disciple can make a constant, cheerful and unconditional surrender to God, then he is or she is the dearest disciple of the Master. Absolute surrender to the Will of the Absolute has no equal in the spiritual life.

The moment you feel that you need a Master and he needs you, the moment you feel the Master inside you, before you and around you, then death no longer exists for you. When the Master is away from your mind, when the Master is not found inside your heart, when you feel that the Master is nowhere near you, at that time death exists for you. Otherwise, where is death? This physical body may leave the earth, but the soul, which is the conscious portion of God, will remain consciously in God and for God throughout eternity.

Question: Why do spiritual Masters get sick if they are in touch with God?

Sri Chinmoy: Many times spiritual figures die of so-called fatal diseases. But these poor Masters are not responsible. What happens is that the Master identifies himself with his disciples; his love and affection for his disciples are boundless. So he tries to take the disciples' imperfections into himself and dissolve them. It is like the case of mother and son. When the mother sees that the child is suffering, she says, "Give me your suffering!" You cannot say that because the Guru is suffering, he is imperfect. No, he is suffering for his own spiritual children. They have done something wrong, and out of his kindness and compassion he draws into himself that imperfection. There are various reasons why the spiritual Masters fall sick.

Question: Was this what happened to Sri Ramakrishna?

Sri Chinmoy: Yes, Sri Ramakrishna took the imperfections of all his disciples. Then he cured them, he saved them. He had to take the cancer and he died. On the strength of his love, intimacy and union, he took their imperfections inside himself. It is very common for a mother to sacrifice her own life to save her child. And the relation between a Guru and his disciple is infinitely more intimate than the relation between mother and son. In this life you have a son, but in the next life you do not know whether he will take birth in India while you may take birth in Japan or somewhere else. In the next life your connection may be broken. But in the case of a spiritual Master, a realized soul, he knows where a particular disciple is going to take birth in his next incarnation and where he himself is going to take birth. His connection and his relationship with his disciple will last throughout eternity. The Guru has to take his disciple to God. Until he has done this, he has not completed his task.

You have to make a living relationship and connection with your Guru. When you pray to your Guru, you have to feel that he is breathing within you. When you have established that relationship, then you can rest assured that the Guru will take you to your destined goal.

Question: Is a liberated soul the same as a spiritual Master who tries to help humanity?

Sri Chinmoy: The world has seen thousands and thousands of liberated souls, but not all liberated souls work in the world of ignorance. Many are afraid that ignorance will threaten them and try to devour them. One who is just liberated has come out of the room which is full of darkness, but this does not necessarily mean he is truly qualified to be a spiritual guide. To be a spiritual guide in the highest sense of the term, one must be commissioned by the Supreme. One may have spiritual knowledge, spiritual power and so forth, but if he is not authorized by the Highest to guide humanity, he cannot be a real spiritual Master.

Question: If someone has realized God, why would he want to leave the higher bliss and come down into the darkness of the earth to help others?

Sri Chinmoy: There are some spiritual Masters who do not care for the manifestation of God's Divinity on earth. They do not care for the transformation of the earth-consciousness. They say to the world, "If I try to help you, your doubts, fears, anxieties, worries, limitations and bondage will all enter into me. I worked hard for my own realization, so the best thing is for you also to work hard for your realization. If you work hard, God will never deny you the fruits."

Again, there are some spiritual Masters who *do* care for the illumination of the earth-consciousness. They see that they are eating most delicious food or drinking nectar in the inner world, while their brothers and sisters are deprived of it. This kind of Master identifies with humanity and feels it is his business to awaken the consciousness of his fellow human beings, his slumbering brothers and sisters. If there are people on earth who are covered by ignorance and are wasting their time in idleness when they really need nourishment, this Master feels sorry. He feels sorry that these people still want to remain in ignorance when they could easily go beyond the boundaries of ignorance.

Since a spiritual Master has himself experienced all kinds of suffering, he does not consider his fellow human beings objects of pity. He identifies himself totally with them. He has realized God, but he feels that unless and until everybody is realized, he himself is imperfect and incomplete. When it is a matter of personal need, the Master does not need anything more from God, but he becomes part and parcel of humanity out of his compassion.

He says, "I shall play the role of a father." In a family we see that the father works very, very hard and amasses some wealth, and then his children do not have to work so hard. He gives all kinds of material help to his children, and they get the benefit of his labor. When a real spiritual Master comes into the world, he has worked very, very hard to realize the Truth, and he possesses boundless peace, Light and bliss in his inner life. He offers this wealth to his spiritual children because they claim him as their very own and he claims them. Those who have established total oneness with the Master and who try to fulfill the Master according to their capacity, those who become extremely close to their Master, receive what the Master has and is. Their realization is entirely up to the Master. It is like the case of the father who has millions of dollars. The son has pleased the father, so the father gives the son his wealth.

Again, the father will always see whether the son is capable of receiving the money and utilizing it in a proper way. If the father sees that the son is going to utilize the money properly, naturally he gives the son money. But if the father sees that the son will squander ten dollars rather than use it for a divine purpose, then naturally he will not lavish his money on this worthless son. In the spiritual world it is also like that. If one is really sincere, if one feels that he can exist without everything, but not without God, then it is possible for him to realize God in one incarnation with the help of a spiritual Master, because he will properly utilize what the Master gives him.

Question: *Will not a person lose his realization if he comes down from the realization-tree and has to face the darkness and ignorance of the world?*

Sri Chinmoy: If you are afraid that a realized soul will lose his divinity and realization if he mixes with ordinary people, then you are mistaken. When you realize God, God gives you more power than He has given His unrealized children. Spiritual Masters have a free access to God's Omnipotence and to all His other qualities. If spiritual Masters did not have more power than their disciples, who still suffer from fear, doubt, anxiety and other undivine qualities, they would never mix with them or even accept them. They would know that they would be devoured, totally devoured by their disciples' imperfections. But they are not afraid because they know that their realization has much more power than any negative forces in their disciples. Before realization, even up to the very last hour, it is possible to fall from the realization-tree. But once you have realized God, you have won the race. This victory is permanent and eternal. Nothing and no one can take it away from you, nor can you lose it.

Question: *Does every person who realizes God become a spiritual Master?*

Sri Chinmoy: There are hundreds of students every year who get their Master's degree from a university. Some then enter into an office or business, while others begin to teach. Similarly, some people who have realized God teach others how to realize God, and some do not. Those who do not teach in the world are God-realized nevertheless. We cannot deny it. But it has taken them many incarnations to cross the barriers of ignorance, and they are now really tired. It is not an easy thing to realize God, and they feel they have acted like real divine heroes in the battlefield of life. They have fought against fear, doubt, anxieties, worries, imperfections, limitations and bondage and conquered these forces. Now they feel that they have every right to withdraw from the battlefield and take rest. These souls speak to God, and if God says they do not have to take conscious part in the Cosmic Game any more, and may just observe, then they withdraw. If they have God's permission, naturally they can remain passive.

But the souls who do not take part in God's manifestation are also doing something very great. They may not take an active part in the world, they may not go from one place to another to teach or open spiritual centers and accept disciples, but in their meditation they try to offer illumination inwardly by offering their conscious good will to mankind. How many people offer their good will to mankind? Ordinary human beings quarrel, fight and consciously or unconsciously do many undivine things against God's Will. But in the case of these realized souls, they do not enter into any kind of conflict with God's Will; their will has become one with God's Will.

We cannot say that he who works outwardly for mankind is greater than he who helps inwardly. What is of paramount importance is to listen to God's Will. If God tells one illumined soul, "I do not need you to move around from place to place. You just give your light inwardly," then that person is great by offering his light inwardly. And if God tells another soul, "I want you to go into the world and offer humanity the light you have," then that Master is great by helping humanity. Everything depends on what God wants from a particular soul.

Question: *Why do you come down to your disciples' level in order to help them?*

Sri Chinmoy: It is not that I just come down to the level of my disciples. I go one step below their standard, because I want to place them on my shoulders. But sometimes it happens that they will not sit on my shoulders. It is here very often that misunderstandings start. If we run after someone in order to give him something, that person may think that we have some motive. They feel that if they are on my shoulders they will be stuck and they will not be able to climb up. They want to climb up on their own so that they can take the full credit. But they are fools if they think this. If they were able to climb up on their own, then why did they come to me?

The mother goes to the market, buys food and then asks her children to come and eat. If the children are wise they will say, "We are so lucky that we have such a good mother. She has gone all the way and brought us this food." Otherwise they will say, "No. We need food, but we want to go out to eat." This is what some unfortunate disciples do. They want to go out to eat somewhere, because they have not been there before. Then on the way they see some candy and are tempted. So instead of getting the proper food, they buy some junk and eat it and get an upset stomach.

You can eat proper spiritual food provided that you feel that there is someone who is constantly expecting something from you. If you feel that there is someone who is constantly expecting something from you, you will give more importance to your life. If your boss is expecting something from you, you are bloated with human pride. And when you feel that Somebody else who is superior to your boss is expecting something from you, then immediately you are nourished with a sense of divine pride. You are nourished only when you feel that your own Inner Pilot needs you. His expectation means His oneness with you. His very need of you is His nourishment. Your Inner Pilot is the Supreme. Your Supreme and my Supreme are the same, but in my case, I have established my constant oneness with Him, while unfortunately in your case you have not done so. When I say, "I," immediately I feel that the Supreme is operating in and through me and I am operating in and through the Supreme. If you can go deep within, then you will also establish your oneness with the Supreme.

Right now, the concept of the Supreme operating in and through you is only a vague idea. When you think of God, you may think that He is in beautiful trees or on top of a mountain. If you think of God in this way, then at any moment He may disappear, and you will wonder where He has gone. But when you think of me, that question does not arise. You know that I am in this house or at the store or some other place. When you think of God, you may try to imagine whether He is in Heaven or hell, but when you think of your Guru, you know where I am. I am something tangible. You will see me because I am on the physical, vital, mental, psychic and spiritual planes. You can visualize me immediately. That is why they say that if you go through the Master, you are reaching the right place. It is much easier and safer to allow the Guru to go to God and bring God to you than to go to the Guru through God. If you go to God, the mind will doubt. If a child goes directly to the father and the father says, "I am your father," the child may not believe it. He will say, "How do I know this?" But if his friends say, "This is your father," then he will believe it.

Question: *Why do not you just give up on us?*

Sri Chinmoy: If I give up on you, then what am I and what do I have? If I give up on all of you who are composed of me, then what do I have to call my own? There is no good or bad in my life. If you people are bad, then I am bad. If you people are culprits, then I am the first and worst culprit. If you are good, then I also am good. Anything that you people are is only an expansion or projection of my own reality. So how can I get rid of my own reality? I am the source. How can the root leave the branches and leaves? You have accepted me. If it is stupidity, then it is my stupidity. I have accepted all my disciples in the inner world long before you have accepted me on the physical plane.

How can I give up? If I give up, then I myself do not exist. I am only what you have for me and what you are with me. My existence is composed of what you people have and what you people are. It is not a matter of putting up with you; it is only an act of wisdom. Since I want to exist, I have to be with you all. It is like an onion. The layers of an onion grow one on top of another. Each layer is part of the rest. If you start peeling the onion to separate the layers, you will peel right down to nothing. Again, when the onion grows, one layer grows on top of the next. It is all oneness, oneness, oneness. So let us try to grow a small onion into a big onion. Only then will the disciple and the Guru be fulfilled.

Question: *When a disciple is far away, how can he get the same force that he feels when he is meditating with his Guru?*

Sri Chinmoy: Physically, the Master cannot be twenty-four hours a day with the disciples; it is impossible. The Master has many, many disciples and also the Master has many, many things to do. Again, a disciple may stay with the Master day and night, but he may not get anything from the Master. Sri Ramakrishna's nephew served him for many, many years, but he got practically nothing from Ramakrishna. Again, look at Vivekananda. In the beginning, he used to come once in two or three months. And then how many days did he stay with his Master?

It is not the physical proximity that counts most. It is the inner awareness of one's relationship with the Master. Where is the Master? Is he in New York or is he inside your heart? If the disciple feels that the Master is something very sacred and secret, and that the Master is something essential in his life, then he cannot stay without the Master. If he feels that the necessity of the Master is of paramount importance, if he feels that he cannot exist without the Master, any more than he can exist without his heartbeat, then only the relationship between the Master and the disciple is secure and complete.

When you go back home, you have to feel that you are carrying me inside your heart, not that you have left me in New York. Do not feel that my existence is only in one part of the world; no, you have to feel that my inner existence is everywhere. My outer existence, my physical body, which is five feet eight inches, can stay only at one place, but my inner existence can roam about many, many places. You have to feel the necessity of the inner relationship, the inner connection with my heart and soul. Then only will you be able to make the utmost progress.

Again, if a disciple has already established his inner connection with the Master, if he has established a secure, most intimate and most surrendering and surrendered relation, then if he stays with the Master, then naturally he will be able to get more benefit. In his case, inside he is already one with the Master; now his outer self is crying to become one with the inside. So naturally he will get a double push and progress infinitely faster if he is physically near the Master.

But, very often, familiarity breeds contempt. When you stay with the Master, cutting jokes and all that, immediately you will say: "He is also like us." In the outer world he eats the same food and takes ice cream and does everything as you do. But he can do quite a few things in the inner world which you cannot do. That is why, first of all, his inner existence has to be approached and adored. If inwardly you have pleased the Master, then rest assured that it is only a matter of a short time before you please the Master in the outer life, not vice versa. In the outer life, if the Master says: "I want to get some stamps," immediately you will go to the Post Office and bring some stamps. But this kind of connection will not help you considerably if your inner connection is not complete. If the inner connection is complete, and if I say, "Please take me to the beach," if you take me and make me happy, then you are pleasing me on all ends. Already you have made the inner connection with me. You have pleased me most, and now the outer connection also you have made by listening to me.

If you had not made the inner connection with me, then what would have happened? During the two hours that you are driving me, our outer connection gives you peace, joy, harmony or some kind of gratification. But at the end of two hours all vanishes again. But in the inner world, when somebody meditates and thinks of me for five minutes and offers me his life-breath, this lasts forever. Then you have fulfilled me and I have fulfilled you.

Question: *Can a Master guide new disciples after he has left this earth?*

Sri Chinmoy: Certainly, it is possible. Look at the Christ, for example. Great Masters such as the Christ, Sri Krishna, the Buddha, Ramakrishna and others can and do guide their followers; they have a free access to the earth-consciousness no matter where they are.

Again, it depends on the disciple. If it is a real first-class disciple, who is always thinking of the Master and meditating on the Master, then it is much easier for the Master to guide that disciple. But if it is a fourth-class disciple, who is all the time occupied with worldly thoughts and ideas, then how can the Master make him conscious of his guidance? So it depends upon the calibre of the Master, and the receptivity of the disciple.

Question: *How can we tell if we have met our Master?*

Sri Chinmoy: I have answered this particular question millions of times. Now, I am a spiritual Master and today we have all come here to pray and meditate and create a spiritual atmosphere. When I called my disciples up to meditate, I saw that everyone else in the audience was meditating in his or her own way, which is absolutely the right thing. Now each individual has to become like a teacher and give marks for whatever he sees in me—peace, Light, bliss or any spiritual quality and also the spiritual atmosphere that he finds here. He should give ten out of a hundred or twenty out of a hundred and so on. If he gives zero out a hundred, it may be absolutely correct according to him. He will know he is with his real Master when he can give at least eighty out of a hundred.

A seeker must prepare himself to be ready for his Master. Otherwise, if he is not ready, he can see the Master face-to-face, but he will not recognize him. The Master knows that that seeker is meant for his path, but he cannot tell him, "You are my disciple." The seeker will think, "Oh, I am so rich or I am very influential, that is why he wants me to be his disciple." This is the way the Master is suspected. Also, if the Master says, "No, you are not my disciple," then the seeker will feel, "Oh, it is because I have nothing to offer him; I am hopeless and helpless." Whatever the Master says will be open to question. So it is the seeker who must choose, and then it is up to the Master to accept him or else to tell him that there is another Master waiting for him.

After the seeker has chosen and is accepted by a Master, he must not feel that he has automatically become a dear, close disciple of the Master. The seeker must see how sincere he is. If he feels, "I need Truth, I need Light," then he is ready for the true spiritual life. The seeker has to know if he is ready to give the Master everything that he has and everything that he is. What the seeker has is aspiration, the inner cry, and what he is, right now, is ignorance. When he is fully prepared to give the Master all that he has and all that he is, then the Master can work most effectively to transform his entire life. The seeker surrenders his existence to the Master, and then it becomes the Master's responsibility to illumine and perfect him.

Question: If the teacher leaves the body, should you try to maintain contact with him?

Sri Chinmoy: It depends on the relationship that the teacher and the student have established. Suppose your teacher has passed away and you did not have any close connection with him. You can say that your teacher was very great, but what kind of connection did you have with him? If the teacher has ten thousand disciples and you are not one of the intimate disciples, then you cannot expect anything from him just because he is very great. Did you ever have any personal contact with him, or any serious conversation with him? Did you have any inner contact with him when he was on earth? These are the things that you have to take into account. Otherwise, just because he is great does not provide any assurance that you can maintain any inner connection with him, if he did not make any solemn promise to you that he would take responsibility for your inner life.

Let us say your father was a very great doctor, and now he is not on earth. If you are suffering from some ailment, will you think of your father in Heaven to cure you? No. Somebody may be infinitely inferior to your father in the medical profession, but you will go to him for immediate cure. He will cure you because he is still on earth.

If you have a Master like Sri Krishna, the Buddha or the Christ, a Master who is fully identified with God-Consciousness, then when you meditate on him, you are offering your very existence to the Ultimate, to the Almighty Father. Otherwise, there are many spiritual Masters on earth who have realized God, but if you have not established any strong inner connection with them while they are on earth, it will be difficult, if not impossible, to maintain any connection once they leave the body.

Question: Does a realized Master who chooses to help suffering humanity lose anything by doing so, especially since humanity is so reluctant to accept his wealth ?

Sri Chinmoy: He is like someone who knows how to climb a tree well. He has the capacity to climb up and climb down. When the Master climbs down, he does not lose anything because he knows that at the next moment he will be able to climb up again. Suppose a child at the foot of the tree says, "Please give me a fruit; please give me a most delicious mango." Immediately the Master will bring one down and then he will climb up again. And if nobody else asks for a mango, he will sit on the branch and wait.

Here on earth, if one human being has something to offer and the other person does not take it, then the first person gets furious. He says, "You fool! It is for your own good that I am giving it." He will scold the other person and be very displeased if his offering is not accepted. In the case of a spiritual Master, it is different. He will come with his wealth, but if humanity does not accept it, he will not curse humanity. Even if humanity insults him and speaks ill of him, he will not lodge a complaint against humanity to God. With his boundless patience he will say, "All right, today you are sleeping. Perhaps tomorrow you will get up and see what I have to offer. I will wait for you." If you are fast asleep and someone pinches you and shouts, "Get up! Get up!" he is not doing you a favor. You will be annoyed. But the spiritual Master will not bother you; he will not ask you to get up. He will stay beside your bed and wait until you get up. The moment you get up, he will ask you to look at the sun.

If he is a real spiritual Master, he will not lose anything if earth rejects what he has because he is well established in his inner life, in his inner consciousness. Again, if humanity accepts what he offers, he does not lose anything either. The more he gives, the more he gets from the Source. Just as in the ordinary life the more knowledge we offer to others, the more we get, in the spiritual life also, it is the same. A spiritual Master will never run short of peace, Light and bliss, because he is connected with the infinite Source of all.

When one is in touch with unlimited capacity in the inner world, his source is like an ocean. One cannot empty the infinite inner ocean. The real Master wants to give everything to his devoted disciples, but their power of receptivity is limited. So he tries to widen their vessels and make them as big as possible so that the disciples can receive the peace, Light and bliss that he brings for them. But he cannot force an aspirant to receive more than he has the capacity to hold. If he does, then the vessel will give way. So a Master can only pour and pour and pour his Light into his disciples, but once the limit of their receptivity is reached, it will all be wasted on them.

Question: When a Master brings down more Light, peace and bliss than those meditating with him can absorb, what happens to it?

Sri Chinmoy: It is not all lost. It is scattered over the earth. It enters into the earth-atmosphere and becomes the earth's possession. When spiritual Masters bring down divine qualities from Above, Mother Earth embodies them as her own. Then, when someone in the street or elsewhere aspires, he will get this peace and Light from the earth-consciousness, but he will not know where it is coming from.

Question: I once read that a Master will come down to help humanity in this world, and then he will continue helping from other worlds. Is this true?

Sri Chinmoy: Whenever there is a necessity, great spiritual Masters come down to help the yet-unrealized souls. They are playing their part in God's Game, His divine *Lila*. Seekers get a tremendous opportunity when they are helped in their aspiration by real spiritual Masters, for by personal effort, without the help of a Master, it is very, very difficult to get realization. Aspiration is of paramount importance, but mere aspiration cannot give realization. There is a necessity for the divine grace. And this grace comes most easily through the intervention of the great spiritual Masters. The world is progressing and evolving as quickly as it is just because great spiritual Masters are coming into the world to help.

After working on earth for a few incarnations, the Master may want to continue his work for humanity from the other world. At that time, he knows all the hidden corners of Mother Earth; he knows every heartbeat of the earth-consciousness, so he is able to work from another plane.

Question: Why is it so difficult for a realized Master to be accepted by the world?

Sri Chinmoy: The world is not ready for spiritual Masters. They come into the world out of their infinite compassion. When they leave, some Masters promise that they will come back as long as there are people still unrealized on earth. They are sincere when they say this, but when they go up to the higher worlds and see earth's ingratitude, they change their minds. They ask themselves why they should waste their precious time if humanity is sleeping, and why they should come back just to be kicked by an ungrateful humanity.

Humanity needs spiritual Masters for awakening and illumination, but in the outer life, people do not feel any urgency. The world is not ready, and perhaps it will never be ready as a whole. When the Masters come, they find unwilling, unaspiring human beings. For spiritual Masters to realize God, it takes quite a few incarnations. Realization is such an arduous task to perform. But it is much more difficult to manifest God on earth. That is why many spiritual Masters do not come down for manifestation.

Although God is inside each human being, unfortunately the animal still predominates in man. When the Masters are dealing with humanity, they see it is all animality. Look at the example of Sri Ramakrishna. He took so many negative and undivine forces from his disciples; he suffered so much from their poison. Otherwise, for such a pure man to be afflicted with malignant cancer would have been impossible.

To realize God is difficult. And after realization, to live in the ignorant world and stay with humanity is more difficult. But to remain in the consciousness of the Highest while working in the lowest, to bring down the highest Light into the lowest and make the lowest receive and accept it, is most difficult. Again, when we say something is difficult or most difficult, we are only belittling ourselves. After all, what are spiritual Masters? They are God's chosen children. God's chosen children are identified with God all the time throughout eternity. God can never be separated from His children, His creation. So nothing is difficult if we see it from the highest absolute point of view—neither to realize God nor to serve God in humanity, nor to take responsibility for bringing humanity to Divinity or Divinity to humanity. Everything is easy, easier, easiest, if there is something called God-touch. If God's Will touches some action, then it is very easy.

Question: *Among those Masters who decide, after realization, to go out into the world to help humanity, why do some accept large numbers of disciples while others do not?*

Sri Chinmoy: Sometimes the Supreme makes the decision, but He does not impose His Will. There are some Masters who, after having their major realization, are asked by the Supreme, "What is your will? What do you want to do?" If the Master says, "I want to work for so many people, I want to do this much work," then the Supreme says, "All right, granted, with My blessings." Then there are some who do not make any hard and fast rule as to how far they want to go. They say, "I will try my best up to the end. I need Your blessings. I need Your grace. I will try to manifest as much as possible. I set no limits."

With some Masters, there is a limit to the number of disciples they want. With others, there is no end to their aspiration to serve. They remain an open channel and tell the Supreme that they will try their best to fulfill Him and manifest Him until the end of their lives. And not only that, but after leaving the body also, they promise to try to continue His work through their disciples. So it depends on the individual Master and how much spiritual responsibility he wants to accept.

The number of disciples a Master may have depends on what kind of people he accepts. If he is very selective and wants only souls that are fully dedicated, intensely aspiring and absolutely destined for the spiritual life, then he will accept only a handful. Sri Ramakrishna, for example, wanted only a limited number of disciples. He was very particular about his disciples. But some Masters say, "Anyone who wants to learn anything about the spiritual life is welcome to my community." Again, some Masters say, "Let everyone progress according to his own standard." So they accept thousands of disciples.

True spiritual Masters will only accept disciples who are meant for them. If I know that somebody will make faster progress through some other Master, then occultly and spiritually I will make that person feel in a few months' time that he is not meant for me. What matters is not the number of disciples a Master has, but whether he takes them to the goal. If I am realized and somebody else is realized, we are like two brothers with one common Father. Our goal is to take our younger brothers and sisters, humanity, to the Father. The game will be complete only when all people are taken to God. If two Masters are real brothers from the same Father, then how can one Master be unhappy or displeased if somebody goes to the Supreme through the other Master? It is not who has done it, but whether the thing is done. Who has done it is only name and form, which will be obliterated in history. What matters is that evolution has taken place on earth.

Question: Why do some spiritual Masters go out into the world to increase their following?

Sri Chinmoy: A true Master is not interested in the number of his devotees, since by God's grace the Master and the aspirant are bound to find each other. But Sri Ramakrishna used to go up to the top floor of his house and cry for spiritual disciples. He used to ask Mother Kali why the disciples he was destined to have did not come to him. Now, people may ask why he could not wait for God's hour. God's hour had come for Sri Ramakrishna, but the ignorance of the world was blocking its path. God told him to do something and gave him the capacity, but ignorance was standing right in front of him and delaying, delaying, delaying his manifestation. Sri Ramakrishna was not crying for disciples who would come and touch his feet. He was crying for disciples who would be his real arms and hands, who would fly with him into the Universal Consciousness, who would work for him, and in that way work for God.

Nobody is indispensable, true. But, at the same time, each person is indispensable so long as he is absolutely sincere in his aspiration and in his service to the Mission of the Supreme. Out of pride and vanity, nobody can feel that he is necessary; but everybody is necessary when he is a sincere, dedicated chosen instrument of God. The Master needs disciples because they are like his hands, his limbs, the expansion of his own consciousness. And when he gets the command from the Highest, then he has to try to find those who are going to be part and parcel of his consciousness to help him fulfill the command.

Traditionally, spiritual Masters used to say, "If you have something, others are bound to come. The pond does not go to the thirsty person; the thirsty person comes to the pond." This is absolutely true if a mature person is thirsty. But if you feel that the thirsty person is just an infant, then it is all different. The baby will cry in his room, and the mother will come running to feed him. The mother does not say to the baby, "You have to come to me, since you want something from me." No, the mother puts everything aside and comes to the baby.

In the spiritual world also, some Masters feel the need to go out into the world, for the outer world is just a baby in consciousness. These Masters feel that there are many children who are crying for spiritual Light, spiritual wisdom, spiritual perfection, but do not know where or how to find it. So the Masters go from place to place and offer their Light with the idea of serving the divinity in humanity. I happen to be one of those. I move around because I feel that there are sincere children who need the Light that the Supreme has given me to offer to mankind. That is why I go to so many countries all over the world because I feel that the outer world is my child.

When the world is crying, if we have the capacity, we have to feed it. If I have the capacity to give you something and I also have the capacity to go and stand right in front of you, why do I have to call you to me? If I have the capacity both to place myself before you and to give you the Light that you want, then I must do so. If I do not have the capacity, then I have to keep silent.

The outer world is very limited in comparison to the inner world. The length and breadth of the outer world is no more than a few thousand miles, but the inner world is without limit. A spiritual person feels, on the strength of his own realization, that all worlds are his, because his Master, the Supreme, is all-pervading. Now, if the Supreme is all-pervading, then why is it beneath the dignity of His son to go from one place to another?

There are various ways to feed the world. Writing spiritual books is one way; giving talks is another. If one has many capacities, why should he not use all of them? Some spiritual Masters do not have these outer capacities. Sri Ramakrishna, for example, did not write. But that did not prevent him from realizing the Highest. At the same time, those who have the capacity to write and give talks are not deprived of their God-realization.

God plays in various ways. If God gives a spiritual Master the capacity to write, to give talks, to mix with people, to travel from place to place, then that is God's business. It is God's Will that the Master is carrying out. And if God does not give the Master the capacity to write and speak, we cannot blame that spiritual Master or say he is inferior. We have to know what God wants from us. If God wants me to write, He will give me the capacity. If God does not want you to write, He will not give you the capacity. In neither case can we find fault.

Question: *Can a spiritual Master who tries to reveal the higher truths be compared in some ways to a poet who tries to express and reveal artistic truths?*

Sri Chinmoy: An ordinary poet may get a glimpse of the Truth, but the spiritual Masters get the Ocean of Truth itself. Spiritual Masters see a much higher truth than any ordinary poets see. Also, in the case of ordinary poets, poetry is everything to them. But in the case of advanced souls or spiritual Masters, poetry is not everything; God is everything.

The poet who brings down higher messages feels that these are everything he has to give. But spiritual Masters feel that their writings represent absolutely nothing when compared with what they know and what they truly are. They say, "In comparison to my realization, my manifestation is absolutely nothing. The Light that I have offered, when compared with the Light that is still unmanifested, is nothing. If, for my realization I get one hundred out of one hundred, for my manifestation I will not get more than one out of one hundred. When I die, I know how much inner wealth will never have a chance to manifest through me." All spiritual Masters have been frustrated this way in their expression, in their revelation, in their manifestation.

Question: *Why is it that realized Gurus sometimes seem to defy the scriptures and accepted rules in what they say and do?*

Sri Chinmoy: It is true that realized Gurus, great Gurus, have their own truth. But they do not defy anything. What they do is give a new orientation. Suppose a great spiritual figure has said something. At the time that he lived, that particular truth was needed. But the world is progressing, and now some higher truth must be manifested. So if we say something different, we are not defying the great Masters of the past. What we are doing is bringing a higher truth and a higher knowledge into the earth-consciousness, which is now ready to receive it. We are enlarging and illumining the Truth.

Only by entering into the truth and transforming it will we achieve a larger and wider truth. If we think that everything to be said with regard to spirituality has already been spoken by our forefathers, we are mistaken. Truth is never complete because we are living in an ever-transcending universe. What the teachers of the past have said is eternally true; what we are saying is also eternally true. But each truth has its own grade, and all the time we are evolving and progressing.

Your father might have imagined or thought of something on the physical plane which was at the time quite striking. Now you have grown up, and you are thinking of something higher and deeper because science has evolved to a new plane. That does not mean that you are defying the achievements of your father. No, you are going beyond him, beyond his capacity, beyond his understanding.

In the spiritual life we do not negate; we just go higher and higher to reach the topmost height. Still the highest Truth, the topmost realization, or what we call the absolute manifestation, has not taken place. Spiritual manifestation has not been completed, and perhaps it will never be completed.

Question: *There were a number of spiritual Masters who used to smoke and drink. How did they realize God?*

Sri Chinmoy: It was because of their aspiration. Spiritual Masters used to drink, dance, eat meat and do all kinds of things without losing their height. For them the world was like a garden, and they were divine children playing there unaffected by anything they said or did.

But you have to know that there is a little difference between their aspiration and yours. It is like the difference between you and a tree. A tree does no harm to anyone; it is pure and innocent. But you will realize God long before the tree does. When it is a matter of inner cry, of aspiration, an ordinary person cannot compare himself with the great spiritual Masters. Once they started meditating, they could go on for hours and become lost in their meditation.

Many Indian spiritual Masters take arsenic, and sometimes when they take large quantities people think they are going to commit suicide. But it does not harm them. Similarly, some occultists meditate for nine or ten hours daily, and the rest of the time they lead a very bad life. But the intensity of their aspiration brings them realization anyway.

Question: Why does a Master give one bit of advice to a devotee today and give another bit of advice tomorrow?

Sri Chinmoy: Sometimes a spiritual Master changes his advice. Then the disciple gets the chance to doubt the Master. He says, "How is it that yesterday he told me to do one thing and today he is telling me to do something else? That means he is not sure of what he said." Unfortunately, here the aspirant is making a mistake. The Master is dealing with the aspirant and the Supreme. The Supreme is omniscient; He knows everything. He is omnipotent; He can do everything. He is the Eternal Player playing the Cosmic Game and has every right to change the course of His Game. The Master is in tune with this Cosmic Play of the Supreme.

Yesterday the Supreme said to the Master, "Tell this disciple to do this." Today the Supreme says, "No, I want to change the course of the Game. Tell him to do that." So what will the Master do? Will he remain faithful to his previous views just because the disciple will say, "How is it that you are constantly changing your opinion?" Or will he be loyal and faithful to his Inner Pilot, the Supreme? If the Master is sincere, immediately he will tell the disciple, "The Supreme has changed His mind. Now please do not do this; do something else."

The spiritual Master will always remain faithful and totally devoted to the Supreme, no matter what the disciple thinks of him. The disciple may think that the spiritual Master is making a mistake, but the Master knows that he is doing the right thing.

HEAVEN & HELL

Question: *Master, speak to us about Heaven and hell.*

Sri Chinmoy: On the highest spiritual level, we have to know that hell, as well as Heaven, is a plane of consciousness. Both Heaven and hell begin in the mind. The moment we think something good, the moment we pray and meditate and try to offer the inner Light that we have gained from our meditation and prayers, we begin to live in Heaven. The moment we think evil of someone, then we enter into hell. Heaven we create; hell we create. With our divine thoughts we create Heaven. With our wrong, silly, undivine thoughts, we create hell within us. Heaven and hell are both states of consciousness deep inside us.

Heaven and hell represent two worlds in our consciousness. Heaven surprises hell with its boundless joy. Hell surprises Heaven with its ceaseless cry. Heaven says to hell, "I know how to dance and I can teach you if you want." Hell says to Heaven, "Wonderful! You know how to dance and you are ready to teach me. But I wish to tell you that I know how to break my legs, and I can break your legs, too, if I want to."

Question: *What about the teachings found in some Western religions that one can see God only after death, if one has been good and goes to Heaven?*

Sri Chinmoy: Heaven and God are not high above us, somewhere far away; they are deep within us, inside our hearts. Heaven is not a distant country where there are trees and houses and other objects; it is a plane of consciousness within us. Seekers of the eternal Truth will realize their eternal Heaven within their aspiring hearts. At every moment we are creating Heaven or hell within us. When we cherish a divine thought, an expanding thought, a fulfilling thought, we create

Heaven in us. When we cherish undivine, ugly, obscure, impure thoughts, we are just entering into our own inner hell.

Question: *Would you care to elaborate on the statement, "The Kingdom of Heaven is within you"?*

Sri Chinmoy: First let me say that it is science that has contributed much to the feeling that Heaven is a place outside of oneself. Science has exercised its power on the conscious and subconscious planes of human thinking.

The Kingdom of Heaven is something that we can feel and not something that we can demonstrate. Science can demonstrate many things. But the Kingdom of Heaven is a matter of one's own inner achievement. If you have realized the Kingdom of Heaven within you, others will look at you and feel that you have something quite unusual, unearthly and supernal. And simply because you have seen, you have felt and you have possessed the Kingdom of Heaven within you, they will see and feel you as a totally transformed divine being.

Needless to say, it is your aspiration, your mounting inner cry that leads you to this Kingdom of Heaven. The Kingdom of Heaven is a plane full of peace and delight. We feel it when we reside deep within ourselves and when we transcend our egocentric individual consciousness. The higher we go beyond our limited consciousness, the quicker we enter into our deepest, infinite consciousness, the more intimately we see, feel and possess the Kingdom of Heaven within us.

To be sure, the Kingdom of Heaven is more than a mere plane. It is a plane of divine consciousness. It is a state of realization. It embodies *Sat-Chit-Ananda*. *Sat* is divine Existence, *Chit* is divine Consciousness, *Ananda* is divine Bliss. When we go deep within, we feel these three together, and when we acquire the inner vision to perceive them all at once, we live verily in the Kingdom of Heaven. Otherwise Existence is at one place, Consciousness is somewhere else and Bliss is nowhere near the other two. When we see and feel Existence-Consciousness-Bliss on the selfsame plane, each complementing and fulfilling the others, we can say that we live in the

Kingdom of Heaven. Yes, the Kingdom of Heaven is within us. Not only can we feel it, but without the least possible doubt, we can become it.

Question: When you say that earth can easily be transformed into heaven, do you mean physically as well?

Sri Chinmoy: What does each human being have? Consciousness. It is through consciousness that we see reality. When we aspire, our finite consciousness becomes infinite; our so-called unaspiring consciousness becomes aspiring. This is Heaven. If we say that we all will become divine, this is certainly true. We will have a divine life, but that does not necessarily mean a physically immortal life. When we think of Heaven, we feel that it is immortal. The consciousness of Heaven is immortal. But very often we feel that the physical will remain immortal as Heaven is something immortal. But this physical body will live for sixty, eighty, one hundred, perhaps even two hundred years and then go.

The very conception of Heaven is of something bright, luminous, delightful and, at the same time, immortal. But we have to know what is immortal in us. It is consciousness, the aspiring consciousness in us. When we say that earth will be transformed into Heaven, that means that anything that is within us or in the world which is now imperfect, obscure or unaspiring will eventually be transformed into perfection.

ILLUMINATION

Question: *Can you speak to us about illumination?*

Sri Chinmoy: In this world there is only one thing worth having, and that is illumination. In order to have illumination, we must have sincerity and humility. Unfortunately, in this world sincerity is long dead and humility is yet to be born. Let us try to revive our sincerity and let us try, on the strength of our aspiration, to expedite the birth of our humility. Then only will we be able to realize God.

Illumination is not something very far away. It is very close; it is just inside us. At every moment we can consciously grow into illumination through our inner progress. Inner progress is made through constant sacrifice. Sacrifice of what? Sacrifice of wrong, evil thoughts and a wrong understanding of Truth. Sacrifice and renunciation go together. What are we going to renounce? The physical body, family, friends, relatives, our country, the world? No! We have to renounce our own ignorance, our own false ideas of God and Truth. Also, we have to sacrifice to God the result of each action. The divine vision no longer remains a far cry when we offer the result of our actions to the Inner Pilot.

In our day-to-day life, we very often speak of bondage and freedom. But realization says that there is no such thing as bondage and freedom. What actually exists is consciousness—consciousness on various levels, consciousness enjoying itself in its various manifestations. In the field of manifestation, consciousness has different grades. Why do we pray? We pray because our prayer leads us from a lower degree of illumination to a higher degree. We pray because our prayer brings us closer to something pure, beautiful, inspiring and fulfilling. The highest illumination is God-realization. This illumination must take place not only in the soul, but also in the heart, mind, vital and body. God-realization is a conscious, complete and perfect union with God.

We want to love the world; the world wants to love us. We want to fulfill the world; the world wants to fulfill us. But there is no connecting link between us and the world. We feel that our existence and the world's existence are two totally different things. We think that the world is something separate from us. But in this we are making a deplorable mistake. What is the proper connecting link between us and the world? God. If we approach God first and see God in the world, then no matter how many millions of mistakes we make, the world will not only indulge our mistakes; it will soulfully love us as well. Similarly, when we see the defects, weaknesses and imperfections of the world, we will be able to forgive the world and then inspire, energize and illumine the world just because we feel God's existence there.

If we do not see God in all our activities, frustration will loom large in our day-to-day life. No matter how sincerely we try to please the world, no matter how sincerely the world tries to please us, frustration will be found between our understanding and the world's understanding. The source of frustration is ignorance. Ignorance is the mother of devastating frustration, damaging frustration and strangling frustration. If we go deeper into ignorance, we see it is all a play of inconscience. Frustration can be removed totally from our lives only when we enter into the Source of all existence. When we enter into the Source of our own existence and the world's existence, we are approaching the reality. This reality is our constant Delight, and Delight is the Breath of God.

This world is neither mine nor yours nor anyone's. Never. It belongs to God, and God alone. So we have to be really wise. We have to go to the Possessor first, and not to the possession. The possession is helpless; it can do nothing on its own. It is the Possessor that can do what He wants to do with His possession. So first we have to become one with God, and then we shall automatically become one with God's possessions. When we become one with God and with His possessions, we can certainly and unmistakably feel that the world is ours and we are the world's.

Ignorance and illumination are like night and day. We have to enter into illumination first, and then bring illumination into ignorance-night. If we try to illumine ignorance the other way around, then the transformation of ignorance will be difficult, slow and uncertain. To enter into the field of ignorance is to take a negative path. If we pursue the path of darkness and try to find Light in darkness, we are taking the negative path. The best way, the positive way to find Light, is to follow the path of Light, more Light, abundant Light, infinite Light. If we follow the path of Light, then illumination will assuredly dawn in us.

Let us look up and bring down the Light from above. The moment we look up, God's grace descends. The very nature of God's grace is to descend upon each individual on earth. When we want to go up to God with ignorance, it is like climbing up a mountain with a heavy bundle on our shoulders. Naturally it is a difficult task. Instead of doing that, we can remain at the foot of the mountain and cry for God's grace, which is ready and eager to come down to us from the Highest. Needless to say, for God to come down into our ignorance is infinitely easier than for us to carry our ignorance up to God.

Illumination is the conscious awareness of the soul. Illumination is the conscious vision of the reality that is going to be manifested. Illumination is possibility transformed into practicality. Illumination is like God's divine magic wand. An ordinary magician in this world uses his wand to make one thing turn into another. When God uses illumination in the world, immediately the finite consciousness of earth enters into the infinite and becomes the infinite.

Illumination is humanity's first realization of God's omnipotent power, boundless compassion, infinite Light and perfect Perfection. It is our illumination that makes us feel what God really is. Before illumination, God is theoretical; after illumination, God becomes practical. So illumination is the divine magic power that makes us see the reality which was once upon a time imagination. When illumination dawns in a human being, God is no longer just a promise, but an actual achievement.

Illumination is in the mind and in the heart. When the mind is illumined, we become God's choice. When the heart is illumined, we become God's voice. Here in the physical world the mind has evolved considerably. Because man has developed his intellectual mind, he has become superior to the animals, for the standard of the mind is higher than the standard of the physical or the vital. Man has cultivated the capacity of the mind, but he has not cultivated the capacity of the heart. When we cultivate the capacity of the heart, we will see that its capacity is far greater than we had imagined. When we cultivate the unique sense in our heart that we are of God's highest vision and we are for God's perfect manifestation, then illumination will take place.

Question: *When I think of all the failings and undivine qualities in myself and my fellow disciples, illumination seems a million miles away.*

Sri Chinmoy: When one is really illumined, one will not see others as imperfect or hopeless human beings. The moment one is illumined, he will feel his real oneness with others and he will see the so-called imperfections of others as an experience God is having in and through them.

Since you are my disciple, I wish to tell you that you see more imperfection, more limitation, more teeming night inside yourself than I can even imagine. To me you are absolutely natural and normal; you are God's child, and you have every opportunity and capacity to realize, manifest and fulfill the Divine here on earth. Illumination is something which you had, but which you now have forgotten; it is not something totally new. One who really cares for illumination has to feel that he is growing from Light to more Light to abundant Light. If a seeker always feels that he is deep in the sea of ignorance, then I wish to say that he will never, never come out of ignorance, for there is no end to the ignorance-sea. But if one feels that he is growing from an iota of Light into the all-pervading, highest Light, then illumination immediately seems easier and more spontaneous.

INDIA

Question: I would frankly like to know what India's spirituality has ever done for her. How is it that in spite of her Yogis and saints, she is still a poor and backward country?

Sri Chinmoy: Firstly, we must understand what has brought this situation about. In ancient India, the material life was not renounced. People in those days aspired for a synthesis of matter and spirit, and to some extent they were successful in achieving it. But there is a great gulf between that hoary past and the present.

In the later periods of India's history, the saints and seers came to feel that the material life and the spiritual life could never go together, that you had to renounce life in order to attain to God. Hence the external life was neglected. This led to foreign conquests and many other troubles. Even today, the attitude of negating material prosperity and beauty is very powerful in India. This accounts for much of her continued poverty.

But at present there are spiritual giants in India who feel that God should be realized in His totality. Creator and creation are one and cannot be separated. So they advocate the acceptance of life, the real need for both progress and perfection in all spheres of human existence. This new approach is widely accepted in India today.

India may be poverty-stricken today, but she will progress quickly by virtue of her new awareness and her new aspiration. She has not only magnanimity of heart, but she has the power to bring her soul's strength to the fore and with this strength to solve all her problems. God is perfect Perfection. This Perfection can be achieved only when there is an inseparable union between matter and spirit, between the outer and the inner life.

196

Question: Could you please tell me why people in India worship so many gods and goddesses and not one?

Sri Chinmoy: Could you please tell me why you worship the Father, the Son, the Holy Ghost and so many angels? Now, to be serious, we in India have millions of gods and goddesses. And we are proud of it. We even feel that each individual must have a god of his own; each man must have his own process of realizing God.

Indeed, these gods and goddesses are simply different manifestations of the sole Absolute. Each deity embodies a particular aspect or quality of the Supreme. Our inability to recognize the all-embracing universal harmony in all these different aspects gives rise to our misunderstandings and disputes. The moment we realize the universal Spirit, the Impersonal One, we can be in perfect harmony with all the different beliefs. Then we can see the truth behind the conception of the gods and goddesses.

Question: Do you not feel that national boundaries, economic disparity and religious dogmas divide human beings into different camps, creating anti-spiritual environments and making peace, for an individual and so for a nation, a distant star?

Sri Chinmoy: I do strongly feel that these national boundaries, etc., are really impairing the growth of our evolving human consciousness. But it is the clarification of the individual's mind and spirit that must precede the awakening of our social institutions such as churches and governments. As we know, the policies of institutions and nations are usually the embodiments of the general consciousness. These policies can be influenced considerably by enlightened individuals. Mother India in particular has not lacked in such enlightened souls, nor does she lack them now.

It is a matter of time, and time itself will create an opening in order for the spiritual consciousness to permeate the individual and his society. On our part, a conscious spiritual effort has to be made so that the higher forces from above can come down and touch the very depths of our seeking hearts. The gap that we see now between our aspiration and its fulfillment in society will then no longer exist.

Question: I understand you to say that some spiritual figures in India claim that today you are here, tomorrow you are not here, that the world is an illusion. But are not those so-called spiritual figures actually corrupting the pure teaching of Shankara on the question of maya [illusion]? Shankara never really disavowed the existence of this phenomenal world. Am I right in saying this?

Sri Chinmoy: Yes, you are right. But the general conception of *maya* has been misinterpreted in the East. Even now ninety-nine percent will say that Shankara advocated the doctrine that the world is an illusion.

What Shankara wanted to say, if I am correct, is: "The world is not an illusion, but we must not give importance to the transitory things. There is something eternal, perpetual, everlasting and we must try to live in the eternal and not in the transitory."

Now at present, or very recently, you can say, about eighty years ago, some of the modern Indian thinkers came to the conclusion, after throwing considerable light on Shankara's philosophy, that he did not actually mean that that the world is a colossal illusion.

"Not this, not this," the Upanishads cried and Shankara echoed. But what is that "this"? It is something that is finite, it is something that is binding us all the time. So people thought that if we leave the world, perhaps there would be a better world somewhere else. It is just like standing on one shore and thinking that the other shore is safe and full of joy and delight. But it is not true.

Each person has his own way of understanding the Truth. You are at perfect liberty to understand it in your own way. How many people can go into the deeper meaning of the Truth? Some people think that the world is an illusion while others feel that it is not an illusion. It is deplorable that we do not or cannot see the world in its totality. We look at the Truth with our finite consciousness, with our limited understanding. When we do that, we see that the world is nothing but an object of ignorance. We feel that we must enter another world, the world of bliss and perfection.

To come back to your question: Shankara's very short earthly existence was surcharged with dynamic energy. He strode the length and breadth of India on foot, preaching his philosophy; he set up temples in key parts of the country. What he offered to the world at large was, in fact, dynamic truth and not the so-called illusion which the world so forcefully associates with his teachings.

Question: *If an Indian living here marries an American girl, will his parents accept them when they go to India?*

Sri Chinmoy: It depends entirely on the parents. If they are orthodox and conservative, they may not accept them. But if the parents are liberal in their ideas and cherish broad ideals, if they value the link between East and West, then they will gladly accept their son and daughter-in-law. From the spiritual point of view, in God's Light, it is not the race, not the nationality, but the true fulfillment of two human souls in union that is of supreme importance.

Question: *In India, the wives surrender to their husbands. Why do they not care for their own individuality?*

Sri Chinmoy: I hope you know the meaning of surrender. In real surrender, we do not lose our individuality. On the contrary, we enlarge it. For example, when we surrender ourselves absolutely to God, we become one with God in our adoration for Him. His power is then added to ours. Surrender is entirely voluntary. Submission, out of fear, to someone more powerful than yourself, is not surrender. True surrender is a great strength which fulfills itself when it becomes one with the object of its adoration.

INDIVIDUALITY

Question: You explained that the soul needs the body. I understand that the soul is the one that is in union with God. Will we retain our individuality or shall we lose our individuality when we realize that union with God?

Sri Chinmoy: God does not want us to discard our individuality, but ordinary individuality and real, divine individuality are two different things. God Himself is, at the same time, One and many. He has produced infinite human beings, human souls. He is One, but in the field of manifestation He has become many. He has selected each person as His chosen instrument, that is to say, each human soul is His chosen instrument. This kind of divine individuality which God has given to us is not the ordinary individuality which is determined by the ego: "I am this, you are that." God's individuality is a unique manifestation of His reality. There is no clash, there is no jealousy, there is no fight, no battle. God Himself is manifesting Himself in a unique manner in you, in me and in others. That kind of individuality, different from the individuality of the ego, God retains for humanity. It is a unique expression of the Divine in His multiplicity. Each one is a chosen instrument of God, but without ego, without pride, without vanity. It is just like the petals of a lotus; each petal has its own beauty and its own uniqueness.

INITIATION

Question: *Master, what exactly is initiation?*

Sri Chinmoy: Real initiation is the total acceptance of the disciple by the Master. The Guru accepts the disciple unreservedly and unconditionally. At the time of initiation, the Guru makes a solemn promise to the individual seeker or aspirant that he will do his best to help the seeker in his or her spiritual life. The Guru will offer his heart and soul to take the disciple into the highest region of the Beyond.

Question: *What are the ways in which a Guru initiates a disciple?*

Sri Chinmoy: The Guru can initiate the disciple in various ways. He can perform the initiation in India's traditional way while the disciple is meditating. He can also initiate the disciple while he is sleeping or even when the disciple is in his normal consciousness, but calm and quiet. The Guru can initiate the disciple through the eyes alone. He can also do a physical initiation, which is to press the head or the heart or any part of the body. That is the purely physical aspect. But along with the physical action, when he touches the heart, the Guru can initiate the disciple in a psychic way. The Guru can feel the soul within the disciple's heart; he can see the soul and he can act upon the soul.

Question: *By what other means do you initiate your disciples?*

Sri Chinmoy: In my case, very often with the aspirants whom I consider to be my disciples, I have initiated them through the eyes. Many times you have observed my eyes when I am in my highest consciousness. At that time, my ordinary eyes, my human eyes, become totally one with my third eye and then they enter into the aspirant's eyes. This way I initiate them. Many times you have observed my eyes radiating divine Light here at this center.

There are various ways, but I prefer the initiation through the third eye, which I feel to be the most convincing and most effective way. Immediately the Light from my eyes, having come from the third eye, enters into the aspirant's eyes and then into his whole body; it percolates there from head to foot. I see my own Light, glowing in the disciple's body. And when I do initiate, it is my Light, the Light of the Supreme, that enters into the person, the disciple.

Question: Should a disciple specifically ask the Guru for initiation?

Sri Chinmoy: I have initiated quite a few disciples of mine. Those who are not my disciples I have no right to initiate. And whoever is my disciple need not ask me to initiate him because I know what is best for him; that is to say, whether the outer initiation will expedite his inner progress or not.

Question: What happens to the relationship when a disciple has a falling out with the Guru after initiation?

Sri Chinmoy: Even if the disciple goes away after initiation, finding fault with the Guru, the Guru will act in and through the disciple forever. The disciple may even go to some other Guru, but the Guru who has initiated a disciple will always help that particular seeker in the inner world. If the latter Guru is noble enough, then he will allow the former to act in and through the disciple.

Question: What happens when all physical contact between the disciple and the Guru who initiated him is cut off?

Sri Chinmoy: Although the physical relation with the former Guru is cut off, and physically the Guru is not seeing the disciple, spiritually the Master has to help the disciple; he is bound to help him because he has made a promise to the Supreme. Sometimes the disciple, in fact, does not go to any other Guru; he simply falls from the path, he deviates from the path of Truth. But his former Guru has to keep the promise that he made to the disciple at the time of his initiation.

Question: What happens if a person falls from the spiritual path for many lifetimes? What remains of the Guru-disciple relationship?

Sri Chinmoy: After accepting the spiritual life and being initiated by a spiritual Master, the disciple may drop from the spiritual path for one incarnation, two incarnations or even several incarnations. But his Guru, whether he be in the body or in the higher regions, disembodied, will constantly watch over the disciple and wait for an opportunity to help him actively when the disciple again turns to the spiritual path. But a time comes when the disciple is bound to come again to the Master's spiritual guidance. The Guru is truly detached, but just because he made a promise to the disciple and to the Supreme in the disciple, the Guru waits indefinitely for an opportunity to fulfill his own promise.

Some of the disciples who came to me to follow the path most sincerely, have also left me most sincerely. But, if in the inner world, they are my disciples, if I had already accepted them and they were my real disciples, if they claim even once to be my disciple, I wish to tell them I have not forgotten them. Neither shall I ever forget my soulful promise to them. They may take one, two, five or six incarnations to come back to the aspiring life; but no matter how long they take, I shall have to help them and I must, in their march towards God-realization.

Question: What does the devotee feel at initiation?

Sri Chinmoy: Those who have been close to their Master must feel the actual flowering of their initiation the moment they have wholeheartedly dedicated to him their entire life—body, mind, heart and soul. This is the flowering of the initiation. It is really more than initiation; it is their revelation of their own divinity. At this moment they feel that they and their Guru have become totally one. They feel that their Guru has no existence without them. Similarly, they have no existence without their Guru. Mutually the Guru and the disciple fulfill each other, and they feel that their fulfillment is coming directly from the Supreme.

Question: *Are there any secrets to be transferred at initiation?*

Sri Chinmoy: The greatest secret one learns from one's Guru is this: only by fulfilling the Supreme first can one fulfill the rest of the world.

Question: *How can the disciple fulfill the Supreme? How can the Guru fulfill the Supreme?*

Sri Chinmoy: The Guru plays his part by taking the ignorance, imperfection, obscurity, stubbornness and unwillingness from the disciple and carrying that individual faithfully and devotedly to the Supreme. The disciple fulfills the Supreme by constantly staying in the Guru's boat, in the innermost recesses of the Guru's heart, and feeling that he exists only for the fulfillment of his Master. Him to fulfill, him to manifest is the only meaning, the only purpose, the only significance of the disciple's life. This is the most important thing that is to be understood about initiation.

Question: *Can the Guru help the aspirant even after the Guru has left the body?*

Sri Chinmoy: If the Master is a realized person, then he can and he has to. Suppose I die today. All the disciples that have accepted me as their Master, genuinely and devotedly—and these do not include my followers, admirers and friends, but only my true disciples— would be served by me and would be taken care of by me. I am bound to them. I am the conscious slave of all my disciples. I shall have to be at their beck and call, no matter where I go. Wherever I go after I leave the earth plane, I shall have to be inside my disciples. If a Master is a realized soul, he can easily maintain an inner contact with his disciples. He can do it because he has made a solemn and soulful promise to them that he will take them to God. The Master has gone back to Heaven and the disciples are still on earth. Yet the Master has to fulfill his promise.

Question: *What happens when the Guru dies and he or she is not God-realized?*

Sri Chinmoy: Gurus are like schoolteachers. If an ordinary guru dies, he will not be able to keep any inner contact with you. In fact, even while he is in the body, the ordinary guru does not have much inner connection with the disciples. If you are on an island and the ordinary guru is on the mainland, he will not be able to have any inner knowledge of you. Even here, if you are in the room and he is in the other room, he will not be able to maintain an inner connection. And when he leaves the body it will be simply impossible for him to have the slightest possible connection with you.

Question: *So what happens to a disciple when a Guru who is not God-realized dies?*

Sri Chinmoy: There are some Gurus who are very sincere and dedicated, but at the same time, they are not fully realized. What they do sometimes is this: when they leave the body, they feel that their disciples who are still on earth need a particular kind of help in their quest for God-realization. If the Guru has no jealousy, he will come to his disciples in a dream and say, "Go to that particular Guru and become his disciple. I have played my part. But you need further help and I know that so-and-so is a sincere person. He will help you in your God-realization." These undoubtedly noble and wise Gurus tell the student to go to another Guru who is still on earth and can teach them how they can realize God.

Question: *Have any followers of deceased Gurus ever been sent to you?*

Sri Chinmoy: In New York, I have six or seven followers who have been asked by their own Guru to come to me. And they came. The first thing that happened was that they saw in me their own Master who had left his body three years earlier. The truly selfless Gurus let others carry on for them.

Question: *And what about the selfish, self-centered, fake Gurus?*

Sri Chinmoy: A mean and possessive Guru would say, "Wait my son, until I come back again to earth. I shall recognize you and you will recognize me. Do not go to any other Guru. You stay alone."

Question: *What do you mean by "the joint initiation of the Earth-reality and the Heaven-reality"?*

Sri Chinmoy: One day a middle-aged man and his wife went to Gambhirananda and asked to be initiated. The Master said, "Not today, but in a few months time I shall initiate you."

It happened that the wife was attacked by a severe illness very shortly afterwards and died. The man was very sad, but he still wanted to become a real disciple of Gambhirananda. So he went to the Master and again asked to be initiated. The Master agreed and set the date. At the time of initiation, the man begged Gambhirananda to initiate his deceased wife as well.

The Master said, "How can I do that? She is dead; she is no longer with you."

The man said, "No, her soul is not dead. You promised you would initiate both of us. While initiating me, you can initiate her too. Please do me this favor." He began crying, and finally the Master agreed.

Gambhirananda placed two small cushions side by side. The man sat on one, and the other remained unoccupied. While the Master was initiating the seeker, he placed one of his hands on the seeker and the other in the space above the empty cushion. In a few minutes' time people saw that the cushion was moving, and they felt certain that it was the wife's presence. In this way, Gambhirananda initiated both of them together.

The true operation of initiation takes place mostly in the soul and not in the body-consciousness. When the Master initiates a seeker, he immediately helps the seeker remember his soul's promise to the Absolute Supreme before the soul entered into the world-arena. When the Master initiates the physical in a seeker, he purifies the seeker's outer existence by touching the seeker's physical-reality. When he initiates the spiritual in the seeker, he pours a stream of illumining Light into the seeker's system. Physical initiation reminds us of our spiritual duty. Spiritual initiation reminds us of the immortality of our consciousness-Light.

Question: How important is initiation?

Sri Chinmoy: Initiation is of paramount importance. The Master can initiate the seeker either outwardly or inwardly. But the traditional outer way, as part of a religious rite, is far less effective than the silence-initiation. In the silence-initiation, the Master offers a portion of his life-breath to the seeker for his ignorance-illumination and his delight-realization. Initiation is purification. No purification, no perfection. No perfection, no satisfaction either on earth or in Heaven.

INNER PEACE

Question: Speak to us about inner peace.

Sri Chinmoy: No price is too great to pay for inner peace. Peace is the harmonious control of life. It is vibrant with life-energy. It is a power that easily transcends all our worldly knowledge. Yet it is not separate from our earthly existence. If we open the right avenues within, this peace can be felt here and now.

Peace is eternal. It is never too late to have peace. Time is always ripe for that. We can make our life truly fruitful if we are not cut off from our Source, which is the peace of eternity. The greatest misfortune that can come to a human being is to lose his inner peace. No outer force can rob him of it. It is his own thoughts, his own actions, that rob him of it.

Our greatest protection lies not in our material achievements and resources. All the treasure of the world is emptiness to our divine soul. Our greatest protection lies in our soul's communion with the all-nourishing and all-fulfilling peace. Our soul lives in peace and lives for peace. If we live a life of peace, we are ever enriched and never impoverished. Unhorizoned is our inner peace; like the boundless sky, it encompasses all.

Long have we struggled, much have we suffered, far have we traveled. But the face of peace is still hidden from us. We can discover it if ever the train of our desires loses itself in the will of the Lord Supreme.

Peace is life. Peace is bliss eternal. Worries mental, vital and physical do exist. But it is up to us whether to accept them or reject them. To be sure, they are not inevitable facts of life. Since our Almighty Father is All-Peace, our common heritage is peace. It is a Himalayan blunder to widen the broad way of future repentance by misusing and neglecting the golden opportunities that are presented to us. We must resolve here and now, amidst all our daily activities, to throw ourselves, heart and soul, into the sea of peace. He is mistaken who thinks that peace will, on its own, enter into him near the end of his life's journey. To hope to achieve peace without spirituality or meditation is to expect water in the desert.

For peace of mind, prayer is essential. To pray to God for peace with full concentration and singleness of devotion even for five minutes is more important than to spend long hours in carefree and easy-going meditation.

We will own peace only after we have totally stopped finding fault with others. We have to feel the whole world as our very own. When we observe others' mistakes, we enter into their imperfections. This does not help us in the least. Strangely enough, the deeper we plunge, the clearer it becomes to us that the imperfections of others are our own imperfections, but in different bodies and minds. Whereas if we think of God, His compassion and His Divinity enlarge our inner vision of Truth. We must come in the fullness of our spiritual realization to accept humanity as one family.

We must not allow our past to torment and destroy the peace of our heart. Our present good and divine actions can easily counteract our bad and undivine actions of the past. If sin has the power to make us weep, meditation has undoubtedly the power to give us joy, to endow us with the divine wisdom.

Our peace is within, and this peace is the basis of our life. So from today let us resolve to fill our minds and hearts with the tears of devotion, the foundation of peace. If our foundation is solid, then no matter how high we raise the superstructure, danger can never threaten us. For peace is below, peace is above, peace is within, peace is without.

Question: *How can we attain lasting inner peace?*

Sri Chinmoy: We can attain lasting inner peace only when we feel that our Supreme Pilot is in the many as one and in the One as many. When we consciously feel this truth in our life, we get lasting peace in whatever we say, whatever we do, whatever we offer and whatever we receive.

The day I feel my existence and my illumining heart in everyone is the day I immediately become one in many. When I receive or bring down peace from Above, immediately I feel that I am many, not one. Then when I assimilate the peace in myself, I see the peace has been assimilated in all of us. Then I have a conscious feeling of oneness, of the oneness in the many and the many as one.

Peace comes in and we lose it because we feel that we are not responsible for humanity, or that we are not part and parcel of humanity. We have to feel that God and humanity are like a great tree. God is the tree, and the branches are His manifestation. We are branches, and there are many other branches. All these branches are part of the tree and are one with each other and with the tree. If we can feel that we have the same relationship with God and with humanity as the branch has with its fellow branches and with the tree as a whole, we are bound to get everlasting peace.

Question: What steps can a person take to find inner peace?

Sri Chinmoy: On a practical level, do not expect anything from others on the physical plane. Just give and give and give, like a mother who gives everything to her child thinking that the child is not in a position to give her anything in return. Do not expect anything from the world; only love the world and offer your capacity, your inner wealth, your joy. Everything that you have, give to the world unconditionally. If you expect anything from the world, then you will feel miserable because the world does not understand you, the world does not care for you. If you can do anything unconditionally, then you will have peace of mind. This is one way.

The other way is to meditate on the heart, where there is constant joy, constant love. At that time you will not cry for appreciation from others. You will all the time depend on your inner Source, where there is infinite joy, infinite love, infinite peace. The best thing is to meditate on the heart. This second way is most effective.

JAPA

Question: *What is* japa?

Sri Chinmoy: *Japa* is the repetition of a mantra. If you want purity, then today repeat the name of God five hundred times. Then every day increase the number by one hundred. That is to say, tomorrow you will repeat the name of God six hundred times, and the day after, seven hundred. After one week you will repeat the name of God twelve hundred times. From that day, start decreasing the number daily by one hundred until you again reach five hundred. Continue this exercise, week by week, just for a month. Whether you want to change your name or not, the world will give you a new name. It will call you by the name Purity. Your inner ear will make you hear it. It will surpass your fondest imagination.

Let nothing perturb us. Let our body's impurity remind us of our heart's spontaneous purity. Let our outer finite thoughts remind us of our inner infinite will. Let our mind's teeming imperfections remind us of our soul's limitless perfection.

The present-day world is full of impurity. It seems that purity is a currency from another world. It is hard to obtain this purity, but once we get it, peace is ours, success is ours.

Let us face the world. Let us take life as it comes. Our Inner Pilot is constantly vigilant. The undercurrents of our inner and spiritual life will always flow on unnoticed, unobstructed, unafraid.

God may be unknown, but He is not unknowable. Our prayers and meditation lead us to that unknown. Freedom we cry for. But strangely enough, we are not aware of the fact that we already have within us immense freedom. Look! Without any difficulty, we can forget God. We can ignore Him and we can even deny Him. But God's compassion says, "My children, no matter what you do or say, My Heart shall never abandon you. I want you. I need you."

The mother holds the hand of the child. But it is the child who has to walk, and he does so. Neither the one who is dragged nor the one who drags can be happy. Likewise, God says, "My divine children, in your inner life, I give you inspiration. It is you who have to aspire with the purest heart to reach the golden beyond."

Joy/Ananda

Question: *Once you said that transcendental delight is one of the divine qualities not manifested on earth. Why is that?*

Sri Chinmoy: On the highest plane there is Existence-Consciousness-Bliss; we call it *Sat-Chit-Ananda*. *Sat* is Existence; *Chit* is Consciousness; *Ananda* is Delight. Consciousness is the source of everything, but Consciousness cannot stay without Delight and Existence. If there is no Existence, there can be no Consciousness. If there is Existence and Consciousness, Bliss is required for self-fulfillment.

Great spiritual Masters from time immemorial have brought down the *Sat* and *Chit* aspects. But *Ananda* is difficult to bring down. Some could not bring it at all. Some brought it, but it lasted for only a few seconds or a few minutes and then went back up again. Peace is accessible; we can bring down peace. Light and power can easily be brought down. But the delight which immortalizes our inner and outer consciousness has not yet been established on earth. It comes and then goes away because it sees so much imperfection in the earth-atmosphere that it cannot remain.

Even spiritually advanced people are often confused. They feel an inner ecstasy which comes from the vital world, and they think this is the real delight. But it is not so. real delight comes from the highest world to the soul, and from the soul it saturates the whole being.

This *Ananda* is absorbed differently from physical delight, or what we call pleasure or enjoyment. The supramental delight is totally different from the world of pleasure and enjoyment. Once you get even an iota of it, you feel your entire inner being dancing for joy like a child with utmost purity, and your outer being feels true immortality in its outer existence. If you get this delight even for a second, you will remember it all your life. All around us is the Cosmic Game, the

214 • *The Wisdom of Sri Chinmoy*

Cosmic Play. The universe is full of joy, inner joy and outer joy. When realization takes place, we have to feel the necessity of manifesting this constant delight in our heart. This delight glows, but does not actually burn. It has tremendous intensity, but it is all softness and absolutely sweet-flowing Nectar.

Question: *Do children sometimes experience this kind of delight?*

Sri Chinmoy: No. Children do not have the highest delight. They get psychic delight. They get some delight from the psychic being, from the inner being, or from the soul, which they express spontaneously. And very often children express their joy through their pure, uncorrupted vital. But the highest delight, which comes from the plane of *Sat-Chit-Ananda*, children do not get. One can feel it only in one's deepest, highest meditation. Children also have to go through meditation, concentration and contemplation in order to experience this quality.

KARMA

Question: What is the relationship between realization and the law of karma?

Sri Chinmoy: When one realizes God, one has the capacity to stand above one's own fate or karma. But if God wants him to accept his own karma and go through the pain and suffering, he will do so and offer it as an experience to God. At that time, he feels that God is having these experiences in and through him. After realization one can nullify the law of karma. Again, if one wants to accept the punishment or retribution of others' karma, one can do it. If it is God's Will, a realized person can nullify his own and others' karma, or he can consciously, deliberately and smilingly accept both his own karma and the karma of others.

Question: Does the law of karma apply to everybody?

Sri Chinmoy: The law of karma applies to everyone and at the same time one can transcend it by one's meditation. The law of karma exists and at the same time it can be transcended by realization, oneness with God and by the power of spirituality.

Question: What is the best way to get rid of bad karma?

Sri Chinmoy: The best way to get rid of bad karma is to enter into the field of aspiration, concentration and meditation. If you want to get rid of your bad karma, the first thing you have to do is to forget about it. If you think of it, unconsciously you are cherishing it, but if you think of good karma, that is to say, aspiration, concentration and meditation, then you are walking along the right path. What you did yesterday, what you ate yesterday or ten years ago is now not at all impor-

215

tant. What you want to do now and be now is of paramount importance. We have to know that we are not the children of the past, but of the golden future. Yesterday did not give you realization. Yesterday did not give you fulfillment. You are going to get it either today or in the distant future or in the near future. You have to know that if you look forward, one day you will reach your goal, but if you look backward, you will remain where you were and where you are. So in order to get rid of bad karma, the only medicine is meditation in the form of aspiration, or concentration in the form of aspiration.

Question: Is all suffering the result of bad karma, either from this life or from a past life?

Sri Chinmoy: Not necessarily. Sometimes what happens is that even though we have not done anything wrong, our soul wants to have an experience of suffering. Our soul wants to enter into the depth of pain just to know what pain is.

Many times we do wrong things and we get the results sooner or later. But again, there are times when we suffer because of the cosmic forces. Sometimes sincere, very devoted parents have children who are absolutely unspiritual, undivine and worthless. Now you will say that perhaps in their past incarnation the parents were also unspiritual and did many wrong things. In some cases, the parents were bad in their previous lives, but in other cases, this may not be true. Sometimes sincere seekers are affected by hostile, animal-like forces that are operating in the world. When these undivine, hostile forces that are hovering around behave like mad elephants or enter into a person, then the person suffers. It is like this: around us are animals fighting, quarreling and destroying each other. A mad elephant, no matter how nice and sincere you are, will simply destroy you. You never know when these animals are moving around. So when a sincere seeker suffers, we cannot immediately come to the conclusion that in his past incarnation he did something wrong.

If we follow the spiritual life all the time, then we stay in the field of divine power, which is like a fort. We are inside the fort being protected by God. When wrong forces, undivine forces, try to attack us, the divine grace stands in their way. Spiritual people try always to be conscious of God's compassion, God's blessing and God's Light because they know that even if they do not do wrong things, they may be attacked by undivine forces. And when they do wrong things, immediately they know that there is someone who can forgive them, who can protect them, who can elevate their consciousness, and this someone is their Inner Pilot, or God.

Question: *Could you please explain how the law of karma affects us in this life and our next life?*

Sri Chinmoy: We are carrying the past inside us. It is a continuous flow. "As you sow, so you reap." If we do something wrong, we have to know that either today or tomorrow, either in the physical world or in the inner world, we will get the result. If I constantly steal, one day I will be caught and put into jail. I may not get caught today, but one day I will be caught. And if I do something good, if I pray, if I meditate and do divine things, I will get the result of this also. Sometimes we see someone who has done something wrong enjoying the world. But perhaps he did something extraordinary, something wonderful in his immediate past incarnation, and now he is having the result of his good action, while the results of his bad deeds have not yet started to bear fruit. In the evening of his life, or in a future life, he will definitely be punished.

In the case of an ordinary, unaspiring person, karmic dispensation is unavoidable, inevitable. The law of karma is always binding; like a snake it will coil around him. He has to pay the toll, the tax; the law of karma is merciless. But again, there is something called divine grace. Suppose I was ignorant and I did a few things wrong. If I shed bitter tears and cry for forgiveness, then naturally God's compassion will dawn on me. When a person enters into the spiritual life, his karma can easily be nullified if it is the Will of God operating through a spiritual Master. Slowly God's infinite grace can nullify the results of his bad karma and expedite the results of his good karma. If a seeker not only wants the spiritual life but also sincerely practices the spiritual life every day, then he can stand above the law of karma, for God is bound to shower His boundless grace on the devoted head and heart of the aspirant. Of course, I cannot go on doing some undivine thing and feel that God will always forgive me. No. But if God sees a soulful cry looming large from within, if He sees that I am sincere and aspiring and want to be free from the meshes of ignorance, He will not only forgive me but He will also give me the necessary strength not to make the same mistake again.

When we come back in our next incarnation, naturally we have to start our journey according to the result of our past karma. If we have done many things wrong, we cannot expect to realize the highest Truth in our next incarnation. But if God's grace is there, we can easily nullify the wrong things we have already done during this life. In this incarnation you feel that you have done a few things wrong and now you are suffering. If you have done something wrong, then you know about it and God knows about it.

Others also know that you have done something wrong, but they cannot rectify your mistake. Only God can help. If you go deep within, God will tell you that your wrong karma is just an experience and that now that experience is over. You have done something wrong and have suffered. That experience was written in God's Heart, and now it is deleted. The moment you suffered, your bad karma entered into God's cosmic flow.

The voice of silence within you tells you to feel that you did something wrong and that you have offered the experience to God. So now you are in no way responsible. Whenever you do something wrong, act like a child. Whenever a child does something wrong, he runs to his mother. He knows that his mother will protect him. The soul is like a mother. The soul will protect you and give you wisdom. If you know you have done something wrong, immediately run to your eternal Mother, the soul inside you. Then the law of karma will not affect you, because the soul has more power than the mistakes that you have committed. The soul gets that power from the Supreme. Even if you have suffered and are afraid that your suffering will come back, you will not suffer if you run towards the soul. In this way the law of karma can be nullified.

LIGHT

Question: Master, quite often you speak of "light." What is it exactly?

Sri Chinmoy: In a very broad sense you can call Light a divine gift. Everything good, in fact, is a divine gift. From the spiritual point of view, everything that a seeker has and is, is a divine gift—an unconditional gift from the transcendental Supreme.

When I say Light, I am speaking about illumination. This illumination will first take place in the realm of the God-manifesting soul. Next it will take place in the aspiring heart, then in the searching mind, then in the dynamic vital and, finally, in the wakeful body. When you can open your third eye—the eye of inner vision—at your sweet will, you can not only see Light but also grow into the Light and spread it around the globe.

Although Light is the most needed spiritual quality of all, unfortunately it is the least wanted. Very often seekers invoke joy, peace or power, but very rarely do they aspire for Light. Instead of feeling that the divine Light will illumine them, they mistakenly identify with their own limitations and imperfections and feel that they are going to be exposed. But the divine Light is not going to expose them. On the contrary, Light embraces humanity with all its imperfections and tries to illumine human ignorance so the human life can be elevated into the divine life.

LONELINESS

Question: *Sometimes in my meditations I come to think about the feeling of eternity. I come to feel that human beings have lived forever and will live forever. This feeling, instead of causing me pleasure and a good sensation, on the contrary causes me great anguish and pain. I feel then that I am all alone, that I am living a life of my own, different from everything. I feel that I have no world left, that by the power of my mind, I have destroyed the world and am alone by myself. This thought causes me a great deal of pain and I have wanted to mention this state of mind. I want to know if I am taking a wrong path.*

Sri Chinmoy: When, in your meditation, you feel that you are lonely, alone, it is not actually the loneliness of the human being. At that time you get a glimpse of the Sole One. This One pervades all. We call it *Brahman*, the One without a second. When you feel that you are lonely, it is really the feeling of your unconscious oneness with that Absolute Oneness. But when the physical, the vital and the mental beings are not transformed to a considerable degree, they are afraid of this super-loneliness. It is not actually loneliness, as I have said, it is the sense of the Oneness. You see the reality; you feel the One pervading everything.

Now, what is actually happening in your meditation is that at times your aspiration, before it reaches its goal or before it finds its abode in the goal, ceases. Your heart's mounting flame rises upward, but there are a few stops and breaks. If there were a gradual and continuous flight and if it were uninterrupted, then you would not feel the loneliness at the lower levels of your consciousness. Please try to keep your aspiration uninterrupted at all times. The inner runner must complete his race divine.

The infinite eternity and the eternity that you are speaking of is in the motto of our Centers: "Man is Infinity's Heart, Man is

Eternity's Breath, Man is Immortality's Life." The breath which eternity possesses is man. Most of us have had countless lives and some of us will have countless more. In your case, it is the divine realization or the spiritual realization that you need. One can attain the achievements of twenty incarnations in one lifetime provided one takes to spirituality in all sincerity and dedication and listens to one's spiritual guide most devotedly. Since you have the intense aspiration, you are accomplishing it successfully. That is why the spiritual Masters say, "Take to the spiritual life and enter into the divine. This divine is your own infinite Self. The sooner you start your journey, the better for you."

When you live the spiritual life, you live in eternity. This eternity does not present itself as a problem, but as an inspiration, encouragement, aspiration and illumination. It is eternity that is constantly carrying us into the immortal Self and that immortal Self is our real Self.

LOVE

Question: *I believe that love is always the same, whether human or divine. Is this true?*

Sri Chinmoy: No, my young friend, human love and divine love are two completely different things. If I give you fifteen cents and you give me a piece of candy, that is called human love. In divine love, you do not wait for my fifteen cents. You give me the piece of candy cheerfully of your own accord. Divine love is sacrifice, and in this sacrifice, you are fulfilling God's Will, consciously or unconsciously. In human love, we display the buyer's and the seller's love, which is synonymous with self-interest. I am not saying that human beings cannot express divine love. They can and sometimes do. But consistent divine love is, at present, rare in human beings.

Question: *How can we teach ourselves to love humanity, not just as a collective whole, but also specifically, when a person's defects and bad qualities are so obvious?*

Sri Chinmoy: When you see that a person's defects and bad qualities are so obvious, try to feel immediately that his defects and bad qualities do not represent him totally. His real self is infinitely better than what you see now. On the other hand, if you really want to love humanity, then you have to love humanity as it stands now and not expect it to come to a specific standard. If humanity has to become perfect before it can be accepted by you, then it would not need your love, affection and concern. Right now, in its imperfect state of consciousness, humanity needs your help. Give humanity unreservedly even the most insignificant and limited help that you have at your disposal. This is the golden opportunity. Once you miss this opportunity, your future suffering will be beyond your endurance. A day will come

222

when you will realize that humanity's imperfection is your own imperfection. You are God's creation; so is humanity. Humanity is only an expression of your universal heart. You can and must love humanity, not just as a whole, but also individually if you realize the fact that until humanity has realized its supreme goal, your own divine perfection will not be complete.

Question: How can we tell if our love is vital or pure?

Sri Chinmoy: You can easily tell whether your love is vital or pure. When your love is vital, there is a conscious demand, or at least an unconscious expectation from the love you offer to others. When your love is pure or spiritual, there is no demand, no expectation. There is only the sweetest feeling of spontaneous oneness with the human being or beings concerned.

Question: Is it possible to prevent oneself from giving off impure vital love and to substitute the heart's pure love for it? How can we consciously give pure love?

Sri Chinmoy: It is not only possible, but absolutely necessary, to prevent oneself from giving off impure vital love. Otherwise one will have to constantly wrestle with the gigantic forces of ignorance. One has to use love, not to bind or possess the world, but to free and widen one's own consciousness and the consciousness of the world. One must not try to substitute the heart's pure love for the impure vital love. What one must do is to bring the heart's purifying and transforming love into the impure vital. The vital as such is not bad at all. When the vital is controlled, purified and transformed, it becomes a most significant instrument of God.

Now you want to know how you can consciously give pure love to others. You can consciously give pure love to others if you feel that you are giving a portion of your life-breath when you talk to others or think of others. And this life-breath you are offering just because you feel that you and the rest of the world are totally and inseparably one. Where there is oneness, it is all pure love.

Question: *In what way does love for one's Guru differ from devotion to him? Is it possible to have one without the other?*

Sri Chinmoy: To have love for one's Guru is to take the first step into the spiritual domain. The second step is devotion. One cannot take the second step unless one has taken the first step. Moreover, true love and pure devotion cannot be separated. They breathe together. Love sees the Truth. Devotion feels the Truth. Surrender becomes the Truth.

Question: *When we concentrate on love and devotion, should we direct it mainly to the Supreme or to our Guru?*

Sri Chinmoy: It entirely depends on the disciple's conscious awareness of the Guru's spiritual status. If the disciple's ignorance compels him to feel that the Guru stands only ten inches higher than he himself stands in the spiritual domain, then naturally he will direct his love and devotion to the Supreme. But if he sincerely, consciously and spontaneously feels that the Guru is a God-realized soul and that there is a yawning gap between him and his Guru in their inner achievements, if he feels that the Guru has established his conscious and constant oneness with the Supreme, that the Guru is the representative of the Supreme for the disciples, that he is the direct channel streaming downward from the Ultimate Source to cultivate the soil of human aspiration, then the disciple, with the least possible hesitation, can direct his love and devotion to the Guru. To be sure, neither the Supreme nor the Guru is hurt when you approach one, leaving aside the other. As a matter of fact, just because they know that they are absolutely one, they are equally and supremely pleased with you when you offer your love and devotion to one of them.

MEDITATION

Question: What is meditation?

Sri Chinmoy: Meditation is man's self-awakening and God's Self-Offering. When man's self-awakening and God's Self-Offering meet together, man becomes immortal in the inner world and God becomes fulfilled in the outer world.

Meditation is the language of God. If we want to know what God's Will is in our life, if we want God to guide us, mold us and fulfill Himself in and through us, then meditation is the language we must use. Spirituality cannot be achieved by pulling or pushing. We cannot pull down spiritual Light by hook or by crook. When it comes down on its own, only on the strength of our aspiration will we be able to receive it. If we try to pull the Light beyond our capacity of receptivity, our inner vessel will break. How can we receive this Light from above? How do we expand our consciousness so that our receptivity will increase? The answer is meditation.

When we meditate, what we actually do is to enter into a calm or still, silent mind. We have to be fully aware of the arrival and attack of thoughts. That is to say, we shall not allow any thought, divine or undivine, good or bad, to enter into our mind. Our mind should be absolutely silent. Then we have to go deep within; there we have to observe our real existence. When we speak of our outer existence, we see our limbs and our body, the gross body, that is all; but when we go deep within, we approach our true existence and that existence is in the inmost recesses of our soul. When we live in the soul, we feel that we are actually, spontaneously doing meditation.

Meditation is that very state of our consciousness where the inner being, instead of cherishing millions of thoughts, wants only to commune with God. Meditation is God's language as well as

225

man's language. Now I am speaking in English and you are able to understand me because you know English well. Similarly, when one knows how to meditate well, one will be able to commune with God.

Question: *Why do we meditate?*

Sri Chinmoy: We meditate because this world of ours has not been able to fulfill us. The so-called peace that we feel in our day-to-day life is five minutes of peace after ten hours of anxiety, worry and frustration. We are constantly at the mercy of negative forces that are all around us: jealousy, fear, doubt, worry, anxiety and despair. These forces are like monkeys. When they get tired of biting us and take rest for a few minutes, then we say we are enjoying peace. But this is not real peace at all, and the next moment they will attack us again.

It is only through meditation that we can get lasting peace, divine peace. If we mediate soulfully in the morning and receive peace for only one minute, that one minute of peace will permeate our whole day. And when we have a meditation of the highest order, then we really get abiding peace, Light and delight. We need meditation because we want to grow in Light and fulfill ourselves in Light. If this is aspiration, if this is our thirst, then meditation is the only way.

If we feel that we are satisfied with what we have and what we are, there is no need for us to enter into the field of meditation. The reason we enter into meditation is because we have an inner hunger. We feel that within us there is something luminous, something vast, something divine. We feel that we need this very thing badly; only right now we do not have access to it. Our inner hunger comes from our spiritual need.

Question: *Is meditation an escape from the world?*

Sri Chinmoy: Meditation is not an escape. If we enter into the life of meditation in order to escape from the world and forget our sufferings, then we are doing it for the wrong reason. If we enter into the spiritual life because of outer frustration or dissatisfaction, then we may not remain in the spiritual life. Today I have failed to satisfy my desires, so I am dissatisfied with the world. But tomorrow I will say, "Let me try again. Perhaps this time I will get satisfaction." But eventually we will feel that desire-life will never satisfy us; we will feel that we need to enter into the inner life. This is aspiration. In the life of aspiration, we want only God. If we sincerely want God, then naturally He will give Himself to us. But He will do it in His own way and at His own time.

Question: *How does one meditate?*

Sri Chinmoy: There are two ways to meditate. One way is to silence the mind. An ordinary man feels that if he silences the mind, he becomes a fool. He feels that if the mind does not think, the mind has lost everything. But this is not true in the spiritual life. In the spiritual life, when we silence the mind we see that a new creation, a new promise to God, dawns in the mind. Right now we have not fulfilled our promise to God; we have not totally dedicated our existence to God. When we can silence the mind, we are in a position to please and fulfill God.

Another way to meditate is to empty the heart. Right now the heart is full of emotional turmoil and problems created by the impure vital which has enveloped it. The heart is a vessel. Right now this vessel is full of undivine things, things that limit and bind us. If we can empty the heart-vessel, there is someone who will fill it with divine peace, Light and bliss, which will liberate us. When we empty our heart of ignorance, God's wisdom-Light will come and fill it.

Question: *Will you please tell me how a beginner should start meditation?*

Sri Chinmoy: First you have to read a few spiritual books in which they teach the various ways to start meditation. Then you start. Soon you will see that reading books is not enough. You will see that you need a particular teacher. The teacher will know which kind of meditation will most suit your nature and soul. If you do not have a teacher, pray to God to reveal within you the kind of meditation you should adopt. Then, during a dream or in your silent mood, God will make you feel what you should do. Now you can begin your journey.

When your meditation is correct, you will feel a kind of joy all over your body. But if you do not feel that joy, if, on the contrary, you feel a mental tension or disturbance, then you will know that that particular kind of meditation is not meant for you and is not advisable. When you get a kind of spontaneous inner joy, then the meditation you have adopted is correct.

Question: *As you evolve spiritually, does your meditation become longer, and does it change its focus or orientation?*

Sri Chinmoy: A person who is highly developed spiritually will naturally be able to meditate for a longer time than a relative beginner. But meditation is not a matter of time; but it is a matter of aspiration. If one has true aspiration, deep aspiration, one will be able to meditate for a longer time, because meditation will be easy for him. He will feel that God-realization is the only objective in his life. Someone with just a little aspiration will meditate for five or ten minutes as a discipline or an obligation, but with little joy or inspiration.

Many people believe that a true seeker must meditate at least eight hours a day. I did it. Even though I attained realization in my past incarnation, when I was thirteen years old in this incarnation I was meditating for eight, nine, ten, thirteen hours a day. But I had the capacity. I do not advise my disciples to do this, because I know their capacity. They would have a mental breakdown. It would be simply impossible for them. It would not be true meditation. I am not saying that they are insincere. No! They are most sincere. But capacity is like a muscle. One has to develop it gradually. You start with fifteen minutes and then go on to half an hour. Those who are now meditating for half an hour will soon be able to meditate for an hour or an hour and a half.

Gradually, gradually, your inner capacity will grow. At the proper time, your inner being will tell you when you can meditate for eight hours. But right now, do not even try. It will simply create a disaster in your life.

After one has achieved realization, it is not necessary for him to meditate the way an aspirant or a seeker meditates. When one has attained realization, which is oneness with the Supreme, his meditation is continually going on—in this world, in that world, in all the worlds. When one has realized God, he does not meditate to achieve something or to go beyond something. He meditates to bring down peace, Light and bliss into humanity or to awaken the consciousness of the seekers.

Question: *If meditation gives you such a marvelous feeling, why do not you stay in your highest meditation twenty-four hours a day? Why do you give lectures, for example?*

Sri Chinmoy: What does one do when he has studied for quite a few years and has received his Master's degree? He starts teaching. In my case, my eternal Father has given me a big heart. I know how I suffered to realize Him; I know what kind of pangs and agonies I went through to realize the Highest. Now I am seeing these pangs in my brothers and sisters. They are suffering as I did. Once upon a time, I, too, was wallowing in the pleasures of ignorance. Now I see that same thing happening to them. Since God, out of His infinite Bounty, gave me love, Light and other divine qualities, let me offer them to that part of suffering humanity which is crying for them. I am for those who really want Light from me. If God wants me to be of service to my brothers and sisters who really need Light, then by serving humanity I am pleasing God.

A God-realized soul is he or she who wants to please God in God's own way. Since God wants me to be of service to aspiring human beings, then that is what gives me greatest joy, and not staying in my highest consciousness, which I could easily do. Very often I show that consciousness to my disciples and students during our meditations. They have seen it often. But if I stay in that consciousness all the time, who will derive any benefit from me? I will be acting like a selfish fellow. I have the wealth, but if I keep it all for myself, then what good is it to the poverty-stricken world? If I use it for others who are desperately in need of it, only then will God be pleased with me. These people need God, and God also needs them. I am the intermediary. I go to God with folded hands because He has something to offer. I take what He has and with folded hands I offer it to mankind. Mankind also has something to offer. Its offering is ignorance. I just exchange God's offering, Light, for man's offering, ignorance. The real work, if there be any, of a Guru is to show the world that his deeds are in perfect harmony with his teachings.

Question: Are there any set procedures one must follow in order to meditate correctly?

Sri Chinmoy: Each one has his own way of meditation. What actually happens in the individual is that the inner being comes forward and tells the individual to pray or meditate in this or that way. Sometimes a spiritual figure comes along who can easily enter into the individual and know the development and the aspiration of the seeker. Then this spiritual teacher can tell him how to meditate and when to meditate.

When you have a teacher, you are extremely lucky, especially if the teacher is a genuine one. If you do not have a teacher, but if you have a genuine aspiration, God within you will tell you the correct meditation. It is not possible for everyone in the world to have a spiritual teacher. If one does not get one, what will happen? We are all God's children. God does not want to deprive us of God-realization. God wants us to realize Him. So, if you get a teacher, well and good. If not, go deep within to discover your own meditation.

Question: I understand. But very often, with the inner self, I may not recognize it to be the true inner self. I do not know whether this is the inner voice or the outer voice and this is extremely confusing.

Sri Chinmoy: I fully understand. But if you get a teacher who is a realized soul, you can go to him for help and find out if what you are doing is correct. If you do not get a spiritual teacher, please go deep, deep within and see if you get a voice or a thought or an idea. Then go deep into the voice or thought or idea and see if it gives you a kind of inner joy or peace, where there is no question, no problem. When you get this kind of peace and inner joy, you can feel whether the voice that you have heard is correct and whether it will help you in your inner and spiritual life.

Question: *When I try to meditate, I get a feeling of oceans and waters before my mind's eye. This creates fear in me, and I cannot meditate very well. How can I meditate without getting this feeling?*

Sri Chinmoy: Please try to see the ocean as something of your own, something in your inner being. Instead of seeing the ocean with its surges, waves and waters, please think of it as your own largest consciousness, and throw yourself into that largest and deepest consciousness. The ocean is not something standing in front of you as an enemy. Water symbolizes consciousness. When you see this consciousness, you should feel happy and fortunate. There are so many seekers who try to imagine the ocean, their consciousness as vast as the ocean.

From now on, try to throw your own consciousness into the waters of the ocean. You will be able to meditate most powerfully and most successfully. You will be able to contact, deep within you, that which is nearest and dearest to your soul.

Again, remember that you are extremely lucky to see the ocean in front of you. Do not focus your attention on the surface of the ocean, but please go, silently and consciously, deep into the ocean, where you will find your true reality, which is all tranquillity.

Question: *Can meditation help people overcome their fear of death?*

Sri Chinmoy: Certainly. Meditation can easily help the seeker to overcome the fear of death. Meditation means conscious communication with God. If one can establish his oneness with God, who is all Life, then there can be no fear of death. He will not only conquer fear of death, but he will also conquer something else. He will conquer his doubt about God's existence in his own life or in others' lives. It is very easy for us to feel that God exists only in us, or only in spiritual people. But if we meditate, then it becomes clear to us that God exists not only within us but also inside the people whom we do not like or appreciate.

Question: *Is it possible for a spiritual person who is dying a painful death to transform his pain to joy through meditation?*

Sri Chinmoy: If one is a sincere seeker, then even while he is dying, great joy will come. Although the physical may suffer, the delight of the soul will come forward, enabling one to meditate consciously. Sometimes, when one consciously enters into the pain, then one's own inner courage in the pain itself is transformed into joy.

One can consciously enter into pain even while undergoing a serious operation. When I was a young boy, eighteen or nineteen years old, I did this during a serious operation. While the doctor was operating on me, I consciously entered into the pain and felt real joy. I was smiling at the doctor, and he simply could not understand it. This anybody can experience.

Question: Is chanting a kind of meditation?

Sri Chinmoy: Chanting is not, strictly speaking, a form of meditation. It is an invocation. You invoke God to enter into you, into your inmost Self, into your inner existence. Meditation is different. While in chanting you usually invoke God to permeate your whole existence, in meditation you try, in a broader way, to enter into God's infinity, eternity and immortality.

Question: Sometimes my cousin and I meditate by looking into each other's eyes, and when we do, sometimes we see one another's faces change and even the hair turns a different color. I was wondering what this means.

Sri Chinmoy: You are seeing his past incarnation and he is seeing yours. But this is not at all advisable. For two people to look at each other and consciously concentrate on the eyes and bring forward the past is very risky, for you may be unconsciously bringing forward your animal consciousness. In India I know people who have done this with their brothers and sisters, and then the undivine forces from the past incarnation of one have entered into the other, and vice versa. Even in this incarnation, as long as we have not realized God, there are many undivine elements in our nature which we have to contend with. So let us not bring forward the past. This past, I always say, is dust. Has the past given you realization? No! If it had, then you would not have come to me. So it is not necessary or advisable to go to the past.

MIND

Question: *Is it the mind that sets limits on man?*

Sri Chinmoy: The desiring mind in man sets limits on everything—whether it is something that he already has or something that he wants to possess. But the aspiring heart in man deals with the infinite—with things that are already infinite or things that eventually will be infinite. When someone lives primarily in the mind or in the desire-world, he is enchained by the limitations of his mind. When the same person enters into the world of the aspiration, that means he wants to liberate himself from the world of limitations.

Question: *Can a seeker live in vast expansion of mind, or is this possible only for a realized soul?*

Sri Chinmoy: Vast expansion of mind the aspirant can have for a few minutes when he is in a very high, deep meditation. Only the realized soul can enter into this vast expansion of mind and stay there indefinitely. But we are actually making a mistake when we use the term "expansion of the mind." In the state I am referring to, there is no mind; the mind has been transcended. We feel that what we experience is the expansion of the mind, but it is actually the transcendence of the mind. In the mind there is form, there are limits; but when we speak of the vast expanse, it is something beyond the domain of the mind. It is a vast expanse of Light, consciousness, peace, and bliss.

When we are meditating, we always try to go beyond the mind. When we want to expand our consciousness, our physical reality, we have to enter into the soul. But when we come back from the highest level of consciousness, we try to understand and express the state we were in with the help of the mind. That is because the mind right now is the highest product of human life. But because the mind is limited, it can never understand and express the infinite, the Unlimited.

Question: I understood you to say that God is not a mental being. I am not sure what you meant by that.

Sri Chinmoy: We have a physical body and a mind. Similarly, we can think of God as a physical being, having a mind like ours. People often imagine God as composed of a gigantic mind, or else functioning like we do with the mind. Up until now, the mind has been humanity's greatest achievement. With the help of the mind, science and our physical world have progressed to an enormous extent. As the mind has been our highest attainment, we tend to think of God as a being with a most highly developed mind. But God is not a mental being. God does not act from the mind. He does not need the mental formulation which we utilize in order to act. God does not need to formulate ideas with a mind.

A human being usually thinks before he acts. But in God's case, it is not like that. He uses His Will power which, while seeing, also acts and becomes. God's seeing, acting and becoming are instantaneous and simultaneous.

Question: When I try to think out a problem and plan a course of action, I find myself unable to make up my mind. Why is this?

Sri Chinmoy: When people use the mind, they constantly suffer from one thing: confusion. They go on thinking and thinking, and the moment they think that they have arrived at the Truth, they discover that it is not truth at all, but just more confusion. The difficulty is this: when we think of someone or something, we form a conception which we think is absolutely true. But the next moment doubt comes and changes our mind. This moment you will think that I am a nice man. The next moment you will think that I am a bad man. Then after that you will think something else. Eventually you will see that there is no end to your questions and that there is no solution.

Each time we think, we are lost. Thinking is done in the mind, but the mind is not yet liberated. Only the soul is liberated. Our problem is that we want to be liberated by thinking. But the mind itself is still in the prison cell of darkness, confusion and bondage, so how can we expect liberation from the mind?

When we plan, we very often are frustrated because we do not see the Truth right from the beginning. We plan to do something because we feel that if we do it we will achieve a certain goal. But between planning and executing, different ideas and different ideals enter into us and create confusion for us. Then our planning goes on and on forever, and we never enter into the world of action because our plans are never complete or certain. There is a yawning gap between our mental plan and the action itself.

But if we have an inner will, the soul's will, which has come to us from meditation, then the action is no sooner conceived of than it is done. At that time there is no difference between our inner will and our outer action. When we enter into the totally dark, obscure, unlit room of action with our mental plans, it is like carrying a candle. But when we enter the room with our soul's light, the room is flooded with illumination.

Right now we are laboring with our mind. The mind says, "I have to achieve something. I have to think about how I can execute my plan." But God does not do that. God sees the past, present and future at a glance. When we are one with God, when by constant aspiration we identify ourselves with God's Consciousness, then whatever we do will be done spontaneously. We will not utilize the mind but will always act from our own inner consciousness, with our intuitive faculty. And when we develop that intuitive faculty, we can easily act without having a plan. At each moment the possibility of the total manifestation that is going to take place will materialize right in front of us.

NIRVANA

Question: What is nirvana?

Sri Chinmoy: When one's cosmic play is done, one enters into nirvana. If one is a tired soul and wants to go permanently beyond the conflict, beyond the capacities of the cosmic forces, then nirvana is to be welcomed. Nirvana is the cessation of all earthly activities, the extinction of desires, suffering, bondage, limitation and death. In this state one goes beyond the conception of time and space. This world, earth, is the playground for the dance of the cosmic forces. But when one enters into nirvana, the cosmic forces yield to the ultimate highest Truth, and the Knower, the Known and the Knowledge or Wisdom are blended into one. At that time one becomes both the Knower and the Known.

If one does not have the experience of nirvana, he usually cannot know what illusion is. According to some spiritual teachers, the world is *maya*, an illusion. When one enters into nirvana, he realizes what illusion is. Nirvana is the static oneness with God. There, everything comes to an end in the static bliss. This bliss is unimaginable, unfathomable, indescribable. Beyond nirvana is the state of absolute oneness. This oneness is the dynamic oneness with God.

Nirvana is a very, very, very high state. However, it is not the highest state for the divine worker. If one wants to serve God here on earth, then he has to come back into the world again and again to serve the Supreme in humanity. If one wants to manifest the Supreme in the field of creation, then he has to work in the absolute dynamism of the Supreme, and not take rest in nirvana. This does not mean that the divine worker cannot have the experience of nirvana. The experience of nirvana is at the command of all God-realized souls. But permanent nirvana is for those who want to be satisfied with the static aspect of the supreme *Brahman*. If one wants

236

to embody both the static and dynamic aspects of the Supreme, then I wish to say that one should go beyond nirvana and enter into the field of manifestation.

Question: *Is there any difference between nirvana and* nirvikalpa samadhi?

Sri Chinmoy: Let us take nirvana and *nirvikalpa samadhi* as two of the tallest mansions. Other mansions are next to nothing in comparison to these two mansions. If you climb up the nirvana-mansion, there is no way to come down, or you do not feel the necessity of coming down to offer what you have received to the world. There is no link with the earth-consciousness. In nirvana you notice the extinction of earth-pangs and the end of the Cosmic Dance. Nirvana is flooded with infinite peace and bliss. From the point of view of absolute Truth, nirvana is the Goal of goals to the seekers who no longer want to take part in God's manifested creation. Of course, if the Supreme Pilot wants an individual seeker of the absolute Truth to go beyond nirvana and enter into the world for earth-transformation and earth-perfection in a divine way, He sends him down. He feels that that particular instrument of His is supremely indispensable for transforming the Supreme's birthless transcendental vision into His deathless universal reality.

When you climb up the *nirvikalpa samadhi*-mansion, there is a way to climb down if you want to. But if you stay there for a long period of time, then you totally forget that there is a way to come down. *Nirvikalpa samadhi* throws illumination-flood into us and makes us feel that there are higher worlds far beyond this world of ours. Further, it reveals itself to the seeker as a connecting link between this world and other high, higher, highest worlds, and it offers him the road to go beyond it and enter into the ever-transcending Beyond.

PATIENCE

Question: What is patience?

Sri Chinmoy: Patience is a divine virtue. Unfortunately, not only are we badly wanting in this divine virtue, but also we neglect it most foolishly.

What is patience? It is an inner assurance of God's unreserved love and unconditional guidance. Patience is God's power hidden in us to weather the teeming storms of life.

If failure has the strength to turn your life into bitterness itself, then patience has the strength to turn your life into the sweetest joy. Do not surrender to fate after a single failure. Failure, at most, precedes success. But once success is achieved, confidence becomes your name.

Have patience in the body; you will be able to accept the whole world. Have patience in the vital; you will be able to hold the whole world. Have patience in the mind; you will neither forget nor lose the world. Have patience in the heart; you will feel that the world is not only with you and in you, but also for you.

Time is a flying bird. Do you want to capture the bird and encage it? Then you need patience. Your fondest dreams will be transformed into fruitful realities if you just know the secret of growing the patience-tree in your heart.

Patience is your sincere surrender to God's Will. This surrender is by no means the effacement of the finite self which you now are, but the total transformation of your finite existence into the infinite Self.

In silence, patience speaks to you: "Try to live the inner life. You will not only see and reach your goal, but also become the goal."

Patience can never be imposed on you from outside. It is your own inner wealth, wisdom, peace and victory.

Question: How can we develop patience?

Sri Chinmoy: In order to develop patience, we have to feel that we have begun a spiritual journey, an inner journey, which has a goal, and that this goal wants us and needs us as much as we want and need it. This goal is ready to accept us, to give us what it has, but it will do this in its own way at God's choice hour. We must know that God will give us His Wealth in time.

Patience will never tell us that it is a hopeless task. Patience will only tell us either that we are not ready or that the time is not ripe. We may have the feeling that we are ready, but we have to know that our integral being, our whole being, is not ready. Our soul may be ready, our heart may be ready, our mind may be ready, but our vital and physical may not be ready to reach the goal, which is Light and Truth. When our whole being is ready, the goal itself will dawn within our aspiring consciousness. When the hour strikes, the goal will draw us towards itself like a magnet.

We have to feel that patience is not something passive. On the contrary, it is something dynamic. In patience we develop our inner strength, our inner will power. It is true that if we have will power we can easily acquire patience. But it is equally true that when we have patience, our inner will power develops itself in a special way.

PERFECTION

Question: What keeps us from attaining perfection?

Sri Chinmoy: What keeps us from attaining perfection? It is our self-indulgence. In self-indulgence we feel that there is something absolutely necessary in our life, and that is pleasure. When we cry for pleasure and want to remain in pleasure, to become pleasure itself, perfection is a far cry. But when we cry for divine joy, delight, bliss, at that time, we enter into the ocean of perfection. If we cry continuously, we learn how to swim in the sea of perfection.

When we have an inner cry for delight, we jump into the sea of perfection. This is the first step. But when this inner cry becomes constant, we swim in the sea of perfection. When we keep joy and delight as our goal, perfection automatically grows in us, and slowly we become the sea of perfection. But what now keeps us from perfection is our fondness for pleasure-life and our indulgence in pleasure-life.

Question: God could have made man perfect to begin with. What was His reason for putting us to all the trouble that we are going through to attain perfection?

Sri Chinmoy: God could have started His creation with perfection. But fortunately or unfortunately, that was not His intention. What God wanted was to go through ignorance to Knowledge, through limitation to Plenitude, through death to Immortality.

In the outer world, we see limitation, imperfection, doubt, fear and death. But in the inner world we see Light, peace, bliss and perfection. When we live in God's Consciousness, there is no imperfection. It is all perfection.

God is a divine Player. He is playing His divine Game and He knows the ultimate end. At each moment He is revealing Himself in

240

us and through us, in spite of the fact that we see, nay create, a vast gulf between ourselves and God. In addition to this, we feel that God is in Heaven and we are on earth. In the physical world, the miseries, troubles, frustrations and despair that we are going through are nothing but experiences on our way to the ultimate goal. Who is, after all, having all these experiences? It is God and God alone. When we consciously identify ourselves with God's Consciousness, we observe that there is no imperfection because God is perfect Perfection. But if we do not live in the divine consciousness, if we feel that we are the doers, naturally we will be yoked to the imperfection of the outer world. What actually is happening is the self-revelation of God in His manifested creation. A seeker of the Supreme, living in the Supreme, being one with the Consciousness of the Supreme, sees and feels that his consciousness, his life, both inner and outer, are the projections of God's ever-transcending Perfection growing into perfect Perfection.

Question: Will the process of striving for perfection ever come to an end?

Sri Chinmoy: It will never come to an end, because God Himself does not want to end His Cosmic Game. Today, what we feel is the ultimate perfection, tomorrow will be just the starting point of our journey. This is because our consciousness is evolving. When our consciousness evolves to a higher level, our sense of perfection simultaneously goes higher. Let us take perfection as a achievement. When we are a kindergarten student, our achievement of perfection may be very good for that stage. But from kindergarten we go to primary school, high school, college and university. When we get our Master's degree in perfection, our achievement is much greater than what it was when we were in kindergarten. Even then we may feel that there are many more things that we have to learn. Then we will study further and enlarge our consciousness still more.

If the child thinks that the Master's degree will always be unattainable, then he is mistaken. The spiritual ladder has quite a few rungs. If we do not step onto the first rung, then how can we climb up to the ultimate rung of the ladder?

PRAYER

Question: What do you say while you are praying? To whom are you speaking? Have you ever prayed for others, for the world, for peace? How have you done this?

Sri Chinmoy: How to pray? With tears in our hearts. Where to pray? In a lonely place. When to pray? The moment our inner being wants us to pray. Why to pray? This is the question of questions. We have to pray if we want our aspirations to be fulfilled by God. What can we expect from God beyond this? We can expect Him to make us understand everything: everything in nothing and nothing in everything, the Full in the Void and the Void in the Full.

When I am praying, I am communing with the Highest Absolute. I speak to Him either like a beggar to an emperor or like a child to his grandfather. I started praying and meditating—you can say unconsciously—at the age of four or five. But since the very beginning of my conscious spiritual journey, I have been praying to the Supreme not only for my own perfection in life but also for a oneness-world founded upon inner peace. At this point in my spiritual journey, all my prayers are for others, for the world, for peace.

Then again, in the highest sense, there is no separation between myself and "others." After I attained my own conscious union with God, I came to realize that there is only one "person," and that is my universal oneness-life.

So when I pray, automatically I include in my prayer all human beings on earth. And when I meditate, that too is for the benefit of all the souls in God's entire universe. Once you have established your oneness with God's Will, it is extremely easy to meditate soulfully, powerfully and unconditionally for God's Will to be executed in and through each human being on earth.

Question: *In calling on God, should we use the pronoun "You"? If not, what language should we use?*

Sri Chinmoy: You can say "You" or "Thou" or refer to God by whatever name you feel comfortable with, or in whatever aspect you like. You can offer your prayers to God the compassionate, God the Almighty, God the Beloved Supreme or any other aspect of God that pleases you.

During prayer and meditation, it is advisable to speak to God in your own mother tongue because the language that you learned from birth has become inseparably one with your life-breath, which is all simplicity, sincerity, purity and divinity. So it is advisable, especially for seekers, to pray to God in the language in which you were brought up.

Question: *To pray to God or to work as God wants us to work—which is the better of the two?*

Sri Chinmoy: I am happy to answer this question. It is a question of questions. But the answer is quite simple. To pray to God or to work as God wants us to work—both are of supreme importance. Both are inevitable means to an end. And that end is God-realization.

Question: *Which is the most beautiful prayer: the prayer of praise and beseeching, where man sees God as omnipotent, or the prayer of acceptance—"Thy Will be done"?*

Sri Chinmoy: The prayer "Let Thy Will be done" is infinitely more beautiful, infinitely more illumining and infinitely more fulfilling than a prayer of praise and beseeching. In our prayers, we appreciate, admire and adore God's infinite capacities and qualities. Unconsciously or consciously, we hope to get some blessingful reward or boon in return. In a sense, it is like trying to flatter God, and in return we expect something.

But when we say, "Let Thy Will be done," it means we have become fully aware of our measureless limitations, incapacities and ignorance, and aware of God's measureless compassion, concern and love for us. Because of our fathomless ignorance, we admit that we do not know what is good for us. We realize we may ask for the wrong thing, which instead of helping or satisfying us will only make us miserable. So we ask our divine Father, who loves us infinitely more than we love ourselves, to take control of our lives and make the decisions for us.

When we offer our earthbound will to God's Heaven-free Will, we feel we are a tiny drop entering into the boundless ocean and becoming inseparately one with the ocean. The ultimate goal of each seeker is to achieve infinite peace, infinite Light and infinite bliss, and this can be done only by fulfilling and pleasing God the Omniscient, God the Omnipotent and God the Omnipresent in His own way.

PRECOGNITION

Question: Do you think that precognition can restrict man's free will?

Sri Chinmoy: Precognition does not necessarily restrict man's free will. It depends entirely on the wisdom-Light of the one who has the knowledge of the future and on his capacity to deal with the prediction. It may be helpful to have the capacity to know the future, but one should not pray to God to give him this capacity. One should pray to God only for the fulfillment of His Will.

Question: Is it good to have a knowledge of the future?

Sri Chinmoy: To know the future is good only if you have patience, faith and the wisdom to use this knowledge in the proper way. Suppose you see that something discouraging, disheartening and destructive is going to take place in your life in the near future. Because you know in advance, you have the opportunity to pray to God to avert the calamity.

On the other hand, if you see something good, divine, inspiring, illumining and fulfilling is going to take place in the near future, then you can start offering your sincere gratitude to God, and also you can pray to God to expedite this fulfilling manifestation. God may listen to your prayers and accelerate the process if He sees that you truly value His blessings.

So if God blesses you with inner vision or with the capacity to know the future, then you have to utilize it properly. There are people who have the vision, but who are not wise enough to use it carefully. When they predict disastrous future events, they create useless and destructive fear in people, instead of inspiring them to pray for protection or illumination.

PRIDE

Question: Could you speak to us about human pride and divine pride?

Sri Chinmoy: My human pride feels that I can do everything. My divine pride, the pride that has surrendered itself to the Will of God, knows that I can do everything only when I am inspired, guided and helped by the Supreme.

My human pride wants the world to understand me, my love, my help and my sacrifice. My divine pride, which is the feeling of oneness with all in God, does not wish the world to understand my selfless activities. It feels that if God understands me and knows my motives, then there can be no greater reward.

My human pride drinks the hot water of life—sufferings, struggles and doubts—without a spoon. The result is that my tongue gets badly burnt. My divine pride drinks the same hot water, nay, infinitely more in quantity, but it uses a spoon to drink with, so I suffer not. This spoon is the spoon of liberation, freed from the shackles of ignorance.

My human pride is afraid of saying and ashamed of doing many things. My divine pride is not afraid of saying and not ashamed of doing anything, for it knows that God is at once the Doer and the action. Whom am I to be afraid of? What am I to be ashamed of?

My human pride crushes humanity with man-acquired power. My divine pride liberates humanity with God-given power.

When I say that God is mine and I can use Him at my sweet will, I harbor my human pride. But when I say that I am God's, and my very existence is at His Behest and at His Feet, I cherish divine pride.

To my human pride, the material world says, "We shall either succeed or we shall fail and perish." To my divine pride, the spiritual world says, "Together shall we endeavor, together shall we succeed."

PROBLEMS

Question: *Would you speak to us about the reason for adversity and problems in our life?*

Sri Chinmoy: Adversity makes you dynamic. Adversity forces your eyes wide apart. Adversity teaches you the meaning of patience. Adversity endows you with faith in yourself. Adversity leads us inward to correct and perfect our march to life. Prosperity leads us onward to illlumine and imortalize our human birth.

In prosperity, our inner strength remains static. In adversity, our inner strength becomes dynamic.

None can deny the fact that every step of progress which the world has made has come from both the smiles of prosperity and the tears of adversity.

Adversity, like poverty, is no sin. One merit of adversity none can deny: it helps us to be stronger within. The stronger we are within, the brighter we are without.

"No suffering, no salvation," so says the teacher adversity to his student, man. "No soul's delight, no salvation," so says the teacher, prosperity, to his student, man.

The world is strewn with difficulties. In a sense, it is full of thorns. But if you put on shoes, you can walk on the thorns. What are these shoes made of? They are made of God's grace.

Problems do not indicate a man's incapacity. Problems do not indicate a man's insufficiency. Problems indicate man's conscious need for self-transcendence in the inner world, and his conscious need for self-perfection in the outer world.

You have a problem. He has a problem. She has a problem. Your problem is that the world does not touch your feet. His problem is that the world does not love him. Her problem is that she feels that she does not adequately help God in the world. To solve your problem, you have to conquer your pride. To solve his problem, he has to conquer his greed. To solve her problem, she has to conquer her self-

247

styled and self-aggrandized, desiring ego. Each problem is a force. But when we see the problem, we feel deep within us a greater force. And when we face the problem, we prove to the problem that we not only have the greatest force, but actually we are the greatest force on earth.

A problem increases when the heart hesitates and the mind calculates. A problem decreases when the heart braves the problem and the mind supports the heart. A problem diminishes when the mind uses its search-Light and the heart uses its illumination-Light.

If fear is our problem, we have to feel we are the chosen soldiers of God the Almighty. If doubt is our problem, then we have to feel that we have deep within us the sea of God's Light. If jealousy is our problem, we have to feel that we are the oneness of God's Light and Truth. If insecurity is our problem, then we have to feel that God is nothing and can be nothing other than the constant and ceaseless assurance that He will claim us as His very own. If our body is the problem, our constant alertness and attention can solve this problem. If the vital is a problem, our soaring imagination can solve this problem. If the mind is the problem, our illumining inspiration can solve this problem. If the heart is the problem, our perfecting aspiration can solve the problem. If life is the problem, our fulfilling self-discovery can solve this problem.

Question: When I have problems, I can not seem to really solve them. Even my friends and parents do not know what way is best.

Sri Chinmoy: There is somebody who knows what is best for you, and that is the Supreme. The Supreme is not a mental hallucination. You will be able to see Him, you will be able to hear Him, you will be able to dine with Him. He is not only your Father, but also your eternal Comrade. You have to give Him responsibility for yourself. If you feel your family or friends are not guiding you properly, then the first thing is to offer them at the Feet of the Supreme as well. Each time you are attacked by a problem, instead of trying to solve it yourself with your limited capacity or wisdom, please offer it to the Supreme.

His Eyes have better vision than ours. His Ears hear more quickly than our human ears. We talk to human beings who have no time to hear us; they have so many things to do in the outer world. But we very often forget that there is somebody else who is eager to listen. The Supreme is always eager to hear from us, but we do not speak to Him. Sometimes we speak to our own mind, to our own dissatisfied vital but rarely do we speak to our inner being. If we discover the secret of speaking to our inner being, we will solve all our problems and discover the true meaning of our human existence. This human existence is a golden opportunity that the Supreme has granted us. We say that we do not have an opportunity, but that is a sheer lie. The Supreme has given us the opportunity, but we do not avail ourselves of that opportunity.

Question: *You said that if we see the problem and if we face the problem, then we have greater force than the problem. Do you mean, then, that a problem is not a problem if we know how to look at it?*

Sri Chinmoy: If we know how to look at a problem, half the strength of the problem goes away. But usually we try to avoid the problem; we try to run away from it. To have a problem is not a crime, so why should we be afraid to face it? Our difficulty is that when something unfortunate happens in our life, we immediately feel that we are at fault, that we have done something wrong. We must know that there are also wrong forces, undivine forces, hostile forces around us. We believe in the law of karma—that if we do something wrong, we suffer later. But even if we do not do anything wrong, the ignorance of the world may come and torture us. Think of the Christ. He was a great spiritual Master. He did not have any bad karma. He did not do anything wrong. But the ignorance of the world crucified him. Of course, we cannot compare ourselves with the Christ, but at our own level we have to feel that we are not necessarily at fault.

By blaming ourselves and then trying to hide, we do not solve the problem. We have to face the problem and see whether we really are to blame. If somebody else is creating the problem, then we have to stand like a solid wall and not allow the problem to enter into us. If it is my house, my wall, I will not allow anybody to break through. But if I am the problem itself, then this problem is infinitely more difficult to solve. In order to solve the problem of myself, I have to practice the spiritual life and develop inner strength, aspiration and inner detachment. Slowly, gradually, I will become inwardly strong, and then I will be able to solve the problems caused by my own inner weaknesses.

As soon as you have conquered a difficulty, you will find that it repeats itself on a higher and subtler level. It is the same essential weakness in yourself which you are made to face in a more refined form.

Question: *By handing over problems to my Guru, is this not burdening him even more?*

Sri Chinmoy: When you give your problems to your Master, you should not feel that you are overburdening him with a heavy load. The Master is ready to accept your ignorance. He has come here with the sea of Light; if you offer him the sea of ignorance, it will not harm him. But unfortunately, you feel your ignorance is so precious that with one hand you give it and with the other you take it back. This moment you feel that ignorance is useless and you are happy to give it to the Master. You feel that you are very clever because you have given him something unimportant and have got something important for it in return. But the next moment ignorance makes you feel that what you gave him was more precious than what he gave you; you feel that vital pleasure is much more important than Light. When you are in your deepest meditation, you feel that Light is more important than darkness. But when you are in the ordinary life, the life of desire, you feel that Light is all false and vague—all mental hallucination.

PURITY

Question: What is the role of purity in the spiritual life?

Sri Chinmoy: Purity! Purity! Purity! We love you. We want you. We need you. Stay in our thoughts! Stay in our actions! Stay in the breath of our life!

How to be pure? We can be pure by self-control. We can control our senses. It is unbelievably difficult, but it is not impossible.

"I shall control my senses. I shall conquer my passions." This approach cannot bring us what we actually want. The hungry lion that lives in our senses and the hungry tiger that lives in our passions will not leave us because of the mere repetition of the thought, "I shall control my senses and conquer my passions." This approach is of no avail.

What we must do is fix our mind on God. To our utter amazement, the lion and tiger of impurity, now tamed, will leave us of their own accord when they see that we have become too poor to feed them. But as a matter of fact, we have not become poor in the least. On the contrary, we have become infinitely stronger and richer, for God's Will energizes our body, mind and heart. To fix our body, mind and heart on the Divine is the right approach. The closer we are to the Light, the farther we are from the darkness.

Purity does not come all at once. It takes time. We must dive deep within and lose ourselves, with implicit faith, in contemplation of God. We need not go to purity; purity will come to us. And purity does not come alone. It brings with it everlasting joy. This divine joy is the sole purpose of our life. God reveals Himself fully and manifests Himself unreservedly only when we have this inner joy.

The world gives us desires. God gives us prayers. The world gives us bondage. God gives us freedom: freedom from limitations, freedom from ignorance.

251

We are the player. We can play either football or cricket. We have a free choice. Similarly, it is we who can choose either purity or impurity to play with. The player is the Master of the game, and not vice versa.

Question: What is the highest kind of purity I can aspire to?

Sri Chinmoy: Purity in the physical. You should always try to invoke Light in the unaspiring body. The lower physical and the emotional vital below the navel have to be purified totally. Human beings have purity to some extent in the heart. In the mind the quantity is very small. In the vital purity is totally mixed with impurity. There dynamism and aggression play together, but aggression is impurity and dynamism is purity. Below the vital is the physical. There, because of inertia and sloth, darkness reigns supreme. And where there is darkness, you can rest assured that impurity is the lord.

You have to aspire for purity in the gross physical. It is the physical in you that needs radical transformation, and for that what you need is physical purity. Purity in the physical can be established only by bringing down Light from above into the physical and lower vital consciousness, especially below the navel center. How can you do it? Through constant elevating prayer and constant inner cry for Light. Light and darkness cannot stay together; it is impossible. Similarly, purity and impurity cannot stay together. When you pray for purity, you have to feel that what you actually need is Light. And you must not just repeat the word "purity" like a parrot. You should meditate on the transcendental Light. When Light descends into your emotional vital and physical body, then automatically, spontaneously, the Light will purify the conscious and the unconscious or lower worlds within you. First it will purify and then it will illumine your consciousness, which is now unconsciously expressing the physical truth: the world of temptation, frustration and destruction.

Question: Is it possible for a person to become unintentionally involved in the vibrations of someone who is impure?

Sri Chinmoy: Yes, it is quite possible. In spite of being absolutely pure oneself, one can become a victim of others' impurity. What actually happens is that the person who has purity does not have enough inner strength to prevent others' impurity from entering into his system. That is why spiritual teachers very often tell aspirants not to mix with people who are not pure. The aspirants may be absolutely pure themselves, but if they are not also very strong, then they are helpless. Their purity can be torn to pieces like a rose. The rose is beautiful to look at, for it is the embodiment of purity. But if someone wants to, he can easily tear the rose to pieces.

In our day-to-day life we very often come across people and places that are very impure. While walking along the street, a spiritual person may sense tremendous impurity at a particular spot where an ordinary person may not notice anything at all. To an ordinary person all places are practically the same.

Question: *Please speak to us about the power of purity.*

Sri Chinmoy: Purity is the Light of our soul expressing its divinity through the body, the vital and the mind. When we are pure, we gain everything. If we can retain our purity, we will never lose anything worth keeping. Today we may have great thoughts or great inner power, but tomorrow we are bound to lose them if we are not pure. Purity is the breath of the Supreme. When purity leaves us, the breath of the Supreme also leaves, and we are left with only our human breath.

Purity means following the dictates of our Inner Pilot without allowing undivine forces to enter into us. Wherever there is a lack of purity, there is obscurity, which is the harbinger of death. What we call obscurity today is death for us tomorrow. If there is no purity, there is no certainty. If there is no purity, there is no spontaneity. If there is no purity, there is no constant flow of divinity inside us.

Purity is like a divine magnet. It pulls all divine qualities into us. When we have purity, the world is filled with pride in us. If Mother Earth houses a single pure soul, her joy knows no bounds. She says, "Here, at last, is a soul I can rely upon."

Once purity is established, especially in the vital, much is accomplished in one's inner life and outer life. In human purity abides God's highest Divinity. Man's purity is God's Breath. Purity is tremendous power. We can accomplish anything with purity. But if we lose our purity, although we may have power, wealth or influence, we can easily fall, we will crumble.

All spiritual aspirants, without exception, have seen and felt the necessity of purity. Today they climb the inner Mount Everest on the strength of their highest purity, but tomorrow they fall down into the lowest abyss. With purity lost, everything is lost; God Himself is lost. With purity won, the world is won; the entire universe is won.

Question: *What do you mean by "Purity is selfless oneness with God"?*

Sri Chinmoy: Once there lived a pious youth named Nagamuddin who came from a Muslim family. He used to study all day and night. His father died when he was still quite young, and suddenly Nagamuddin had to support his poor mother. He started looking for a job here, there and everywhere, but he did not succeed in getting one.

One day he went to a Muslim priest and begged him to give him a job in any line, although he said he would be very happy if he could also become a priest. The priest said, "I will give you a job, but I cannot make you a priest, for you will far surpass me and every other priest on earth. You have no idea how great you are. One day everybody will come to know of you. Even the Emperor of Delhi will come to you to honor you."

A burning desire to realize God had long been consuming Nagamuddin. He had been looking for his Guru everywhere. Finally one day he went to a very spiritual man named Phariduddin and said to him, "Please become my Guru. I am tired of searching for a Guru."

Phariduddin accepted Nagamuddin as his devoted disciple, and Nagamuddin learned to cook so that he could prepare meals for his Master. He enjoyed the Master's deep affection for him. But the Master and the disciple were very, very poor. Sometimes for days on end they had no food to eat. They spent most of their time praying and meditating and totally neglected the demands of the body.

One day somebody gave Nagamuddin some flour so he could make some bread. Nagamuddin did not have money, and he knew that his Master also had no money to buy one of the necessary ingredients to make bread—salt. So he went to the village market and borrowed some salt from a shop. The shopkeeper readily gave him the salt because he knew that Nagamuddin was a spiritual man, and that his Master was very great.

Nagamuddin brought the salt back and made delicious bread for his Master. But when he offered Phariduddin a few pieces of bread, something unusual happened. On other days when he would give something to his Master, the Master would eat it happily and bless Nagamuddin for the food. But that day Phariduddin said, "I shall not eat your food. There is tremendous impurity in it."

Neither the Master nor the disciple had eaten for three days, but because there was tremendous impurity in the food, the Master would not eat it. Nagamuddin felt miserable. He could not account for it.

Then his Master said, "I can clearly see that you have borrowed salt from a shopkeeper to make this bread. This is indeed a disgraceful act. Never borrow anything from anyone. If you borrow, your consciousness descends and you become impure. The man who gave you the salt is so proud that he has given you something, so he is treasuring impurity. And when you borrow something, you become a victim to worries and anxieties. Worries and anxieties are also a kind of impurity. If you do not have total purity in your system, in every cell of your body, then you will not be able to realize God. So from now on, do not borrow anything, money or material gifts. Worries and anxieties will assail you and purity will leave you."

If you have purity, then you have everything. There are two ways to have purity. One is by seeing God inside everyone, consciously and constantly. The other is by imagining God and consciously repeating His name as many times as possible. If you have purity, you do not have to go to God. God Himself will make you see His infinite Divinity. What God is will be reflected in you. You will be an exact replica of God.

Purity expedites God's hour. Purity embodies God's power. If you have purity, then there is nothing that you cannot accomplish. Purity is the harbinger of selfless oneness, eternity's perfect, selfless oneness with God.

REINCARNATION

Question: What is the purpose of reincarnation?

Sri Chinmoy: In one lifetime on earth we cannot do everything. If we remain in the world of desire, we will never be able to fulfill ourselves. As children we have millions of desires, and even when we reach the age of seventy we see that a particular desire has not been fulfilled and we feel miserable. The more desires we fulfill, the more desires we get. We want one house, then two houses; one car, then two cars, and so forth. There is no limit to it. When our desires are fulfilled, we find that we are still dissatisfied. Then we become the victims of other desires or larger desires.

Now our dearest is God. Do you think that God will allow us to remain unfulfilled? No! God's very purpose is to fulfill each individual, and Himself through us. He will have us come back again and again to fulfill our desires. If someone is eager to become a millionaire in this incarnation, and at the end of his journey he sees that he has not become a millionaire, then if his desire is really intense, he will have to keep coming back until he really becomes a millionaire. But by becoming a millionaire, he will see that he still remains a beggar in one sense, for he will have no peace of mind. If he enters into the world of aspiration, he may have no money, but he will have peace of mind, and this is the real wealth.

If we live in the world of desire, we see that there is an endless procession of desires. But if we live in the world of aspiration, we see the whole, we enter into the whole and eventually we become the whole. We know that if we can realize God, inside God we will find everything, for everything exists inside God. So eventually we leave the world of desire and enter into the world of aspiration. There we diminish our desires and think more of peace, bliss and divine love. In order to get a little peace, a drop of nectar, it may take years and years. But a spiritual person is ready to wait indefinitely for God's hour to fulfill his aspiration. And his aspiration to achieve this peace, Light and bliss will not go in vain.

Now if our aim is to enter into the Highest, the infinite, the eternal, the immortal, then naturally one short span of life is not enough. But again, God will not allow us to remain unfulfilled. In our next incarnation, we will continue our journey. We are eternal travelers. We have to continue, continue until we reach our goal. Perfection is the aim of each individual. We are trying to perfect ourselves in an imperfect world. And this perfect perfection we can never have in one life.

It is through aspiration and evolution that the soul develops the full possibility of realizing the Highest and fulfilling the Divine. The physical, the human in us, has to aspire to become one with the Divine in us—the soul. Right now the body does not listen to the dictates of the soul; that is to say, the physical mind revolts.

The workings of the physical mind cover up the soul's divine purpose, and the soul cannot come to the fore. At the present stage of evolution, most people are unconscious and do not know what the soul wants or needs. They have desires, anxiety over success, intensity and excitement. All these stem from the vital or ego, whereas anything done with the soul's consciousness is always all joy. At times we may hear the dictates of the soul, or the message of our conscience, but still we do not do or say the right thing. No, the physical mind is weak; we are weak. If we start aspiring, however, with the mind, and then go beyond the mind to the soul, we can easily hear and also obey the dictates of the soul.

A day will come when the soul is in a position to exercise its divine qualities and make the body, mind and heart feel that they need their self-discovery. The physical and the vital will consciously want to listen to the soul and be instructed and guided by the soul. Then, here in the physical, we will have an immortalized nature, an immortal life, for our soul will have become totally and inseparably one with the Divine on earth. At that time we will offer our inner wealth to the world at large and manifest our soul's potentialities. It very often happens that realization can take place in one incarnation, but for manifestation the soul has to come down again and again to earth. Unless and until we reveal and manifest the highest

Divinity within us, our game is not over. We have not finished our role in the Cosmic Drama, so we have to come back into the world again and again. But in the march of evolution, in one of its incarnations, the soul will fully realize and fully manifest the Divine in the physical and through the physical.

Question: You said that we are all evolving and progressing. But where did this whole process start? Was there a beginning?

Sri Chinmoy: We came into existence from God's delight. When we entered the creation, we evolved through the lower stages: mineral life, plant life, animal life. Although we have now entered into the human life, we are still half animal. There are some who want to kill or hurt others, and exhibit all kinds of animal and destructive tendencies.

But in the case of a spiritual aspirant, it is different. He tries to transcend his lower nature and aspires to be aware of and live in his divine nature, where he experiences peace, joy and love.

In the beginning we came from delight; we are now growing in delight; and we shall consciously return to delight.

Question: Why did we go from Light to darkness when we took birth?

Sri Chinmoy: Actually, we did not go from Light to darkness when we entered into the world. It is a very complicated matter. Each birth is part of the process of evolution. Each person has a soul. The soul enters into matter and from matter it aspires. Mother Earth has the inner urge, the aspiration to be one with the Highest, the cosmic Self, and eventually all human beings on earth will become one with the highest Spirit. This is an evolutionary process leading towards perfect perfection. Some will say that God is everywhere; God is inside us and likewise God is inside a thief. When He is not in creation but beyond creation, He is all Light and He enjoys the Light of the beyond. But when He enters into manifestation, He wants to enjoy Himself in a million ways. The cosmic Self wants to fulfill its Cosmic Play in each individual and in each creature here on earth. For that, evolution is proceeding.

Our soul is all Light. But on earth the atmosphere is not aspiring. When somebody takes birth, the first thing he sees is ignorance and illusion all around. In the highest plane, we are all perfect, but now in the material plane, we are experiencing the play of ignorance. During our meditation, we raise our level of consciousness a little and find ourselves hundreds of miles above the bed of thorns. Yet, if we remain only where our meditation takes us, above the thorns, and if we cry for perfection, our cry is only partially fulfilled. We are not eating the full fruit. God is inside everything. He must be realized in the material plane also.

In the deepest philosophy, what we call night is not absolutely night. There is some Light there also. A person who is realized naturally has more inner Light than a person who is not realized. The world will say that the unrealized person is all ignorance because he has not realized God. We are always comparing someone with someone else. What is really happening is that we are growing from little Light to more Light, to abundant Light, each according to his own understanding and capacity. What we call night is also Light in an infinitesimal form. It is because we are marching forward that we see the difference between effulgent Light and darkest night. Strictly speaking, in everything there is Light. Our human understanding makes us see both light and darkness. But from the highest point of view we should always feel that we are marching from Light to more Light, to abundant Light.

Question: *Why do you believe in rebirth? I know pretty well that I shall go to God when I die. And that's all.*

Sri Chinmoy: My friend, as you will go to God when you leave the body, so will I. Let us be wise. Our business is to go to God; it is God's business if He wants to keep you in Heaven and send me back to earth. Or vice versa. The best thing for us is to surrender to God and let Him fulfill us in His own way. Having thrown aside all our preconceived ideas regarding the existence or non-existence of rebirth, let us do the only thing of importance: be one with His Will and Consciousness.

Question: *Is reincarnation an entity in itself or is it a religious belief of Hinduism?*

Sri Chinmoy: There are religions which accept the belief in reincarnation, whereas there are other religions which do not. The Hindu religion believes in reincarnation. But reincarnation in itself has very little to do with Hinduism or any other religion.

What is reincarnation? It means that the soul comes into the world with a new garment. Now we are wearing garments. At any moment we can throw them off. They are at our disposal. Similarly, when the soul finds the body to be no longer capable of receiving the highest Truth or when the soul finds that the body needs rest or when the soul feels that God wants it to leave the body, it leaves; and again, when God wants the soul to enter into a new human body, the soul enters. I wish to add that this concept of reincarnation is not only the Hindu idea or the Hindu philosophy or the Hindu way of approaching life, but it is a truth to which many, many people in the West adhere.

In the Gita, one of our most sacred books, sometimes called the Bible of India, we find a beautiful verse on reincarnation. I wish to cite it.

[Sri Chinmoy chants Verse 22, Chapter 2 of the Bhagavad Gita in Sanskrit.]

"As a man discards his old and worn-out clothes and takes on new ones, so does the embodied soul discard this body and migrate from body to body."

This is what we call reincarnation from the Hindu spiritual point of view.

Question: *Why do some realized souls return to earth and some not?*

Sri Chinmoy: You get joy when I ask you to do something for me, to work for me. I get joy if I ask you to work for me and also if I ask you not to work. It is the same with the spiritual Masters. The Supreme asks some souls to work for Him on earth and some not to. Some souls, when they realize God, do not want to manifest Divinity on earth and, with God's approval, they remain in the soul's region. But those who want to manifest are like divine soldiers. They come down again and again and work for the Supreme for the transformation of humanity. For these souls, manifestation is always necessary. They feel that if manifestation does not take place, then realization is useless.

Question: *Does the soul make any promises before it incarnates?*

Sri Chinmoy: Please do not be forgetful of your great promise to God. Before you came into the world, before you donned the human cloak, you told God, your sweet Lord, with all the sincerity at your command, that you would participate in His divine Drama. He said to you, "My child, fulfill Me and fulfill yourself at the same time on earth." You were divinely thrilled; your joy knew no bounds. You said, "Father, I shall. May my soulful promise be worthy of Your compassionate command."

Question: *Who were you in your last incarnation?*

Sri Chinmoy: In my immediate past incarnation I was a spiritual Master in India with just a handful of extremely soulful and devoted disciples. In that incarnation, I lived in circumstances of extreme simplicity, perhaps I should even say austerity. Although I offered my inner good will to the world, my role in that lifetime was not to work in the world but to concentrate on my own spiritual progress and that of a few excellent disciples. Both God's justice and compassion are needed for the transformation of earth's consciousness. In my immediate past incarnation, God used His justice-Light for me, in me and through me more than He used His compassion-Light. In this incarnation it is absolutely the reverse. Right now it is God's compassion that is playing a greater role in inspiring, uplifting, illumining and fulfilling countless God-seekers through me.

Question: *Did you then choose your present life-role?*

Sri Chinmoy: No, I did not choose my life-role. My Inner Pilot commanded me to serve those who want and need my inner guidance, and to be their spiritual teacher. There are many God-seekers all over the world who are searching for a spiritual teacher.

Question: And who will you be in your next incarnation?

Sri Chinmoy: With regard to future lives, my Beloved Supreme, out of His infinite bounty, has repeatedly told me that this incarnation of mine marks the unmistakable end of my earthly pilgrimage. In the future I will continue to love, serve and please my Lord Supreme in His own way from the inner and higher worlds.

Question: When the soul is going to reincarnate, is it forced to do so or does the soul have the privilege of making this decision?

Sri Chinmoy: When the soul leaves the body, it gradually goes back to its own region, after leaving the physical, vital, mental and psychic sheaths. Nobody can compel the soul to reincarnate, save the Supreme. The Supreme has the power to compel the soul, but He does not do it. The Supreme does not compel anybody to do anything. The soul has an inner urge to fulfill the Divine here on earth. Some souls want to take rest for a few years, say ten, twenty, forty or sixty years, while others who are not developed and are full of earthly desires, who want to fulfill their countless unfulfilled desires, come back to the physical world sooner. To be sure, they are not going to fulfill anything spiritual here on earth. They just come back to the world of manifestation to fulfill their countless human desires.

The soul, as I have already said, is not compelled to reincarnate; but if a soul wants to descend, before doing so, it investigates the family, the environment, the circumstances and a few other things. Before actually entering into the family, the soul has to have an interview with the Supreme. Then the Supreme either approves of the soul's decision or He may merely tolerate it. There is a great difference between approval and tolerance. I am sure you know this.

Then there are some souls who have had enough of earthly experiences, that is to say, sufferings and frustrations. These particular souls usually take the oath of nirvana. They do not come down again. They remain in the Void. But there are aspiring souls who will not accept any defeat. They will come down to have the divine Victory in spite of their repeated defeats. These souls will come and go until the divine Victory has been fully established on earth.

Something more I wish to add. The soul is not compelled. The human father says to his son, "You are my son. You have to listen to me." But the Supreme Father does not do that. It is only the ignorant human being who commands. The higher we go, the clearer this becomes to us. Normally, the Supreme puts into our consciousness what he actually wants us to do in order to fulfill Himself in infinite ways in us and through us. Compulsion is only in this world, not in the higher worlds. It is the inner urge that compels the soul to reincarnate and not any outer force. My Father, the Infinite, is the most compassionate Being here on earth as well as in Heaven. It is my boundless duty to fulfill Him here on earth, there in Heaven. Finally, I must realize that by fulfilling Him, I am fulfilling myself unmistakably, totally, divinely and supremely.

Question: *Religion has told us that we have come from the Spirit and we go back to the Spirit at the end of our present incarnation. Now if we go back to our Father, then what is the use of reincarnation, realization and so forth?*

Sri Chinmoy: There are many religions on earth that do believe in reincarnation. Reincarnation is an undeniable fact. Now let me explain to you briefly what we mean by reincarnation. You play a game, but you cannot play it forever. You cannot play it for twenty-four hours at a stretch. You have to rest from time to time. Similarly, in the process of evolution, through a long series of reincarnations, we are trying to complete the game. This divine game that we are all playing is called the *Lila*. We cannot complete the game in its fullness during one span of life. Also, we are not playing the game in a divine way. We have not reached the goal. Our goal is still a far cry. Now if you want to embody your Father's infinite Consciousness on earth, and want to reveal and manifest your Father, then you have to play His divine Game of reincarnation. There is no other way. When we go to Him after each lifetime, it is only for a rest.

Question: There are many books on reincarnation on the market that you can buy. But are the laws of reincarnation something that can be understood by the intellect?

Sri Chinmoy: The laws of reincarnation can never be understood by the intellect. After one has realized the ultimate Truth, one can not only understand the laws of reincarnation, but seize the entire picture of the whole system of reincarnation from the beginning to the end. In order to understand the laws of reincarnation, one has to enter into the region of the soul and abide therein. One has to go far beyond the domain of the intellect. By studying books, even if you study millions of books on reincarnation, you cannot enter into the region of the soul. To enter into the region of the soul, you have to aspire and meditate. All you can understand by the intellect are certain very insignificant principles in the boundless realm of reincarnation.

Question: Is there a special evolution for advanced souls?

Sri Chinmoy: A holy man in his next incarnation can become a Yogi, and then he can become a real spiritual Master. In each life he will only increase his capacity. Each time he becomes stronger, so he will dare to challenge and transform ignorance more. First, as a holy man, he is afraid and does not want to challenge ignorance. He feels that he will lose his purity and divinity. Then, when he becomes a spiritual Master, he is not at all afraid; he knows he can dare to accept it because he has the capacity to transform it. Even without touching it, he can throw ignorance into the Universal Consciousness and he can transform the nature of humanity. He starts as a holy man. There he is strengthened and his power has increased infinitely. Each time it increases, he becomes a greater manifestation, a greater perfection, a greater fulfillment of the Supreme.

Question: Must a person evolve in every incarnation?

Sri Chinmoy: Each incarnation is meant for progress. You can take one step or ten steps or ten million steps. Progress depends on how much aspiration one has. Each incarnation indicates that the soul is entering into the world-arena to manifest something. The soul enters into the physical. It has made a fervent promise to God, but because of earthly pleasures and human ignorance, the soul finds it very difficult to make progress. In each life the soul comes to the physical with one sincere will: to go forward. So each incarnation is meant for that. The only thing is that some can cover only one step with greatest difficulty while others can take countless steps. Each incarnation is meant for gradual progress.

Question: Do you have the divine power to reduce the number of our future incarnations?

Sri Chinmoy: Most of the sincere, dedicated disciples have already made such progress in the spiritual life that they have eliminated the need for quite a few incarnations. First-class disciples have already made such progress that although it will take them many more incarnations to realize God, they will be realized much sooner than they would have otherwise been.

It depends on how fast you run. If you are a slow runner, it will take you forty or fifty seconds to run one hundred meters. But a first-class runner will do it in eleven seconds because he has the capacity to run faster. If someone has the eagerness to learn from a coach or an instructor, naturally he will run the fastest. But if somebody does not practice or take instruction from the coach, then how will he run as fast as someone who does? So speed is of utmost importance. In the case of running a race, it is a matter of ten or twenty or thirty seconds. But in the case of the spiritual life, it is a matter of ten or twenty or forty or sixty incarnations. If you run the fastest when a spiritual Master enters into your life, at that time you have a golden opportunity. All spiritual Masters have said that when spiritual figures descend, it is like an oceanliner that can carry many people very fast. The individual seeker is like a little tiny boat that may capsize at any moment.

Question: Is it possible that this is my last incarnation? I have been through so much suffering that I do not want to come back again.

Sri Chinmoy: You are not the only person on earth who is miserable.

There are billions of people on earth who will say that they are miserable if you ask them. But you are going to come back anyway. God is very clever. He wants His Game to continue and continue. Unless He sees that you are playing the Game extremely well, that is to say, until you have realized Him, God will not allow you to retire. Even after you have realized God, still you may have to work.

Again, who am I to say that this is your last incarnation? If I say yes, then difficulties will arise; and if I say no, then you will really feel miserable. So I will not say. Only let us offer our prayer to God to remove suffering from this earth.

Question: *If I have to come back to earth in another incarnation, who is going to take care of my soul? If you do not come into this world again, will you name someone else to take care of me?*

Sri Chinmoy: I will not come back anymore. I have played my role. Once the game is over, you do not play again. When you are playing your part in a game, sometimes you lose the game and sometimes you win. But you will only be concerned that you have played your part. In your case, the most important thing you have to feel is whether or not you have achieved an inseparable oneness with my soul in this incarnation. In the ordinary human life we see the bond between mother and son. You are in Puerto Rico and your son may be in New York. But although you are here working in the office, your heart is inside your son, who may be studying in New York in the university. His heart is also inside you, his mother. From New York the message of all his affection, love and concern is coming to your heart. Even human love, a human bond, has crossed thousands of miles. Your human body will stay on earth for perhaps seventy or eighty years. But in this body you have got something which is called a heart. How it is crossing the distance of thousands of miles! This is your offering and his offering.

In the spiritual plane the teacher himself represents God. His soul is infinitely more illumined than his disciples' souls. But each disciple's soul also wants to be as illumined as the Master's soul.

It is most important for the disciple to establish a real feeling, a radiant feeling of oneness with his Master. If the disciple does not realize God in this incarnation, there will be a definite, direct, express connection between that disciple and his Master. Then in the next incarnation, or in one or two incarnations, the disciple can realize the Highest, the Absolute.

Everybody has to realize God. You may say that you will not eat anything. But there is one thing that you will have to eat, and that is the fruit of the tree of realization. Other food you may deny, but realization-food you will not be able to deny. God will say, "All right, if you do not want to eat, do not eat, but this food, the realization-food, you have to eat sooner or later, in this incarnation or in ten incarnations."

When your Master is in the physical, it is the greatest opportunity, because at that time your physical mind is bound to be convinced. When a spiritual Master descends to earth, you get the greatest opportunity. Ramakrishna used to say, "The cow is already there. The cow has milk, but where does the actual milk lie? In the udder. When you milk the cow, you should not try to get milk from the leg of the cow or from the tail of the cow or from the ear of the cow. There is no milk there." So also, divine Bliss is everywhere. But there is a particular time when infinite grace and compassion can descend consciously and constantly. And that is when a realized Master descends to earth.

Question: *Is it possible for the individual to remember the details of past incarnations?*

Sri Chinmoy: The soul can easily remember its past incarnations, but it does not want to do so. Let us say that in a past incarnation you were living in Connecticut and now you are living in Puerto Rico. Why should you care to remember every day what your home in Connecticut was like or how many rooms you had there? Your business now is to stay in Puerto Rico in your present house. If anyone asks you where you live, you will say, "I live in Puerto Rico." And if anyone asks you how many rooms you have in your house, you will immediately think of this house and not your previous house.

Please do not pay any attention to the past. Right now you have to do your own work. You have to manifest the qualities that God has given you. You have to do everything here and now. The soul does not care for the body in which it lived during a previous incarnation. The soul can remember that in a previous incarnation it had better circumstances, surroundings and opportunities. But actually the soul will not care. It just wants to fulfill God in His own way.

You have accepted your fate. You are going to work and study here in Puerto Rico. The soul also feels this way. It says, "Now I am in this body. Let me go on manifesting as much as I can. To think about what I could have done in the past will not solve my problems. Only what I am going to do right now can solve all my problems."

If you go backward, it is a waste of time. Our goal is in front of us, not behind us. The soul does not care at all for the past. It only wants to reach the goal. God-realization lies ahead of us, not in our past.

Question: Do all souls have hundreds or thousands of incarnations before realization?

Sri Chinmoy: Yes, it is only spiritual Masters who do not take so many incarnations. There are some exceptions among spiritual Masters, but most of them do not want to go through so many incarnations.

Question: Will the whole world eventually become a better place as a result of the evolution that takes place through reincarnation?

Sri Chinmoy: The world is constantly evolving and progressing, consciously or unconsciously. It is like a tiny seed which is sprouting into a plant and then growing into a tree. There was a time when we were in the mineral world, then in the vegetable world, then in the animal kingdom. Now we are humans; but if we are sincere enough, we will see that although we have a conscious, developed mind, we still have not cast off our animal propensities and qualities. We are still half animals, quarreling, fighting, struggling. But a day will come when there will be divine people on earth. We will see them just as we are now seeing human beings in front of us.

Question: How can a spiritual Master like yourself convince others who do not believe in reincarnation that it is really true?

Sri Chinmoy: If someone asked me to convince him that he had previous lives, even if that individual did not believe in reincarnation, I would be able to prove it to him. I would ask that individual to meditate with me for a few minutes and I would enter into him and bring to the fore his immediate past incarnation. I would bring the image of one or two of his past activities to the fore to such an extent that what he was in his past incarnation would become vivid to the person. I have done it quite a few times. But sometimes it is not right for the person to know his past incarnations, and then I do not tell him.

One of my most devoted disciples one day asked me about his past incarnation. I told him that in his past incarnation he was a boatman in Japan. I told him he could go deep within to see it. I had not even completed my sentence when he himself saw that he was a boatman. But for those who are arrogant, for those who will not believe, and there are people who will not believe when you speak about reincarnation, we have to see if it is worthwhile to convince them about the past. If they are satisfied with their own notion that there is no reincarnation, then let them be satisfied. After all, who is the loser?

Question: *If somebody lives a good life and reaches nirvana, does this mean he will not reincarnate again?*

Sri Chinmoy: Reincarnation does not mean that if somebody does good things, divine things, he will not come back, and if somebody does bad things, wrong things, he will come back. No, everyone will come back into the world, but one who does good things will naturally have a better life in his next incarnation than the one who does bad things.

Nirvana is the path of negation. Those who follow the path of nirvana want to remain in ultimate Bliss. These people do not want to reincarnate. When they enter into nirvana, there the journey ends for them. The soul feels that it will not walk or run further. It does not want to involve itself with earthly activities.

But there are some souls that want to take a conscious part in God's *Lila* or divine play. They know that reincarnation is absolutely necessary for those who want to serve God here on earth. One has to realize God on earth; on no other planet or plane can there be any realization. Then after realization, some make the promise that they will come back, like Swami Vivekananda and Sri Ramakrishna, who both said that if a single unrealized person remained on earth, then they would be ready to come back.

Question: *Can the soul reincarnate in other worlds after death?*

Sri Chinmoy: The soul that has entered into a human body cannot and does not reincarnate in other worlds. The soul can go through other planes: the physical, vital, mental and psychic sheaths. As soon as the soul leaves the body, it goes through these planes to its own proper region. But there the soul does not reincarnate. The soul is only passing through these places, which are part of its journey of discovery. It is visiting these places, but it does not reincarnate there. The soul reincarnates only in the physical world on earth. Here alone the soul has to manifest its divinity.

There are seven higher worlds and seven lower worlds, and during sleep or meditation everybody's soul travels to these other regions. It may cross through one world after the other, going to the highest world; or again, it can go through the lower regions. An ordinary person is not able to see the soul or feel the soul's movements, but a great spiritual aspirant or a spiritual Master can know what the soul is doing and in which plane the soul is. But reincarnation takes place only here on earth, in this world.

Question: *Will you please explain how it is that the soul evolves only on the planet Earth?*

Sri Chinmoy: The soul manifests only on this planet because this planet is in evolution. Evolution means constant progress, constant achievement. When one wants to make progress, when one wants to go beyond, then this is the place. In other worlds, the cosmic gods and other beings are satisfied with what they have already achieved. They do not want to go one inch beyond their achievement. But here on earth, you are not satisfied, I am not satisfied, nobody is satisfied with what they have achieved. Dissatisfaction does not mean that we are angry with somebody or angry with the world. No! Dissatisfaction means that we have constant aspiration to go beyond and beyond. If we have only an iota of Light, then we want to have more Light. Always we want to expand.

When the creation started, the souls took different paths. Those that wanted the ultimate Truth, the infinite Truth, accepted the human body so that they could someday possess, reveal and manifest the Truth here on earth. According to our Indian tradition, there are thousands of cosmic gods. There are as many presiding deities and gods as there are human beings. These presiding deities and gods remain in the higher worlds, either in the vital world or in the intuitive world or in some higher plane. Right now, according to their limited capacity, they have more power than we have. But when we are liberated and realized, when we are totally one with the Supreme's Consciousness, with the Supreme's Will, then we shall transcend them.

Our human capacity is infinitely greater than that of the so-called presiding deities because they are satisfied, whereas we are not satisfied with what we have. But actually it is not a case of dissatisfaction; it is a case of constant aspiration. We know that our Supreme Father is infinite. We feel that we have not yet become the infinite, but we cry to expand, expand. This planet has that inner urge. On the one hand, it is obscure, it is ignorant, it does not care for divine life. On the other hand, it has that tremendous inner urge of which most human beings are not yet aware. When the inner urge is functioning, then there is no end to our possibilities, no end to our achievements. And when we achieve the infinite, then naturally we surpass the achievements of other worlds.

Question: *Does the soul decide what it is going to go through on the earth plane?*

Sri Chinmoy: It is the soul that determines what we will do here on earth. But our human mind very often makes friends with ignorance and darkness. So what happens is that some souls have minor difficulties while other souls have great difficulties. The soul has accepted human fate. If the physical mind continues to enter into worldly desires and worldly enjoyments, then naturally the soul will have to fight harder to come out of ignorance. For some time it may be completely covered by ignorance.

But at the same time there are some souls that do not have personal problems. They are very large and wide. That kind of mighty soul feels that all humanity is his family. With all sincerity he takes others' problems upon himself, as if they were his own. These souls are most gracious and most willing to accept and harbor others' sufferings. The great spiritual Masters accept the difficulties of humanity as their very own. If they wanted to be completely separated from humanity, they would not suffer. But they choose to suffer by accepting humanity, and they do suffer most intensely for humanity. An ordinary human being who tries to help others who are suffering is himself caught by their suffering. But a realized soul will accept everyone and everything and at the same time he will be flooded with absolute delight. Even while suffering, he has inner delight because he is constantly one with the Divine, with the Supreme.

Question: *In the future, will people always have to aspire like us? Or at some point will people no longer be born on earth?*

Sri Chinmoy: People will continue to be born and evolution will also continue. We are human beings right now, not animals. But we have so many animal qualities: we quarrel, we fight, we have wars, we do so many undivine things. We strangle one another with our hatred and jealousy. Again, we claim that as human beings we are a superior species, we lead a higher life. But in what way? When we enter into ourselves, we see that we are human animals. Still, we have made a little progress. We do not want to remain ferocious animals. Among us, some people are really aspiring and crying for God. Eventually, they will see the Truth and grow into the Truth. This is evolution.

We cannot say that after four hundred or five hundred years there will be no more animal or human incarnations. There will be animals, there will be people, but they will be more perfect. Now, out of ten thousand people, one person may aspire. But the time will come when it will be just the opposite. We will have made such progress that only one person out of ten thousand will not aspire.

We cannot say that there will be another type of evolution in which everybody will descend fully illumined to earth. No! I have worked hard for centuries in order to realize God. Will someone else not have to work at all? Will God do everything for him immediately? No, everybody has to work. God's grace descends only when we work hard, when we aspire most soulfully. True, some people realize God when they are in their teens. You may say, "Oh, I have been meditating for twenty or thirty years, while he has meditated only for five or ten years. How is it that he has realized God?" But you do not know that fifty or seventy years ago in his previous incarnation he meditated intensely for many years. Similarly, the world is now imperfect and only gradually, gradually will it become perfect. It is not that at a fixed time the Light will dawn and all unaspiring people will suddenly run toward the goal. No! Evolution is a slow, gradual process.

Question: How long do we have to continue to reincarnate?

Sri Chinmoy: If one aspires, one expedites one's realization. Otherwise, an ordinary human being takes hundreds and hundreds of incarnations before actual realization takes place. Aspirants who consciously enter into the path of spirituality and try to discipline themselves on the strength of their inner cry will naturally gain their realization sooner than those who are still sleeping and are not yet conscious of the inner life.

Now, after one realizes God, if it is God's Will, that person need not take any more incarnations. If the person is tired, then he may say, "No, I do not want to be of any help to humanity; I only want to realize God. After realization I would like to stay in some other plane of consciousness." But some realized souls will want to go back to the earth-consciousness and serve aspiring humanity. It all depends on the individual and on God's Will.

Question: Do the same souls keep coming back to earth?

Sri Chinmoy: The same souls do return, but the Supreme also creates new souls. For various reasons many souls have asked to take rest before completing their part in the Cosmic Game. Those who strictly followed the Lord Buddha's path and entered into nirvana have not come back. So the Supreme sends new souls into the world to take their place.

Question: *Will the soul usually look the same throughout its incarnations?*

Sri Chinmoy: Yes, it will usually remain the same. But inside the soul is the psychic being, which will grow. Once it takes a form, the soul usually stays that way; but the psychic being grows gradually like a small child. At first, it is very small, but then it grows up. In spiritual seekers the psychic being is more developed than in other human beings.

Question: *Does a beautiful soul always choose a beautiful outer being?*

Sri Chinmoy: All souls are beautiful in origin. But if a certain soul is a special soul, then naturally in its outer manifestation also we will observe sweetness, beauty, serenity, purity and all other divine qualities. What we are within, we are without.

Some people have very fine souls, wonderful souls, yet in their outer manners they are unfortunately very crude, unlit and uncivilized. Why is this? It is because the mind and the vital have not been properly touched with the soul's Light. These individuals do not care for the soul's Light and want to remain very crude, so their lives are lacking in harmony. In their outer manifestation they are absolutely unfortunate and miserable.

There is another reason for disharmony between the outer life and the inner life. If we sow the seed of a mango tree, then naturally we will get mangoes. But at times there are other trees around this tree which ruin its beauty. Similarly, if the members of the family do not care for the spiritual life, if they are absolutely unlit, unaspiring, then they can simply crush the finer qualities of a child. How is it that this wonderful child has come into such an undivine family? That is his fate. But generally if one has a beautiful soul, then the outer expression of the soul will also be beautiful.

Question: *I have read that when the soul takes incarnation in the world, it is like entering a battlefield. Is this true?*

Sri Chinmoy: Each time we come back into the field of manifestation and enter into the world, it is like going into a battle. Here the spiritual seeker, the divine soldier, must fight against fear, doubt, anxiety, worry, limitation, bondage and his worst enemy, death. He is constantly fighting against ignorance, and death is the child of ignorance. He fights and then he either loses the battle and dies, or he conquers all these imperfections and negative forces and goes back to God victorious.

Question: When a child incarnates into a family, is it possible that the child's soul is less highly evolved than the parents' souls?

Sri Chinmoy: Sometimes the parents are inferior, far inferior to the children, and at other times the parents are superior. But just as in the outer world, parents try to make their children wise and well-educated, in the inner world, if parents pray and meditate on their children, the children will make progress and grow.

Question: Do a person's relatives in this incarnation have any connection with his relatives in a past incarnation?

Sri Chinmoy: It depends on God's Will. Your grandfather in this incarnation may not want to keep any connection with your family, so in his next incarnation he will enter into some other family. Sometimes souls try to change the game. They do not want to continue the same game. One soul will say, "I have played my part. Now I want to have a connection with another family." Again, someone may be your grandfather in this incarnation, but if he wants to remain in the same family he can come back to you in another incarnation as your grandson. Naturally, he will come in a different form, as a grandson, a nephew or cousin. In the same way, the mother can come as a daughter, a cousin or a sister. So there is no hard and fast rule.

Question: Did any of your disciples know each other in past incarnations?

Sri Chinmoy: On rare occasions when the Supreme tells me to make disciples aware of their past incarnations, I do so. When the Supreme asks me to do it, that means it is going to help the persons concerned and also others who are present.

It is a great joy to see the members of our family coming back to us from past incarnations. In this incarnation, if the relationship is based on spirituality, then the members can really help each other considerably. If the dear ones, the brothers and sisters, come back again together and they are conscious of what they were, that does help them make real progress. Their progress will be very fast because they will get some benefit from the past. I always say that the past is dust. Yes, the past did not give the disciples realization, but if in the past they had a feeling of oneness or closeness with someone, then when they learn of their past association, they recover that closeness and that oneness. It is not actually the past, but only the disciples' sense of oneness, only their larger Self, that I am bringing back into the disciples' own consciousness.

Question: *What is the relationship of the individual soul to the soul of the country that it is born into?*

Sri Chinmoy: There are many countries. Why does a particular soul enter into a particular country? There are two basic reasons: either the soul has been commanded by the Supreme or the soul has a specific preference for that country. Why will a soul care for a particular country? It is because the soul has its own inner propensities. It feels that it has some inner intuitive capacity or other quality which can be easily brought into manifestation if it takes incarnation in a particular country. If a particular soul has dynamism, it will try to take incarnation in America, not India. Again, if it cries for inner harmony and peace, then it will try to take incarnation in India. If the soul wants vastness and a combination of the mind and the heart in mental and psychic awakening, then it will incarnate in Australia.

The individual soul may want a particular country, and at the same time the soul of a country also wants a particular type of soul, so that its own reality can be manifested. Each soul has something special to offer to its country. So, the soul of each country meditates upon the highest reality to get souls which will be of help to it.

If the soul likes a specific country, the Supreme can accept or reject the soul's choice. But ninety-nine times out of a hundred the

Supreme approves the soul's choice. However, if the Supreme makes the choice, then usually the individual soul cannot alter the Supreme's Will. Again, just as we sometimes do not listen to our boss, the soul also may do this. But usually the individual soul listens to the Supreme because souls have more Light than earthbound beings.

Each individual soul has a special role to play in the country that is accepting it. But once it plays its role, its goes to another country. Of course, the soul can have two or three incarnations in a particular country and then go to another place. Again, some souls may want to take more incarnations in a particular place.

What is the role that the individual soul plays? It is the role of a flower on a tree. When there are many flowers on a tree, then the tree looks beautiful. Each soul is like a flower and each country is like a tree.

Question: When does the soul enter the body?

Sri Chinmoy: Between six and eight months before birth is the usual time for the soul to enter into the body. On rare occasions it may enter at the time of conception. The latest time for the soul to enter is usually about thirteen or fourteen days before the child is born. In very rare cases, the soul enters into the body just two or three days before birth and sometimes it may even come shortly after birth. At that time the soul may be waiting until the last moment before making a decision because it is doubtful about the family. Some souls feel that by waiting for a longer time they will be able to make a better decision. Again, some souls simply take longer to make the decision just as some people take more time to make a decision than others. But some souls do not wait; they know immediately what to do and it is done within a few months after the time of conception.

Question: What does the soul do in the body before birth?

Sri Chinmoy: The soul remains absolutely silent in the body. It is like a witness. It just observes the physical organs. But what it sees when it comes into the world for the first time at birth will give it a kind of fear and frustration. The soul is a spark of the Divine, but when it enters into the world, immediately it sees ignorance. The soul has accepted the world, but the moment the child is born, the soul sees through the eyes of the child and what it sees creates fear within the soul. The soul at that time does not see anything wonderful; it sees something ferocious like a lion that wants to devour it. Then the soul says: "It is I who have taken this body. I have to fight. Why should I act like a coward? Why should I leave the body? In this body, with this body, I shall have to fight for God and establish His Kingdom here on earth."

Question: Is the soul always assured that it will find its true mission during each new lifetime on earth?

Sri Chinmoy: Before taking human incarnation, the soul gets the inner message about its divine purpose on earth. It is fully conscious of its mission and it comes here with the direct approval or sanction of the Supreme. But during the lifetime, the workings of the physical mind sometimes cover up the divine inspiration and the true purpose of the soul. Then the mission of the soul cannot come forward. However, if we start aspiring with the mind, the heart and the soul, then we can learn the purpose of our existence here on earth.

There is a constant battle going on between the divine and undivine in each human being. The ignorance of the world tries to devour human aspiration. At the present stage of evolution, most human beings live in the undivine vital, where all is desire, anxiety and excitement. That is why they are unconscious of the soul's needs.

Question: Is it predestined how far the soul will progress in an incarnation?

Sri Chinmoy: In some cases it is predestined and in some cases there is no fixed limit; it depends on how much grace the soul receives.

Question: Can you help me to leave the body as soon as possible, and help me to reincarnate in a place that is high and very cold, with plenty of fog and snow?

Sri Chinmoy: I have the power to do what you are asking me. But if

I go to the Supreme with your petition, immediately He will laugh at me and say, "What kind of disciple do you have who, when he is just starting to open his eyes, wants to close them again?" Climate has nothing to do with God-realization. Sri Ramana Maharshi and Sri Aurobindo were from South India, which has a very hot climate, but this did not prevent them from realizing God. There are many aspirants living in caves far up in the Himalayas, in the eternal snows, who have not been able to realize God. The climate has nothing to do with it. It is the inner heat of aspiration that can bring God-realization, not outer climate conditions.

Rabindranath Tagore, India's greatest poet, used to write six or eight poems daily. He once thought that if he could retire to a solitary place he could write much better poetry. So he left his house and confined himself to a solitary place in the mountains. While there, he was not able to write a single piece of poetry. He discovered that it is not the environment that is most important, but the inner inspiration. God has chosen the conditions under which you are living your present life. It is like a play. The stage is set and the curtain has been raised for you to perform your part and advance along the spiritual path. Your present conditions are the best possible ones for your advancement. Now you want to leave the body and enter into a new body in a future incarnation so you can have an environment that you think will suit you best. But this kind of life would be worse than your present one because it is chosen by your mind, whereas your present life was chosen by God.

If your past actions of this incarnation are bothering you, I wish to tell you that my philosophy is "the past is dust." Whatever you did a few years ago or even yesterday should not concern you. The past is not important. It is what you do from now on that can expedite your progress. Now you have a spiritual Master in a physical body to help you. It is the present and the future flowing into the present that can give you liberation.

Question: *When the soul reincarnates in a new body, what happens to the spiritual heart? Does it also go from one lifetime to another like the soul does?*

Sri Chinmoy: When the soul leaves the body, it takes with it the quintessence of the experiences that the body, mind, vital and heart had in this present life. But when it goes to the soul's region, it does not take the heart, vital or mind with it. When it reincarnates in a new body, the soul—or you can say, the psychic being or *Purusha*—is the same. It still carries the realizations and experiences from its past lives. But it accepts a new heart, new mind, new vital and new body.

Question: *When the soul comes back, does it take back the same vital?*

Sri Chinmoy: It may take either the same one or a vital that is more evolved. It is like buying things in a shop. You leave something in the shop and then you come back and get your own thing or you get something more beautiful. Instead of keeping your old wristwatch, you may buy a new one. And somebody else, who has less money, will like your old one.

Question: *If a disciple does not realize God while his Guru is in the body, how would the Guru be able to help the disciple in that person's next incarnation if there were no other living Guru through whom he could work?*

Sri Chinmoy: The Guru does not need another Guru to work through. Four thousand years ago Lord Krishna had disciples when he was actually on earth, and even now there are still many of his disciples who have not accepted another Master. They reincarnate, for instance, into a family which is following the path of Krishna, so that Krishna will be able to give them liberation in his own way. It is similar with the other great Masters. There are many of Sri Ramakrishna's disciples who have come back to earth. They have not gone to any other Guru, yet they are being fulfilled. But if they wanted another Master, Ramakrishna would naturally tell them to go to another one. Some disciples of great Masters have accepted other Gurus. Some of my own disciples, in fact, were with Lord Krishna.

How can a spiritual Master help his disciples if they do not go to some other Guru? He can do it through his conscious will, his soul's will. I am here on earth, and although I am not in England or Puerto Rico, through my conscious will, early in the morning after 2 a.m. I concentrate on all those who are my disciples there. To concentrate for a fleeting second is enough, but I use more than that to know what the soul is doing, and how far the soul has gone. So even while remaining in the physical, which is real bondage, a spiritual Master can help his disciples in different parts of the world. Then when he leaves the body, he is totally free. From the other shore the spiritual Master works through the soul's Light or will power. The soul's Light can be offered from any plane of consciousness, from the highest plane right down to the earth plane. From the higher worlds the Master can easily connect with the disciple's aspiring soul, and the disciple can respond to the Master's Light. It is in this way that the Master can, does and must help the disciple.

Question: *If one is a spiritual person, will his next incarnation be different from that of an ordinary person?*

Sri Chinmoy: Certainly. If a soul is very spiritually advanced, it will not take an ordinary life because it will have already gone through the ordinary life. Each incarnation is a stepping-stone towards our ultimate God-realization. When one has consciously aspired in his last incarnation, his future birth will hold more opportunities for his spiritual progress. Now if a seeker actually started his spiritual life in his past incarnation, if he was really sincere in his spiritual practices in his previous life, then naturally in this life he will start aspiring at a very young age. He will be born into a spiritual family where he will be encouraged to lead the spiritual life from his very birth, and he will start aspiring when he is ten or twelve or fourteen or sixteen. It may happen, however, that his circumstances are bad. Then even if he had started his spiritual life in his past incarnation, in this incarnation he will go slowly because he will not get help from his parents or from his environment. But it is not a risk; it is a journey. In the process of evolution the soul covers thousands of inner miles, gaining different experiences, and it is these experiences that eventually give the soul its fullest realization.

But if the person was a very great aspirant who was about to realize God, then he will almost definitely come into a very highly developed spiritual family, and from the very beginning he will be able to enter into the true spiritual life. Most of the real spiritual Masters enter into very highly developed spiritual families. God may send a spiritual Master into an unaspiring family, since He is not bound by any plan, but in most cases spiritual Masters come into spiritual families.

Question: You said before that each incarnation is a stepping-stone towards our God-realization. Does that mean that we can not reach God in this life?

Sri Chinmoy: No, not at all. It is a matter of previous background and aspiration. If one has been aspiring and meditating in previous lifetimes, then there is no reason why he cannot attain realization in his present incarnation on the strength of his aspiration. Since we are all progressing towards realization, in one incarnation or another, this realization is bound to take place. As I said, it is a matter of the aspirant's spiritual development.

Question: If a seeker dies, do all his responsibilities and work cease in the period between his death and his rebirth? Or is he able to work consciously, or in some way continue the work that he started, before he comes back to earth?

Sri Chinmoy: It depends on the achievement of the individual seeker. Suppose an advanced seeker has left the body, and suppose there were many things he had wanted to accomplish on earth when he was here, but he could not. What will he do? When he leaves the body, he has to go through the physical sheath, vital sheath, mental sheath and other sheaths, and then he will enter into the soul's region. If it is not his own will to come back to the earth for ten or twenty years, and if it is also not God's Will for him to come back, then in the meantime he can get his work done on earth through someone still on earth who is dearest to him. Because he is an advanced soul, he can apply his soul's will from where he is to his dearest one on earth. But ordinary human beings cannot do this when they leave the body.

Say, for example, someone wants his children to get their Master's degree. After leaving the body, as long as the soul is in the vital world, in the subtle sheath, it can send these desires and ordinary wishes to the children. Through the vital, the soul still keeps some contact with earth. Ordinary earthly desires can be fulfilled or enhanced by the will of the deceased person who has left the body a year or two earlier.

But when the soul goes back to the higher planes, at that time it will not desire, it will not operate in this way on sons or daughters who are still on earth. The soul will not care for the children's earthly satisfaction, for the fulfillment of their teeming earthly desires. But if the soul has Heavenly aspiration for its dear ones, from the higher worlds it will try to increase their aspiration and help them in every possible way. The soul will go to mighty souls who are still on earth and beg them to help the dear ones in the spiritual world. But if the soul is very highly evolved and it sees that somebody is really sincere and aspiring, then the soul itself can help that person.

Question: When someone dies, in his next incarnation does he maintain the same level of aspiration?

Sri Chinmoy: When someone dies, in his next incarnation he definitely maintains the same level of aspiration within his new body and new consciousness. But this aspiration usually cannot come to the fore immediately because the earth-consciousness is full of darkness and ignorance. He has to fight against tremendous opposition for a few years or, in most cases, quite a number of years. But again, if the soul is most powerful, if the seeker himself has unusual inner strength, then either from the very dawn of his life or in a few years' time he regains his old aspiration and continues to march and run towards his destined goal.

Question: Is the length of time the soul remains in the soul's world between incarnations determined by the aspiration of the previous incarnation? If it is an elevated soul, will it incarnate sooner?

Sri Chinmoy: It is according to the aspiration and according to the necessity. You may have the aspiration to do something, but at the same time God may not feel the necessity for you to do it. From your side aspiration is necessary. You are aspiring to come back again and to start the game again immediately. It is as if you have played for half an hour and now you are taking a short rest. Then, if you do not want to rest any longer, you say: "Give me the opportunity to finish the game and go back." But God may say, "No, I want you to take rest for a while longer." At that time you cannot return. But if your aspiration and God's necessity become one, then certainly you can come back.

Some souls reincarnate almost immediately, without even going to the soul's region. Suppose somebody dies prematurely in an accident. At that time his soul may go only up to the vital sheath and from there, if a spiritual figure or the divine grace intervenes, in seven or eight months it will take incarnation in a new family.

Most ordinary souls come back again after staying in the soul's world for six or seven or, at most, twenty years. The time in the soul's world is used by the soul to assimilate its experiences on earth. Great people, such as great scientists or spiritual figures, do not take birth again as rapidly as ordinary people. Very rarely will you see a great figure in any field who will take incarnation again very soon. Some stay in the soul's world for seventy years or more. In certain cases, spiritual Masters wait a hundred or two hundred years before reincarnating. But there is no hard and fast rule. If the Supreme wants them to come back to earth, they have to come back even if they do not want to. It is the soul's own decision, plus the approval of the Supreme, that determines how long it takes for a person to reincarnate.

Question: *If someone is gifted in one area, does this mean that his soul was originally given this potentiality, or did he try to achieve this for many lives and then finally achieve it?*

Sri Chinmoy: Potentiality everybody has, like a lump of clay. When one potter shapes it, the pot becomes most beautiful, and another potter makes a pot that is not so beautiful. The essence of both pots is the same clay. Likewise, in spirit we are all one. But while the one potter is molding, you may ask, "Why has he molded that particular pot so attractively?" There is something in that particular potter that is called conscious aspiration. In every other respect my essence, your essence, everybody's essence remains the same. But while that particular potter is molding, there is something inside him which gives him the opportunity to make something unique.

So it is not that right from the beginning a particular potentiality was given. No, it was destined for each person to receive very limited freedom, which started right from the beginning of creation. Now this freedom means potential. Some use this potential for the spiritual life, some use it for music, some for poetry and so on. Some do not use it at all. But potentiality will not develop into reality unless and until it is brought to the fore and developed by its possessor.

Question: Do the physical abilities we possess have anything to do with our achievements in our previous incarnations?

Sri Chinmoy: No, our physical abilities depend on how much determination, perseverance and aspiration we have. If we have very few abilities, it does not mean that we were undivine in our previous incarnations. No, it is only that some people do not try; they do not work hard. In this world, nothing can be achieved without working very hard for it.

Question: According to reincarnation, our next life is supposed to be a reflection and extension of this life. Could you please elaborate on this?

Sri Chinmoy: Our next life need not be a reflection of the previous life. Suppose somebody has played his role most satisfactorily. Suppose you were a great artist in your previous incarnation and your soul does not want to have that experience again. If your soul wants you to have the experience of being a politician, then your previous experience as an artist may not come to the fore at all. If the soul has not completed its role in a specific field and wants to continue the same process, only then will one life be a reflection of the previous life. Otherwise, the soul may change the characteristics, nature and propensities of the human being totally.

Question: Does it help you to know what kind of animal you were in your past incarnations, or what kind of person you were?

Sri Chinmoy: When we enter into the inner life and develop our inner consciousness, our inner capacity, we get reminiscences of our past incarnations. Deep in our meditation we can easily feel that we had previous lives. And if we know that we had a past, and if we know that the present is not yet complete and that we ourselves can never remain incomplete, then the urge of the present will take us to the future where we will achieve our completeness. At the same time, we can expedite our progress if we have a Master. If we are most dedicated to the inner life and if we have a Guru, then we can make twenty incarnations' progress in one lifetime.

Now suppose we know that we were a deer in our last animal incarnation. The only advantage is that we can think of our speed and say: "In the animal incarnation I ran so fast, and at that time I did not have the advanced soul which I now have. In this incarnation let me run even faster!" As soon as we remember that we ran fast in a previous incarnation, we feel inspired to run fast in this incarnation. If we know our past incarnation, then we can utilize it positively; at that time inspiration comes forward very quickly. If somebody knows that he was a seeker, then he gets a little joy and confidence. "I started my journey in my past incarnation, but it was a very long and arduous road. In this incarnation I am still walking along the same path, but I do not have as far to go this time. Also, it is easier because I have a little help. I have the capacity. I have the willingness. I have the experience. With a spiritual Master guiding me, I shall easily reach my goal."

But only on very rare occasions do we utilize knowledge of our past incarnations properly. Most of the time it does not give us any encouragement at all. If we know that in our past incarnation we were a thief or something undivine, will this give us any inspiration or aspiration? No! Immediately we will think: "Oh, I was a thief and in this incarnation I am trying to become a saint. Impossible! It is hopeless to try to become spiritual in this life." Even in this incarnation if we do a few things wrong, it takes us a long time to come out of despair. We think: "I was so bad. I did this. I did that. Now how am I going to become pure? How am I going to realize God?" Even if we did something wrong four years ago, it may still bother us.

On the other hand, suppose we know that in our past incarnation we were someone very great and in this incarnation we see that we are nothing. Then we will feel miserable. We will curse God and we will curse ourselves. We will say: "If I was so great, how is it that in this incarnation I am so useless? What unthinkable thing have I done to deserve this fate? God is harsh; He does not care for me." But we misunderstand God. God wants to have a different experience through us in this incarnation, and we think that God is just being unkind.

An aspirant wants inner joy, the joy that fulfills him and fulfills God. This he will never get from his past incarnations. If he enters into some past incarnation and sees that he was the President of the United States, still he will get no satisfaction. He will see that as President, his life was full of misery, frustration and all kinds of suffering. For real joy, an aspirant has to go forward in the spiritual life with his own aspiration and inner cry, with his own concentration and meditation.

The best thing for us is not to think of the past. Our goal is not behind us; it is ahead of us. Our direction is forward, not backward. For a spiritual person I always say: "The past is dust." I say this because the past has not given us what we want. What we want is God-realization. Knowing our previous incarnations does not help our God-realization. God-realization depends entirely on our inner cry. The important thing is not the past, but the present. We must say: "I have no past. I am beginning here and now with God's grace and my own aspiration. Now let me start to run. How far I have run in the past is immaterial. Let me think only of how far I am going to run in this life."

Right now we see the past as something totally different from the present, and the present as something totally different from the future. Once we realize God, at that time the past, present and future become all one. They form a circle, which is our own inner being, our entire life. At that time, we can easily see back to our previous incarnations and know what we were.

If you want to know about your past incarnations, certainly God will give you the capacity. But the most important thing is not past incarnations or future incarnations, but what you want here and now. You want God, and if you meditate soulfully, God is bound to grant you that boon. You will possess Him and you will claim Him as your very own.

Question: If a person is a very advanced seeker and develops the ability to see his past incarnations, will this actually hinder his progress? In other words, is it always harmful if you discover you were a thief or something in the past?

Sri Chinmoy: If you are meditating most sincerely in this life, your inner strength will automatically develop and you will reach the point where you will not be disturbed even if you see that you were the worst possible criminal in a previous incarnation. You know that you have come here to transform yourself, to go towards the Divine. The Lord Buddha disclosed his previous incarnations: he was a goat and many other things. But because he had realized God and had entered into the highest Truth, it was easy for him to say what he was in his previous births. To him it was immaterial if he was most ordinary in his previous incarnations.

Question: If a man dies and he is very fond of a dog or other animal, and if he has compassion for that animal, will this cause him to reincarnate as an animal?

Sri Chinmoy: The greatest scripture in India and the largest in the world is called the *Mahabharata*. In the *Mahabharata* there are quite a few stories in which a man later reincarnates as an animal. There is a famous story about a king named Bharata, who was very fond of deer and who supposedly became a deer in his next incarnation. Now Sri Ramakrishna was very fond of his dearest disciple Naren, who later became Swami Vivekananda. He used to seek out the disciple and to talk to him, and people thought that Ramakrishna was mad. So one day Naren said to him: "What are you doing? Do you not know the story of King Bharata, who was so attached to a deer that he became a deer in his next incarnation? Your fate is also going to be like that, if you constantly think of an ordinary human being like me." Ramakrishna took Naren seriously and asked Mother Kali: "Is this true that my fate will be also like that of King Bharata?" She said: "That is stupid! You are fond of Naren because you are seeing God in him. It is not because he is beautiful or something else. No! You are fond of him because the manifestation of God is expressed in him. That is why you are so delighted when you see him."

If you show compassion to someone, that does not mean that you are going to become that person. If a beggar comes to you for alms and you show your utmost compassion to the beggar and give him some money or food, it does not mean that you are going to become a beggar yourself. Similarly, if you have a dog, you can show your love for the dog because it is extremely faithful to you and so on. But this does not mean that you will become a dog because you admire the qualities of the dog that you love. The good qualities that the dog has, the faithfulness the dog has, you can have in your human existence, without taking an animal life. Just by showing attachment to an animal you are not going to become an animal. You have already passed through that stage. What you get is the good qualities of the animal.

RELIGION

Question: *What is religion?*

Sri Chinmoy: Religion is God. Religion is Truth. God and Truth are one. But when I say that my religion is God, there is a possibility that you may misunderstand me, while if I say that my religion is Truth, immediately you will see eye to eye with me. Let me be a little clearer. If I say that my religion is Lord Krishna and you must accept him, your eyes will emit fire. But if I say that my religion is Truth, you will jump up and say, "So is mine." Now, instead of saying, "You must accept my religion," if I say, "Let us accept the universal Truth," you will cry out, "Already accepted, thank you, my friend!"

Religion is an act of vision that guides and leads us to the Beyond. Religion is intuitive. Religion is so near and dear to each of us, so familiar to our soul and so intimate to our heart, that it requires no definition. Religion is that very intuition which defies explanation but which is self-embodying and self-explanatory Truth.

Religion is not fanaticism. Religion, in the purest form, is a feeling of the universal oneness of Truth. A fanatic never sees the Truth in its totality, even in his wildest imagination. A fanatic has nothing to offer the world precisely because he has not kept his heart's door open wide, and because he lacks the capacity to commune with his soul.

Religion speaks. It speaks more significantly than words. Unfortunately, its message is often subject to ruthless distortion. Nevertheless, in the long run, it triumphantly voices forth the Truth.

When we think of religion, our attitude should be sympathetic and appreciative rather than critical and competitive. Criticism and competition create disharmony, which is a destructive force. Sympathy and appreciation create harmony, which is a creative force. Harmony, moreover, is the life-breath of existence.

Religion is a living challenge to the highest in human beings to face the stormy problems of life. True, there are countless problems. But there is also an omnipotent power. Strangely enough, this power utilizes our problems as true instruments for the blessing of humanity.

The divine aim of religion is to release the pent-up reservoir of human energy. Life itself is religion—intimate, continuous and fulfilling. Let us live openly and freely. Let us have the religion which includes all human beings who have ever lived on earth, those who are now on the world stage, and those who shall dwell here during untold ages to come. Ours is the religion that will perfect the order of the world. Ours is the religion that will ply between the shores of Eternity and Infinity.

Question: *What are the signs of a true religion?*

Sri Chinmoy: Forgiveness, compassion, tolerance, brotherhood and the feeling of oneness are the signs of a true religion. If you live in your oneness-heart, you will feel the essence of all religions, which is the love of God.

True religion has a universal quality. It does not find fault with other religions. False religions will find fault with other religions; they will say that theirs is the only valid religion and their prophet is the only savior. But a true religion will feel that all the prophets are saviors of mankind.

Question: *Why do we need religion?*

Sri Chinmoy: We need religion because we want to go beyond the finite in order to commune with the Infinite. This is not only possible but also inevitable, for in us, there is a conscious being which envisions God's reality in totality.

Religion is a spontaneous experience and never a theoretical knowledge. This experience is immensely practical, and we can use it consciously at every moment of our earthly existence.

Religion has never been thrust upon man. It has sprung from the deepest need of his inner being. When this inner being comes to the fore and looks around, it feels God's all-permeating Immanence; when it looks up, it feels God's all-surpassing Transcendence as its own divine heritage. Religion has two lives: the outer and the inner. It offers its outer life to seekers in the preliminary stage of vital and emotional aspiration. It offers its inner life to the universal meditation and God-realization.

Question: *You have written: "Sri Krishna meditated and became God the divine Light. Christ meditated and became God the divine compassion. God wants us to meditate to become God the divine Life." Why do you not also include Abraham, Moses and Mohammed here?*

Sri Chinmoy: Indeed, Abraham, Moses and Mohammed were also God's representatives on earth. God's conscious servants are like a family with many members. Suppose there is a family with ten members, who are all endowed with exceptional musical talents. You happen to be one of the brothers, and you give preference to some of your brothers and sisters over others because of your own inner feelings. You are in no way saying that the ones you prefer are the only musicians in the family, whereas the others are not musicians at all. You are just more fond of some of your brothers and sisters than of others.

Question: *My wife, who is otherwise the most reasonable of beings, insists that all religious beliefs are delusions brought about by existential anxiety. Most people find the thought unbearable that there is no meaning in life except for the biological and rational fact of life itself. This, she feels, should satisfy anybody. The fact of death, she believes, is to be similarly faced as a biological reality. It is an old theory, which, I realize, can neither be proved or disproved at an intellectual level.*

Sri Chinmoy: The ultimate Truth concerning life and death can never be adequately explained or expressed. It can only be felt by the aspirant. I concur fully with you that this view, as well as that expressed by your wife, cannot be verified intellectually. However, what she feels about life and death may not necessarily be so. Another view is that life is the link between birth and death, and at the same time, it is life that precedes birth and succeeds death.

Human memory is not the first and last word of creation. If, at the age of eighty, I fail to recollect an incident that took place in my own life at the age of four, it does not mean that I did not exist then.

Just as a series of years passes by between the ages of four and eighty, so is there a series of lives which connects the present with the distant past and projects itself into the imminent future.

Then, too, there is something beyond the comprehension of our limited body-consciousness. Even while a man is grossly involved in his most ordinary physical activities, he may feel within himself, at times, some strange truths. These are usually unfamiliar and greatly elevating. These truths come from a higher or deeper world, from a different plane of consciousness, and they knock at his mental door. Thus he possesses and is possessed by forces beyond his ordinary awareness.

It is when we put ourselves in tune with these higher forces, indeed with the universal harmony, that life ceases to be unbearable. I entirely agree with your wife's point of view that when a person sees no meaning in life, no goal or purpose, the thought, nay, the life itself, becomes intolerable. However, regarding religious beliefs, I wish to place before her an analogy: I am now living in a New York apartment. If a child calls on me and asks, "Is there a place called Cologne?" I shall reply, "Certainly, my child, it is in Germany." Suppose he says, "You must prove it to me!" Now how can I prove it to him, apart from showing him maps and photos? I can only tell him that I have personally visited Cologne and that there are millions of others who have also done so. His doubt cannot negate the existence of the city.

Similarly those who have realized God fully have every right to tell us that there is a God. Simply because we have not realized Him, we cannot deny the existence of God. Just as the child has to satisfy his physical eyes by going to Cologne, we can only prove to ourselves the reality of God by seeing Him. And this quest for realization would give to an otherwise purposeless life an unparalleled meaning and direction.

Question: *Is there any difference between one religion and another religion? Does Yoga demand renunciation of all religions?*

Sri Chinmoy: There is no fundamental difference between one religion and another because each religion embodies the ultimate Truth. So Yoga does not interfere with any religion. Anybody can practice

Yoga. I have disciples who are Catholics, Protestants, Jews and so forth. One can practice Yoga irrespective of religion. Now if one has been taught Hinduism, he may be afraid of accepting Catholicism and vice versa. But the real aspirant who has launched into spirituality and Yoga will find no difficulty in remaining in his own religion. I tell my disciples not to give up their own religion. If they remain in their own religion and practice the spiritual life and the inner discipline, they will go faster because their own religion will give them constant confidence in what they are doing and confirm what they are actually practicing in their life.

Question: I have studied a good many scriptures. I also indulge in preaching about spirituality, religion, the inner life and so forth. But personally, I feel a barren desert within me. There is no satisfaction at all from what I am doing. I feel I am wasting my own precious time and that of others along with it. Could you possibly enlighten me regarding this?

Sri Chinmoy: I fully sympathize with you. You are not alone. There are a good many human souls sailing in the same boat. The study of books and scriptures can give us information to quote from, and a certain understanding; they can give us, at most, inspiration, but nothing more. By borrowing others' ideas, we can never be truly enlightened in our inner life. It is by studying the eternal book of Truth within us, by listening constantly to the voice of the inner Self, that we can become spiritually illumined. It is then that we find joy in our inner life. We must see God first and then we shall be godlike. To be truly godlike, talking must give way to becoming. Let me tell you a true story.

In a certain village in Bengal, India, a rich man's servant arrived daily at his Master's house by crossing a river in a ferry boat. One day there was a violent storm. The ferry could not ply across the raging river and the servant was late in arriving. His Master was furious. "You fool," he shouted, "if you utter Krishna's name three times, you will see that you do not need a boat. You will be able to walk across the river!"

The following day, as the storm showed no signs of abating, the poor servant was threatened with the same situation. But in his simple faith, he obeyed his Master's instructions. From the very depths of his heart, he uttered the name of Krishna. Lo! The miracle of miracles. He felt a power propelling him towards the water. He was able to walk upon the very waves. Thus he crossed the river.

On hearing the story, the Master's joy knew no bounds. A swelling pride rose from his heart. Was it not his advice that had brought about the success? "I never knew that my advice had such great power," he thought. "Let me enjoy this miracle myself."

He went to the river, whose waters were now calm and serene. He uttered Krishna's name three times and began to cross. But fear and doubt tortured his whole being, and although he shouted the sacred name hundreds of times, his attempt was fruitless. He was drowned.

Now what do we learn from this story? The servant had sincere faith in his Master. He also had an implicit faith in Lord Krishna. It was this absolute faith in a divine power that saved him and proved the power of Krishna's grace.

Similarly, a speaker, in spite of his own lame faith, can inspire a genuine faith in his listeners. But it is by being truly spiritual himself that he can help others most significantly. If we want to convince others of the Truth, our highest authority must come only from the direct knowledge of Truth and not from any scripture. In the divine play, unillumined authority plays the role of a lamp, while Truth in realization plays the role of the Light.

Question: *Master, does your spiritual philosophy incorporate the Christian concept of redemption?*

Sri Chinmoy: In a very broad sense my philosophy does include the concept of redemption, but it puts more emphasis on human liberation from ignorance. It is through conscious liberation from ignorance that today's man the finite grows into tomorrow's God the infinite. According to my understanding, the Savior Christ lived and died to liberate humanity from ignorance and imperfection—sin—through the example of his own earth-experience.

Question: *Will following your path be in conflict with Jesus when he said, "I and the Father are one. No one can go to the Father except through me"?*

Sri Chinmoy: The conflict is in the seeker's mind, not in the seeker's heart. The Christ was saying that only aspiration will lead you to realization. If you think of the Christ as just someone who stayed on earth for thirty-three years, you will be mistaken. Think of the Christ as the representative of the One who is birthless and deathless. Again, if you think that he was the first God-realized soul, then you are again mistaken. Sri Krishna and Lord Buddha lived before that. We have to know that the Christ-Consciousness, the Buddha-Consciousness and the Krishna-Consciousness are all part and parcel of the same Supreme reality. If you have a Master in whom you have faith, he will help you realize the Christ-Consciousness, Buddha-Consciousness and Krishna-Consciousness. On the one hand, these great spiritual Masters represent the Absolute; on the other hand, they are the Absolute. No matter what path you follow, it will lead you to one destination. You may call it Christ-Consciousness, another will call it Krishna-Consciousness or Buddha-Consciousness. But there can be no conflict, since Truth is one. Any path you follow will help you realize the Truth.

Question: *In the Hindu tradition one speaks of* atman *equals* Brahman, *the individual soul equals the universal Soul. Jesus Christ once said, "I and my Father are one." Are these two statements, coming from two different spiritual backgrounds one and the same?*

Sri Chinmoy: It is the same statement. We say in Sanskrit *atman* and *Paramatman*, the individual soul and the Supreme Self. God comes down into the manifestation and takes the form of the individual soul. Then the individual soul, in the process of its evolution, reaches and becomes the Supreme Self, *Paramatman*. But to fulfill Himself integrally and wholly in the material world, God needs the individual soul, the *atman*.

The statements are the same. When Christ said, "I and my Father are one," it was like saying that *atman* and *Paramatman* are one. That is why in India we say, "*Atmanam viddhi*"— "know thyself."

If you know yourself, then you have known God, because in essence there is no difference between you and God. Self-realization is God-realization and God-realization is Self-realization. For this reason, in India we also say, "*Soham asmi*"— "He am I," and "*Aham Brahma*"— "I am *Brahman*."

In the same vein, all the esoteric traditions have always maintained that true knowledge is seeking within. How may I know this. Jesus said, "The Kingdom of Heaven is within you." The modern conception of Heaven, in the West at any rate, is of some far-off place in the beyond where there is perpetual milk and honey. The modern twentieth century achievement is pressing us backward even more in our conception of Heaven.

Question: What has to prevail in religion—reason or the sentiment of the heart?

Sri Chinmoy: In religion, the feeling of a oneness-heart has to prevail, and nothing else. Religion is not a matter of reason. If we live in our oneness-heart, we will feel the essence of all religions, which is love of God. But if we live in the mind, we will only try to separate one religion from another and see how their ideologies differ. It is the heart that can have a true intuitive understanding of the height and breadth of all religions. It is the heart that sees and feels the inner harmony and oneness of all religions.

Question: Why does God allow antagonism between people of different religions?

Sri Chinmoy: Why does God allow some individuals to be undivine and hostile? The only answer I can give you is that His compassion right now is infinitely more powerful than His Justice. God allows everything, but the individual has to know what he should do. We exist only because God allows us to exist on earth. You may say that other people are worse than we are, that some people quarrel and fight or doubt God more than we do. But we have to ask ourselves whether we sometimes do quarrel and fight, whether we at times cherish doubt. The answer will be, "Yes, we do, although perhaps a little less than others." If God allows us to do something, then we cannot blame God if He allows somebody else to do the same thing. It is only a matter of degree. We may doubt God, say, once in six months; someone else may doubt Him at every second. But if we say, "In this incarnation I have never doubted God," then that will be a mistake. Again, if we do something wrong and another person also does it to an infinitely greater degree, that is still no excuse to criticize and attack that other person. Let us worry about perfecting our own nature. God will take care of others.

RENUNCIATION

Question: Speak to us about renunciation.

Sri Chinmoy: From the strict spiritual point of view, the so-called earthly renunciation is not necessary for an aspirant. If renunciation means leaving aside one's family, if renunciation means not caring for society or humanity, then I wish to say that no matter what we renounce today, there will be something else tomorrow to stand in our way. Today our family is the obstacle; tomorrow it will be our friends; the day after tomorrow it will be our country, and the day after, the world. There is no end to this kind of renunciation.

Certainly we have to renounce in the spiritual life. What are we going to renounce? We are going to renounce fear, doubt, imperfection, ignorance and death. We are not going to renounce individuals; we are going to renounce qualities which stand in the way of our union with the Divine. When we enter into the spiritual life, we get the opportunity to renounce, or rather, to transform these qualities. When we speak of renouncing or transforming something, we immediately think of ignorance. Truly it is the one thing that we have to transform in our spiritual life.

If somebody says he is going to renounce the world in order to realize God, then I wish to say that he is mistaken. Today he will renounce the world and tomorrow he will find that the God he is seeking is nowhere else; He is in the world itself. What is preventing him from seeing God in the world? It is his attitude. In order to see God in humanity, he has to remove the veil of ignorance that lies between him and the rest of the world. When the veil is removed, there is nothing to be renounced. One sees God, one feels God, one is in God, here and beyond.

A perfect renunciation and a complete self-surrender are the obverse and reverse of the same ambrosial coin.

299

Question: *Am I correct in saying that the Buddha is one of those who advocated a kind of escape from the world?*

Sri Chinmoy: If you say that the Buddha's philosophy is one of escape, that would be a misinterpretation. What the Buddha actually wanted was to put an end to human suffering in the world. Like a divine warrior, he played his part on the world-scene. He did not use the term "God," but he used the terms "Truth" and "Light." He stayed on earth for forty years after his own realization, trying to elevate the consciousness of humanity. He went here and there, always preaching, preaching. Even though he had such a frail body, he went on giving talks and trying to bring down peace, Light and bliss. But he saw that the people he was trying to help were not receiving, and he came to feel that it was almost impossible to end human suffering.

Then he discovered there is something called nirvana, where all desires are extinguished, where all earthly propensities are extinguished, where all limitations are extinguished. There you go beyond the domain of the physical, and all is inner existence. So he said, "Now I am very, very tired. Let me enter into that blissful state and take rest." He decided to let other divine soldiers come into the world to fight for the full manifestation of God. Now, if one soldier fights bravely for many years and then takes rest, and if another soldier coming after him decides to keep on fighting until he can manifest the Highest, naturally we feel that this second person is playing his role with more strength, more energy, more stamina. If one wants to manifest after realization, naturally he is leading humanity one step ahead, because manifestation God also needs.

But to say that the first person did not play his role or wanted to escape is wrong. As an individual, the Buddha did play his role. Realization the Buddha had. Revelation he had. He also started manifesting, but ultimately he did not want to play a conscious part in the field of manifestation. He did not want to participate in the Cosmic Play anymore. As an individual, the Buddha never advocated escape or negating the world. What he advocated was prayer and meditation to enter into the everlasting blissful state of consciousness. You can say he opened up another path, or you can call it a house. Those who enter into that particular path or house do not come back into the world after God-realization, whereas those who enter into some other house do come back to the world.

It is not that if you enter into nirvana you are caught there. No, if you enter into nirvana, usually you do not come back because you do not want to. But there are some Masters who go beyond the state of nirvana and do return to the world. They do not stay in the house. The dynamic urge of the Supreme compels these Masters to come back into the world again even after they have lived one life as a God-realized soul, to work for His manifestation.

Question: I just wondered if by creating the highly materialistic form of life we have now, have we put barriers between ourselves and the Divine?

Sri Chinmoy: This is, to some extent, true, but at the same time, in the West, you have been aspiring for material perfection, which will help you hold the Divine most solidly. The Western soil is spiritually fertile. The West can easily and effectively express the Divine through the most advanced material development in the physical world. The East does not have that material development. The sense of material development is absolutely necessary for the East.

Here in the West, your material development need not stand as a barrier. On the contrary, it can be of great advantage. You have both dynamism and material development. Like the East, if the West is ready to accept and feel the truth that the Divine is not only in Heaven, but here on earth, and if the West cultivates, develops and adds Eastern silence to its matchless dynamism and material development, then God's all-transforming Smile will dawn on the West.

Question: Would you kindly advise me as to whether I should leave my wife and child in order to enter deeper into the spiritual life?

Sri Chinmoy: In your case, I feel that you must remain with your wife and child. Today you want to leave them, tomorrow you may want to leave God. It is not in the act of leaving aside humanity that you will be able to realize God. In remaining with them, your realization will be deeper and more fulfilling. True, at a certain stage of our spiritual journey, the renunciation of the gross material life is necessary, but at a higher stage it is no longer necessary. At the highest stage, we neither seek nor renounce anything.

SAINTS

Question: If any human being can so transform his consciousness as to identify with the Universal Consciousness, certainly this human being deserves to be revered. At the same time, you have madmen who go around posing as elevated beings. What then are the distinguishing marks between a saint and a madman?

Sri Chinmoy: Saints are intoxicated with the divine ecstasy. Great spiritual saints, when they attain their spiritual perfection, are drinking ambrosial nectar. They are living in that delightful consciousness in which they feel that the world itself is holding the spiritual ocean of bliss. Some of them try to bring down that highest delight, *Ananda*, from a very high plane where they have received it, and sometimes they find it difficult. When they find it difficult to touch the material plane carrying this bliss, they may lose their inner balance and for a short time become forgetful of the physical consciousness. At that time they may not be able to function normally on the physical plane. A seeker may forget his name, for example, and others may say he is acting like a madman.

But an ordinary madman is mentally, vitally or physically dislocated. He never knows what he should do, what he should say or how he should act. He has permanently lost the connection between the physical world and his own existence on earth. So whenever he says or does something, there is no harmony with the Universal Consciousness. That is to say, he cannot project himself into the Universal Consciousness in which we are all abiding. All of us are living in the Universal Consciousness, although we may not be conscious of it. At the same time, we are not violating the rules of the Universal Consciousness. A madman is also unaware of the Universal Consciousness, but at the same time, he is violating the laws of the Universal Consciousness, owing to his ignorance.

As we have preconceived ideas, the madman too has preconceived ideas, but he cannot formulate his ideas as we formulate ours. We know our mind. We know how one thought can follow another thought. In a madman's case, it is not like that. All the thoughts and ideas of the higher and lower worlds come into him in a flash, and he loses all his inner and outer balance. The forces and the pressures of the other worlds enter into him and get a free channel in him to express themselves.

An ordinary madman will never open to the Light or the Truth which can save his very existence on earth; whereas the God-intoxicated man, the true saint, is mad with the divine beauty, the divine Light, the divine purity and all that is divine. He wants to possess and to be possessed by Divinity itself. This is the difference between an ordinary madman and a God-intoxicated saint.

Question: *What do you mean when you say that "a saint is beyond temptation"?*

Sri Chinmoy: Troilanga Swami weighed over three hundred pounds. He lived in Benares and used to spend most of his time bathing in the water of the Ganges. Once he was walking along the street naked, when he passed a new magistrate who had just come to the area. The magistrate became furious and ordered a policeman to arrest the Master and lock him in a small room. The following morning the magistrate saw Troilanga Swami walking outside the room. "How did you come out?" he demanded.

Troilanga Swami answered, "It was so easy. I came out because I felt like coming out. During the night I emptied myself and now it is smelling; therefore, I thought it would be better for me to come out of the room."

This time the magistrate himself put the Master under lock and key, using a double lock. The following morning, the magistrate was working in his office when all of a sudden he saw Troilanga Swami in one corner of the office, smiling at him. The magistrate said, "How is it possible for you to be here?"

Troilanga Swami told him, "You should not disturb the innocent Hindu Yogis. They can do anything they want to. I am walking along the street naked, but I am not interested in any women. In the case of ordinary men, they are full of lust. They have all kinds of emotional problems, lower vital problems, sex problems. But I am not like that. Also, people who look at me see that my body is so heavy and odd. So who will be interested in me? I have renounced the whole world, and at the same time nobody is interested in me in an impure way. So why do you bother me? I am not creating temptation and I am not tempted by anyone. If you want to torture the Hindu Yogis, you will be embarrassed and at every moment you will fail, because we are far above human torture."

A truly God-realized person is he who has the capacity not to be affected by others and, at the same time, not to affect others. He protects himself from the rest of the world and he protects the world from himself. This miraculous achievement of his is due to the inseparable oneness of his body's divinity with his soul's supreme universality. The body enjoys the soul's freedom. The soul enjoys the body's acceptance of the soul's reality.

SAMADHI

Question: *Could you please describe the different levels of* samadhi?

Sri Chinmoy: There are various minor *samadhis*, and among the minor *samadhis*, *savikalpa samadhi* happens to be the highest. Right after *savikalpa* comes *nirvikalpa samadhi*, but there is a great yawning gulf between *savikalpa* and *nirvikalpa*. However, even though *savikalpa samadhi* is one step below *nirvikalpa*, we do not use the term "lower." We do not call *savikalpa samadhi* lower than *nirvikalpa*; they are two radically different *samadhis*. Again, there is something even beyond *nirvikalpa samadhi* called *sahaja samadhi*. But *savikalpa* and *nirvikalpa samadhi* are the most well-known *samadhis*.

In *savikalpa samadhi*, for a short period of time, you lose all human consciousness. In this state the conception of time and space is altogether different. With the human time you cannot judge; with the human way of looking at space you cannot judge. In that *samadhi*, for an hour or two hours you are completely in another world. You see there that almost everything is done. Here in this world there are many desires still unfulfilled in yourself and in others. Millions of desires are not fulfilled, and millions of things remain to be done. But when you are in *savikalpa samadhi*, you see that practically everything is done; you have nothing to do. You are only an instrument. If you are used, well and good; otherwise, things are all done. But from *savikalpa samadhi* everybody has to return to ordinary consciousness.

Even in *savikalpa samadhi* there are grades. Just as there are brilliant students and poor students in the same class in school, so also in *savikalpa samadhi* some aspirants reach the highest grade, while less aspiring seekers reach a lower or a middle rung of the ladder, where everything is not so clear and vivid as on the highest level.

In *savikalpa samadhi* there are thoughts and ideas coming from various angles, but they do not affect you. While you are meditating, you remain unperturbed, and your inner being functions in a dynamic and confident manner. But when you are a little higher, when you have become one with the soul in *nirvikalpa samadhi*, there will be no ideas or thoughts at all. There nature's dance stops. There is no nature, only infinite peace and bliss. The Knower and the known have become one. Everything is tranquil. There you enjoy a supremely divine, all-pervading, self-amorous ecstasy. You become the object of enjoyment, you become the enjoyer and you become the enjoyment itself.

Nirvikalpa samadhi is the highest *samadhi* that most spiritual Masters attain, and then only if they have achieved realization. It lasts for a few hours or a few days, and then one has to come down. When one comes down, what happens? Very often one forgets one's own name. One forgets one's own age. One cannot speak properly. But through continued practice, gradually one becomes able to come down from *nirvikalpa samadhi* and immediately function in a normal way.

There were spiritual Masters in the hoary past who attained *nirvikalpa samadhi* and did not come down. They maintained their highest *samadhi* and found it impossible to enter into the world atmosphere and work like human beings. One cannot operate in the world while in that state of consciousness; it is simply impossible.

Generally, when one enters into *nirvikalpa samadhi*, one does not want to come back into the world again. If one stays there for eighteen or twenty-one days, there is every possibility that he will leave the body. But there is a divine dispensation. If the Supreme wants a particular soul to work here on earth, even after twenty-one or twenty-two days, the Supreme takes the individual into another channel of dynamic, divine consciousness and has him return to the earth-plane to act.

Sahaja samadhi is by far the highest type of *samadhi*. In this *samadhi* one is in the highest consciousness, but at the same time he is working in the gross physical world. One maintains the experience of *nirvikalpa samadhi* while simultaneously entering into earthly activities. One has become the soul and at the same time is utilizing the body as a perfect instrument. In *sahaja samadhi* one walks like an ordinary human being. One eats. One does the usual things that an ordinary human being does. But in the inmost recesses of his heart, he is surcharged with divine illumination. When one has this *sahaja samadhi*, one becomes the Lord and Master of Reality. One can go at his sweet will to the Highest and then come down to the earth-consciousness to manifest.

After achieving the highest type of realization, on very rare occasions, one is blessed with *sahaja samadhi*. Very few spiritual Masters have achieved this state, only one or two. For *sahaja samadhi*, the Supreme's infinite grace is required, or one has to be very powerful and lucky. *Sahaja samadhi* comes only when one has established inseparable oneness with the Supreme, or when one wants to show, on rare occasions, that he is the Supreme. He who has achieved *sahaja samadhi* and remains in this *samadhi* consciously and perfectly manifests God at every second, and is thus the greatest pride of the transcendental Supreme.

Question: *Is the* turiya *consciousness a form of* samadhi? *Is it in any way related to* sahaja samadhi?

Sri Chinmoy: The *turiya* consciousness is the transcendental reality. It is not a form of *samadhi* in the accurate sense of the term. When an individual soul establishes permanent and constant union with the Supreme Being, we say that he is enjoying the *turiya* consciousness. The possessor of *turiya* consciousness usually does not come down for manifestation because he likes to remain immersed in *Sat-Chit-Ananda*—Existence-Consciousness-Bliss. Here the seeker reaches the absolute height of evolution. This loftiest realization has no direct link with *sahaja samadhi*.

Sahaja samadhi holds the *turiya* consciousness. A possessor of *sahaja samadhi* embodies the *turiya* consciousness, and it is he who challenges earth-ignorance with a view to transforming it into the perfect creation. He embodies the highest transcendental Truth, Light, peace, bliss, power and all divine qualities in boundless measure in his being, and he manifests these divine qualities in the easiest and most effective way in his multifarious day-to-day activities. In his outer life, he acts like a divine child who has eternity's height and infinity's Light at his disposal, sharing them with aspiring humanity cheerfully and unreservedly.

Question: *Could you speak a little more extensively about the experience of nirvikalpa samadhi?*

Sri Chinmoy: *Nirvikalpa samadhi* cannot be explained by any individual, no matter how great he is. It is an experience which can be understood only by trying to identify and become one with someone who has attained the experience. We must try to enter into the experience rather than ask the experience to come to our level. When we enter into *nirvikalpa samadhi*, the experience itself is the reality. But when we want to tell others, to put it into words, we have to come down very far and use the mind; we have to couch the experience in human concepts. Therefore, the consciousness of *nirvikalpa samadhi* can never be adequately explained or expressed. The revelation of the experience can never be like the original experience.

I am trying my best to tell you about this from a very high consciousness, but still my mind is subtly expressing it. In *nirvikalpa samadhi* we have no mind. We see the Creator, the creation and the observer as one person. There the object of adoration and the person who is adoring become totally one; the lover and the Beloved become totally one. We go beyond everything, and at the same time we see that everything is real. Here in the ordinary world, I will say you are unreal and you will say I am unreal because of our different opinions. But in *nirvikalpa samadhi* we go beyond all differences; there the mind does not function at all.

When we enter into *nirvikalpa samadhi*, the first thing we feel is that our heart is larger than the universe itself. Now we see the world around us, and the universe seems infinitely larger than we are. But this is because the world and the universe are now perceived by the limited mind. When we are in *nirvikalpa samadhi*, we see the universe like a tiny dot inside our vast heart.

In *nirvikalpa samadhi* there is infinite bliss. There is nothing in comparison to the quantity, not to speak of the quality, of that bliss. Bliss is a vague word to most of us. We hear that there is something called bliss, and some people say they have experienced it, but most of us have no firsthand knowledge of it. When we enter into *nirvikalpa samadhi*, however, we not only feel bliss, but we grow into that bliss. The third thing we feel in *nirvikalpa samadhi* is power. All the power that all the occultists have put together is nothing compared with the power we have in *nirvikalpa samadhi*. But the power that we can take from *samadhi* to utilize on earth is infinitesimal compared with the entirety. It is like what we require to blink our eye. All this I am expressing through the mind; it is not exact. But I cannot express with words more of the Truth that I have realized.

I wish to say only that to enter into any level of *samadhi* is infinitely easier than to transform the human consciousness into the divine consciousness. That I have been trying to do, you have been trying to do, the Supreme has been trying to do. All of us here are trying for only one thing, and that is the transformation of human nature — physical, vital, mental and psychic. When that is done, perfect perfection will dawn both here on earth and there in Heaven.

How can this transformation take place? Through aspiration. The world has to aspire, creation has to aspire. Only then can the spiritual Masters bring down Heaven onto earth. Heaven, as we say, is a state of consciousness. In *samadhi*, all is Heaven, all is bliss, Light, peace. But when we come down into the world again, all is suffering, darkness, fear, worry. How can we make a conscious connection between this world of ours and the highest state of *samadhi*? Through constant aspiration. There is no other medicine but constant aspiration, not for a day or two, but for a whole lifetime. To realize God takes many, many incarnations. But when you have a fully realized spiritual Master, it becomes much easier. It may take you one incarnation, or two, or three or four. Otherwise, for a normal human being it takes many, many hundreds of incarnations, even to attain the higher experiences or so-called minor realizations. But a realized Master knows the souls and stays in the souls. Since he can do this, it is easy for him to deal with each aspirant according to his soul's necessity, for his soul's development and fulfillment.

Question: *What is the difference between* samadhi *and God-realization?*

Sri Chinmoy: *Samadhi* is a realm of consciousness. Many people have entered into *samadhi*, but realization comes only when we have become one with the highest Absolute. We can enter into some *samadhis* without realizing the Highest.

Entering *samadhi* is like knowing the alphabet, but realization is like having a Ph.D. There is no comparison between *samadhi* and realization. *Samadhi* is a state of consciousness in which one can stay for a few hours or a few days. After twenty-one days, usually the body does not function. But once one has achieved realization, it lasts forever. And in realization, one's whole consciousness has become inseparably and eternally one with God.

There are three stages of *samadhi*: *savikalpa samadhi*, *nirvikalpa samadhi* and *sahaja samadhi*. *Savikalpa samadhi* is an exalted and glowing state of consciousness, whereas realization is a conscious, natural and manifesting state of consciousness. When realization dawns, the seeker enjoys freedom from the human personality and human individuality. He is like a tiny drop of water which enters into the ocean. Once it enters, it becomes the ocean. At that time, we do not see the personality or the individuality of the one drop. When one realizes the highest Truth, the finite in him enters into the infinite and realizes and achieves the infinite as its very own. Once realization has taken place, a Master can easily enter into *savikalpa samadhi*. *Nirvikalpa samadhi*, too, is not difficult for a God-realized soul to attain. Only *sahaja samadhi*, which is the highest type of *samadhi*, is a problem, even for the very highest God-realized souls.

Question: *In the highest state of* samadhi; *when you look at other human beings, what kind of consciousness do you feel in them ?*

Sri Chinmoy: When one is in the highest transcendental *samadhi*, the physical personality of others disappears. We do not see others as human beings. We see only a flow of consciousness, like a river that is entering into the ocean. He who is in the highest trance becomes the ocean, and he who is in a lower state of consciousness is the river. The river flows into the sea and becomes one with the sea. The one who is enjoying the highest *samadhi* does not notice any individuality or personality in the others. A human being who is not in this state of *samadhi* is a flowing river of consciousness, while the one who is in *samadhi* has become the sea itself, the sea of peace and Light.

Question: How long can a realized soul remain in savikalpa samadhi?

Sri Chinmoy: One need not be a realized soul in order to enter into *savikalpa samadhi*. If someone is a great aspirant and if he has been meditating for many years, he can enter into *savikalpa samadhi*. It is not that difficult. *Savikalpa samadhi* can last for several hours. When Sri Ramakrishna used to touch seekers and give them a kind of trance and *samadhi*, it was for a few hours. In *savikalpa samadhi* one does not stay more than a day or two, because it is not necessary and not advisable. Only *nirvikalpa samadhi* goes on for seven, eight, nine, ten days, because *nirvikalpa samadhi* is more important in terms of our inner life.

For a spiritually realized person, there is no definite boundary to his *savikalpa samadhi*. At his will he can come and go. At any moment he can enter, and he can stay a few hours or days. Certainly, it is not an easy thing for an aspirant to do, but it is not the most difficult thing for a Yogi. If someone is a realized soul, if he is a real Yogi, spiritual Master or Avatar, for him *savikalpa samadhi* is just like playing with toys. In his case it is very simple, but for an ordinary aspirant, certainly it is difficult.

Question: I understand that a liberated soul can prolong his stay in the physical world for twelve or fifteen days even while he is in nirvikalpa samadhi.

Sri Chinmoy: A liberated soul can stay for twenty-one or twenty-two days in *nirvikalpa samadhi* if God wants that particular soul to continue on the path of dynamic manifestation. If God wants the individual to remain in the *Brahman* of static realization, then his soul will not return to the earth-consciousness after he has attained *nirvikalpa samadhi* and he will have to leave the body. Otherwise, after eleven, twelve or thirteen days, God will say: "I want you to work for Me in the world. You must go back."

The name of the plane from which the Masters come back is the Super-mind. This is where the actual creation starts. Higher than this is the level of *Sat-Chit-Ananda*—Existence-Consciousness-Bliss. The spiritual Masters who want divine manifestation here on earth are trying to manifest first the Super-mind, which is the golden Consciousness from which the creation descended. When that is manifested, the spiritual Masters who are here to bring down the highest Consciousness will then bring down *Sat-Chit-Ananda.* These three qualities can never be separated. They have to come together here on earth. The Supreme wants the whole divine manifestation to take place here on earth, not in Heaven or anywhere else.

In our Indian scriptures, it is said that man is greater than the cosmic gods because the cosmic gods are satisfied with the bliss of Heaven, whereas man is not satisfied until he actually achieves liberation. If the cosmic gods want to make progress, if they want liberation or manifestation, even they have to take human form and come to earth. Manifestation cannot take place anywhere else. In India there are thousands of gods, and we appreciate, we admire, we adore them because right now they are superior to us. When we suffer from a headache, if we soulfully invoke a god, then he will come and take it away. But the cosmic gods can do nothing further than that. When man realizes God, at that time these cosmic gods are of no help to him. At that time man is superior, because he is attaining constant and conscious union with the absolute Supreme.

Question: Will a Master know beforehand if he is to leave the body during samadhi?

Sri Chinmoy: Yes, he will know. Even an ordinary man often knows when he is going to leave the body. Sometimes his departed relatives will appear and say, "Come, my friend, now it is your time to follow us. How long we have waited for you! It is time to take birth here, to enjoy Heaven." They want to celebrate his arrival. Here on earth we die, but there in Heaven we are born to all our departed dear ones.

Question: Could you explain the difference between opening the heart-center and nirvikalpa samadhi?

Sri Chinmoy: These are two different things. In the heart center, you do not get *nirvikalpa samadhi. Nirvikalpa samadhi* you get only when you go beyond the domain of the mind—far beyond, to the very highest level of consciousness. When you go inside the heart, deep, deeper, deepest, there you get the feeling of inseparable oneness with your Inner Pilot, the Supreme. So these are two different things.

Question: *Is there anything higher than* samadhi?

Sri Chinmoy: There is a stage which is superior to *samadhi*. That is the stage of divine transformation, absolute transformation. You can be in *samadhi*, but *samadhi* does not give you transformation. While you are in your trance, you become exalted, for you are one with God. But when you come back into the material plane, you become an ordinary man. But if you have transformed your outer and inner consciousness, then you are no more affected by the ignorance of the world.

Question: *If a Master is in* sahaja samadhi *all the time, which is the highest form of* samadhi, *is it a sort of conscious descent when he goes into* nirvikalpa samadhi?

Sri Chinmoy: It is not like that. *Sahaja samadhi* encompasses the other *samadhis—savikalpa* and *nirvikalpa*—and it goes beyond, beyond. *Samadhi* is like a big building with many floors. When one is in *sahaja samadhi*, he is the owner of the whole building. He has the height of *nirvikalpa* and the heights far above that, and at the same time he has achieved the perfection, wealth and capacity of all the other floors. On the one hand, he has encompassed within himself all the floors, and on the other hand, he is above them. *Nirvikalpa* is like one height, say the thirtieth floor; it is very high, but it has only its own limited capacity. It cannot bring any of its capacity to the basement. If one has *nirvikalpa*, he is afraid to go down into the basement, because he may not be able to go back up again. But *sahaja* consciousness is above the thirtieth floor and, at the same time, it can be in the basement also. *Sahaja samadhi* will not be satisfied with thirtieth floor; it will be satisfied only when it touches the basement, the first floor, the second floor, all the floors. The power of *sahaja samadhi* is such that it can take one to any floor.

Right now, for example, I am talking with you. You can say that I am on the lowest floor. Not in terms of consciousness or achievement, but in terms of height, that is my actual location. But if I own the building, if my consciousness has captured the entire building, then I can be anywhere. When it is a matter of actual location, I may be in the basement; but when it is a matter of possession, I have earned, I have achieved and I constantly have all the floors as my own.

Question: If a Master is in sahaja samadhi *all the time, does that mean* nirvikalpa samadhi *is not fulfilling to him?*

Sri Chinmoy: If one is in *sahaja samadhi*, in one sense, nothing can fulfill him because he is already fulfilled in his inner life. As an individual, he has gone beyond fulfillment. When one is in *sahaja samadhi*, there is nothing more for him to achieve or learn. The Master may not be a carpenter, but he has such oneness with the universe that he can identify with a carpenter and make himself feel in his own living consciousness that he *is* that carpenter. At that time, the Master's being and the carpenter's whole being are totally one.

But when it is a matter of the fulfillment of everyone, within the Master—fulfillment in him and for the Supreme—that is not yet done. When it is a matter of manifestation, he is stuck. In that sense, he is not fulfilled. My own personal realization I achieved long, long ago. But when it is a matter of the fulfillment of those whom I call my own, in that I am not yet fulfilled. In the outer life, in the manifestation, I will be fulfilled only when you are fulfilled, when he is fulfilled, when she is fulfilled. If somebody leads a better life, if somebody prays for five minutes most soulfully, that is my fulfillment. If you pray most sincerely, one minute more than you did yesterday, that is my real fulfillment, because of my oneness with you.

Question: When you bring down peace and Light to us, do you have to go into nirvikalpa samadhi?

Sri Chinmoy: No, I do not have to go to any particular state of consciousness to give you something. All spiritual qualities are inside me, in the spiritual heart. The spiritual heart is infinitely larger than the universe itself. The whole universe is inside the spiritual heart. When I want to offer Light, I may look up, and you may think that I have gone very high, beyond the heart. But the heart is like a globe which encompasses the whole universe. Inside the heart is the plane for love, the plane for Light, the plane for peace. Each plane is like a different house. Some planes have a little of everything, and some planes are specialized. But all are inside the heart, which is where a spiritual Master lives, and from there he brings everything.

One has to develop the spiritual heart. Everybody does not have the same capacity. Everybody has potentiality, but it must be developed. It is not like our oneness with God, which is something we all possess equally but have misplaced. No, the capacity of the spiritual heart is something we actually have to achieve in the process of evolution. Gradually it grows from a seed to a plant to a huge banyan tree, as our oneness with God increases. With unconscious oneness we enter into the world. Through the process of prayer, meditation, love, devotion and surrender, we develop conscious oneness. The heart develops from the consciousness of a child to the consciousness of the eldest member of the family, who knows everything that the father knows. When we have developed the spiritual heart, at that time we come to realize our identity with the Mother and Father of the universe.

Question: Do you teach your disciples any specific technique for attaining samadhi?

Sri Chinmoy: No. *Samadhi* is a very high state of consciousness. If the beginner comes to kindergarten and asks the teacher how he can study for his Master's degree, the teacher will simply laugh. He will say, "How can I tell you?" Before we are ready to try to attain *samadhi*, we have to go through many, many, many inner spiritual experiences. Then there comes a time when the Master sees that the student is ready to enter into *savikalpa samadhi*. *Nirvikalpa samadhi* is out of the question for seekers right now. One has to be a most advanced seeker before he can think of attaining *nirvikalpa samadhi*. But before that, *savikalpa samadhi* is enough. If one gets *savikalpa samadhi*, it is more than enough for quite a number of years, even for this lifetime.

One gets *nirvikalpa samadhi* only in the highest stage of his aspiration. Unfortunately, I do not have anyone among my disciples now whom I can help to enter into that state. I am very proud of my disciples. They are very sincere, very devoted, and they are making very fast progress; but the time has not come for them to enter into *nirvikalpa samadhi*. For all seekers I wish to say that the spiritual ladder has quite a few rungs. We have to climb up one step at a time. *Nirvikalpa samadhi*, for my disciples at least, is a far cry right now.

SERVICE

Question: How can we love and serve our brothers and sisters?

Sri Chinmoy: First things first. To love others, to serve others, try to love and serve God first. Then automatically you will be in a position to love and serve all human beings, your brothers and sisters.

Question: How can I best serve you?

Sri Chinmoy: You can serve me best if you can all the time think of me, pray to me and meditate on me. When I say "me," I mean the Supreme in me, who is your Guru, my Guru, everybody's Guru. Try to feel that I am not only your best friend but also your only friend, here on earth and there in Heaven. Your wife is here, but she has to forgive me; I am your only friend. You have to know that I am your best friend in Heaven and on earth for eternity. I am not only your best friend for eternity, but also your only friend for eternity. You can get rid of all your unfortunate experiences of life only by constantly feeling that I am your only friend.

Question: After a disciple has realized God, will he always serve you in the inner world?

Sri Chinmoy: After you have realized God, why should you serve me? You will not serve me, but you will serve God, the Supreme, the boundless infinite Consciousness. If you serve the infinite Consciousness of the Supreme, you serve me, because I am part and parcel of that infinite Consciousness; that is where I dwell in my inner life. But whom will you actually be serving? You will not be serving me, you will not be serving the Supreme; you will be serving yourself, your own highest aspect. The Supreme is not a third person, and I am not a third person. Once we are realized, we are all one. On the strength of your highest oneness with the infinite Consciousness, you will be serving the One in three forms: the Supreme in His own aspects, the Supreme as your spiritual teacher and the Supreme as yourself. But the personality, the individuality that I have in this incarnation, you will not serve when you have realized the Highest.

Right now I am serving, serving, serving. I am serving my disciples and trying to manifest the Supreme on earth. Right now you, my disciples, have a little faith in me; that is why you are trying to manifest the Supreme. But practically nobody is serving Him consciously. If you had really been serving the Supreme, by this time you could have offered abundant Light to the world at large. You are serving in a way, but not spontaneously, wholeheartedly and lovingly.

When you realize God, at that time you will really know me. Now you do not know me. Among my disciples, not even a single one knows me. You say, "Sometimes Guru goes into a very high consciousness," but you do not actually know where my consciousness is. What I am you will realize only the day you realize God, not one second before. Right now when I talk of infinity or eternity, it is all meaningless to you. Some of you try to digest what I say, even though you find it difficult to assimilate. But when you realize God, at that time you will understand me.

SEX

Question: Do you practice celibacy?

Sri Chinmoy: Of course. Without celibacy, there can be no true spiritual life, not to speak of God-realization.

Question: Speak to us about the temptation of sex.

Sri Chinmoy: One day, during the period that Nigamananda was practicing austerities, he passed by a temple owned by an elderly woman. The woman begged the sadhu to stay in her temple for some time, and he kindly listened to her request. Finally, she begged him to take charge of the temple and he agreed. Afterwards, both of them became very fond of each other. She showed him all her motherly affection and he showed her all his heart's good qualities.

One day a beautiful young woman came into the temple. She became deeply enraptured with Nigamananda's soulful beauty, and she did not want to leave the temple. Nigamananda and she had serious spiritual conversations, and he was very moved by her sincere spiritual qualities and deep spiritual understanding.

The owner of the temple did not like this at all. She felt that Nigamananda's spirituality was being ruined. She insulted the young woman in order to make her leave the temple. But the young woman had fallen desperately in love with Nigamananda, so she was adamant about staying there. And gradually Nigamananda also became weak.

One day the young woman said to him, "I have amassed wealth, and I will take you to my house. I assure you, your spirituality will not be ruined. On the contrary, I shall help you to meditate all day and night. Let us get married. If we get married, then it will be natural for me to help you, and society will not criticize us. You

319

will be able to expedite your Godward journey." So they decided to get married in two weeks time.

Before the two weeks had elapsed, Nigamananda's Master appeared before him one night in a dream with a luminous face. The Master had a stick, and soon Nigamananda was shocked to see his Master striking and beating his girlfriend black and blue. The Master insulted her and beat her senseless. Then he blessed Nigamananda and said to him, "Leave this place immediately! This woman will not help you in your God-realization, but will take away all the aspiration that you now have and turn you into a street beggar."

Needless to say, Nigamananda obeyed his Master immediately.

The sincere seeker has to be extremely alert all the time, for the forces of the lower vital can easily rob him of his aspiration. Until God-realization dawns, he can always be tempted, and he can easily swerve from the path of Truth and Light. The very nature of the outer world is temptation. In order to overcome temptation, the seeker has to be constantly vigilant and always abide by the dictates of his inner will, not by the suggestions of the outer world.

Question: Speak to us about the transcendence of sex.

Sri Chinmoy: Do not try to suppress sex. With your inner wisdom, inner experience and inner Light, sex can be transcended, and it has to be. But by fighting, struggling and suppressing it, sex cannot be conquered. The easiest way to transcend something is to pay no attention to it, to feel that it is unnecessary. If you think that it is necessary, then it comes to tempt you, and you will feel that you are caught.

If you want to conquer your desires, there is only one thing to do. You have to pay more attention to the Light, in a positive way. But not by hook or by crook! If you try to subdue your vital urges in any kind of repressive way, then you will never be able to conquer this physical need. You have to open yourself toward the Light and reach or feel the Light within you. By thinking constantly of your desires, vital, sex life, you will never be able to conquer them. It is impossible. Even if you want to think of them with a view to conquering them, you are making a mistake. But think of the other things, like Light and joy, which you need and which you actually want. Through concentration and meditation, you can have inner joy and inner Light. You will try to bring them into your gross physical, and your physical being will also feel divine joy and divine Light. At that time, the life of destructive pleasure will leave you and the life of fulfilling joy will embrace you.

Question: *I have read that when one uses sexual energy he is using up some spiritual energy at the same time. Is this true? If so, what can be done if one wants to lead a spiritual life?*

Sri Chinmoy: What you have read is absolutely true. Animal human life and divine God-life do not and cannot go together. To attain the highest Truth, the seeker needs total purification and transformation of his lower vital. If one wants to have real joy, everlasting joy, then he has to transcend the need of sex. If the seeker wants to be inundated with boundless peace, Light and bliss, then he has to eventually transcend this physical need. Otherwise, the transcendental peace, Light and bliss will remain a far cry for him.

But you cannot realize God overnight. It is impossible! You do not get your Master's degree in a day, or even in a year. It may require twenty years of study to achieve. And God-realization is a far more difficult subject. It requires many incarnations of aspiration and spiritual discipline for anyone to realize God. In each life-time the possibility of your God-realization depends on both your present aspiration and your previous spiritual life.

If you tell a beginner that he will have to give up his lower vital life, his sex life, all at once, he will say, "Impossible. How can I do that?" If he has to do it all at once, he will never enter into the spiritual life. But slowly and steadily he can make headway towards his goal. If he tries to run too fast and does not have the capacity, he will simply drop in the field. He will lose what limited aspiration he has.

Transforming one's sex life is like giving up a bad habit, but for many people it is more difficult and it takes a longer time. Suppose somebody drinks a lot. If he drinks six or seven times a day, let him first come to realize the fact that this is something harmful for his God-realization. Then let him try to drink less. If he drinks six times a day, let him change to five times. After a while, let him drink four times a day. Then, after a while longer, let him drink three times a day. Gradually, let him diminish his desire for alcohol.

In our ordinary human life we have many weaknesses. If we try to conquer them all at once, the body will resist and break down. The body will revolt, and we shall be torn to pieces. We have to have a real inner will, the soul's will, to conquer our desires slowly and steadily. Gradually we have to diminish our need for sex on the strength of our aspiration. There will be a tug-of-war between aspiration and the gross physical desire, and slowly our nature will be purified.

On the strength of our inner urge, we have to run towards the Light. Then we will see that there is a great difference between pleasure and joy. Pleasure is always followed by frustration, and frustration is inevitably followed by destruction. But joy is followed by more joy and abundant joy, and in joy we get real fulfillment.

If one enters into the spiritual life and says, "Today I shall conquer all my lower propensities," he is just fooling himself. Tomorrow his physical mind will torture him with doubts. His impure and cruel vital will try to punish him in every way. He will be frustrated, and inside his frustration his own destruction will loom large. The lower vital life must be transformed completely before God-realization can take place, but I advise my students to do it gradually and with sincere determination.

Question: *Whenever I see a beautiful woman, sex thoughts enter my mind. I try to destroy them, but they persist.*

Sri Chinmoy: There are two ways to solve this problem. As soon as you see a beautiful woman, just try to concentrate and lift her up with your will so that, like a kite, she is flying. The other way, the easiest way, is when you see a woman to look only at her feet. Indian sadhus say to look only at the feet, not at the eyes, not at the face. Look only at the feet if you want immediate release from temptation. Look at the feet and then try with your whole consciousness to go deep within yourself. This takes only a second. Either lift this woman up or look at her feet. Then immediately lower vital thoughts will be controlled. Many have done it and have been very successful. There was a great Indian Avatar named Sri Chaitanya. He used to tell all his disciples, "Even if it is your mother, do not look at her eyes; just look at her feet."

But these methods are only for beginners. A day will come when you will have to look at women with your eyes open and, with your inner experiences, with your own inner realization, go beyond the feeling of man and woman. There is only one universal Consciousness; there is no masculine, no feminine. There is only one Consciousness flowing in two different forms. This feeling can be developed only along with our own inner development. It is a very advanced state. Right now perhaps we do not even feel oneness with our limbs. If I can throw a shotput farther with my right hand than with my left hand, I give more importance to my right hand and I ignore my left hand. I have seen many athletes who curse their left hand because they need the help of the left hand even though it is not as powerful as the right. If we cannot feel oneness even with our own two hands, how can we be one with another person? With aspiration and with our inner spiritual development, the whole creation becomes ours. At that time, there is no difficulty.

Question: For what purpose is the union between man and woman?

Sri Chinmoy: When union takes place between a man and a woman, each one gives a significant or insignificant meaning to the action. But in the highest, deepest spiritual life, when the realization of oneness with all humanity is coming to the fore, this ordinary human union does not serve any purpose. One can have physical relations with someone hundreds of times, but the real union, the inner union, does not take place. Only when we can establish our soul's union with a person will we be fulfilled. When we can liberate ourselves from the meshes of ignorance, and when we can realize the entire earth as our own, when we feel that all of mankind is our very own, then only can we have proper union. Physical union is no union in comparison to the all-pervading union of spiritual oneness which we can have.

I am telling you all this from the strict spiritual point of view. We have to reach a certain level before we can reject the ordinary human relation. Many times disciples in India come to their Master and say that there is no joy in human union. These very students then enter into deeper spiritual life and get the highest joy and purest delight from inner union with their Supreme Beloved.

Delight and pleasure are two different things. If one cares for the inner spiritual life, one will get delight. If one cares for the ordinary human life, one will get pleasure. Pleasure is bound to be followed by frustration because in pleasure there is no permanent fulfillment. But delight itself is all-fulfilling. This delight we get only in the spiritual union with the Divine, with our inner being. We have to know what we want. If we want pleasure, the union between man and woman is enough for a while. But if we want delight, which is the nectar of immortality, the immortal bliss, then we have to launch into the path of spirituality and establish the supernal union between man and God.

Question: *Can you please speak about marriage with regard to the spiritual life?*

Sri Chinmoy: Since each soul is a divine portion of God, marriage can be something very spiritual. When both husband and wife are with the same Guru and have utmost faith in the Guru, then they can make very fast progress together. Because they have faith in the Guru, he brings down the supreme power to help them, guide them and mold them, and they also help each other. But in many marriages we see that the husband is spiritual and the wife is unspiritual, or vice versa. When this happens, both are caught in a tug-of-war. One cannot make satisfactory inner progress, and the other cannot make satisfactory outer progress.

Question: *Should husband and wife try to feel the same kind of love and devotion for one another as they try to feel for their Guru or should it be of a different kind?*

Sri Chinmoy: There is a slight difference between a couple and a great spiritual Master in their spiritual attainments. The love and devotion that you will show to your husband and the love and devotion that he will show to you will no doubt make you two inseparably one in your inner life and outer life. But if you two expect realization, illumination and liberation from each other on the strength of your mutual love and devotion, I think you have to wait until the eternal time enters into infinite ignorance. The love and devotion that you must necessarily have for the spiritual Master in order to realize the transcendental Truth should spring from the inmost recesses of your crying, searching and aspiring heart. The kind of love and devotion you offer to your spiritual Father is infinitely purer, deeper, higher, more surrendered and more illumined than the kind of love and devotion that the husband and the wife can possibly offer to each other.

The husband and the wife can truly, soulfully, unmistakably and unreservedly become one if and when they discover their oneness with their Master first. One partner has to feel the living presence of the other partner in the heart of the Master. Then only will the divinity of the one be reflected in the life of the other. Let the husband and wife together show their love and devotion to their Guru. The Guru, in no time, will show them what he has for them, the infinite flood of Liberation.

Question: *Why is detachment from our family spiritually preferable to attachment?*

Sri Chinmoy: Attachment is the root of desire; ignorance is the root of attachment. In this world we are attached to the body, vital, the mind and the heart. Why? Because we want to possess. Unfortunately, we forget that there is nothing on earth we can possess forever. No, not even for a long time.

India's great philosopher Shankaracharya said, "Who is your wife, who is your son? This world is very peculiar. Brothers, think of the One who is eternally yours." This is the message of detachment. If you are attached to a physical person—the wife, the husband, the son, the friend—then you are only binding yourself and the other. But if you see the true object of adoration inside the wife, inside the husband, inside the son, then divine knowledge can dawn in you.

Lord Buddha left his beautiful wife and his little child when they were asleep. Before departing he said, "I loved you. I still love you. But I have to love the entire world also. Only if I can love the entire world will my love for you be complete." His human attachment had to surrender to the divine love in him.

While they were leaving the kingdom, Buddha's charioteer asked him a significant question: "Are you not mean? How is it that you are leaving behind your wife who has been so affectionate to you? You are her treasure; you are her peerless wealth."

The Buddha said, "You are mistaken. My wife's affection was binding me, and my affection was binding her. Now I am entering into the world at large, where there is no one to bind me, and where I will not bind anyone. I am going to free myself and others."

A real philosopher is one who is detached. He alone can have the vision of Truth. Once he has this vision, he can easily be indifferent to success and failure, joy and sorrow, pleasure and pain. His detachment does not mean that he will not help the world or receive help from it. It means he will not be bound to those he is helping or to those who are helping him. If we are attached, we are frustrated; but if we are detached, we are fulfilled. If we can feel that it is God who is operating in us and through us, as well as in and through the world, then we can be truly free.

It is said that before marriage a man is a woman's aspiration, and after marriage he is a woman's exasperation. But what is the woman aspiring for? She is aspiring for the fulfillment of desire. When the object of desire is attained, disappointment and frustration reign. When we fulfill any desire of ours, we will find that we are not eating the delicious fruit that we expected, but rather something destructive, poisonous and unsatisfying. In India there is a proverb that whoever has not eaten the Delhi ka laddu (sweet cake of Delhi) feels denied and whoever has eaten it feels disgusted. That is always the case with desire unfulfilled and desire fulfilled. Fulfillment may follow desire, but it will not be the fulfillment that energizes us and gives us greater inner strength to do the right things. On the contrary, it will only destroy the little aspiration we already have.

Question: *How does one transform attachment into detachment?*

Sri Chinmoy: Attachment does not diminish with age. Only through aspiration can we conquer attachment. In order to be free from attachment, we have to go through several stages. We have to study the scriptures and spiritual books. We have to associate with spiritual aspirants who have studied these books and are now crying for the real Light, or with those who have already attained some Light, insignificant or considerable, in their life of aspiration. We have to see or feel that in the ordinary world all around us is temptation that at any moment we may fall victim to it, and that we must valiantly fight against it. We have to take our minds away from physical consciousness and bodily demands. We have to enter into a world of expanded consciousness. We have to feel the necessity of attaining the divine goal. We have to follow the guidance of the Inner Pilot who is God, either in the form of a God-realized spiritual Master or in His own unembodied form.

To love those who love us is to do the right thing. To love those who do not love us is to do the good thing. To love God, who always loves us, is to do the wise thing. When we do the right thing, we are free. When we do the good thing, we are safe. When we do the wise thing, we are fulfilled.

SILENCE

Question: What does it mean when you say, "when silence speaks, silence answers"?

Sri Chinmoy: There was once a very great spiritual Master whose name was Troilanga Swami. He was the possessor of tremendous occult power and spiritual power. Sri Ramakrishna went to see him a few times. According to Sri Ramakrishna, he was the moving Lord Shiva. Once, Sri Ramakrishna asked him, through gestures, about God. Also through gestures, Troilanga Swami made it clear to Sri Ramakrishna that high above in Heaven, God is One, but when we are in the body, then the body becomes the only reality for us and God becomes many.

When silence answers a question, the answer is most effective. Here, in silence one spiritual Master put the question, and in silence another Master answered. The giver and the receiver were extremely pleased with each other.

Indeed, the body sings the song of God's multiplicity and the soul sings the song of God's unity or God the transcendental vision.

Question: What are "questions and answers in the silence world"?

Sri Chinmoy: Once a seeker named Bijoykrishna went to visit the spiritual Master Ramdas Kathiya Baba while he was holding a meeting. The disciples of Ramdas Kathiya Baba were asking their Master questions, but Bijoykrishna remained silent. When he was about to go away, the disciples of Kathiya Baba said to him, "You came all the way from a distant village to meet with our Master. Do you not have anything to ask?"

Bijoykrishna said, "I have already asked him many, many questions. He has answered all my questions inwardly."

Ramdas smiled and said, "It is absolutely true."

When silence asks a question and silence answers, both the question and the answer are most powerful, for the question and answer start their journey in the silence-heart and end their journey in the silence-heart. When the question and answer are not from the silence world, the mind wants to add something to the question and to the answer. What the mind adds is nothing but a doubtful, hesitant and discouraging existence-reality. When the mind is involved, the reality-experience is not and cannot be spontaneous; therefore, it is infinitely inferior to the reality-experience which lives in the heart, with the heart and for the heart. In the heart, spontaneity always reigns supreme.

SIN

Question: What does sin mean to you?

Sri Chinmoy: To me, sin is a kind of imperfection or ignorance. It is not necessarily something very bad, ugly or untouchable. In the process of evolution we are aiming at perfection, but right now most people are still wallowing in the pleasures of ignorance and self-indulgence. As long as you remain in ignorance, you will do things wrong, you will commit sins. But you must not feel that you are completely lost or covered in darkness. You are just progressing from less Light to more Light, and ultimately to liberation from ignorance-imperfection-sin.

Question: How does one get liberated from sin? Does liberation happen suddenly?

Sri Chinmoy: One can liberate oneself from sin only by invoking God's constant grace. God's grace always descends abundantly and powerfully, but most human beings do not try to receive it. If the individual wants to free himself or herself from ignorance, and cries to receive God's compassion-rain, then definitely he will be liberated from the snares of imperfection-sin. But this liberation comes gradually as the seeker becomes more illumined. You must not expect sudden and miraculous overnight transformations, although these do occasionally occur.

SOUL

Question: *Has each soul a special mission?*

Sri Chinmoy: Your soul has a special mission. Your soul is supremely conscious of it.

Maya, illusion or forgetfulness, makes you feel that you are finite, weak and helpless. This is not true. You are not the body. You are not the senses. You are not the mind. These are all limited. You are the soul, which is unlimited. Your soul is infinitely powerful. Your soul defies all time and space.

Has your soul a special mission? Yes. Your mission is in the inmost recesses of your heart, and you have to find and fulfill it there. There can be no external way for you to fulfill your mission. The deer grows musk in his own body. He smells it and becomes enchanted, and tries to locate its source. He runs and runs, but he cannot find the source. In his endless search, he loses all his energy and finally he dies. But the source he was so desperately searching for was within himself. How could he find it elsewhere?

Such is the case with you. Your special mission—which is the fulfillment of your divinity—is not outside you, but within you. Search within. Meditate within. You will discover your mission.

Question: *Can one ever realize the soul? Can you be fully conscious of the soul and be one with it?*

Sri Chinmoy: Certainly you can. In fact, you are nothing other than the soul. It is your soul that represents the natural state of consciousness. But doubt makes it difficult to realize the soul. Doubt is man's fruitless struggle in the outer world. Aspiration is the seeker's fruitful confidence in the inner world. Doubt struggles and struggles. Finally it defeats its own purpose. Aspiration flies upward to the Highest. At its journey's end, it reaches the goal. Doubt is based on outer observation. Aspiration is founded on inner experience. Doubt ends in failure because it lives in the finite physical mind. Aspiration ends in success because it lives in the ever-climbing soul. A life of aspiration is a life of peace. A life of aspiration is a life of bliss. A life of aspiration is a life of divine fulfillment.

Question: *How does one know what one's special mission is?*

Sri Chinmoy: To know what your special mission is, you have to go deep within. Hope and courage must accompany you on your tireless journey. Hope will awaken your inner divinity. Courage will make your inner divinity flower. Hope will inspire you to dream of the Transcendental. Courage will inspire you to manifest the Transcendental here on earth.

To feel what your special mission is, you have always to create. This creation of yours is something which you ultimately become. Finally, you come to realize that your creation is nothing other than your self-revelation.

True, there are as many missions as there are souls. But all missions fulfill themselves only after the souls have achieved some degree of perfection. The world is a divine play. Each participant plays a part in its success. The role of the servant is as important as that of the Master. In the perfection of each individual part is the collective fulfillment. At the same time, the individual fulfillment becomes perfect only when the individual has established his inseparable connection and realized his oneness with all human beings of the world.

You are one from the sole of your foot to the crown of your head. Yet at one place you are called ears, at another place you are called eyes. Each place in your body has a name of its own. Strangely enough, although they all are part of the same body, one cannot perform the action of another. Eyes see, but they cannot hear. Ears hear, but they cannot see. So the body, being one, also is many. Similarly, although God is one, He manifests Himself through many forms.

God tells us our mission. But we do not understand God's language, so He has to be His own interpreter. When others tell us about God, they can never tell us fully what God is. They misrepresent, and we misunderstand. God speaks in silence. Also, He interprets His message in silence. So also let us hear and let us understand God in silence.

Question: *Is the soul always with the person during his lifetime, or can it leave him temporarily, even making its home elsewhere?*

Sri Chinmoy: As a rule, the soul always remains with the person during his lifetime, but it can leave the body for a few minutes, or a few hours at most, while the person is asleep. It can also leave the body for a short period while the aspirant is in a deep state of meditation. Then one can see one's own body. One may see it as a dead body or a dynamic body or as a shaft of light facing one's soul, or in many other ways. Of course, at that time, one sees the body with the eye of one's own soul.

Question: *During sleep, does the soul make journeys?*

Sri Chinmoy: Yes. The soul makes journeys to different levels of consciousness. There are seven higher worlds and seven lower worlds. Generally, the soul travels in these worlds during sleep. Almost everyone's soul is fortunate enough to have access to some of these worlds, but very few are conscious of these experiences while they are happening, or remember them after they awake.

Question: *How does one know if his soul is happy?*

Sri Chinmoy: First of all, one has to believe that one has a soul. One has to know and feel where the soul abides, that is, its location in the body. In order to know and feel the soul, one has to aspire. During his ardent aspiration, his spiritual journey, he can actually discover whether the soul is happy or not. He will feel that his soul is happy only when he sees and feels joy within and without, and also when he does not find fault with God's creation and God's divine dispensation.

Question: *Can the soul be equally represented in dreams by an old woman, wrinkled and wise, as well as by a young baby, babbling a new language?*

Sri Chinmoy: Yes. The soul can be represented in dreams by an old woman or by a young baby. In order to give a particular experience to the outer being, the soul can assume any form in dreams. One's own soul can be compared to the gradual growth of a seed into a tree. This is what we call the evolution of the soul.

Question: Is the soul both male and female?

Sri Chinmoy: The soul itself is neither male nor female. But when the soul starts its journey and takes a female body, then in all its incarnations it will take a female body. If it once takes a male body, then in all its incarnations it will take a male body. It is impossible to change the sex. In the whole history of mankind, there have been a few exceptions here and there, but very rarely.

Question: Is it the soul that must surrender to the cosmic Self?

Sri Chinmoy: Yes. The soul has to surrender to the Self, which in Indian terms is called *Paramatman*—that which is unmanifest. This Self does not take human incarnation nor enter into creation, whereas the soul accepts a human body and accepts limitation, imperfection and ignorance. Each human being has an individual soul. This individual soul, which takes a human body, is not all-pervading, omniscient or omnipotent. The Self is. The soul, in its upward evolution, can someday merge into the Self and become as powerful as the Self.

Question: Is it the soul that makes the decision in selecting a new body in each incarnation?

Sri Chinmoy: Yes. It is the soul that makes the decision in selecting a body, but with the direct approval of the Supreme or the Self. The choice is made to give the soul the opportunity to manifest more and more of its inner divinity in each incarnation and to fulfill the Will of the Divine here on earth.

Question: Does the soul experience loneliness? If so, how does this differ from the superficial need to have the company of others, whether we like them or not, but simply because we want someone to talk to?

Sri Chinmoy: The soul experiences loneliness only when the body, vital, mind and heart, which are supposed to cooperate with the soul in fulfilling its divine mission on earth, do not cooperate. But it does not act like a human being. It does not waste its time, as a human being would, feeling that just by talking to others, the sense of loneliness will disappear. The soul, in its loneliness, aspires most intensely to bring down peace, Light and power from Above into the physical, the vital, the mind, so that the total being can cooperate with the soul to fulfill the Divine. When peace, Light and power descend into the physical, vital and mind, the person becomes conscious of his inner life and true happiness. With peace, Light and power, a higher consciousness descends. With this higher consciousness, the person will naturally respond to the soul's need.

Question: Does the soul make demands on a person so that he has to change his ways?

Sri Chinmoy: The soul does not make demands as such. It is not like a mother making demands of her child at every moment, saying, "I am telling you such and such for your own good." What the soul does is to send a divine inspiration. This inspiration can, at times, be so vivid and spontaneous that the person may feel it to be almost an inner imposition made by his inner Self on his outer personality. The soul does not demand. On the contrary, it sympathizes with human failings and imperfections and tries to identify itself with these failings. Then, with its inner Light, it tries to help the person to change his ways.

Question: How different is this from the demands the ego makes?

Sri Chinmoy: When the ego makes a demand, it is all self-centered— "I," "me" and "mine." The ego wants to possess and be possessed. When the soul wants to have something, it is not for its own personal benefit, but is for the fulfillment of the Divine. The ego, by feeding the outer personality, wants to fulfill itself, and this is simply impossible, as there is no end to its cravings. The ego eventually meets with frustration, whereas the soul, by fulfilling the divine Will, realizes its own absolute fulfillment.

Question: *Does the soul cry when it is unhappy?*

Sri Chinmoy: No. The real soul, which is a portion of the cosmic Self is all delight. Since it cannot be unhappy in the human sense of the term, it does not cry. It is the unsatisfied and demanding vital, which we often take for the soul, that suffers unhappiness and cries pitifully.

Question: *Do things or places have a soul? For example, does a chair have a soul; does a city have a soul?*

Sri Chinmoy: Each thing and each place has a soul. Like all other cities, the city of New York has its soul. The Supreme has graciously shown me the soul of New York City a number of times. The difference between the soul of things and the souls of humans is a difference in their degree of evolution, in the degree they manifest their divine potentialities. It is through the process of reincarnation that the soul gradually manifests its hidden powers within, that the soul eventually reaches its absolute fulfillment.

Question: *Does the earth have a soul?*

Sri Chinmoy: Certainly. The earth represents the Mother aspect of the Divine. It is on earth that matter and spirit will find their absolute fulfillment in their reciprocal help and complete union. Matter will see through the eye of the spirit's vision. Spirit will flower by awakening and energizing matter to become a perfect basis of physical immortality and human transformation on earth. The two main characteristics of the soul of the earth are aspiration and compassionate tolerance.

Question: *When the vital or mind tries to satisfy itself without the soul's approval, what happens to the soul?*

Sri Chinmoy: In such cases, the soul usually remains silent. But at times the Supreme may put some pressure on the vital and the mind when they are going too far. He does this through the soul.

Question: Can the gross ever give the subtle anything? That is, can the soul become stronger by the right use of the body, such as exercise, right food, and so on?

Sri Chinmoy: Certainly. The gross can and must help the subtle. The body is gross, but in its sound and perfect condition, it helps the mind and the subtle existence considerably. One cannot, of course, make the soul stronger merely by taking vigorous exercises or by eating judiciously. But if the physical consciousness aspires to grow in the Light of the soul and tries to fulfill the Divine in the physical itself, then the progress of the soul becomes easier, faster and more fulfilling.

Question: Can the soul select what the individual is to experience in the manifested world?

Sri Chinmoy: Normally it is the soul that determines the experiences that the individual will have in his lifetime. As a matter of fact, if the individual consciously puts himself into spontaneous flow of the experiences that the soul wants to give him, he will eventually grow into abiding peace, joy and fulfillment. Unfortunately, the individual, being a victim of ignorance, is not aware of the soul's selection of the experience or, in spite of knowing, does not care for the selection made by the soul.

Question: Approximately where in the physical body does one feel a sense of the soul?

Sri Chinmoy: It is in the spiritual heart. According to medical science, the heart is slightly to the left of the center of the chest. According to Ramana Maharshi, the great sage of Arunachala, the spiritual heart is slightly to the right of the center. Some spiritual figures say that the spiritual heart is in the middle of the chest. Again, according to another spiritual figure, the spiritual heart is located between the eyebrows! Of course, he also has his reasons for saying this.

The true spiritual heart, four finger-breadths in width, is located twelve finger-breadths directly above the navel and six finger-breadths directly below the center of the throat. It is here that one feels the "quickening" of the soul.

Question: *If the personality is the newcomer and the soul is the real land-lord, or lord, then how is it that the newcomer, which is always seeking satisfaction, can so suffocate the soul that its inspirations cannot be heard?*

Sri Chinmoy: The *Katha Upanishad* says that the body is the chariot, the soul is the Master of the chariot, the intellect is the charioteer and the mind is the reins.

You are the landlady of the building in which we have our Center. You own this building. We are your tenants. We are all new-comers. You try your best to satisfy our requirements. Nevertheless, some of the tenants, not all, make your life a hell. Their demands are at times outrageous and absurd. Further, they cherish an uncompromising attitude. What do you do then? I believe you become quite helpless, if not hopeless, in spite of the fact that it is you who own this building. It is not easy to drive away the disturbing, demanding, uncompromising tenants all at once. Similar is the fate of the soul, which is attacked by the pleasure-seeking, demanding and unaspiring newcomer, the personality.

Question: *When someone is described as having a young soul or an old soul, what does this mean?*

Sri Chinmoy: From the spiritual point of view, when one has higher and deeper experiences, acquired from previous incarnations, one is called an old soul. The one who is wanting in such experiences is called a young soul. As you can see, it is not the number of incarnations that determines the "status" of the soul, but what one has learned and achieved in those lives.

Question: *Do things move faster with a young soul because there is less overlay of previous incarnations?*

Sri Chinmoy: Things do move faster with a young soul, provided he is a sincere and dedicated aspirant and listens to his spiritual guide unreservedly; provided also that he has not been burdened with too many worldly experiences.

Here again, it is not the number of incarnations that impede the soul's rapid journey towards its ultimate goal, but the old unlit human habits and propensities which present themselves as great obstacles, since they do not open so easily to the Light for purification and transformation.

Question: What is the difference between "strength of soul" and "strength of character"?

Sri Chinmoy: Strength of character is the pride of morality and humanity. Strength of soul is the pride of spirituality, eternity and infinity.

Having said this, I do not want to leave you with the impression that morality has no value in the inner life. On the contrary, a solid morality is preparatory to a deep spirituality. Further, the role of morality is of paramount importance in true spirituality.

The strength of the soul is the inner power or certitude that comes from the Divine within you. You have seen your soul, you have felt God's Will within you, and you have been given the strength to manifest His Will here on earth.

Question: Could the soul that inhabits a human body have inhabited an animal body or plant in previous times?

Sri Chinmoy: I am sure you are well acquainted with the theory of evolution. Charles Darwin, in the modern world, discovered the process of the evolution of species, that is, the change from a lower level to a higher one. But long before Darwin, a thousand years before the advent of the Christ, the great Indian sage Kapila had discovered the theory of spiritual evolution. According to his unique philosophy, the Eternal, Unchangeable and Imperishable at every moment evolves. "Nothing came from nothing." The Indian sage discovered this truth and offered it to the world at large.

The total process of evolution on earth includes the soul as well as the physical form. In the march of evolution, each soul has to undergo the plant life and the animal life in order to launch into the human life.

Question: Do souls differ in their characteristics?

Sri Chinmoy: There is actually no basic difference among souls except in the degree of their manifestation. All souls possess the same possibilities, whether they are housed in the lowest or the highest form of life.

We have to remember, however, that the Supreme manifests Himself in infinite ways through the different souls. They express His varying aspects of divinity. For example, one soul may manifest Light, another power, a third beauty, and so on.

It is by manifesting the hidden powers through the process of reincarnation that some souls have become great spiritual Masters. And all souls shall eventually follow them.

Question: What is the connection of the soul to past and future karma?

Sri Chinmoy: Actually, karma cannot be deeply understood apart from the soul. It is for the sake of the soul's growth that karma exists. You know, I am sure, what the word "karma" means. It is a Sanskrit word, derived from the root "*kri*," to do. Whatever we do, say or think is karma. The universe is governed by a law which we call the law of karma. You have read much about the law of karma, so I need not explain it here, except to say that all one's deeds and thoughts leave their impression upon one's causal body and bring about certain results.

At the same time, the soul is far beyond the snare of cause and effect. It is the hyphen between all that precedes and all that succeeds. It is enriched by all the experiences which the personality derives through the laws of karma.

Question: Where does the soul rest when it first leaves the body? Does it carry over its bodily or earthly limitations?

Sri Chinmoy: When the soul leaves the body, it first stays in the vital world for a short period. Some souls suffer there, while others do not. It is like visiting a strange, new country. Some are fortunate enough to mix freely with the people of the new country and understand its culture in almost no time, while others are not so fortunate.

The soul does not carry over any earthly limitations to the higher worlds. The soul or the psychic being, while leaving the body and going back to its own region, gathers together the quintessence of its earthly experiences. It stays for some time in its own region and then it comes back into this world with new determination and new possibilities to realize and fulfill the Divine here on earth.

Question: *When one sees through the Light of the soul, does he see through hundreds of lifetimes?*

Sri Chinmoy: When one sees through the Light of the soul, one can see the future possibilities of one's present incarnation, and at the most, one or two future incarnations, not hundreds of lifetimes. This statement applies to past incarnations as well. These glimpses need not be in any chronological order. However, in the cases of great spiritual Masters like Sri Krishna and Lord Buddha, this principle is not applicable, for the remotest past and the farthest future, in exact chronological order, is at their command.

Question: *When we see through the Light of the soul, is it always with the feeling of joy?*

Sri Chinmoy: Yes. It is always with a feeling of inner joy and this joy may often be expressed by the shedding of tears. This shedding of tears is the outer expression of the soul's delight and has nothing to do with human sorrow, grief or frustration. It is like a mother shedding tears when she sees her son returning home from abroad. Her tears are the expression of her inner joy.

Question: *When the soul chooses a new body, does it have a blueprint laid out as to its mission, or does the soul's mission evolve during one's lifetime, depending on circumstances and environment?*

Sri Chinmoy: The soul always comes down to earth with a certain mission. However, the earthly environment can help or hinder this mission. It also happens that the soul, at times willingly, makes an adjustment to its surroundings. Then it gradually tries to fulfill its mission with the full recognition and cooperation of the environment.

Question: Does the soul have many missions, or just one, in a lifetime?

Sri Chinmoy: There is only one mission, but there are many aims. One soul may wish to become a poet, an artist or an engineer in a lifetime. Each soul may aim at various creativities, but these are aims. They are not to be confused with the soul's mission. The soul's mission is always first and foremost: God-realization; then comes the manifestation of God-realization on earth. However, one's aim may help him in his God-realization or it may delay him, depending on the individual's approach to Truth.

For example, if one is a writer, it is well and good. If he goes on writing without aspiration for God-realization through his writings, he may one day become a very great writer, but he has not necessarily progressed in his Self-discovery. On the other hand, if one writes to express the Divine in his writings, if one's outer expression is the result of one's inner aspiration, and if one has taken to writing as a self-dedicated service to the Supreme in humanity, then certainly the aspirant in the writer is leading him to the realization of God. To come back to your question, from the standpoint of absolute Truth, there is only one mission and that is nothing but Self-realization.

Question: Does the vital have a mission separate from the soul's or is it related to the soul's mission?

Sri Chinmoy: The vital and the body do not have a separate mission. But when they collaborate with the soul's mission, it becomes theirs too. The vital hungers for name and fame, which are only aims. When the vital identifies itself with the soul and willingly accepts the soul's mission, then the soul's mission undoubtedly becomes the mission of the vital.

Question: How does one know if he is attending to his soul's mission or simply satisfying his vanity?

Sri Chinmoy: One can distinguish between the two only when one works without being motivated by desire and without being affected by the results of his actions. When one is in that state of consciousness, one can easily know whether one is attending to one's soul's mission or just satisfying one's vanity. Work done in Self-dedication leads the aspirant toward the fulfillment of his soul's mission. Work done for self-gratification drives man toward the pleasures that end in self-annihilation.

Question: It is often said that the soul needs certain experiences even though they may seem adverse at the time. How are we to distinguish between the experiences the soul needs and our own desire to forge ahead through egoistic stubbornness?

Sri Chinmoy: The soul does not have any experience which is unnecessary. Whenever the soul has an experience, there is a divine purpose behind it. But on the physical plane, we often fail to see that divine purpose. We see it as a mere incident in our journey here on earth. There are many things which our physical mind cannot comprehend while our soul is having the experiences. It is also true that through our stubbornness, we impose some insignificant experiences on the soul. But what we call "adverse experiences" are not adverse to the soul because in the soul's wide vision of Light, these experiences are all possibilities to grow, to develop, to manifest a higher truth or to fulfill a greater mission on earth.

Question: There is always talk about this world destroying itself; then people become personally alarmed. Would the end of the physical world as we know it be a threat to the soul?

Sri Chinmoy: If the physical world is destroyed, it would not be a threat to the soul, for the soul can stay in the soul's region. But if the soul wants to manifest the divine in all its aspects, then it must incarnate in a human body in the physical world.

SPIRITUALITY

Question: *What is spirituality and what is it not?*

Sri Chinmoy: Spirituality is man's boundless freedom in his life-boat: the freedom of his life-journey, the freedom from his life-pangs and the freedom beyond his life-achievements.

In spirituality is man's farthest vision. In spirituality is man's nearest reality. God has compassion. Man has aspiration. Spirituality is the consciousness-Light that unites man's aspiration and God's compassion. Spirituality tells man he is God veiled and that God is man revealed.

Spirituality is not an escape from the world of reality. Spirituality tells us what the true reality is and how we can discover it here on earth. Spirituality is not the denial of life, but the purest acceptance of life. Life is to be accepted unreservedly. Life is to be realized soulfully. Life is to be transformed totally. Life is to be lived eternally.

Spirituality is not the song of ignorance. It is the mother of concentration, meditation and realization. Concentration takes me dynamically to God. Meditation silently brings God to me. Realization neither takes me to God nor brings God to me. Realization reveals to me that God is the blue bird of infinity's reality and I am the golden wings of Divinity's Truth.

Question: *Do the words "psychic" and "spiritual" mean the same thing?*

Sri Chinmoy: No, the word "psychic" and the word "spiritual" are not the same. Let us use the term "the psychic being" instead of "psychic." It then simplifies the matter. The psychic being is the conscious representative of the soul. It is the aspiring, divine spark in us. It is supremely beautiful and is the fondest child of the

Supreme. The psychic being is an entity which only humans have. Animals, plants and material objects do not have a psychic being. However each object, animate or inanimate, does have a soul.

Anything that concerns this divine being or pertains to it is described as "psychic." But the word "spiritual" is something general and all-pervading. It includes and envelops everything, including the psychic being. You can liken the word "spiritual" to a garden and "psychic" to a most beautiful mango tree bearing countless, delicious, energizing mangoes.

Question: What is the difference between spiritual strength and spiritual power?

Sri Chinmoy: When we use the word "strength," we usually refer to the physical strength, the vital strength, the mental strength or even we go as far as the inner strength. When we use the word "power," we try to indicate a divine power which is the night-chasing capacity and the soul-fulfilling capacity of one's inner being. In the spiritual life, it is always better to use the word "power" instead of "strength." For power, unlike strength, immediately gives us the feeling of an essential aspect of God. Strength is bound in the physical and it can be used only in the physical world. Power too can be used in the physical, for the physical, but it is not bound there. Its home is high, very high, in the loftiest regions of the infinite Consciousness.

Question: Is the spiritual life an escape from reality?

Sri Chinmoy: The spiritual life is never an escape from reality. On the contrary, the spiritual life is the conscious and spontaneous acceptance of reality in its totality. For a spiritual seeker the idea of an escape from reality is absurdity plus impossibility, for spirituality and reality need each other to be supremely fulfilled. Without reality's soul, spirituality is worse than useless. Without spirituality's breath, reality is more than meaningless. Spirituality with reality means man's inner cry for perfect Perfection. reality with spirituality means God's omnipotent Will for total and absolute manifestation.

The acceptance of life with a divine attitude is not only a lofty idea but the very ideal of life. This ideal of life is realized, revealed and manifested through God's soul-elevating inspiration and man's life-building aspiration. Acceptance of life is the divine pride of true spirituality. To live a spiritual life is our only responsibility.

Escape is a base thought. It acts like a thief, the worst possible thief. Into the heart of tenebrous gloom escape gains easy and free access. He who indulges in the idea of an immediate escape unmistakably commits lingering suicide.

No, we must never make a cowardly escape. We must always be brave. Divine courage is our birthright. We are the hero-warriors of the supreme reality, chosen to fight against the teeming, brooding and threatening ignorance-night.

Question: *What happens if a person wants to enter the spiritual life but has to adjust himself to the material life?*

Sri Chinmoy: Yoga and life must go together. We have to go deep within to discover the spiritual life, but without negating the material life. From inside we have to come outside; we cannot go inside while holding on to the values of the outer life. We need the inner life and in the inner life is to be found infinite joy, peace and bliss. From the inner life, we bring to the fore our inner, divine qualities. The material life can then be easily adjusted. The material life, in fact, has its true significance only when it is supported by the inner life. At present, what is actually happening is that we are trying to separate the material life from the spiritual life. Actually, there is no such division, but unfortunately people think that either one has to accept the material life and wallow in its pleasures or else one has to be a complete ascetic, that there can be no compromise. This is not true. The material life has to be accepted, but not in a sense of total indulgence. The material life is to be accepted for the manifestation of our divine, inner qualities. Through the material life, we shall have to fulfill the message of our inner life. Now how can we do this?

One should try to aspire in one's day-to-day life to combine both the material and the spiritual life. One can do this through the remembrance of something higher or deeper. What is that higher and deeper thing? It is God, the Divine. If God comes to one's mind before anything else, then only will God flow through, from the spiritual life into the material life. God has to be placed first in one's life, without negating the material life or the outer world. If we place God first, then God enters, on our behalf, into the outer world, into the material world. But if we place the material world first, then we cannot reach God because the process is wrong. It is from God that we have to enter into the material life. God looms large in the inner life and from the inner life we can and must bring Him into the outer life. This is how we can adjust ourselves to the material life and make it one with the spiritual life.

Question: I am studying to be an actor at the Drama School here at Yale. Is it possible to follow the spiritual path and also have this earthly value, or must I totally devote myself to the spiritual path and be devoid of everything else?

Sri Chinmoy: This is a very wrong conception of spirituality. True spirituality never, never negates our earthly life and our significant earthly values. True spirituality only simplifies our earthly life; it purifies and illumines our human existence. We are now in ignorance. We know that we are caught in the meshes of ignorance, but spirituality shows us how we can come out of ignorance, how we can free ourselves from the bondage that we have consciously or unconsciously created. If you want to be an actor, spirituality will never prevent you from being one. On the contrary, spirituality will inspire you in your acting line. Spirituality never negates. It is like your private tutor. It will teach you privately and secretly to be successful and meaningful in your outer, as well as your inner, life. Nothing has to be given up. Everything has to be divinized and transformed. If you give up this world, then what are you going to achieve? It is here on earth that you have to realize God, reveal God and fulfill God.

Question: How many people turn to the spiritual life just in desperation?

Sri Chinmoy: I will say a majority turn to the spiritual life out of desperation and not out of the soul's necessity. Very few people start from the dawn of their existence to build an inner life out of the soul's necessity. Most people turn to the inner life out of sheer frustration, when they see that the world is torturing them mercilessly and that there is no hope. But if people enter into the inner life, they have to know that they should not accept it as an escape. Many people will think that the outer life has deserted them, so they want to accept the inner life as an escape. But no, the inner life is not an escape. The inner life will show us Truth and Light. And more than that, it will guide us and give us the message of illumination and transformation.

Question: What would be the first step for an ordinary person who has not been in contact with spiritual teachings and wants to enter into the path of Self-realization?

Sri Chinmoy: The important thing is the ultimate goal. If a person wants to have Self-realization, then the first step, the very first step, should be the acceptance of the spiritual life. Without accepting the spiritual life, one cannot realize God. It is simply impossible. The spiritual life, of course, is a very vast field—one has to know where one actually stands right now. If, as the first step in the spiritual life, one wants to have a better life, a more harmonious life, a more peaceful life, and if he feels that the peace, joy and harmony that he seeks are still beyond his reach, then he has to start by reading from a few scriptures; he should get some illumination from religious and spiritual books. These books will inspire him to some extent to enter into the inner life. Then when the person has studied the books and is getting some inspiration, but is unable to go farther, at that time he has to put into practice what he has studied in the books. When he is practicing these new principles, if he is not satisfied with his achievements, then he has to search for a spiritual teacher. It is the teacher who can help him in his spiritual life, who can tell him what kind of spiritual discipline is needed for him.

I must emphasize again that at the very outset he has to determine that he needs the spiritual life. There is no other life that can give him Self-illumination. When he is sure that it is the spiritual life that can give him that, then he has to enter into his deeper part. Through his inner cry, through prayer, through aspiration, through concentration and meditation, he has to start on his divine journey.

SUFFERING

Question: Why do we have to pass through sad experiences such as suffering and sorrow?

Sri Chinmoy: Why do we experience suffering? In this world, we are always consciously or unconsciously making mistakes. When we consciously make mistakes, we are quite aware of it. But unfortunately, we do not realize how many things we are doing wrong unconsciously. These unconscious mistakes manifest themselves in the physical world, and the results come to us as suffering. In the case of ordinary, unaspiring human beings, after tremendous suffering, sincerity dawns and the soul leads them to knowledge and wisdom. If people who repeatedly make mistakes have sincere aspiration and want to know why they are suffering, then the soul's Light comes to the fore and tells them. If we are spiritual people, consciously we will try not to do anything wrong, but unconsciously we do many things wrong. We can prevent unconscious mistakes only through our aspiration, prayer and meditation. If we aspire, then God's grace and compassion protect us.

Question: Is pain necessary?

Sri Chinmoy: There is a general notion that if we go through suffering, tribulations and physical pain, then our system will be purified. This idea is not founded upon reality. There are many people who are suffering because of their past karma or because undivine forces are attacking them, but we can not say that they are nearing their destination. No! They have to aspire sincerely in order to reach their destination. We shall not welcome pain; we shall try to conquer pain if it appears, since very often pain, whether physical, mental or emotional, only interferes with our aspiration.

Physical pain, vital pain and mental pain have to be either con-

349

quered or transformed into joy through our constant inner cry for something that will give us real and permanent satisfaction. The best thing is to take unavoidable pain as an experience which has to be transformed into an experience of joy. Joy is the only eternal reality, the only permanent and everlasting reality. It is absolutely wrong to say that each time we suffer we go one step closer to our goal.

It is not necessary to go through suffering before we enter into the kingdom of delight. Many people have realized God through love. The Father has love for the child and the child has love for the Father. This love takes us to our goal. Our philosophy emphasizes the positive way of approaching Truth. We have limited light. Let us increase it. Let us progress from more Light to abundant Light to infinite Light.

The highest discovery is this: We came from delight, we grow in delight and at the end of our journey's close, we retire into delight. Delight is now in the inner world, while the outer world is all suffering. We see people quarreling and fighting. Fear, doubt, anger, jealousy and other undivine elements torture us. But when we go deep within, on the strength of our highest meditation, we discover that delight was our origin, our Source. We see that in delight we play the Cosmic Game and at the end of the Cosmic Game, we again retire into delight.

SUICIDE

Question: *Some persons are disturbed by the problems surrounding them. They think they can find escape in suicide. Do you think this is a door that we can open at our sweet will to escape from responsibility and suffering?*

Sri Chinmoy: Suicide is by no means an escape. There is no escape; there can be no escape. We can escape from this room, but we will be caught in another room. We think that we can escape from this world by killing ourselves.

Unfortunately, this is not the only world. There are other worlds as well. In this world I can take my life, but in another world I will have to continue my existence. Nay, I will be caught. God's Consciousness is all-pervading and He will be able to catch me, the thief.

Why do people commit suicide? They commit suicide because they feel that they are miserable, frustrated; others do not understand them. They feel that by committing suicide, they will be freed from countless responsibilities, inner turmoil and pain. Or they feel that as they have committed many wrong actions, they will be mercilessly punished, and they prefer to take their life first. So they need an escape. Now who escapes? Not a divine hero. A hero fights; a coward escapes. If I am on the right path, I will not try to escape. He who wants to commit suicide is a coward. He does not face the world.

First of all, you have to face the world, live in the world, in order to establish your divine qualities on earth. If we do not accept the world, what are we going to face? When we face the world, if there is anything wrong with the world, we can try to rectify it. So those who are committing suicide are committing the worst possible mistake. To be sure, there is no escape for them either in this world or in any other world. They are not only killing themselves, but are also killing the fruitful possibilities of their future incarnations.

351

Question: If someone is violently killed, does his soul undergo the same suffering as that of someone who has committed suicide?

Sri Chinmoy: No, it is not the same. If someone becomes a victim in a war or if someone is violently killed in a car accident, then it is some wrong forces that have killed the person. On the other hand, if somebody destroys his body, he becomes the aggressor. So the victim and the aggressor cannot be in the same category.

Question: What if a political prisoner commits suicide to end the unbearable suffering? Would that person have the same punishment as someone who simply takes his own life in a mood of escapism?

Sri Chinmoy: It depends on merits and demerits. During the war, how inhumanly and brutally the people in concentration camps were tortured and killed. What if they themselves wanted to destroy their lives because they did not want to be killed or mercilessly beaten without any reason? Here we have to know that there is something called God's dispensation. Let us say that these people are innocent and they are being killed. Or they fought for their lives and lost and now they are being killed. In order not to be killed by the enemy, they may want to destroy themselves.

In India and elsewhere it has happened many times that two warriors are fighting, and one knows definitely that the other one has won and it is a matter of a minute or a second before he will be destroyed. Immediately he will put an end to his life. His suffering will not be the same as if he had just committed suicide.

Question: Will the soul suffer if a person commits hara-kiri, a form of suicide which regarded as honorable in Japan?

Sri Chinmoy: It entirely depends on the individual case. Ordinarily, people commit suicide because they cannot face reality; they have emotional problems or their desires are not fulfilled. But each case is different and only God can decide. In the case of spiritual Masters, they can leave the body at will. But they do not harm the physical. The soul leaves occultly and spiritually. But first they take permission from the Supreme.

Question: *If someone makes an almost impossible attempt to save some-one else's life and he dies in the attempt, is this like suicide?*

Sri Chinmoy: You have to know the motive. The mother sees that the child is drowning. She may not be able to know that it is God's inten-tion that she stay on earth and look after her other children. Only she sees that her son is drowning, so she tries to save him. Then, if she dies, this is not suicide.

Question: *Your philosophy states that the soul is always making progress, but how do you reconcile that with the fact that when someone commits suicide his soul falls?*

Sri Chinmoy: When one commits suicide, the soul of that person actually does not fall. But it remains at a particular place and is cov-ered by infinitely more veils of ignorance. It is absolutely covered by ignorance—layer upon layer of ignorance. It is the consciousness of the individual that falls. It goes backwards right to the starting point, almost to the mineral consciousness, where there is no evolution. The soul is eclipsed by teeming ignorance, that is to say, by infinite layers of ignorance. Before, the soul had perhaps ten layers, but now it has countless layers of ignorance. The soul has to begin again removing them one by one. Of course, it becomes infinitely more difficult for the soul to carry the individual to perfect perfection, liberation or sal-vation.

But if the Supreme wants to operate in a particular human being who has committed suicide, on very, very rare occasions, the Supreme asks the spiritual Masters, who have the capacity, to take care of that soul and not to allow it to be enveloped by teeming ignorance. In these cases, whatever the soul already has is enough to bring the grace and compassion of the Supreme, and He will not allow a veil to cover the soul more than usual. But this is done only on very rare occasions.

Otherwise, if a person commits suicide, evolution stops for that individual indefinitely—for one hundred, two hundred, five hundred, six hundred years or even more. He cannot go forward, and the heav-iest possible load is placed on his shoulders. The process of his evolution stops. Because he has violated the laws of the Cosmic Game, he has to undergo the cosmic punishment. This punishment can never be imagined by any human being on earth. The worst possible earthly torture is simply nothing in comparison to the cosmic punishment the individual gets when he commits suicide.

You cannot say to the cosmic forces, "I have done something wrong and it is none of your business. I shall reach my goal when I feel like reaching it." You have jumped out of the Cosmic Game intentionally, without God's permission and against His intention. He has not allowed you to leave the game, but you have actively and openly defied Him and tried to ruin the game. For this wrong action the punishment is most severe. This punishment is so intense that with our human heart we cannot feel it, with our human mind we cannot imagine it.

Question: Sometimes people burn themselves to death as a protest against war. From the spiritual point of view, what does this accomplish?

Sri Chinmoy: In a family, very often the brothers will fight. Then the mother says, "If you do not stop, I am going to commit suicide." I know of many cases where the parents have committed suicide when they found it impossible to keep harmony in the family. Then the children immediately changed. When they saw that their parents died on account of their fighting, they turned over a new leaf. But this did not last, and soon they were fighting once again.

Now from the spiritual point of view, suicide does not serve any purpose. The mother has sacrificed herself for her children. By her own physical sacrifice she thought that she would create harmony, but in the vital world there is no escape, no forgiveness for her. To the vital world she will go for her stupidity, and there she will stay. Why did she not have the wisdom to see that the children are not her children but God's children? God gave her these children, so why did she not approach God to illumine their consciousness? Why did she not pray to God for their harmony and peace?

The world will remain ignorant unless and until the Supreme illumines the world consciousness. If we sacrifice our individual lives in order to bring about peace, the world's problems will never be solved.

Many martyrs, aspirants and spiritual figures have killed themselves, but it did not solve the problems of the world. These problems will be solved only by aspiration, by praying to God to illumine the world while we are here on earth. Our individual death can never transform the face of the world. But if we invoke God's blessing, God's grace and God's Concern, then all the world's problems can eventually be solved.

SURRENDER

Question: Speak to us about spiritual surrender.

Sri Chinmoy: The present-day world wants individuality. It demands freedom. But true individuality and freedom can breathe only in the Divine. Surrender is the untiring breath of the soul in the Heart of God.

Human individuality shouts in the dark. Earthly freedom cries out in the deserts of life. But absolute surrender universally sings of divine individuality and freedom in the lap of the Supreme.

In surrender we discover the spiritual power through which we can become not only the seers but also the possessors of Truth. This Truth is the omnipotent power. If we can surrender in absolute silence, we shall ourselves become the reality of the real, the life of the living, the center of true love, peace and bliss. We shall become an incomparable blessing to ourselves.

A lovely child attracts our attention. We love him because he conquers our heart. But do we ask anything from him in return? No! We love him because he is the object of love; he is lovable. In the same way we can and should love God, for He is the most lovable Being. Spontaneous love for the Divine is surrender, and this surrender is the greatest gift in life. For when we surrender, the Divine in no time gives us infinitely more than we would have asked for.

Surrender is a spiritual miracle. It teaches us how to see God with our eyes closed, how to talk to Him with our mouth shut. Fear enters into our being only when we withdraw our surrender from the Absolute.

Surrender is an unfoldment. It is the unfoldment of our body, mind and heart into the sun of divine Plenitude within us. Surrender to this inner sun is the greatest triumph of life. The hound of failure cannot reach us when we are in this sun. The prince of evil fails to touch us when we have realized and founded our oneness with this eternally life-giving sun.

Surrender and wholeheartedness play together, eat together and sleep together. Theirs is the crown of victory. Calculation and doubt play together, eat together and sleep together. Theirs is the fate that is doomed to disappointment, destined to failure.

Our surrender is a most precious thing. God alone deserves it. We can offer our surrender to another individual, but only for the sake of realizing God. If that individual has reached his goal, he can help us in our spiritual journey. If, however, we offer ourselves to someone just to satisfy that person, then we are committing a Himalayan blunder. What we should do is offer ourselves unreservedly to the Lord in him.

Every action of ours should be to please God and not to gain applause. Our actions are too secret and sacred to display before others. They are meant for our own progress, achievement and realization.

Question: *Could you speak to us on the necessity of surrender?*

Sri Chinmoy: There comes a time in our spiritual life when we realize that we are not satisfied with what we have, whether it is material wealth or inner wealth, or with what we are. At that time we are ready for surrender. How does one surrender? It is very easy. When we feel the need for surrender, automatically the means will come. If we are desperately in need of surrender, if we feel the soul's inner urge, if our entire being wants to surrender to God's Will, then automatically we will be given more than the necessary capacity, assurance, compassion and Light from above and within. When we surrender, we empty all our impurity into God and He replaces it with His Purity and His Divinity.

Surrender to God's Will entirely depends on our necessity. If we feel that our life is meaningless, that we will not be satisfied or fulfilled without surrendering our earthly existence to God's Will, then surrender will be possible for us.

God can never compel us to surrender; it is we who have to feel the necessity of loving God and devoting ourselves to God at every second. We start with love. Even in the ordinary life, when we love someone, we gladly devote our life and our entire being to that person. In the spiritual life also, if we really love God, who is all Light and infinite wisdom, then we have to devote ourselves to Him. So love and devotion must always go together.

When we devote ourselves to God we may have an ambition or a hankering for a personal way of getting the Truth. Some will say to the Supreme, "I am doing this for You; I have devoted all my life to You and expect You to give me something in return." This is quite natural, but from the highest spiritual point of view, it is wrong. Others will say, "I shall give what I have and what I am to God. If God does not like me or want me, then He may give me nothing; it is up to Him. My duty is to serve Him with what I have and what I am; it is His duty to give to me or not to give to me, to utilize me or not to utilize me." A real seeker will try to please God in God's own way.

Spiritual surrender is our absolute oneness with our own highest part, with the Supreme. We do not surrender to somebody other than ourselves. No! When our Master stands in front of us and bows down, to whom is he bowing? He is bowing to the Supreme in us. And when we bow down with folded hands to the Master, we are bowing to the Supreme in him. His Highest and our Highest can never be two different things; they are the same.

Our path of love, devotion and surrender will lead to the same goal as the path of *jnana*, wisdom. But we feel that the path of love is easier. The very word "God" conquers our heart, not because God has infinite power, but just because God is all love. God is the mightiest on earth. But our human nature is so feeble that if we concentrate on God as infinite power, we shall not be able to approach Him. If we say, "God" and immediately feel that He is all love, infinite love, then we are right; His love is His power. If we approach God through love, this is the easiest and quickest way.

Question: *How can we surrender to the Supreme?*

Sri Chinmoy: Let us say that as a child, when you were about three years old, you used to always listen to your mother. Perhaps you do not always listen to her now; but when you were a child, there were many things your mother asked you to do or not to do. Did you do anything wrong at that time by listening to her? No. Your mother asked you not to touch fire and you believed her. If you had touched the fire, it would have burnt your hand. But just because you were obedient and you surrendered to your mother's will, you escaped being burnt.

You have to have this same kind of faith in the spiritual life. You need to feel that your spiritual Master, like your mother, will not disappoint you or deceive you. You are now a child, a baby in the spiritual life. Your spiritual Master will not deceive you; your Inner Pilot will not deceive you. No! Surrender comes only when one has faith in somebody else, when one has more faith in that particular person than he has in himself.

You can also become a child just by unlearning. Ignorance and darkness have taught you many things which you have now to unlearn. A child knows practically nothing; he knows only how to love his mother and father, and that is more than everything for a child. Everyone has to unlearn things that the mind has taught him. So when we pray, when we meditate, the first thing we should do is get rid of doubts, suspicions and other negative qualities.

If you please your parents when they want you to do something, then if you ask them for money or for some other material help, immediately they will give it to you. They will give it to you because they have much more money than you have, much more capacity in various fields. But if you do not please them, they will give you nothing.

When a child comes running to his father with a nickel he has just found in the street, he says, "Look, Father, I have found a nickel!" The father is so happy that his son has come to him. The child's sole possession, his only wealth, is a nickel. With this nickel he could have gone to a shop and bought candy or used it some other way, but he did not. Instead, he came home to his father with this little nickel. Naturally the father is pleased and gives the child a quarter or dollar instead of the nickel.

In the spiritual life also, you give a little aspiration, which is your nickel, during your prayer or meditation for a few minutes early in the morning. Then immediately the spiritual Master will invoke so many things for you: peace, Light, bliss, joy and delight. But you have to give an iota of aspiration, for five minutes or half an hour of meditation in the morning.

God will never be indebted to you. You do have a little capacity; you meditate on God for a few minutes each day. The moment he sees that you are regular in your meditation, that you are sincere and earnest and have accepted the spiritual life wholeheartedly, God showers His boundless compassion on you in the form of Light, delight and peace.

So give to God what you have: your childlike faith and inner cry. If you can give Him your inner cry and have implicit faith in Him, then surrender will automatically loom large in your life of aspiration.

Question: *Could you speak to us about the joy in surrender?*

Sri Chinmoy: When an aspirant is totally surrendered to God's Will, he will get abundant joy. He will feel all joy in his heart and he will live in constant joy. He will not be able to account for it or give any meaning to it. Early in the morning when he first gets up, he will get a very sweet feeling or sensation. If he touches a wall, he will get joy; if he touches a mirror, he will also get joy. His own joy enters into everything he sees. At times, he may see that a solid wall is full of joy; a tree will be full of joy. If a taxi cab goes by, he will see intense joy in the driver, even in the car itself. His inner joy will enter into each person, each object; and it will pervade everything.

If there is total surrender, then there can be no failure. Surrender means the greatest joy, deepest joy, most soulful joy, even in so-called failure. Success also brings the same joy. When we are successful in something, immediately we derive joy from our success. Similarly, if our inner and outer lives are surcharged with surrendering Light, then at every moment we derive pure unalloyed joy from the highest Source. If we have this kind of spontaneous inner joy, then we can feel that it comes only from our total surrender to the Inner Pilot, the Master, the Guru, God.

Question: Can you tell us a story about spiritual surrender?

Sri Chinmoy: India is the land of surrender. This surrender is not a blind submission, but rather the dedication of one's limited self to one's unbounded Self. There are a good many stories in the *Mahabharata* dealing with surrender. They all have great spiritual Truth in them. Let me tell you a short but most inspiring and revealing story about Draupadi, who was the Queen of the Pandavas. While the evil Dhushasana was ruthlessly attempting to disrobe her, she was praying to the Lord to save her. Yet all the while she was holding her garments tightly with her fists. Her surrender was not complete, and her prayer was not granted. Dhushasana continued his efforts to pull off the garments of the unfortunate Queen. But the moment came when Draupadi released her hold on her robes and began to pray to the Lord with hands upraised. "O Lord of my heart, O Boatman of my life, may Thy Will be fulfilled," she prayed. Lo, the strength of her absolute surrender! God's silence broke. His grace rained down on Draupadi. As Dhushasana tried to pull off her sari, he found that it was endless. His pride had to kiss the dust.

God's all-fulfilling grace descends only when man's unconditional surrender ascends.

Question: Is there a limit to surrender?

Sri Chinmoy: There is no limit to our surrender. The more we surrender, the more we have to surrender. God has given us capacity. According to our capacity, He demands manifestation of us. Manifestation beyond our capacity God has never demanded and will never demand.

In man's complete and absolute surrender is his realization: his realization of the Self, his realization of God the Infinite.

Question: Is there a relationship between surrender to God and the opening of the chakras?

Sri Chinmoy: There is no direct relationship between one's surrender to God and one's progress in the opening of the chakras. One may totally surrender to God, but God may not or need not open that person's chakras. The full opening of the chakras may give the aspirant some occult powers, but that does not indicate that his surrender to God is stronger or going to be stronger as the result of the opening of the chakras. Far from it. If the surrender to God's Will is not complete, the occult powers that you get from the opening of the chakras is a veritable curse, instead of a covetous boon. One's misuse of occult power can and does lead one astray. To be sure, if one uses the occult power to draw the attention and admiration from the world and not in conformity with God's Will, the realization of the highest Absolute will always remain a far cry.

Question: *Is surrender a passive thing?*

Sri Chinmoy: There is a great difference between the surrender of laziness or utter helplessness and dynamic surrender, which is surcharged with aspiration. If out of laziness or helplessness we say, "I have surrendered. Now I do not want to do anything," this is not enough. Our surrender has to be dynamic, constantly aspiring to grow into or merge into the Infinite. Our surrender has to be conscious and spontaneous. When we surrender consciously and spontaneously to the infinite Truth, peace, Light and bliss, we become a perfect channel for these qualities to manifest in and through us on earth. In the West, surrender has been badly misunderstood. Here surrender is seen as submission to something or to somebody else. It is seen as a loss of individuality, an extinction of individuality. Then, where is the question of a perfect channel? But this view of spiritual surrender is a mistake. If we really want to be one with the Infinite, then we have to enter into it. When we enter into the Infinite, we do not lose our so-called little individuality. On the contrary, we become the Infinite itself. On the strength of our total oneness, we and the Infinite become indivisible.

Question: *Could you explain the difference between dependence and surrender?*

Sri Chinmoy: In real surrender we feel that our darkest part is surrendering to our brightest part, that our unlit part is surrendering to our fully illumined part. Let us say that my feet are in darkness and my head is in Light. My feet are surrendering to my head, knowing perfectly well that both the feet and the head are parts of the same body. This is the surrender of oneness. One enters into surrender knowing well that the brighter part is equally his.

We have to know what kind of dependence a seeker has. Some people are clever; they depend on the spiritual Master or on some higher authority, but only with a motive behind their dependence. But there is another type of dependence: a child's dependence. An innocent child feels that his father and mother will do everything for him. He feels that he is helpless. He has the sincere inner conviction that he cannot budge an inch or do anything without his mother's help, so he gets the mother's help.

To have true dependence, one has to feel that he is hopeless without the divine grace of the Supreme. This kind of dependence helps us immensely. Some of my disciples feel that if they leave me even for one day, they will be totally lost, like children in the desert. Those who have that kind of sincere feeling will make real progress. They are dependent, but not like beggars. They are dependent on the higher Light. When they depend on me, they feel that they are depending on something higher, which belongs to them.

If we have a free access to that higher plane and feel that the higher plane is also ours, then naturally we can depend on the higher plane. In that sense, dependence is very good. Otherwise, most of the time people are telling a lie when they say they depend on God's Will or they depend on the Master's will. By saying this, they only try to draw the attention of other disciples. They say, "Oh, Guru has said to do it? Then we will do it." Yet inwardly, two hundred times they have refused to do it. Outwardly they may do it, but with utmost inner unwillingness. So this kind of dependence is not good at all.

If your dependence is absolutely sincere, if you feel that without the help of the Supreme you cannot breathe, then this is surrender. When you breathe in, you depend on your life-breath. If your life-breath goes away, then you do not exist. Similarly, if you can feel that you are totally depending on the Will of the Supreme, which is far more important than your life-breath, then this dependence is true surrender.

Question: *Does the achievement of complete surrender assure that one will accomplish Self-realization in this lifetime, or are there other factors that enter the picture?*

Sri Chinmoy: Mere achievement of complete surrender does not assure Self-realization in this lifetime. There are other factors that must enter into the picture; God's choice hour, the aspirant's receptivity in its fullest measure and the full readiness of the entire being, to name only a few, are required for realization to dawn on the aspirant. Again, I wish you to know what complete surrender means. It means that the aspirant's surrender is joyful, soulful, spontaneous, unconditional and constant—forever and forever.

Question: *Am I correct in assuming that surrender necessarily precedes realization, or can it occur at the time of the first realization experience or later?*

Sri Chinmoy: You are correct in assuming that surrender precedes realization. It is inevitable. Now as for realization and experience, they are two totally different things. Realization is oneness with Oneness Itself. Experience is, at the most, a momentary or limited feeling of oneness with the highest Truth. So you cannot speak of "the experience of realization." Realization is not an experience; it is reality itself. You can correctly say "the oneness of realization in the realization-consciousness."

Question: *Having once surrendered completely, is there any possibility of backsliding, or will the strength of the disciple's aspiration and oneness with the Guru's consciousness prevent this?*

Sri Chinmoy: In one of my previous answers, I have told you what complete surrender means. If surrender has already achieved that kind of perfect perfection, then there can be no possibility of backsliding on the part of the disciple. A disciple who achieves perfect perfection in his or her surrender will undoubtedly be the highest pride of the Guru.

Question: *Realizing that the ability to surrender is 99% dependent upon grace, I have been using part of each meditation time to pray for the grace of God and my Guru. In view of the fact that you have said that prayer is a lesser form of devotion than meditation, I wonder whether what I am doing is a worthwhile effort.*

Sri Chinmoy: I am extremely glad to learn that you have realized the fact that the ability to surrender is 99% dependent on the Divine grace. That you are praying for grace is an excellent thing. Unfortunately, however, there has been a slight misunderstanding. I have not said that prayer is a lesser form of devotion than meditation. What I stated was that prayer is a lesser form of aspiration and that the rung of meditation is by far the highest in the spiritual life. Since you are meditating devotedly, you are undoubtedly doing the right thing in also praying. Needless to say, your effort is entirely worthwhile.

Question: *At times, when praying and meditating on surrender, I am moved to copious tears. I feel these tears as different from those tears of soul's joy which I have experienced at times. The anguish which accompanies them makes me feel that these are not even tears of aspiration, but merely of frustration, and this disturbs me. How can I aspire for, and concentrate on surrender without becoming so emotional? Even writing this question, I find myself moved to tears.*

Sri Chinmoy: I am sure you know that when the soul expresses its joy with tears it means that the soul is expressing its deepest gratitude through the physical being. As you know, in the soul's joy, there can be no frustration. There you get only the feeling of a vast and total oneness with the Highest on the strength of your surrender. During your meditation and prayer, at times what you feel is the uncertain drive of your yet-uncontrolled emotional vital. Since you have, a few times, experienced the tears of your soul's joy, which are a kind of divine Light, the frustration that lies in your unlit emotional vital cannot last for long. Again, if your prayer is flooded with purity and your meditation is surcharged with luminosity, even in the domain of the gross vital, instead of frustration you will have a partial sense of psychic realization, of Truth in the form of the heart's spontaneous joy. The spontaneous joy of the heart can easily enable you to meditate on total and integral surrender. Please try to illumine your emotional vital through your soul's Light. Once the limited emotional vital is illumined, it enters into the boundless sea of all-achieving and all-fulfilling surrender.

Question: *I have the feeling that when our heart and our soul have surrendered, we can know it ourselves, in fact, do know it in our heart, but, other than being told by the Guru, are there any ways in which we can know positively that our vital and physical being have surrendered?*

Sri Chinmoy: It is not always inevitable that one knows definitely when the heart and the soul have surrendered to the Will Divine. There are many cases where we have seen that in spite of the heart's surrender and the soul's surrender to the Divine, the aspirant still gropes in the dark, playing with uncertainty. Here is the need of a Guru. If the Guru says that your heart and soul have both surrendered, then rest assured that they have certainly done so.

There is one positive way of knowing that one's vital and physical being have surrendered and that is through widest expansion and enlargement of one's vital and physical being. In the constant flow of inner delight and outer dynamic, confident urge, one invokes the Highest to descend into the lowest, thus bringing the Supreme atmosphere into the earth atmosphere.

Question: *As one may consciously feel that one deeply wishes to surrender and may, in fact, do so intellectually, without yet ridding oneself of the fear within the physical mind, this would seem to indicate that the different levels of mind each have an independent relationship to surrender. Would you please explain what the relationship is?*

Sri Chinmoy: You know well that there are the physical mind, vital mind, subtle mind, intellectual mind, intuitive mind apart from the infinitely higher ranges of the mind, the Overmind and Super-mind, etc. If you want to offer the different levels of the human mind proper, then you have to give due importance to each, individually and collectively, with your aspiration. You have to create a basic and fundamental union amongst them. You have to feel that these are petals of a lotus and the lotus is your own aspiring life. Unless and until the lotus is offered totally, and fully bloomed, the realization cannot be complete and the acceptance of the Inner Pilot will not be for eternity.

Question: *When fear holds back the physical mind from surrender, it operates like an invisible enemy. This fear, being subconscious, is something of which we may be totally unaware, and even when told that it exists and is holding us back, it remains a fear that we do not feel. I daily offer my fear to the Supreme, but this offering has a feeling of unreality. How may we overcome an invisible obstacle such as this?*

Sri Chinmoy: I am glad that you feel that fear acts like an invisible enemy. If you become more aware of your inner life and deeper existence, you will realize that fear is not only a visible, naked enemy but your worst possible foe. It is absolutely true that fear holds back the physical mind from total surrender. If a spiritual Master tells the disciple that he has inner fear, then he should have perfect faith in the Master, although he may not feel the existence of this fear. The Master's vision is always faultless. The Master has no need to tell a lie. He gains nothing by telling a certain disciple that deep down in his being there is real fear. If the aspirant is not aware of fear, the culprit, that means that either in the subconscious or unconscious part of his being, he gets some joy when he identifies himself with fear. Here at this point, the Master can say, if he wants to, that the unaspiring and insincere part of the disciple is unconsciously in collusion with fear to prevent the Light from descending from above.

You say that you offer your fear to the Supreme daily. This is something absolutely necessary, wonderful and praiseworthy. But to my surprise, you say that this offering of yours has a feeling of unreality. If only once you cared to believe that the Supreme does exist on earth to accept your offer and your unconsciously cherished fear, then your feeling of unreality would disappear. The Supreme will make you feel, on the strength of your implicit sincerity, that you do have fear.

You want to know how you can overcome this invisible obstacle. I wish to tell you that you can overcome all obstacles, visible and invisible, on the way towards your God-realization if you have genuine faith in the Master's inner inspiration, outer dispensation, higher guidance and deeper wisdom.

Question: *How does surrender affect rebirth into our next incarnation? Does it in any way assure that we will be able to pick up where we left off without the loss of time which often occurs?*

Sri Chinmoy: If one's surrender is complete and constant, then the result of surrender, which is conscious oneness with the Divine, will bring the aspirant into a first-class spiritual family in his next incarnation. From the very beginning, he will be inspired and nurtured spiritually by the parents. He will not have to wait for seventeen or eighteen years to convince his physical mind about his inner spiritual thirst. His will be the life of conscious awareness in the field of spirituality right from his birth.

    I just said that the parents would inspire the child. It is equally true that the child, the very divine face of the child, will inspire the parents to dive deep into the sea of spirituality.

Question: *What happens when I make a conscious surrender to the Supreme in the Master?*

Sri Chinmoy: You become everything that he has and is. The tiny drop enters into the boundless ocean and becomes the ocean itself. This surrender is the surrender of your unillumined part to your highest part, which is represented by the Supreme in your spiritual Master. In this case, your Master represents your own highest Self.

    One day Sri Ramakrishna and two of his very close disciples were returning to their ashram in a boat. The two disciples and Sri Ramakrishna were extremely hungry. While they were in the boat, Sri Ramakrishna asked one of them to bring him some juice and food. When the disciple brought them, Ramakrishna did not give the others a morsel. He ate and drank everything himself! But because of their identification with their Master, because of their oneness with him, these two disciples really felt that their hunger and thirst were appeased. They no longer felt hungry or thirsty at all.

    If a disciple has established this kind of inner oneness with his Master, then he will not expect anything. The child does not expect things from his mother. He knows that his mother has given him and will continue to give him everything, for it is the mother's bounden duty to take care of the child. Similarly, it is your spiritual Master's bounden duty to be of constant service to you. You serve him with your aspiration and dedication; he serves you with his concern and compassion. You play your role with aspiration. He plays his role with his concern and compassion, which uplift your consciousness.

THOUGHTS

Question: In the spiritual life, the importance of purity is always stressed. Are pure actions worthwhile if thoughts are impure? How can we purify our thoughts?

Sri Chinmoy: Yes, in the spiritual life the importance of purity is always stressed. It is not only unavoidable but supremely necessary, for without soulful purity, the aspirant's life will have to dance with futility. It is true that when you act, your thoughts must be pure. That is why the spiritual Masters say that it is not so much what you do but how you do it. Since I am one of them, I wish to add that at the beginning, even if your thoughts are impure and motives conditional, do not be upset. Start your inner journey from where you are right now. If you wait for purity to flood your outer consciousness before you start your inner and outer work, then you are doing something absurd. If you stick to the spiritual path, then the divine purity is bound to dawn on your inner life and your outer life in the course of time.

You want to know how you can purify your thoughts. You can purify them just by feeling that your thoughts are coming out of your devoted and consecrated inner life and not from your doubting, suspecting, scrutinizing, reasoning, fault-finding and correcting mind.

Question: What is the best way to prevent wrong thoughts from attacking us?

Sri Chinmoy: The thoughts that we have to control are the thoughts that are not productive, the thoughts that are damaging, the thoughts that are destructive, the thoughts that are silly, the thoughts that are negative. These thoughts can come from outside and enter into us; or they may already be inside us and merely come forward. The thoughts that come from outside are easier to control than the thoughts that are already inside. If an undivine thought comes from outside, we have to feel that we have a shield all around us or right in front of us as a protection, especially in front of the forehead. If we feel that our forehead is something vulnerable, delicate, exposed, then we will always be a victim to wrong thoughts. But the moment we consciously make ourselves feel that this forehead is a shield, a solid wall, then wrong thoughts cannot come in. We have to make ourselves feel consciously that we are protected by a solid wall or a fort with many soldiers inside. We have to be constantly vigilant and, when an attack of wrong thoughts comes, we have to know that we have inside us soldiers stronger than they are. The strongest soldiers are our purity, our sincerity, our aspiration and our eagerness for God. These divine soldiers inside us will be on their guard the moment a wrong thought comes, and they will serve as bodyguards to us.

The thoughts that are already inside us creating problems are more difficult to throw out, but we can do it. We can do it through extension of our consciousness. We have a body, and inside this body are wrong forces that have taken the form of thoughts. What we have to do is extend our physical consciousness through conscious effort and aspiration, as we extend an elastic band, until we feel that our whole body is extended to infinity and has become just a white sheet of infinitely extended consciousness. If we can do this, we will see that our consciousness is all purity.

Each pure thought, each pure drop of consciousness, is like poison to impurity or to wrong thoughts in us. We are afraid of impure thoughts, but impure thoughts are more afraid of our purity. What often happens to us is that we identify ourselves with our impure thoughts and not with our pure thoughts. But the moment our physical existence can identify with purity, when we can say, "This pure thought represents me," then impurity inside us immediately dies. Wrong thoughts are inside us just because we identify ourselves with these thoughts. If we identify with something else, immediately they have to leave us.

Vegetarianism

Question: *Are you a vegetarian?*

Sri Chinmoy: I am a vegetarian. I stopped eating meat and fish when I was twelve years old, the age that I entered seriously into the spiritual life.

Question: *What role does the vegetarian diet play in your teachings?*

Sri Chinmoy: In my teachings the vegetarian diet plays a most important role. In order to become pure, a vegetarian diet helps us considerably. Purity is of paramount importance in our spiritual life. This purity we must establish in the physical, the vital and the mind. When we eat meat, fish and so forth, the aggressive, animal consciousness enters into us. Our nerves become agitated; we unconsciously become restless and aggressive. The mild qualities of vegetables, on the other hand, help us to establish in our inner life, as well as in our outer life, the qualities of sweetness, softness, simplicity and purity.

But again, if you ask me whether by becoming a strict vegetarian you can realize God or not, then I would say "No," a definite "No." There are millions and millions of people on earth who are strict vegetarians, but I do not think there are millions and millions of God-realized souls on earth. For God-realization we need aspiration. But in answering your question, I wish to say that it is always advisable, if possible, to have a vegetarian diet in order to further one's progress in the inner discipline, so that one can feel that even the body, with its purity, can help one's inner aspiration to become more intense and more soulful.

Question: *Do you feel it is important for the aspirant to follow the vegetarian diet?*

Sri Chinmoy: The answer will be yes and no. It depends on the individual aspirant. We all know that we have come from the animal kingdom. We believe in reincarnation. So once upon a time, we were all animals. Now, we have come into the human creation. We are progressing and evolving and all of us will realize God on the strength of our aspiration. For an aspirant, it is advisable to be a vegetarian precisely because when he eats meat, the aggressive quality of the animal enters into him. We are trying to live a life of peace and tranquility. If we sincerely want that kind of life, then it is foolishness on our part to eat something that would diminish our peace and tranquility and stand in the way of our meditation, concentration, etc. So it is always advisable to accept the vegetarian life.

Again, there are some parts of the world where it is exceptionally cold and there it is impossible to live on vegetables alone. There only if they eat meat can they remain on earth. Then, again, there are some sincere seekers whose physical constitution is very weak. Some children, for example, who are very ill require meat for a short time to regain their strength. Others from the beginning of their lives have been eating meat and now they have formed such a habit, such a bad habit, you can say, that they cannot manage without it even for a day. What are they going to do? On the one hand, they have sincere aspiration, genuine aspiration, but their body revolts. I feel, in such rare cases, that they should eat meat.

But as a general rule, it is always advisable to be a vegetarian because we are trying to throw away the animal qualities and propensities from our nature. Already when we go deep within, we see that we have two different qualities or natures—the divine and the undivine. The undivine is the animal in us and the animal within us will always be aggressive and destructive. The divine in us will always be progressive and illumined. If we want to march and run towards our goal, then we have to do away with our animal life. To do that, whatever animal qualities we take into us in the form of meat or in some other form have to be discontinued.

Now if one says that one has to be a vegetarian in order to realize God or that one cannot achieve God-realization unless he is a vegetarian, that it is pure foolishness. There are many meat-eaters who have realized God: the Christ and Swami Vivekananda, to name just two. A few months ago someone told me that in order to have purity in abundance, he stopped eating meat, but he also felt that just by becoming a vegetarian, he would be able to realize God. He would not have to meditate, he would not have to concentrate; only by becoming a vegetarian, he could achieve union with the Absolute. So I told him that in India, all widows without exception are forbidden to take meat. When their husbands die, on that very day, they have to stop taking meat. Now in spite of my deepest love and respect for Indian widows, I do not think that they are all God-realized souls. That kind of feeling towards the vegetarian life is absurd. We have to strike a balance. For a sincere aspirant, it is certainly advisable and helpful to be a vegetarian.

Question: *I find that when I eat meat I cannot meditate very well; I feel restless. But if I do not eat meat, I feel very weak.*

Sri Chinmoy: You know very well that animals are restless, aggressive, destructive and unevolved. We have transcended the animal consciousness to some extent, and we have come out of the animal kingdom. We are only one step ahead on the ladder of evolution, but the difference between an animal and a human being is very vast. Now, when you eat something, naturally you will absorb the qualities of that thing. What you have within you will unavoidably manifest itself outwardly in some way. When you eat meat, the immediate result is restless, aggressive and destructive impulses and thoughts, and lowering of the consciousness.

It is not true, however, that if you do not eat meat you will lose strength, power or energy. There are millions of people on earth who do not eat meat, but who are physically very strong and healthy. You may say that your constitution is different from theirs, but I wish to say that in God's creation there is something called inner food. What is this food? It is peace, Light and bliss and all other divine, fulfilling qualities. When you aspire properly, meditate properly, you will be able to draw this inner food into your body. It may take quite a number of years for you to attain this degree of inner proficiency, but in the meantime try to go deep within and see what actually gives you most of your strength. I have known people to claim it is meat that gives them strength, but when they go deep within, they discover that it is their own feeling and idea about meat that is giving them strength.

WORDS

Question: *In the old books they talk about* nama-rupa, *name and form. Words are* nama-rupa, *right? Ideas are* nama-rupa. *Now this is not really God. These are human concoctions, something you make out of nothing. So naturally, words by themselves, that is, the objective words that we speak or write, have no inherent meaning. The meaning is a manufactured thing. There is no reality in the word itself.*

Sri Chinmoy: As you know, the study of Semantics has gone into this problem very deeply. We know that it is not the actual word but the concept which we attach to the word that creates most of our difficulties. The spiritual approach to this problem of words is that we have to go from the form to the Formless. We have to go to the infinite through the finite. So at the beginning, we have to give a form to something. For example, at the beginning we say that God has a form. Then we go deep within and we see that God is not a human being or a mental being but a vast, infinite Consciousness. For a beginner on the spiritual path, a form is absolutely necessary; the form is everything to him. Then he goes beyond the form to the Formless. He can get the infinite Consciousness, he can feel God, the infinite Consciousness. But again, God, being infinite, can also be finite. Otherwise, He is not infinite. He is omnipotent because He can be in the atom and at the same time in the vast universe. Through the form we have to go to the Formless. Through the finite we have to go to the infinite. Indeed, this is the divine logic. Form at the beginning has a peerless value, but not necessarily at the end.

Again, it is not the word by itself that has an intrinsic value, but what it conveys. Certain spiritual words are surcharged with a meaning or a condition or a consciousness that has developed in them from thousands of years of a special spiritual usage. When we enter deep into the significance of such a word, and reveal the very breath of the word and manifest its inner urge on the outer level, then the word fulfills its purpose, both inwardly and outwardly.

WORRY

Question: I do not know what is going to happen to me in the future, and I worry a lot about my destiny. Is this right?

Sri Chinmoy: No, we should not worry. We should have implicit faith in God, in our Inner Pilot or in our spiritual Master. We have to feel that not only does God know what is best for us, but He will do what is best for us. We worry because we do not know what is going to happen to us tomorrow, or even the next minute. We feel that if we do not do something for ourselves, then who is going to do it? But if we can feel that there is someone who thinks of us infinitely more than we think of ourselves, and if we can consciously offer our responsibility to Him, saying, "You be responsible. Eternal Father, Eternal Mother, You be responsible for what I do and say and grow into," then our past, our present and our future become His problem. As long as we try to be responsible for our own life, we will be miserable. We will not be able to properly utilize even two minutes out of every twenty-four hours we have. When we can feel that we are God's conscious instruments and He is the Doer, then we will not worry about our destiny; we will not be afraid of our destiny, for we will know and feel that it is in the all-loving Hands of God, who will do everything in us, through us and for us.

Let us consciously offer our very existence—what we have and what we are—to God. What we have is aspiration to grow into the very image of God, into infinite peace, Light and bliss. And what we are right now is just ignorance, the ignorance-sea. If we can offer our aspiration-cry and our ignorance-sea to God, then our problem is solved. We should not and we need not ever worry about destiny. On the strength of our surrender, we become inseparably one with God's cosmic Will.

Question: How can one conquer worry?

Sri Chinmoy: Ignore it deliberately. To be sure, worry also has its own pride. It will ignore you totally. It will feel that it is beneath its dignity to come to you and offer all its problems and responsibilities. Why do you worry? Just pray in the morning, concentrate at noon, meditate in the evening, contemplate at night. That is all! Look, your worries are buried in oblivion-hush.

Why do you worry? Turn around; look, God is looking at you. Enter into your mind; look, God is devotedly thinking of you. Enter into your heart; look, God is all for you. Enter into your soul; look, God has already done everything for you.

YOGA

Question: *What is actually meant by Yoga?*

Sri Chinmoy: "Yoga" means "union." This union is between man and God. Yoga tells us that we have a divine quality called aspiration within us and that God has a divine quality called compassion. Yoga is the common link between our aspiration and God's compassion.

Yoga is the language of God. If we wish to speak to God, we have to learn His language. What is Yoga? Yoga is that which discloses God's secret. If we wish to know God's secret we have to launch into the path of Yoga. What is Yoga? Yoga is the breath of God. If we wish to see through God's Eye and feel through His Heart, if we wish to live in God's Dream and know God's reality, if we wish to possess the Breath of God, and finally if we wish to become God Himself, Yoga will beckon us.

What we have to do is accept life and fulfill the Divine in ourselves here on earth. This can be effectuated only by transcending our human limitations.

Yoga tells us how far we have progressed in relation to God-realization. It also tells us about our destined role in God's Cosmic Drama. The final word of Yoga is that each human soul is a divine representative of God on earth.

Now let us focus our attention on the practical aspect of Yoga. There are various kinds of Yoga. *Karma Yoga*, the path of action; *Bhakti Yoga*, the path of love and devotion; and *Jnana Yoga*, the path of knowledge. These three serve as the three main gates to God's palace. If we want to see and feel God in the sweetest and the most intimate way, then we have to practice Bhakti Yoga. If we want to realize God in humanity through our selfless service, then we have to practice Karma Yoga. If we want to realize wisdom and the glories of God's transcendental Self, then we have to practice Jnana Yoga.

One thing is certain. These three paths lead us to Self-realization in God-realization and God-realization in Self-realization.

Question: *Would you speak to us about Bhakti Yoga?*

Sri Chinmoy: Ask a man about God, and he will speak endlessly. Ask a *bhakta* to speak about God, and he will say only two things: God is all Affection, God is all Sweetness. The *Bhakta* even goes one step further. He says, "I can try to live without bread, but I can never live without my Lord's grace." A *bhakta's* prayer is very simple: "O my Lord God, do enter into my life with Thine Eye of Protection and with Thy Heart of Compassion." This prayer is the quickest way to knock at God's Door and also the easiest way to see God open the Door.

A karma Yogin and a jnana Yogin may suffer a moment of doubt about God's existence. But a *bhakta* has no suffering of that type. To him, the existence of God is an axiomatic truth. More than that, it is his heart's spontaneous feeling. But alas, he too has to undergo a kind of suffering. His is the suffering of separation from his Beloved. With the tears of his heart's devotion, he cries to re-establish his sweetest union with God. The reasoning mind does not charm the *bhakta* devotee. The hard facts of life fail to draw his attention, let alone absorb him. He wants to live constantly in a God-intoxicated realm.

A devotee feels that when he walks towards God, God runs towards him. A devotee feels than when he thinks of God for a second, God cries for him for an hour. A devotee feels that when he goes to God with a drop of his love to quench God's ceaseless thirst, God enfolds him in the sea of His ambrosial love.

The relation between a devotee and God can only be felt, never described. Poor God thinks that no man on earth can capture Him, for He is priceless and invaluable. To His greatest surprise, to His deepest joy, His devotee's surrendered devotion is able to capture Him.

Question: *Would you speak to us about Karma Yoga?*

Sri Chinmoy: Karma Yoga is desireless action undertaken for the sake of the Supreme. Karma Yoga is man's genuine acceptance of his earthly existence. Karma Yoga is man's dauntless march across the battlefield of life. Karma Yoga does not see eye to eye with those who hold that activities of human life are of no importance. Karma Yoga claims that life is a divine opportunity for serving God. This particular Yoga is not only the Yoga of physical action; it includes the aspirant's moral and inner life as well.

Those who follow this path pray for a strong and perfect body. They also pray for a long life. This long life is not a mere promulgation of life in terms of years. It is a life that longs for the descent of the divine Truth, Light, and power into the material realm. The karma Yogins are the real heros on the earthly scene, and theirs is the divinely triumphant victory.

A karma Yogin is a perfect stranger to the waves of disappointment and despair in human life. He feels himself to be the hyphen between earthly duties and heavenly responsibilities. He has many weapons to conquer the world, but his detachment is the most powerful. His detachment defies both the crushing blows of failure and the ego-gratifying surges of success. His detachment is far beyond both the snares of the world's excruciating pangs and the embrace of the world's throbbing joy.

Many sincere aspirants feel that the devotional feelings of a *bhakta* and the penetrating eye of a *jnani* have no place in Karma Yoga. Here they are quite mistaken. A true karma Yogin is he whose heart has implicit faith in God, whose mind has a constant awareness of God and whose body has a genuine love for humanity.

It is easy for a *bhakta* to forget the world, and for a *jnani* to ignore the world. But a karma Yogin's destiny is otherwise. God wants him to live in the world, live with the world and live for the world.

Question: *Would you speak to us about Jnana Yoga?*

Sri Chinmoy: The *bhakta's* faith in God and the karma Yogin's love for humanity do not interest a Jnana Yogin, much less inspire him. He wants nothing but the mind. With his mental power he strives for the personal experience of the highest Truth. He thinks of God as the Fount of Knowledge. He feels that it is through his mind that he will attain his goal. At the beginning of his path, he feels that nothing is as important as the fulfillment of the mind. Eventually he comes to realize he must transcend the mind if he wishes to live in the Supreme Knowledge.

Life is a mystery. So is death. A jnana Yogin wants to fathom these two apparently insoluble mysteries of God's creation. He also wants to transcend both life and death and abide in the Heart of the Supreme reality.

Man lives in the sense world. He does not know whether this world is real or unreal. An ordinary man is satisfied with his own existence. He has neither the thinking capacity nor the sincere interest to enter into the deeper meaning of life. He wants to escape the problems of life and death. Unfortunately, there is no escape. He has to swim in the sea of ignorance. A jnana Yogin alone can teach him how to swim across the sea of ignorance and enter the sea of knowledge and Light.

Question: *Can anybody practice Yoga?*

Sri Chinmoy: Yes, anybody can practice Yoga and it can be practiced irrespective of age. But we must understand what Yoga really involves. Unfortunately, there are many people who think that Yoga means physical postures and breathing exercises. This is a deplorable mistake. These postures and exercises are preliminary and preparatory states, leading towards concentration and meditation, which alone can take us to a deeper, higher and fuller life.

Yoga is not something unnatural, abnormal or unearthly. It is something practical, natural and spontaneous. Right now, we do not know where God is and what God looks like. But by practicing Yoga, we see Him first hand. As in the material world we achieve success in our chosen activity by constant practice, so also in the spiritual world, by practicing Yoga, we achieve the Goal of goals—God-realization.

Question: *Who is fit for Yoga?*

Sri Chinmoy: Who is fit for Yoga? You are fit for Yoga. He is fit for Yoga. I am fit for Yoga. All human beings without exception are fit for Yoga.

The spiritual fitness can be determined by our feeling of oneness, our desire for oneness. The tiniest drop has a right to feel the boundless ocean as its very own, or to cry to have the ocean as its very own. Such is the case with the individual soul and the universal Soul.

Where is God and where am I? God is on the third floor and I am on the first floor. I come up to the second floor. He comes down to the second floor. We both meet together. I do not forget to wash His Feet with my tears of delight. Nor does He forget to place me in His Heart of infinite compassion.

What is Yoga? Yoga is self-conquest. Self-conquest is God-realization. He who practices Yoga does two things with one stroke: he simplifies his whole life and he gets a free access to the Divine.

In the field of Yoga, we can never pretend. Our aspiration must ring true. Our whole life must ring true. Nothing is impossible for an ardent aspirant. A higher power guides his steps. God's adamantine Will is his safest protection. No matter how long or how many times the aspirant blunders, he has every right to come back to his own spiritual home. His aspiration is a climbing flame. It has no smoke, it needs no fuel. It is the breath of his inner life. It leads him to the shores of the Golden Beyond. The aspirant, with the wings of his aspiration, soars into the realms of the Transcendental.

God is infinite and God is omnipresent. To a genuine aspirant, this is more than mere belief. It is the reality without a second.

It is a mistaken idea that the spiritual life is a life of austerity and a bed of thorns. No, never! We came from the Blissful. To the Blissful we shall return with the spontaneous joy of life. It seems difficult because we cater to our ego. It looks unnatural because we cherish our doubts.

The realization of God is the goal of our life. It is also our noblest heritage. God is at once our Father and our Mother. As our Father, He observes; as our Mother, He creates. Like a child, we shall never give up demanding of our Mother, so that we can win our Mother's love and grace. How long can a mother go on unheeding her child's cry? Let us not forget that if there is anybody on whom all human beings have a full claim, it is the Mother aspect of the Divine; She is the only strength of our dependence; She is the only strength of our independence. Her Heart, the home of infinitude, is eternally open to each individual.

We should now become acquainted with the eight significant strides that lead a seeker to his Destination. These strides are: *yama*, self-control and moral abstinence; *niyama*, strict observance of conduct and character; *asana*, various body postures which help us enter into a higher consciousness; *pranayama*, systematic breathing to hold a rein on the mind; *pratyahara*, withdrawal from the sense-life; *dharana*, the fixation of our consciousness on God, joined by all parts of the body; *dhyana*, meditation, the untiring express train speeding toward the goal; and *samadhi*, trance, the end of nature's dance, the total merging of our individual consciousness into the infinite Consciousness of the Transcendental Supreme.

Yoga is our union with Truth. There are three unfolding stages of this union. In the first stage, man has to feel that God needs him as much as he needs God. In the second stage, man has to feel that, without him, God does not exist even for a second. In the third and ultimate stage, man has to realize that he and God are not only eternally one, but also equal, all-pervading and all-fulfilling.

Question: *Can Yoga help us in our everyday life?*

Sri Chinmoy: Certainly. Yoga helps us in our everyday life. As a matter of fact, it is Yoga that can serve as the supreme help in our daily lives. Our human life is full of doubt, fear and frustration. Yoga helps us to replace fear with indomitable courage, doubt with absolute certainty and frustration with golden achievements.

Question: *Can a person remain in his own religion and at the same time practice Yoga?*

Sri Chinmoy: It is quite possible. It is always easier and safer, in fact, for one to practice Yoga at the beginning while remaining in his own religion. But once one has reached God by practicing Yoga, he transcends all barriers of religion. God-realization reveals to him that each religion is nothing but a river that ultimately has to merge into the boundless ocean. The ultimate aim of each religion is God-realization. Here also, Yoga comes as an inevitable aid, to transport the finite human being into the infinite divine Self.

Religion is inspiration. Yoga is aspiration. Divinity is perfection. Inspiration, aspiration and divinity can easily and fruitfully blossom here on earth in transcendental harmony.

Question: I wonder if Yoga itself is a part of another religion of India or is it a religion in itself?

Sri Chinmoy: Yoga is not a religion. Yoga transcends all religions. It is something infinitely deeper than religion. Yoga is the living breath that makes us feel that God is within us, of us and for us. Yoga is direct communion with God. It is our union with God that Yoga teaches us. And at the same time, it is the language of our inner spiritual life. Right now, I am speaking in English in order to convey my feelings, thoughts and ideas. Similarly, if I want to speak to God, commune with God, then the language that is required is called Yoga.

Question: In Yoga, how do you communicate with God?

Sri Chinmoy: In Yoga we pray, we concentrate and we meditate. When we pray, we get an inner feeling of going upwards, that is to say, with our hearts we feel that we are crying for something from above. When we concentrate, we focus all our intense attention on something—it may be an object or it may be a person—in order to identify ourselves with it. When we meditate, we enter into the deeper planes of consciousness. These three ways, prayer, concentration and meditation, are the most effective ways to commune with God.

Question: Most of us in the Western world who are ignorant of Yoga have a tendency to think of a Yogi as someone sitting with his legs crossed, or someone standing on his head, someone doing particular exercises or things that seem strange to us. How or why does a Yogi perform these feats?

Sri Chinmoy: Some people take these exercises to keep the body fit, free from physical ailments and so forth, while others take them in order to get realization. But realization can never be had by merely doing Hatha Yoga exercises. What these exercises actually do is to help the seeker enter into the true spiritual life.

In the beginning, a child reads aloud in order to convince his parents that he is reading. A grown-up person reads silently. Now in the physical world, there is a similarity. Right now most of us are physically very restless, no better than monkeys. We cannot stay more than a second without getting restless. But there are aspirants who can just sit down and make their minds calm and quiet and then they enter into the deeper regions of the being. It is these physical exercises and postures which relax our body and give us peace of mind for a short period of time.

But these exercises will never give us realization. These are the preliminary stages. The beginners in Hatha Yoga are like kindergarten students. One can easily skip kindergarten. But we have to go from kindergarten to elementary school, high school, college and then to university. Concentration, meditation and contemplation are taught in the higher courses. Otherwise, just by taking physical exercises and making the body strong, the athletes, the boxers, the wrestlers would all have realized God by this time.

Hatha Yoga exercises are superior to some other exercises which are done abruptly, vigorously and, to some extent, violently. When Hatha Yoga exercises are done calmly, quietly, in a meditative mood, they strengthen the nerves and calm the mind.

The body is necessary. We must have a sound and healthy body so that the soul can act in and through the body in the field of manifestation. But if we expect something more from the body, then we are being foolish.

Question: Recently, I read about a person who was buried alive for eighteen days and then was able to come back alive. Is there any relation between this sort of thing and Yoga?

Sri Chinmoy: My teaching is not a kind of miracle-mongering. My business is to help the aspirant to reach God. When one wants to realize God, I try to help the person. But by being buried underground for eighteen days or by performing other feats, I cannot lead my students to God nor are the students helped in their spiritual search. What leads us to God is our aspiration, our inner, mounting cry. So I do not advocate this kind of miracle.

What I want from my students is this inner cry. A child cries for his mother's love; a spiritual child needs and wants to have infinite love from God. And how can he get it? Only by reaching and realizing God. My philosophy and spirituality are different from those who are meant only for displaying and teaching their supernatural capacities.

Question: So what that person did has nothing to do with Yoga?

Sri Chinmoy: It has very little to do with true Yoga. Yoga means "union with God." If somebody performs miracles, he is not helping you directly or indirectly to realize God. At most, we learn from him that there is no end to human capacity. If one enters into the secret domains where the inherent powers of the cosmic realities exist, one can get the capacity to do anything.

I know an amusing incident in connection with a *fakir* in India who used to perform this very feat you mention. He could remain buried for long periods of time and often lay underground for as long as twenty-one days. Once it happened that when he was dug up from his long burial, the moment he regained consciousness, he looked around frantically for his girlfriend who was standing amidst his relatives, friends and admirers. Having found his paramour, he left the spot immediately with her. Now did his unusual achievement help the audience in any way in their aspiration for God-realization? You tell me. By performing these miracles, we in no way inspire others to unite themselves with God, whereas in helping someone in his aspiration, his concentration and his meditation, we do help the person to realize God.

Question: If a person practices Yoga, what kind of life will he lead in his daily activities?

Sri Chinmoy: In his daily activities he has to be, first of all, sincere, honest and pure. He has to have purity in his mind, in his body, in his speech and in his ideas. Anyone can practice sincerity, honesty and purity. Then if he really wants to practice Yoga, the deeper Yoga, each day for about fifteen minutes he must devote himself to his inner search, to his self-discovery. These fifteen minutes of meditation have to be learned from someone who can teach him. He needs a teacher for meditation, for his inner illumination. The individual has to know how sincere he is or how far he wants to go, how deeply he wants to accept Yoga. If he feels that he wants to go to the end of the road, that he wants to reach the goal, then he has to follow some strict inner discipline and he has to meditate, concentrate and so forth. But if he wants to remain satisfied with obtaining a little peace, joy and Light, then what I said at the beginning, in answering your question, applies here: let him be perfectly sincere in all his activities.

Question: *Does a person who has not practiced Yoga have the same grade of unity with God after death as one who practices Yoga?*

Sri Chinmoy: No. One who has practiced Yoga alone will eventually experience conscious oneness with God. He will see God here on earth and there in Heaven. Just by leaving the body, one does not immediately go to God. For God-realization, one has to be here on earth. It is mere foolishness to think that when we leave the body, we immediately fly to God. No! It is not like that. One has to realize Him here on earth. It is by listening to the dictates of the soul that one realizes God here on earth. Otherwise people only need commit suicide in order to realize God after death. Anyone would be able to leave the world and fly to God.

Question: *What does God-realization really mean? Is it connected to Yoga?*

Sri Chinmoy: God-realization, or *siddhi*, means Self-discovery or Yoga, union with God, in the highest sense of the term. One consciously realizes his oneness with God. As long as the seeker remains in ignorance, he will feel that God is somebody else who has an infinite power, while he, the seeker, is the feeblest person on earth. But the moment he realizes God, he comes to know that he and God are absolutely one in both the inner and the outer life. God-realization means one's identification with one's absolute highest Self. When one can identify with one's highest Self and remain in that consciousness forever, when one can reveal and manifest it at one's command, that is God-realization.

When one achieves God-realization, one remains in God's Consciousness and speaks to God face to face. He sees God both in the finite and in the infinite; he sees God as both personal and impersonal. And in this case, this is not mental hallucination or imagination; it is direct reality. This reality is more authentic than my seeing you right here in front of me. When one speaks to a human being, there is always a veil of ignorance—darkness, imperfection, misunderstanding. But between God and the inner being of one who has realized Him, there can be no ignorance, no veil. At that time one can speak to God more clearly, more convincingly, more openly than to a human being.

As ordinary human beings, we feel that infinite peace, infinite Light, infinite bliss and infinite divine power are all sheer imagination. We are victims to doubt, fear and negative forces which we feel are quite normal and natural. We cannot love anything purely, not even ourselves. We are in the finite, quarreling and fighting, and there is no such thing peace, Light or bliss in us. But those who practice meditation and Yoga go deep within and see that there is real peace, Light and bliss. They get boundless inner strength and see that doubt and fear can be challenged and conquered. When we achieve God-realization, our inner existence is flooded with peace, poise, equanimity and Light.

Question: What is the eternal question of man?

Sri Chinmoy: Man's eternal question is: "Who is God?" God's immediate answer is: "My child, who else is God, if not you?"

SELECTED LIST OF SRI CHINMOY CENTERS

USA
Chicago 773-271-7330

New York 718-297-6456

Seattle 206-526-0742

Washington, DC 202-332-7649

CANADA
Montreal 514-489-5692

Ottawa 613-232-2387

Toronto 416-588-7767

Vancouver 604-732-8997

UNITED KINGDOM
London 020-7729-6319

FRANCE
Montpellier 467-64-54-70

GERMANY
Augsburg 0821-716-247

SWITZERLAND
Zürich 01-743-4020

AUSTRALIA
Melbourne 03-9853-3432

NEW ZEALAND
Auckland 09-309-3437

Selected List
of Divine Enterprises
of the Sri Chinmoy Centers

USA

New York:

Annam Brahma
(vegetarian restaurant)
84-43 164th St.
Jamaica, NY 11432
718-523-2600

Divine Robe Supreme
(boutique)
86-06 Parsons Blvd.
Jamaica, NY 11432
718-523-2082

Guru Health Foods
86-18 Parsons Blvd.
Jamaica, NY 11432
718-291-7406

Guru Stationery
86-24 Parsons Blvd.
Jamaica, NY 11432
718-523-3471

Madal Bal Bakery
80-06 Surrey Place
Jamaica Estates, NY 11432
718-380-8828

The Manifestation-Glow
(printing press)
146-01 Union Turnpike
Flushing, NY 11367
718-380-5259
fax: 718-380-7651

The Oneness-Fountain-Heart
(vegetarian restaurant)
157-19 72nd Ave.
Flushing, NY 11367
718-591-3663

Pole-Vision-Life-Strength
(health food store)
189-07 Union Tpke.
Fresh Meadows, NY 11366
718-454-3663

Smile of the Beyond
(luncheonette)
86-14 Parsons Blvd.
Jamaica, NY 11432
718-739-7453

Chicago:

Victory's Banner Restaurant
(vegetarian)
2100 W. Roscoe
Chicago, IL 60618
773-665-0227

Massachusetts:

Divinity's Splendour-Glow
(gift and card shop)
311 Broadway
Arlington, MA 02474
781-648-7100

Florida:

Consciousness-Blossoms
(vegetarian restaurant)
3390 Tampa Rd.
Palm Harbor, FL 34684
727-789-1931

Washington:

My Journey's Dawn
(bookstore)
5615 University Way N.E.
Seattle, WA 98105
206-527-8099

Silence-Heart-Nest
(vegetarian restaurant)
5247 University Way N.E.
Seattle, WA 98105
206-524-4008

California:

Jyoti-Bihanga
(vegetarian restaurant)
3351 Adams Ave.
San Diego, CA 92116
619-282-4116

Ananda-Fuara
(vegetarian restaurant)
1298 Market St.
San Francisco, CA 94102
415-621-1994

The Heart-Road-Traveller
(health food and bookstore)
1828 Euclid Ave.
Berkeley, CA 94709
510-665-1838

The Strength-Length of a New Life
(health food store)
235 Gough St.
San Francisco, CA 94102
415-863-1947

Washington, DC:

Transcendence-Perfection-Bliss of the Beyond
(gifts)
3428 Connecticut Ave. NW
Washington, DC 20008
202-363-4797

CANADA

Halifax:

Satisfaction-Feast
(vegetarian restaurant)
1581 Grafton St.
Halifax, N.S. B3J 2C3
902-422-3540

Ottawa:

Peace Garden
(café)
47 Clarence St.
Ottawa, Ont. K1N 9K1
613-562-2434

Perfection-Satisfaction-Promise
(vegetarian restaurant)
167 Laurier Ave. East
Ottawa, Ont. K1N 6N8
613-234-7299

Phulero Dola
(flower shop)
World Exchange Plaza
111 Albert St., 2nd Floor
Ottawa, Ont. K1P 1A5
613-234-8217

Toronto:

Annapurna Vegetarian Restaurant
1085 Bathurst St.
Toronto, Ont. M5R 3G8
416-537-8513

UNITED KINGDOM

The Golden Path
(book store)
St. James Market off 52
Haymarket
London SW1Y 4RP
020-7925-1777

Health My Most Precious God-Given Wealth
(health food shop)
41 Turnham Green Terrace
Chiswick London W4 1RG
020-8995-4906

Run and Become, Become and Run
(running store)
42 Palmer St.
London SW1H OPH
020-7222-1314

Run and Become, Become and Run
(sporting goods)
56 Dalry Rd.
Edinburgh EH11 2BA
0131-313-5300

FRANCE

Tripti-Kulai
(vegetarian restaurant)
20, rue Jacques Coeur
34000 Montpellier
467-663-051

Courez le but Vous Appelle
(running store)
164, rue de Charonne
75011 Paris
01-4371-0104

La Victoire Supreme du Coeur
(vegetarian restaurant)
41 rue des Bourdonnais
75001 Paris
01-4041-9395

GERMANY

Perfection-Glory Press
(printing)
Partnachweg 1
D-86165 Augsburg
0821-716-247
fax: 0821-716-162

Madal Bal
(health food store)
Nussmannstr. 14
79098 Freiburg
0761-381-386

Sangit Sushama, Music-Beauty
(music store)
Märzgasse 4
69117 Heidelberg
06221-160-649

The Golden Shore
(Sri Chinmoy book
publishing)
Glockendonstr. 31
D-90429 Nürnberg
0911-288-865
fax: 0911-288-412

AUSTRIA

Gandharva Loka
(musical instruments)
Linzergasse 47
A-5020 Salzburg
0662-874727

Madal Bal
(health food store)
Radetzkystrasse 13
8010 Graz
0316-831654

NETHERLANDS

Madal Bal
(health food shop)
Denneweg 51-53
NL-2514 CD Den Haag
070-365-1863

SWITZERLAND

Madal Bal
(health food store)
Universitätsstr. 102
CH-8006 Zürich
01-363-2410

AUSTRALIA

My Rainbow-Dreams
(health food store)
Shop 8, Manuka Court
Bougainville St.
Manuka, A.C.T. 2603
02-6295-6594

The Rainbow Silence-Heart
(vegetarian café)
280 Bridge Rd.
Richmond, Victoria 3121
03-9428-3225

NEW ZEALAND

The Blue Bird
(café)
299 Dominion Rd.
Mt. Eden, Auckland
09-623-4900

JAPAN

Sujata's Vegetarian Café
3-6 Kamibetto-cho
Kitashirakawa Sakyoku
Kyoto 606-8275
75-781-8275

The Blue Dove Foundation

The Blue Dove Foundation is a non-profit, tax-exempt organization Our purpose is to deepen the spiritual life of all by making available works on the lives, messages, and examples of saints and sages of all religions, paths, and traditions, as well as other spiritual titles that provide tools for inner growth.

The Blue Dove Foundation is not affiliated with any particular path, tradition, or religion.

For more information on the Blue Dove Foundation, contact us at:

The Blue Dove Foundation
4204 Sorrento Valley Blvd. Suite K
San Diego, CA 92121
Phone: (858)623-3330 FAX: (858)623-3325
Orders: (800)691-1008
e-mail: bdp@bluedove.com
Web site: www.bluedove.org

Lights of Grace
Catalog
from
The Blue Dove Foundation

The Blue Dove Foundation distributes spiritual works from Blue Dove Press and other publishers, including hundreds of titles from India, through our *Lights of Grace* catalog.

From Saint Teresa of Avila, to Sri Ramana Maharshi, to Milarepa, the Tibetan yogi—from *The Koran*, to *The Zohar*, to *The Mahabharata*—we have assembled an inspired collection of spiritual works at its most diverse and best.

For a free 68-page Catalog contact:

The Blue Dove Foundation
4204 Sorrento Valley Blvd. Suite K
San Diego, CA 92121
Phone: (858)623-3330 FAX: (858)623-3325
Orders: (800)691-1008
e-mail: bdp@bluedove.com
Web site: www.bluedove.org